Languages at War: External Language Spread Policies in Lusophone Africa

DUISBURGER ARBEITEN ZUR SPRACH- UND KULTURWISSENSCHAFT

DUISBURG PAPERS ON RESEARCH IN LANGUAGE AND CULTURE

Herausgegeben von / edited by
Ulrich Ammon, René Dirven und / and Martin Pütz

Band / Volume 97

Carla Figueira

Languages at War: External Language Spread Policies in Lusophone Africa

Mozambique and Guinea-Bissau at the Turn of the 21st Century

PETER LANG
EDITION

Bibliographic Information published by the Deutsche Nationalbibliothek
The Deutsche Nationalbibliothek lists this publication in the Deutsche
Nationalbibliografie; detailed bibliographic data is available in the internet
at http://dnb.d-nb.de.

Research and publication supported by the Ministério da Ciência,
Tecnologia e Ensino Superior, Portugal, (PRAXIS XXI / BD / 21356 / 99).

Cover Design:
© Olaf Gloeckler, Atelier Platen, Friedberg

Library of Congress Cataloging-in-Publication Data

Figueira, Carla, 1968-
    Languages at war : external language spread policies in Lusophone Africa :
    Mozambique and Guinea-Bissau at the turn of the 21st century / Carla Figueira.
    pages cm. — (Duisburg papers on research in language and culture ; Bd. 97)
    Originally presented as the author's thesis (doctoral)—City University, Lon-
    don, 2010, under the title: Languages at war in Lusophone Africa.
    ISBN 978-3-631-64436-2
    1. Language policy—Mozambique. 2. Language policy—Guinea-Bissau. 3.
    Portuguese language—Political aspects—Mozambique. 4. Portuguese lan-
    guage—Political aspects—Guinea-Bissau. 5. Language spread—Government
    policy—Mozambique. 6. Language spread—Government policy—Guinea-
    Bissau. 7. Language and international relations—Africa, Portuguese-
    speaking. I. Title. II. Series: Duisburger Arbeiten zur Sprach- und Kulturwis-
    senschaft ; Bd. 97.
    P119.32.M85L36 2013
    306.4496657—dc23

                                                              2013011816

ISSN 0934-3709
ISBN 978-3-631-64436-2

© Peter Lang GmbH
Internationaler Verlag der Wissenschaften
Frankfurt am Main 2013
All rights reserved.
Peter Lang Edition is an Imprint of Peter Lang GmbH

Peter Lang – Frankfurt am Main · Bern · Bruxelles · New York ·
Oxford · Warszawa · Wien

www.peterlang.de

Dedication

This book is dedicated to my parents, Fortunata and António, to my husband, Jonathan, without whose help this task would have been impossible to fulfil, and to my sons, David and Daniel, both born during the course of the research, a source of inspiration that kept me going, although with a lot of distractions along the way!

Foreword by Robert Phillipson

The warfare analysed by Carla Figueira is the battle for hearts and minds and influence, the goal of Westerners being to profit from the economies of vulnerable former colonies, often through continuing to exploit them. Portuguese is in combat with French and English in a new scramble for Africa and its resources - with language as a key battering ram. New alliances have emerged, countries identified as Lusophone, Francophone and Anglophone / Commonwealth. However, in such countries only a small fraction of the population is proficient in these languages. The challenge for Carla Figueira has been to relate the forces and pressures impacting on national and international power to national identity and diversity, to linguistic imperialism and linguistic human rights, and the roles of the various constituences, including non-governmental organizations. She describes the theoretical ramparts for analysing the complex interlocking of these various factors. The instruments and agents of linguistic warfare are diagnosed, as are the implications for the citizens of the countries involved.

Carla Figueira's book fills an important gap in the research literature. It explores cultural and linguistic diplomacy through a comparative empirical study of the policies of France, Germany, Portugal and the UK in the 'external' spread of their languages. It relates the activities to their reception in two former Portuguese colonies. Brazil was included because of the link between Portuguese-speaking Brazil and Portuguese former colonies in Africa. The study integrates approaches from the fields of international relations, development 'aid', sociolinguistics, language diversity, language rights, and language policy, especially in education. It judiciously presents a great deal of information on under-researched topics, and brings the issues together in astute and interesting conclusions. This is therefore an important book for the study of North-South links, and how agendas that are of major significance for social cohesion in postcolonial states are set.

European countries are heavily committed to promoting their languages in Africa and elsewhere. Language is of decisive importance in maintaining strong links with the European 'mother country' as well as being of regional significance - English in southern Africa, French and English in West Africa. Success in learning a European language is assumed to correlate with economic, political and geostrategic clout.

There is extensive coverage of many aspects of international development 'aid' policies, for instance the role of the World Bank, in postcolonial, politically independent African states. There is a wealth of literature on the language policies that evolved in the British Empire and in former British colonies. There

7

is rather less on the experience of the colonies of the French Empire, and much less - at least in English - on the Portuguese Empire and its postcolonial aftermath.

Language policies were not been left to chance. The Alliance Française dates from 1883. The British and Americans began coordinating strategies for English as a 'world' language in the 1930s (Phillipson 2009a). Winston Churchill recognized that American Empire was supplanting the British, and insightfully noted, when receiving an honorary doctorate from Harvard University in 1943, the need for Western powers to shift from physical control to psychological and mental colonisation: 'The empires of the future are the empires of the mind.'

In *The diffusion of English culture outside England* (Routh 1941) the British government is advised to form an 'army of linguistic missionaries' to preach the gospel of English worldwide. The batallions of this army were established in the 1950s, and plotted with USA-UK collaboration (Phillipson 1992). I was in fact commissioned into this army in the mid-1960s, though clearly the commanding officers in London feel that I have let the side down by exploring and denouncing linguistic imperialism.

With the British and Americans 'divided by a common language' (as George Bernard Shaw put it), there has always been rivalry between these two partners. This tension between a common interest, the establishment of English worldwide, and each individual country's wish to benefit has similarities with the focus of Carla Figueira's study. There is the reality of a European country (the UK, Portugal) having more powerful offspring elsewhere (the USA, Brazil), a family bond that is often tricky. Likewise, there is a mismatch between the European Union formally having a joint or common foreign policy, but the linguistic armies of France, Germany, Portugal, and the United Kingdom lining up against each other throughout Sub-Saharan Africa. Their 'external language spread policies' are not coordinated with each other and definitely not 'joint'. The study relates insightfully and in depth how the battle for 'empires of the mind' is being fought out.

Robert Phillipson is a graduate of Cambridge and Leeds Universities, UK, and has a doctorate from the University of Amsterdam. He worked for the British Council in Spain, Algeria, Yugoslavia and London before settling in Denmark, where he is a Professor Emeritus at Copenhagen Business School. He is best know for his book *Linguistic Imperialism* (OUP, 1992). For more information see: http://www.cbs.dk/staff/phillipson.

Acknowledgements

This book is a lightly edited version of my PhD dissertation "Languages at War in Lusophone Africa: External Language Spread Policies in Mozambique and Guinea-Bissau at the Turn of the 21st Century" submitted to City University, London, in July 2010, in fulfilment of the requirements for the degree of Doctor of Philosophy in Cultural Management and Policy. This study is thus a product of my original research, based on literature and interviews. Any mistakes or inaccuracies are inadvertently my responsibility. Translations are my own and originals are given in footnotes. In addition to this declaration of responsibility for my work, I wish to acknowledge all those that have contributed to this process.

I wish to express sincere appreciation to the Fundação para a Ciência e para a Tecnologia, Ministério da Ciência, Tecnologia e Ensino Superior, Portugal, and the European Social Fund, for awarding me a PRAXIS XXII scholarship that enabled to conduct this research, and to my external supervisor, Professor Naz Rassool, University of Reading, for her assistance in the preparation of the final document.

In addition, special thank you to all interviewees and those who helped during research in Europe and in Africa.

In Lisbon, I am indebted to: The Aga Khan Foundation for help on the preparation of the study trip to Mozambique; Perpétua Santos Silva (Instituto Camões); Mário Matos e Lemos, Jorge Encarnação (Instituto da Cooperação Portuguesa), Isabel Palha (Instituto Português do Livro e das Bibliotecas), Lino Bicari, Margarida Moreira and Toni Tcheca whose knowledge on Guinea-Bissau was most valuable.

For help in Mozambique, I would like to express my gratitude to: Artur Costa for his general help and information on Mozambique; DFID, Maputo: Marie Castelo Branco and Paulo Gentil for their precious help locating some resources people; Aga Khan Foundation, Maputo: Karim Merali for arranging the transfers between Nampula and Mozambique Island; Ali Daudu, Paulo Monteiro and family for their care and friendship in Nampula and Mozambique Island; Oikos, Maputo: Luís Filipe Pereira for booking my accommodation in Mozambique Island; Casa de Hóspedes / Oikos in Mozambique Island: Dulce Daúdo and Xavier for their care and help locating my interviewees.

In Bissau, I wish to thank: Daniel Perdigão, then Portuguese Cultural attaché, and Vítor, responsible for the Bairro da Cooperação, for their general help and information on Guinea-Bissau; The Portuguese teachers living in Bairro da Cooperação, especially Rute Miranda, Paulo Rodrigues and Marta, for sharing their professional experiences; Jorge Fernandes (Instituto Camões) for all the information provided; D. Berta Bento, António, Isabel and Nelo Fróis at Pensão Central, and Fernanda Dâmaso, for making me feel at home in Bissau; Teresa Montenegro for her gift of books that introduced me to Guinean literature.

Thank you also to the staff of the City University's Department of Cultural Policy and Management for their input, namely to the Senior Tutor for Research, Dr. Juliet Steyn, Michael Quine and Professor Patrick Boylan for guidance in the early stages of the PhD process, to Professor Anthony Everitt for supervision during the course of research and to Professor Sara Selwood for supervision in the writing up stage, to Mary Dines for always been there for the administrative stuff, and to Professor Tim Connell, Director of Language Studies, for his interest and advice. I am grateful to Professor Robert Phillipson who, as external examiner, played a fundamental role in bringing this process to an end. Thanks to Carol Benson for the precious contacts in the last stage of the process. Thank you to all my family and friends for their support.

List of Abbreviations

ACALAN	African Academy of Languages
ACP	African, Caribbean and Pacific Group of States
AEMO	Associação de Escritores Moçambicanos / Mozambican Writers Association (Mozambique)
AIDAB	Australian International Development Assistance Bureau
AMOLP	Associação Moçambicana da Língua Portuguesa / Mozambican Association of Portuguese Language
APAD	Agência Portuguesa de Apoio ao Desenvolvimento / Portuguese Development Support Agency (Portugal)
BBC	British Broadcasting Corporation (UK)
BC	British Council (UK)
CCBM	Centro Cultural Brasil - Moçambique
CCBGB	Centro Cultural Brasil – Guiné-Bissau
CCFM	Centro Cultural Franco - Moçambicano / Franco-Mozambican Cultural Centre (Mozambique)
CCFGB	Centre Culturel Franco-Bissao-Guinéen
CCP/IC	Centro Cultural Português / Instituto Camões
CEB	Centro de Estudos Brasileiros / Brazilian Studies Centre
CIDAC	Centro de Intervenção para o Desenvolvimento Amílcar Cabral (Portugal)
CLP/IC	Centro de Língua Portuguesa / Instituto Camões
CPLP	Comunidade dos Países de Língua Portuguesa / Community of Portuguese Language Countries or Community of Portuguese-Speaking Countries
DAC	Development Assistance Committee, part of OECD
DENARP	Documento de Estratégia Nacional de Redução da Pobreza
DFID	Department for International Development (UK)
DGCID	Direction Générale de la Cooperation Internationale et du Développement (MAE, France)
ECOWAS	Economic Community of West African States
EFA	Education for All
ELT	English Language Teaching
ENSTT	Escola Normal Superior Tchico Té (Guinea-Bissau)
FEC	Fundação Evangelização e Culturas / Evangelisation and Cultures Foundation (Portugal)
FRELIMO	Frente de Libertação de Moçambique / Liberation Front of Mozambique

GBP	British Pound
IC	Instituto Camões / Camões Institute (Portugal)
IC-CCPM	Instituto Camões – Centro Cultural Português de Maputo
ICALP	Instituto de Cultura e Língua Portuguesa / Portuguese Culture and Language Institute (Portugal)
ICMA	Instituto Cultural Alemanha - Moçambique
IILP	Instituto Internacional da Língua Portuguesa / International Institute of Portuguese Language
IMA	Instituto Machado de Assis (Brazil)
IMF	International Monetary Fund
INDE	Instituto Nacional de Desenvolvimento e Educação / National Institute for Development and Education (Guinea-Bissau) Instituto Nacional de Desenvolvimento Educacional / National Institute for Educational Development (Mozambique)
INEP	Instituto Nacional de Estudos e Pesquisa / National Institute of Studies and Research (Guinea-Bissau)
ISCTE	Instituto Superior de Ciências do Trabalho e da Empresa (Portugal)
IT	Information Technology
JEN	Junta de Educação Nacional / National Education Board (Portugal)
LSP	Language Spread Policy
MDGs	Millennium Development Goals
MINED	Ministério da Educação / Ministry of Education (Mozambique)
NEPAD	New Partnership for Africa's Development
NGO	Non-Governmental Organisation
NORAD	Norwegian Agency for Development Cooperation
ODA	Official Development Assistance (OECD)
ODA	Overseas Development Administration (UK)
OECD	Organisation for Economic Co-operation and Development
OEI	Organizaciòn de Estados Iberoamericanos / Organisation of Ibero-American States
OIC	Organisation of the Islamic Conference
OIF	Organisation Internationale de la Francophonie / Francophone International Organisation
PAIGC	Partido Africano da Independência da Guiné e Cabo Verde / African Party for the Independence of Guinea and Cape Verde (Guinea-Bissau)
PALOP	Países Africanos de Língua Oficial Portuguesa / African Countries with Portuguese as an Official Language
RENAMO	Resistência Nacional Moçambicana / Mozambican National Resistance.

SADC	Southern Africa Development Community / In Portuguese Comunidade de Desenvolvimento da África Austral
SCAC	Service de Coopération et d'Action Culturelle / Cooperation and Cultural Action Service, France.
Sida	Styrelsen För Internationell Utveckingssamarbete /Swedish International Development Cooperation Agency
SNV	Stichting Nederlandse Vrijwilligers / Foundation of Netherlands Volunteers
STEP	Secondary and Technical English Project
TEL, 3EL	Trois Espaces Linguistiques, Tres Espacios Linguisticos, Três Espaços Linguísticos / Three Linguistic Spaces
UEM	Universidade Eduardo Mondlane (Mozambique)
UK	United Kingdom
UL	União Latina / Unión Latina / Latin Union
UN	United Nations
UNDP	United Nations Development Programme
UNESCO	United Nations Educational, Scientific and Cultural Organisation
USA	United States of America
USAID	United States Agency for International Development
USD	United States Dollar
USSR	Union of Soviet Socialist Republics
VSO	Voluntary Service Abroad (UK)
WAEMU	West African Economic and Monetary Union

Table of Contents

Chapter 1 Introduction

1.1 Research Topic

This study explores the argument that Postcolonial Africa has been the setting for competing external language spread policies (LSPs) by ex-colonial European countries at the turn of the 21st Century. This is what the metaphorical title of this study, *Languages at War in Lusophone Africa*, refers to. The study focuses on the external LSPs developed by the governments of Portugal, Brazil, United Kingdom, France and Germany towards Mozambique and Guinea-Bissau from the 1990s to the present.

Lusophone Africa is composed of five countries that represent former colonies of Portugal: Angola, Cape Verde, Guinea-Bissau, Mozambique and São Tomé and Príncipe. The group is commonly designated as PALOP (Países Africanos de Língua Oficial Portuguesa), African countries with Portuguese as an official language. Lusophone is a linguonym for Portuguese-speaking. It derives from the Portuguese word *Lusitanos* that designates a set of Iberian pre-roman tribes that gave origin to Portugal. I agree with Skutnabb-Kangas (2000, p.232), that the use of linguonyms about a country or group of countries, highlighting former colonial languages, "make the fact that people have been colonised by a specific country the most important linguistic characteristic of them, at the same time as the false impression is given that most people know and/or use the old colonial language". English, French, Portuguese or Spanish have not *replaced* African languages, as Spencer (1985, p.389) notes with regard to the "fallacious use of the French loan-words *anglophone* and *francophone*": "They have been *superposed* (as second languages) upon the existing vernacular language mosaic". The label of Lusophone is used critically in this study as it features in contemporary discourse.

External language spread policies (LSPs) are government policies aimed at spreading the language of a state abroad (Ammon 1992a). In the context of this study they are seen as part of foreign policy, often viewed as activities developed under cultural diplomacy, penetrating diverse areas from education, culture, to development aid. Thus external LSPs are part of the set of instruments available to governments to project their national image and power and pursue their national interests.

This study offers a perspective on the web of relationships involving European ex-colonial powers and the African postcolonial countries of Guinea-Bissau and Mozambique. It seeks to examine the development of external (European) language spread policies and the construction of politico linguistic blocs

19

in a complex context whilst taking into account the colonial heritage and its lingering dependencies, the construction and maintenance of nationhood and the increasing globalisation of the world.

As was the case with other European languages in Africa, Portuguese made the transition from the language of the coloniser to the language of administration and education in the newly independent countries. In the early 1970s, following independence, the Portuguese former colonies 'chose' Portuguese (European variety) as their official language and used it as a tool for the construction of their state and nationhood. Mother tongue education had no place in the colonial times a fact reflected in the postcolonial primacy of Portuguese language in the African countries. Its status as official language has never been challenged and government attention given to African languages, either symbolically in legislation or in the practice of education, has always maintained that status quo.

During the 1980s and 1990s, the Portuguese press cyclically published articles pertaining to the Portuguese language being threatened in Africa, especially by English in Mozambique and French in Guinea-Bissau - these countries are geopolitically situated in regional areas dominated by, respectively, 'Anglophone' and 'Francophone' countries. Frequently ignoring the African countries' own political personas, the media and some in academia transmitted the image of France and the United Kingdom as linguistic competitors of Portugal in those countries, under a realist logic of international relations. That perception of competition among the mentioned former European colonial countries resonates with the 19th century Scramble for Africa, when, at the Berlin Conference (1884-1885), the European powers decided that only effective occupation should justify claims to territory in Africa. Could this historical competition continue into the postcolonial era, now through language? And, regardless of the answer, why has that perception surfaced in discourse?

The fostering of the 'special relationship' between former coloniser and colonised, using the communality of language as a symbol, is typical of the countries involved in this study. Besides bilateral relations that include the development of language spread activities *per se* (language teaching, teacher training, scholarships) or set in the context of broader development aid (general capacity building activities such as the training of government officials), these countries are part of political blocs that use language as an identity label. Portuguese language countries' relationship, often designated Lusophony, was in 1996 given an organisational form with the creation of the Community of Portuguese Language Countries (Comunidade dos Países de Língua Portuguesa, CPLP) and of the International Institute of Portuguese Language (Instituto Internacional da Língua Portuguesa, IILP). Many English language countries belong to the

Commonwealth of Nations, a relationship sometimes referred to as Anglophony. This term is mostly used by Portuguese and French writers and seldom used by English-speaking authors. In fact there is no entry for 'anglophony' in the Oxford English Dictionary (OED). The closest approximation in the OED is 'Anglophone' meaning English-speaking. However the term 'anglosphere' has emerged in the United States as a new concept in geopolitics (Bennett 2002). Countries connected to French language cooperate through the Organisation Internationale de la Francophonie (OIF) and partner organisations, generally designated Francophony. Membership of these organisations is not mutually exclusive. The very inclusive Francophony accepts members from other cultural and linguistic blocs. And even the more exclusive Commonwealth, has among its members: Francophone Canada, Mauritius, Seychelles, Dominica, St. Lucia, Vanuatu and Cameroon and Lusophone Mozambique. Recently there have been attempts to developed closer relations between linguistic blocs as it is the case of the Three Linguistic Spaces group (also known as TEL or 3EL) created in 2001 including organisations from Francophony, Hispanophony and Lusophony.

The end of colonialism and the increased globalisation of the world, and of languages, has created the opportunity for language to be used as a political symbol and managed as an entity at international and multilateral level. Portuguese-speaking countries have gone as far as managing Portuguese language multilaterally by signing amongst themselves an agreement establishing a uniform norm of writing for Portuguese now being implemented. The mentioned politico linguistic blocs are thus multilateral arenas that, among other functions, serve the establishment, development and reinforcement of language spread policies, but do they serve the member countries in the same way?

The history, structure and functioning of the international system has fostered and supported the pervasiveness of global European languages, reinforcing their place in the world hierarchy of languages. Disseminated by colonialism, associated with access to modernity and development, the languages of international organisations and agreements, European languages, in particular English, dominate or have a particular sought after linguistic/cultural capital in most of the linguistic spaces in the world. In the case studies on this study, English as international/regional lingua franca, French as a second international/regional lingua franca, and Portuguese, as the former colonial language and now official language, as language of national unity and as language of a substantial international linguistic bloc, are seen as substantial contenders in the competition for linguistic space in Sub-Saharan Africa. This linguistic inequality reflects the power relations enacted in society and internationally. It further raises issues of linguistic/cultural human rights and the defence of language and cultural diversity that this study argues for.

21

The main research question of this study is: "Are there languages at war in Lusophone Africa?" The answer to this question will allow this study to fulfil the main objective of contributing to the development of knowledge in the area of external language spread policies (Ammon 1992a) amongst ex-colonial European governments in postcolonial African countries. It is hoped to do so by clarification of the underlying motivations, at the same time as understanding how these policies operate, what their consequences are and how they are perceived by the actors involved (both in the source and in the target countries). Associated with this question is the use of external language spread policies in the construction and maintenance of national images. I am particularly interested in exploring the discursive use of language spread serving to reinforce Portugal's self image, as banal nationalism (Billig 1995). I discuss this concept in Chapter 2. Additionally, the issue of external language spread policies implies a careful examination of the national context in which they operate, namely, in this study, the legacy of the colonial language, its use in the construction of the postcolonial nation and the relationship of the European languages with the African languages. This study views language relations within the framework of linguistic imperialism (Phillipson 1992).

The 1990s were rich in events and theories that led to the increased prominence of culture in international relations (Walt 1998, p.42). The fall of the Berlin Wall in 1989 marked a major turning point in the contemporary postcolonial global international system and in the conceptualisation of international relations. The subsequent collapse of the Soviet Union put an end to the Cold War (1947-1989) and to the East-West bipolarisation of world politics. The end of apartheid in the Republic of South Africa (1994) also had a major impact in sub-Saharan Africa, where the case studies are located, as it allowed South Africa to shed its international isolation and pursue aspirations as a regional leader. Africa, a favourite long distance battlefield of the former two world powers, the United States and the Soviet Union, became free from communist ideological constraints (Schraeder 2004, p.272) and many countries embarked on a political route to democracy and a path to economic regeneration. This, nevertheless, still has been insufficient to break the world's North/South divide between the haves and the have-nots, or to stop lingering spheres of influence that maintain the hegemony of the North over the South. As Dunn (2001, p.3) observes, Africa occupies a central position in the theory and practice of international relations: "Africa is the *Other* necessary for the construction of a mythical Western *Self*. ...the ever-present and necessary counterpart that make the dominant theories complete. It is the periphery to the core; the small states upon which the 'great' powers act".

As the ideological bipolarisation of the world between capitalism and communism faded with the widespread adoption of western liberal democracy and economy, political scientists started to search for new paradigms to interpret the post-Cold War international system. Theories such as Francis Fukuyama's (1989, 1992) *The End of History*, Benjamin Barber's (1996) *Jihad vs MacWorld* and Samuel Huntington's (1993, 1996) *The Clash of Civilizations and the Remaking of World Order* became prominent in interpretations of the new world order. Culture is central to some of these new paradigms. For instance, Huntington (1996, p.20) in *The Clash of Civilizations* - a theory that gained increased attention after the 2001 terrorist attacks in the USA - describes how "culture and cultural identities, which at the broadest level are civilization identities, are shaping the patterns of cohesion, disintegration, and conflict in the post-Cold War world". For Huntington, a shared language, religion, values, institutions constitute markers of cultural identities.

Additionally, the constitution of blocs in international relations, often political and economic, also made use of the cultural connections between countries. Koening (1998, p.8) draws attention to the cultural dimension of globalisation, diminishing the role of traditional identities and helping in "the emergence of ethno-political movements drawing on nationalism, religious or sectarian belonging, race and language as resources for the construction of particular identities and for their political mobilization". In the 1990s, several initiatives bringing countries together on the basis of culture and language became visible in the international arena. Since 1991, there have been conferences of Dutch-speakers from eight or more communities as well as Ibero-American summits; Turkish-speaking summits have been held since 1992, with delegates from six independent countries of Europe, Central Asia and small ethnic communities elsewhere (Breton 2000). Since 1996, the Community of Portuguese Language Countries (Comunidade dos Países de Língua Portuguesa, CPLP) has brought together eight countries; in 2001 the Three Linguistic Spaces group (also known as TEL or 3EL, acronyms from the French *Trois Espaces Linguistiques*; Spanish, *Tres Espacios Lingüísticos*; Portuguese *Três Espaços Linguísticos*) was created gathering Lusophony, Hispanophony and Francophony, with the declared objective to protect and promote cultural diversity in the world.

The 1990s were also an important decade in raising awareness of sustainable development and of the ecological problems faced by humanity and planet Earth. These integrated and global frameworks to view the problems faced by humankind, concomitantly highlighted the struggles of indigenous cultures, languages and habitats.

For all the above reasons, I see the period of the 1990s to the present, coinciding with the turn of the century, as a rich period that offers the possibility to provide a complex context for the analysis of external language spread policies.

This study has a Portuguese perspective, as I was born, raised and mainly educated in Portugal and my interest in the topic has been influenced by those circumstances. This is further discussed in Chapter 3 Methodology. Portugal and Portuguese external language spread policy represents a major thread throughout. This study hopes to contribute to the broader debate on Portuguese language spread.

1.2 Literature Review

In the preface to the first volume of the *International Journal of the Sociology of Language* on the language spread of former colonial powers, Ammon noted that both he and Kleineidam had found language spread policy to be "a topic which has mainly been dealt with by politicians for practical purposes" (1992a, p.6). That volume, and a second published in 1994, was invaluable to furthering the research on the spread of other languages besides English and contributing to the establishment of a terminology, typology and framework for analysis of the subject.

Not surprisingly, given its reach, English language spread has been a favourite subject of analysis, as the works of Fishman *et al.* (1977 and 1996); Phillipson (1992, 2009a); Pennycook (1994, 1998a, 2006); Graddol (1997, 2006); and Crystal (1997) demonstrate. A similar interest in French language spread is shared by numerous authors; amongst the most important are Calvet (1994), Roland Breton, and Chaudenson (2000).

Although the study of the Portuguese experience is extremely relevant in the context of external language spread policies and linguistic imperialism, it has not had the same international coverage, in breadth or depth, as English or French language spread. For instance, the Portuguese-speaking world does not feature in Routledge's book series 'Language in Society' (1997) designed as practical guides to sociolinguistic issues: *The French-speaking world* by Ball; *The Spanish-speaking world* by Mar-Molinero; *The German-speaking world* by Stevenson. Other interesting books in the area are Mar-Molinero's *The politics of language in the Spanish-speaking world: from colonisation to globalisation* published in 2000 and Totaro-Genevois's *Culture and Linguistics Policy Abroad: The Italian Experience* in 2005. Portuguese language spread still lacks a major volume in English for an international audience – with this remark I do not dismiss all the important work that has been written in Portuguese, nor do I wish to defend the problematic dominance of English language in academia, but merely state the present reality.

Portuguese external language spread is a topic that has grown in interest since the 1990s. The setting up of the Instituto Camões (the institution responsible in Portugal for language and cultural spread abroad) in 1992 demonstrated the importance of Portuguese external language policy in the national strategy (even if often without being backed by the adequate financial means). In 1996 with the setting up of the CPLP and the IILP, the multilateral establishment of international language spread policy was a possibility – still only tentatively being undertaken today. Amidst this political evolution, the policies of diffusion of Portuguese language abroad have been associated with the concept of *Lusofonia*. The idea of Lusophony integrates a variety of meanings (Medeiros 2005), however the concept is usually applied to the set of Portuguese-speakers, regardless of nationality and level of fluency, identified as a (real and/or imagined) community of language and culture, often used in Portuguese political, academic and journalistic discourse.

In Portugal, many authors accept unquestionably the idea of communality provided by the linguistic commonness. Others see Lusophony as a myth. For Lourenço (1998, 1999), Margarido (2000) and De Almeida (2004, 2008) *Lusofonia* is a neocolonial project. According to Lourenço (1998, p.180) it is a Portuguese invention to still be able to inhabit the imperial spaces, because it is symbolically and unconsciously dreamt about. De Almeida (2004, p.45) regards Lusophony "as a device that helps to regain – in both the "spiritual realm" of the cultural products (language, with "Lusophony") and in the institutional one, with CPLP – that which has been lost in the political and material one (Empire as such)". In the same line of thought, Margarido (2000, p.12) points to a messianic function of Lusophony to assure Portugal a promising future.

By exposing the neocolonial character of Lusophony, these authors do not dismiss the value of the cultural and linguistic ties, nor its importance for Portuguese national identity. Authors such as De Almeida (2008) and Cristovão (2008) believe that Lusophony has the potential to be built. The need to take into account the '*Other*' is pointed as the way forward. Lourenço (1998, p.164) observes: "to seriously dream it [the Lusophone dream] means not to be the only dreamer of it and to know that the others would not dream of it as we do."[1] Margarido (2000, p.57) highlights the need to consider the will of the '*Other*' and

---

[1] "sonhá-a a sério significa não ser o único sonhador dela e saber que os outros a não sonharão como nós."

revise the "theoretical garbage"[2] that makes language the most efficient agent of the unity between people and territory marked by the presence of the Portuguese.

Unlike much of the theoretical work mentioned above, Errante's (1998) article 'Education and National Personae in Portugal's Colonial and Postcolonial Transition' is based on grounded research in Mozambique. It explores the dynamics emerging from the metropole-colony relationship for Portugal's identity as a colonizing and postcolonizing society through the analysis of the role of primary school education. She argues for the long-term importance of imperialism for empires, in the Portuguese case resulting in the defence of the artefacts crucial to a narrative of an *imagined* Portugal. I am interested in exploring, on a contextualised basis, the importance of the discourses of external language spread policy in the construction of Portugal's identity and how these discourses, and in particular the concept of Lusophony, are perceived by the *'Other'*, especially in the African countries targets of the external LSPs.

Regarding the perception of Lusophony by the *'Other'* it is important to note briefly the position of Brazil, before focusing on Africa. Brazil, as the country with the largest number of Portuguese speakers, an emergent economy and a vibrant culture with international appeal, is regarded as a potential challenger of Portugal as source country in the spread of the language (Da Silva and Gunnewiek 1992, Graça 1992, Lourenço 1998, Zúquete 2008). Nevertheless that prospect does not appear to have materialised. In Brazil, according to Faraco (forthcoming) the subject is hardly discussed or mentioned - and when it does it is done in the academic arena. Lusophony seems to be used merely as a facilitator of Brazilian presence in Africa (Faraco, forthcoming p.13). In this study I restrict my brief investigation of Brazil's policy in the context of the case studies to the potential competition/concurrence in the spread of Portuguese with the one developed by Portugal, since my main concern is the competing policies of European Western countries.

The perception of threats to Portuguese language in Africa has often been signalled in literature. The earliest reference identified was by Pierre Alexandre (1967 cited in Graça, 1992, p.247-248). Trying to forecast the trends for the linguistic future of Africa, he highlighted the cultural competition (*concurrence culturelle*) between Western powers. In a section entitled "'Competitors' of Portuguese as official language", Da Silva and Gunnewiek (1992, p.89) identify in Africa: French as a serious rival of Portuguese in Guinea-Bissau; Spanish, sup-

---

2   "estrume teórico". The direct translation for estrume is compost , however, since I interpret Margarido uses the expression in a derogatory sense, I opted to translate it as garbage.

ported by Spanish and Cuban governments, as a potential rival in Angola; Swahili and English in Mozambique, as respectively "*langue véhiculaire*" in large areas of the country and dominant language at the University of Maputo. Da Silva and Gunnewiek (1992, p.89) identified some causes for the competition cases that are connected with the historical and political circumstances of the countries and therefore go beyond the linguistic processes and geopolitical location. In Angola, the rivalry with Spanish was presented as being due to the presence of Cuban troops and the educational support given by the Spanish and Cuban governments; and in Mozambique, the displacement of people due to the civil war determined the use of Swahili as regional lingua franca. Ten years later, Vilela (2002) also identified "linguistic pressures" affecting the PALOP:

> There are linguistic pressures affecting the language situation both from within the countries and from without. Within the countries, this pressure comes from the competing demands of the various languages spoken within the country. …Externally, it is necessary to consider the pressure from other official languages as they relate to Portuguese. In a general way, it can be said that *Portuguese-speaking African countries experience linguistic pressure from languages of their neighbours, notably English and French, and the power of these as international languages influences language planning in the PALOP.* (2002, p.308, my emphasis in italics).

Vilela does not define linguistic pressure, its process, nor are the causes and motives explicitly, given:

> Guinea-Bissau is completely surrounded by polities with French as their official language, while internally Creole also exerts pressure. São Tomé and Príncipe is in a zone dominated by both English and French. Angola has four neighbours of whom the northern ones (the Democratic Republic of Congo and Congo) have French as their official language while those in the south and east have English. Mozambique is completely surrounded by polities with English as their official language (Tanzania, Malawi, Zambia, Zimbabwe, South Africa and Swaziland). (Vilela 2002, p.308-309)

Hamilton (2001) acknowledging the juxtapositions between indigenous African languages, Creoles, and Portuguese, points to an exaggerated, real or imagined, threat to Portuguese's survival in Africa coming from English and French, which "a number of Portuguese and Brazilian government officials and intellectuals, along with not a few of their counterparts in Lusophone Africa, have come together under the banner of lusofonia" (Hamilton 2001, p.185-186).

From the above examples of literature reviewed concerning the policies of Portuguese language spread in Africa what is sorely missing is a more contextualised and complex analysis. Much of the work operates within fairly strict disciplinary theoretical backgrounds such as postcolonial studies, linguistics and political science, restricting the variables with which one can deal. Additionally, a substantial part of the research reviewed, particularly that by Portuguese researchers, appears to follow Portuguese authorities' agendas, as often its objectives seems to be to clarify, justify and improve existing policies, or at least to reinforce the official discourse.

The political use of the concept of Lusophony to designate the populations of the Portuguese-speaking countries and other communities scattered throughout the world is seldom challenged. Even Zúquete's (2008, p.495) enlightened article about the context and politics of the spelling reform of Portuguese language falls prey of the official rhetoric regarding the spread and number of Portuguese speakers: "No longer an empire but confined to its present European borders, the heritage of Portugal's colonial period nevertheless lives on, particularly through a Romance language that is spoken by more than 200 million people around the world." However the official number crunching of Lusophony does not add up in reality, as, for instance, large numbers of the African countries' populations do not become fully proficient in the Portuguese language.

Studies into the economic value of languages, providing economic justifications for external language spread are present in the literature reviewed and evidence linkages between policy agendas and academic research and the predominant liberal market ideology. Examples include Galito's (2006) doctoral study on the economic impact of Portuguese language as work language and ISCTE's study of the economic value of the Portuguese language, commissioned by the Instituto Camões: Esperança (2008) *An Eclectic Approach to Language Valuation: The Global Influence of the Portuguese Language.*

The economic justification for Portuguese language spread enhances the existing justifications connected with Portuguese foreign policy objectives. The following example provides an updated version of terminology utilized in the political justification. Teles' (2009) approach to the cultural dimension of Portuguese foreign policy - from the 1990s to present - examines the use of Portuguese language and culture, *Lusofonia*, as a display of *soft power* (Nye 2004). She calls for a revaluation of strategy implying a debate about the national interest of Portugal with view to a clear definition of the Portuguese *national brand*. She also argues that France, the UK and Germany have the concept of *mutuality and reciprocity* as a distinct feature of their cultural diplomacies – which is highly contentious - and that Portugal should follow their example. However she does not approach the hegemonic role of language in society (nationally and internationally), thus seriously undermining the assertions of her master's degree thesis.

Moreover, there still appears to be a lack of information and awareness regarding the '*Other*'s' (that is of the African countries, Timor-Leste and the Diaspora) positioning in the topic of Portuguese language spread and Lusophony both in Portugal and in Brazil (Faraco, forthcoming). For instance, Portuguese author Teles (2009, p.2) observing the task of the Instituto Internacional da Língua Portuguesa (IILP) in the "defence of Portuguese language and different Portuguese speaking cultures", endorses the neutral vision of language often present in official discourse: "Starting as an imperial language during the Portuguese colonial empire that only fell after the revolution of 1974, in Lisbon, in the 21st century Portuguese is looking to become a language that is effectively shared by all peoples and societies that express themselves in Portuguese" (Teles 2009, p.3). From a contrasting point of view, Mozambican author Do Rosário (2007, p.4) argues that the IILP is strangled by the fact that:

> the Portuguese representatives with the neutral complicity of the Brazilians consider that organisation should essentially look after the interests and the defence of Portuguese language, the common denominator of the countries it represents. The Africans seek to remind their partners that the linguistic space of the three continental African countries and Timor-Leste is that of linguistic diversity. And if the IILP is an institution sprouting from CPLP it does not make sense that that reality is dealt with in another organisation with the same objectives.[3]

This example highlights the different universes in which the topic of this study can be viewed, and the relative ignorance about the different contexts in which Portuguese external language policy operates. Besides the ignorance of the '*Others*'' interpretation of a supposedly common project such as Lusophony, there is also a danger of oversimplification of the processes involved. An interesting position about the neocolonialism in Lusophony is that of Do Rosário (2007, p.3) who places the anglophone and francophone communities issued from the independence of the African countries as a linguistic component of the neocolonialist strategy (fuelled by political and mainly economical interests) of the ex-colonial powers, Britain and France respectively. However, Do Rosário (2007, p.5) is adamant that Portugal "did not build a plan or design a strategy of neocolonial type to continue in the colonies"[4]. I presume that his position derives from the known fact that Portugal does not have enough financial resources to back such a project. However, what Do Rosário may be overlooking

---

3   "os representantes portugueses com a neutralidade cúmplice dos brasileiros considera-rem que aquela instituição deve velar essencialmente os interesses e defesa da língua portuguesa, denominador comum dos países nele representados. Os africanos procuram lembrar aos seus parceiros que o panorama linguístico dos três países africanos conti-nentais e Timor Leste é de diversidade linguística. E se o Instituto é uma instituição que emana da CPLP, não faz sentido que essa realidade seja derrogada daquela estância para uma outra com o mesmo fim."

4   "não construiu nenhum plano nem esboçou qualquer estratégia do tipo neocolonial para continuar nas ex-colónias".

is the colonial construct of Portuguese that is reconstructed in the postcolonial 'lusophone' countries (in the same way Pennycook (1998a) exposes the cultural constructs of English and its contemporary reconstruction, or as Phillipson's denounces the neoimperial character of English and Global Englishes (2008a)).

1.3 Theoretical Framework

Conceptual frameworks of language spread policy are characterised by their transdisciplinarity and vastness. As Ammon (1992b, p.47-48) observed:

> A reasonable comprehensive explanation of a specific LSP would at least have to draw on sociology (economic, power, and value structure of the society in question), politicology (form of government and international relations), psychology (motives of politicians), and sociolinguistics (for example, beliefs about languages and about their status/functions). Such a comprehensive approach usually transcends the research capacity of individuals or smaller research units; thus only certain aspects of the phenomenon can, as a rule, be explored within an explicit theoretical (explanatory) framework.

In this study I resort to the sociology of language, sociolinguistics, political science and international relations to explore aspects of the external language spread policies undertaken in Mozambique and Guinea-Bissau. These aspects are:

- Clarify the source countries justifications for external LSPs, briefly explaining their strategies, organisation and activities, examining how those policies and the relations between them are perceived and why from the perspective of different actors (government, academia, media in Africa and in Europe);
- Analyse the national context (from the point of the source and target country) in which these policies emerge and are deploy, concentrating on the role of language in the construction and reinforcement of nationhood, and highlighting the legacies of colonialism;
- Examine the international context that sets the scene for the deployment of such policies, including: the globalisation of languages and the multilateralisation of external LSPs; the dependency of African postcolonial countries on Western agendas, concepts and aid; issues of linguistic human rights and of the defence of cultural and linguistic diversity.

The theme of language and power permeates this whole study. Different facets of the interpenetration of these two concepts serve as theoretical framework for the research inquiry developed. The transdisciplinary theoretical framework (further presented in Chapter 2 Language and Power) has as main theories, principles and concepts:

- External language spread policy, as part of a government's foreign policy (Ammon 1997), is an instrument to project national image and power and to pursue national interest;
- Issues of language and power in society and culture are grounded fundamentally in relations of power. National language policies are at the very heart of the state (Lewis 1980 cited in Rassool 1995);
- National identity as a constructed ideology. Nationhood is constructed in a battle for hegemony, official national languages illustrate that (Billig 1995);
- National identity remains one of the most important multiple categories of individual and collective identities (Smith 1991, Sen 2006);
- Colonialism has made a major imprint on the history of Africa that lingers in the contemporary world through continual dependency of postcolonial societies on the 'developed' world (Laitin 1992, Pennycook 1998, Rassool 2007);
- The spread of international (European postcolonial) languages is supported by structural power. Linguistic imperialism entails unequal exchange, communicative rights and benefits between people/groups defined in terms of their competence in specific languages in a system that legitimates such exploitation (Phillipson 1992, 1998);
- Linguistic human rights and the defence of cultural and linguistic diversity are valid principles (Skutnabb-Kangas 2000);
- Access to language does not guarantee its use, participation in dialogue or access to certain discourses (Giroux 1987, Pennycook 1998, Rassool 2008);
- The contemporary world political system is still a system of states (Jackson and Sørensen 2007). States and their decision-makers are important actors in the global system, where they purposely use competition and collaboration strategies to further their national interest, gaining material and non-material benefits, according to their capabilities and solidarities;
- Non-state actors have an increasing importance in the international system; these include transnational corporations, international organisations, supranational organisations, blocs of states, non-governmental organisations, groups of individuals and individuals. They participate in the definition, decision process and management of important issues in the international system (environment, human rights, end of poverty and oppression);
- Globalisation is a set of processes and discourses relating to the worldwide interconnection and integration of a multitude of areas through globe-spanning networks that has deep historical origins (Fairclough 2001, 2006, Frank and Gills 1995/2000).

Since language became a symbol of nationalism in the modern world, governments have been interested in spreading and/or maintaining the language associated with their nation, internally and externally, as a means to extend and maintain their influence and power. Language spread policies were thus an intrinsic part of the colonial project of European countries. In the colonial setting the European languages were closely associated with the exercise of power and maintenance of domination by the metropole in the colonial territory.

The role of European languages in Africa is complex. Introduced in Africa through the first contacts developed by European explorers and merchants, the European languages created Creoles in their mixing with African languages serving trade and commerce. As colonialism developed, the European languages, incorporated into social and political infrastructure in the colonies, mirrored the underlying inequalities. In that process, they acquired a vast amount of cultural, economic, social and political capital that placed them at the top of the linguistic hierarchy. As it will be discussed later this situation was perpetuated in the postcolonial world. The former colonial European countries develop external language policies as part of the regular business of the state conducting its foreign affairs, as cultural diplomacy. Those policies are often presented by their source countries as innocuous/neutral policies, fostering international understanding and/or helping the target countries in their own linguistic policies. However, being part of a government's foreign policy, external LSPs are "part of the business in the projection of power and influence, of gaining friends and deterring enemies" (Fox 1999, p.1). Their deployment in multilateral arenas, such as the mentioned politico-linguistic blocs, may therefore raise questions regarding the beneficiaries.

The motivations of these relations, based on previous colonial links, can thus be questioned. Can they be characterised as a continuation of colonial relations, in which ex-colonisers seek to maintain and/or promote the dominance of their culture and language, as in cultural and linguistic imperialism? Might they constitute another form of domination and exploitation of the developing world by the West, as in neocolonialism? Do they represent spheres of influence that overlap and compete in a new scramble for Africa, as a means for the European countries to promote their status internationally? Are they an opportunity for the African countries to obtain more funding and support for development projects? Can they be interpreted as an expression of multiple identities in an increasingly multicultural world, which is no longer bounded by territorial constraints or the idea of the nation-state?

1.4 Overview of the Study

The study is set out in five main chapters. *Chapter 1, Introduction*, introduces the subject, justifies the choice, and sets the starting point for the rest of the study. *Chapter 2, Language and Power*, provides the underlying theories in which the study is grounded. It includes three main sections: *Language and the State*, which explores the role of language in the construction and maintenance of nationhood; *Language, Colonialism and Postcolonialism*, examines the importance of the colonial legacy in the linguistic situation of Sub-Saharan African and explores theoretical perspectives regarding language relations; and *Language and Globalisation* approaches the contemporary construction of politico linguistic blocs and the issues of Africa, languages and states in the setting of an increasingly globalised world. *Chapter 3, Methodology*, provides a detailed account of the research approach chosen for the study, including the guiding research questions and assumptions, the research design and techniques and analyses used in the research. *Chapter 4* presents the *country case studies*, Mozambique and Guinea-Bissau, along the parameters defined in Methodology. *Chapter 5, Discussion and Conclusions*, returns to the research questions and in the light of the theories and findings discusses the topic and presents the final conclusions.

Chapter 2 Language and Power

This study is concerned with the role of language policy and, particularly, external language spread policies (LSPs) in structuring language relations in society. A key underlying principle is that issues of language in society and culture are grounded fundamentally in relations of power. Indeed it is argued that national language policy lies at the very heart of the state (Lewis 1980 cited in Rassool 1995). The key role of language policy in defining postcolonial nationhood, within a rapidly evolving interactive global context, clearly needs to take into account of colonial language relations as well as the discursive power relations operating within the international terrain. These issues are examined within an interdisciplinary theoretical framework using key concepts and issues from the sociology of language, sociolinguistics, political science and international relations.

Colonialism has made a major imprint on the history of Africa that lingers in the contemporary world. This chapter offers a perspective on the web of relationships involving European ex-colonial powers including Portugal, the United Kingdom (UK) and France and postcolonial contexts relevant to Lusophone Africa, and in particular, Guinea-Bissau and Mozambique. It seeks to examine the impact of the colonial heritage on the development of external (European) LSPs and in the construction of politico linguistic blocs.

The chapter is organized in three broad sections namely: Language and the State; Language, Colonialism and Postcolonialism; and Language and Globalisation. The first section explores the use of language in the construction of nationhood by the State. It provides the necessary background concepts related to language, state and identity to understand the use of external LSPs by ex-colonial countries to project their image and further their influence. The second section analyses the long-term impact of the colonial legacy on language relations in postcolonial states in Africa. It explores theoretical perspectives regarding language relations, with particular relevance to linguistic imperialism – this theory is considered most important as it highlights a structural imbalance in the international system. The final section provides a contemporary outlook on the construction of political blocs based on culture and language, focusing on the case study countries that are part of my research study, and analyses the issues of Africa, languages and states within the setting of an increasingly globalised world.

2.1 Language and the State

Language represents an important means to create and maintain a sense of nationhood in the sovereign political association that is the State. Governments at least since the emergence of the modern nation state during the 19th century have selected specific languages and varieties of languages to symbolise their nationhood and mediating meanings *intra*nationally and *inter*nationally (Bickley 1982, p.100). States in which nationhood provides a key organizing principle - a social construct with which the grouping of people in a particular state tends to identify - are normally called nation-states. Our world of nations is also a world of formally constituted languages (Billig 1995, p.35). The main concern of this section is to examine the use of languages in the construction of nationhood by the State.

2.1.1 Definitions of Nation-State and National Identity

The search for objective criteria to define a nation has often elected territory, language, history, ethnicity, etc, as elements indispensable for the construction of a nation. Within the ideology of linguistic nationalism, Stalin's objective definition of nation in 1912 is one of the most well known: "A nation is a historically evolved, stable community of language, territory, economic life and psychological make-up manifested in a community of culture" (cited in a footnote in Hobsbawm 1990, p.5) According to Hobsbawm (1990, p.10) it represents "a particular kind of territorial state or the aspiration to establish one ...in the context of a particular stage of technological and economic development". Hobsbawm further stresses the multidimensionality of nationality and identity in a globalising world. I will further explore identity in relation to language and culture in section 2.3.1 when looking at political blocs based on culture and language. For the moment, I would like to stress that the multiple categories of the individual self - gender, language, space and territory (local and regional identities in terms of origin, residence), socio-economic (social class, occupation, employment), culture (sports, music, food, etc), religion, ethnicity and national identity (Smith 1991, Sen 2006) - in a world increasingly interdependent and interconnected by easiness of travel and communication, meet in a multiplication of changeable individual and collective identities. Of these categories, national identity remains one of the most important (Smith 1991, p.170).

At this point it is interesting to observe Billig's (1995) rejection of the explanation of nationalist consciousness purely in terms of identity. Billig (1995, p.24) argues that "(p)sychological identity, on its own, is not the driving force of history, pushing nation-states into their present shapes. National identities are forms of social life, rather than internal psychological states; as such, they are ideological creations, caught up in the historical process of nationhood". Nationalism is "an ideological movement for attaining and maintaining the *autonomy*, *unity* and *identity* of a nation" (Smith 1991, p.74), an aspiration to the state of being a nation, nationhood. However this ideology should not be taken as homogenising. According to Billig (1995, p.87) "(i)n common with other ideologies, nationalism includes contrary themes, especially the key themes of particularism and universalism". I return to this issue when discussing globalisation below (2.3.2.1).

The construction of the nation is an ongoing process. Social and political analysts, concerned with emergent nationalist movements, often overlook the importance of the daily reproduction of national identity. This study is concerned with the role of language in postcolonial countries, in Guinea-Bissau and Mozambique, as a means to construct nationhood, as well as with its role in the maintenance and reinforcement of national identity in the ex-colonial countries, in particular Portugal, as the former coloniser of the fore-mentioned African countries. The study analyses how the ex-colonial language is used as a symbol of unity and national identity in postcolonial states and examines the daily reproduction of nationality in the ex-colonising countries through the analysis of discourses regarding external LSPs. External LSPs can be seen as ways in which an ex-colonial country tries to maintain its former reach; thus they can be seen as serving to reinforce a certain self-image of the country. This is very clear in the broad national consensus backing the promotion of Portuguese culture and language worldwide and in the official justifications provided. For instance, in 1992 the then Minister of Education in Portugal, Couto dos Santos (Instituto Camões 1992, p.1), in the speech signalling the creation of the Instituto Camões (IC), the organisation responsible for the promotion of Portuguese abroad, under the aegis of that ministry, highlighted four main challenges faced by Portugal:

- assertion of Portuguese national identity in the face of the European Union integration process;
- maintenance of Portuguese language and culture in the former colonies;
- language as an important component of cooperation relations;
- support of Portuguese communities abroad.

These challenges represent the reasons behind the creation of the IC and, ultimately, for external LSP in the 1990s. The first 'challenge', assertion of identity, clearly connects with the role of external LSP in the permanent construction of national identity - here in face of a potential 'threat' of dilution by Portugal's integration into the EU. The other 'challenges' point to the reinforcement of

Portugal's self-image as a centre – in this case – of diffusion of language and culture. At present, in relation to the factors mentioned, which are all still valid today, there is in Portugal an additional factor related to internal LSP that involves the integration/assimilation of the increasing number of cultural and linguistic minorities originating from the former colonies and, more recently, from Eastern European countries. To help in the task of uncovering the daily reproduction of national identity it is important to note Billig's (1995, p.6) extended notion of nationalism as covering the "ideological means by which nation-states are reproduced" and the use of the expression *banal nationalism* to "cover the ideological habits which enable the established nations of the West to be reproduced". According to Billig (1995, p.6) "national identity in established nations is remembered because it is embedded in routines of life, which constantly remind, or 'flag', nationhood. However, these reminders, or 'flaggings', are so numerous and that are such a familiar part of the social environment, that they operate mindlessly". Billig (1995) sees nationalism as an ideology that deeply penetrates our consciousness and results in common sense assumptions. In this study I will explore how discourse as ideology is translated in language as a system of communication.

The discussion thus far has briefly examined what a nation-state is and the ideological basis of national identity. The following subsection will examine the centrality of language to the concept of nation-state and focus on the hegemonic role of common languages in nationhood. As Billig (1995, p.27) observes "The battle for nationhood is a battle for hegemony, by which a part claims to speak for the whole nation and to represent the national essence". One of the ways in which this can be illustrated is by "the triumph of official national languages and the suppression of rivals" (Billig 1995, p.27).

2.1.2 Language and the Nation-State

Whilst it is not an aim of this study to examine in depth the birth of the nation-state, several perspectives will be examined briefly as a means of providing a theoretical framework to the study.

Anderson (1991) argues that the historical causes of the concept of nation are rooted in the lexicographical revolution that took place in 16th Century Europe:

> [that] created, and gradually spread, the conviction that languages (in Europe at least) were, so to speak, the personal property of quite specific groups – their daily speakers and readers – and moreover that these groups, imagined as communities,

were entitled to their autonomous place in a fraternity of equals. (Anderson, 1991, p.84)

These political communities that Anderson (1991, p.4,6) mentions are the imagined nations, which he views as cultural artefacts: imagined because in the minds of their members "lives the image of their communion", a fraternal and finite sovereign state (1991, p.6-7). By highlighting the cultural roots of nationalism, Anderson moves away from political ideology. He explains nationalism as a product of and a reaction to the historically preceding cultural systems: the *religious community* and the *dynastic realm* (1991, p.12). Language is, in Anderson's conception, closely intertwined with the birth of the modern nation: "the convergence of capitalism and print technology on the fatal diversity of human language created the possibility of a new form of imagined community" (Anderson, 1991, p.46). Common languages create a proto-national community of intercommunicating elite and provide a more fixed and stable platform that can be easily disseminated through the educational and administrative structure of the state (Andersen 1991). However, Anderson (1991, p.133) warns that languages should not be treated as "*emblems* of nation-ness", language builds "*particular solidarities*".

Others (in Billig 1995) have highlighted other problems in the modernizing world of the 18th and 19th Century to which the nation-state provided a solution: industrialization's demand for standardized skills provided by a centrally control system of education (Gellner 1983, 1987); professionalisation of the army providing military advantage (Kennedy 1988); the role of commercial capitalism (Mann 1992); the development of peripheral regions (Nairn 1975).

As pointed out, often, language is seen as a unifying force within a state - "the natural domain of a particular language" (Wardhaugh 1987, p.3) - or indeed as a symbol of national sentiment (Safran 1999, p.77). In contrast, Billig (1995, p.30) argues that this banal sense of language may be "an invented permanency, developed during the age of the nation-state", that is, nationalism "creates 'our' common sense, unquestioned view that there are, 'naturally' and unproblematically, things called different 'languages', which we speak." Billig exemplifies his thesis by contrasting the Medieval Europe vernacular continuum of communication between villages to the present boundaries of standardised communication (dividing countries and languages).

This sub-section briefly discussed the importance of language in the creation of nationhood. I now examine how states are able to act on languages and discuss the concepts related to external LSP.

2.1.3 Acting on Languages

In the modern world, with the rise of nationalism in the late 18th century, language became a political symbol at the disposal of the state, and could be used as: "a focus for political and cultural struggle", "expand a state's power both within and without and to resist similar expansionist policies of other states" (Wardhaugh 1987, p.4). Language thus became an area of government intervention, a tool and symbol to use in the construction of the nation and in the operationalisation of the state. States establish their national language regimes planning language(s) choices for internal and external communication, between the state and its citizens, between its citizens (to an extent) and between the state and other states and developing policies to implement those choices. The next section will focus on how states act on language - that is, how they establish and manage language regimes by exploring selected concepts in the area of language policy and planning and how they also have established channels to influence language beyond their borders through their foreign policies and specifically using what is referred to as external LSP. However, the establishment and management of language regimes (Coulmas 1998) have increased in complexity, in particular due to the increasing globalisation of the world (section 2.3).

2.1.3.1 Language Policy and Language Planning

Language policy and planning is a vast and permeable area with no overarching theory (Spolsky 2004, Ricento 2006). The concepts of language policy and language planning appeared, within the field of sociolinguistics, at the end of the 1950s and were developed through the 1960s and 1970s, in the aftermath of the decolonisation of many African and Asian countries (Calvet 1996, p.8-9; Kaplan *et al.* 2000, p.1, Ricento 2000).

The concepts of language planning and language policy can be clearly differentiated. Language planning has been characterised by Kaplan and Baldauf Jr. (1997, p.xi) as "an activity, most visibly undertaken by government (simply because it involves massive changes in society), intended to promote systematic linguistic change in some community of speakers". Language policy represents "a body of ideas, laws, regulations, rules and practices intended to achieve the planned language change in the society, group or system" (Kaplan and Baldauf Jr. 1997, p.xi). Underlying the definitions of language policy and planning is the assumption that only the state has the power and the means to pursue them. The state, through language policies, "can promote, prescribe, discourage or prevent the use of languages and thereby empower or disempower speakers of languages by giving higher or lower status to their languages" (Wolff 2000, p.340-341).

Despite the prominent role of the state, there are signs of change in the universe of the linguistic stakeholders. Some groups of states sharing the same language are managing some aspects of their language as a bloc (this is the case of Lusophone countries with the Portuguese orthographic agreement). Additionally the effects of international organisations (e.g. the United Nations fostering cultural diversity and mother tongue education, the World Bank through development policies) and transnational corporations (such as media conglomerates, publishing houses, internet search engines) cannot be overlooked in the management of language in the contemporary world. Language planning by states, or any other agents, also has limits. As noted by Ricento (2000, p.16) linguistic behaviour is social behaviour, motivated and influenced by attitudes and beliefs of speakers and speech communities, as well as macro economic and political forces. In this study the perspective focuses on the state and its agents; when found relevant the other actors are mentioned.

Having established a general idea of the concept of language policy and planning, the next section examines the concept of LSP.

2.1.3.2 Language Spread Policy

At the start of the 1990s, the concept of external LSP emerged concentrating particularly on government promotion of a language abroad (Phillipson, 1992, p.82). However LSPs have been implicit in imperialist conquest and colonial enterprise, for example, the spread of Latin in Roman Empire, European colonial exploitation of Africa and elsewhere in the colonized world, and in general cultural relations. As stated in the introductory chapter, the *International Journal of the Sociology of Language* published in 1992 and 1994 a double issue on the subject of (contemporary) external LSPs. German Professor Ulrich Ammon (1997, p.51) and editor of the mentioned journal defines the concept thus:

> *Language-spread policy (LSP)*, which is carried out by numerous nations, aims at spreading the own language, either to speakers or domains. It can be internal or external, declared or undeclared, overt or disguised, and related in different ways to national language policy. The interests of receivers usually diverge from those of agents, who strive to increase their native-language advantage in international communication, to disseminate their ideology, to create binding economic ties, to profit economically from language teaching, or to pamper their national pride. At the basis of LSP is a power vision or market view of languages, other rhetoric notwithstanding.

Ammon (1997, p.53) points to connections between LSP and national language policy, which overlap "insofar as national language policy entails, as a rule, *internal* language spread policy". In the case of external LSP there are also relations to other countries' internal and external LSP. For example, "some countries, particularly the developing countries, are often supported in planning or implementing their national language policy by institutions of other countries, sometimes precisely those that are at the same time the agents of those countries' external language-spread policy" (Ammon 1997, p.53). The UK, the United States of America (USA), France, Germany, Portugal, Italy and many other countries promote their languages, in different scales according to their political strategies and economic means. However, as Phillipson (1992, p.35) states, there are "essential similarities in the way that western nations promote the continued use of their languages abroad, both in education and in society at large." Language spread theory, according to Phillipson (1992, p.79-80) "can provide a useful framework for analysing processes of language spread and for synthesizing the results of such studies", but is no more than "a heuristic formula and not specifically concerned with analysing structural forces in society". Indeed, frameworks and typologies do have their inbuilt biases and constraints. In a later work, Phillipson intensifies his critique and classifies language "spread" as "another apparently innocuous term that refers to a seemingly agentless process, as though it is not people and particular interests that account for the expansion of a language" (Phillipson 2000, p.89). However, Ammon (1997, p.51) in the definition of LSP quoted at the beginning of the subsection does highlight the interests of the agents and writing on external LSP, particularly in developing countries, notes the "possibility of pressures from outside in favor of certain languages" through "financial or technical aid to countries" which "may be connected, though in a subtle way, to an improved status of the donor's preferred language" (Ammon 1997, p.53). Whilst acknowledging Phillipson's critique of language spread theory, this study will use the concept as a framework in which to examine issues related to the state sanctioned export of powerful ex-colonial languages. Issues of power imbalances will be highlighted.

The next subsection examines specifically the concept of external LSP, which is at the heart of this study, within the broad context of foreign policy and cultural relations.

2.1.3.3 Foreign Policy, Cultural Relations and External Language Spread Policy

The contemporary world political system is still a system of states, an *interna*tional system. States interact with each other in the international system. Foreign or external policy is the "substance, aim and attitudes of a state's relations with others" (Evans and Newnham 1998, p.128-129). This relationship has different dimensions, of which culture is one. Political scientists usually rank culture as the third or fourth 'pillar of foreign policy', after politics, trade and, for some, defence (Mitchell 1986, p.1). Cultural diplomacy is therefore "part of the business in the projection of power and influence, of gaining friends and deterring enemies" (Fox 1999, p.1). Historically, in relation to power and the state, power was seen as 'the use of coercion, influence, authority, force or manipulation to change the behaviour of others in a desired direction" (Cox 1981, p.131). Sources of power have traditionally been associated with territory, population, military and economic assets and direct exercise of power observed in military action or through economic pressure. However, political units have used culture to relate to one another since before the Ancient Greek and Roman empires. The development of the concept of the modern nation-state in Europe and the creation of the cultural nation to fit the territorial, political and economic state unit, along with increased structuring of the international system around balances of power has reinforced the association of cultural relations with the projection of national power and the pursuit of national interest, namely through the projection of the nation's image abroad or any cultural means (Taylor 1997, p.80; Fox 1999, p.3).

Presently, cultural relations, which were placed traditionally in the domestic/international boundary of the sovereignty of the state, are increasingly developed by other actors and moving away from a national base, for example, the development of relations directly between arts organisations, (see later in the case studies) denoting the increasing interconnectedness of the world - no wonder the field is characterised by a dispersion of work and a multitude of concepts. In parallel, changes of paradigms have forced language policy and planning to come to terms with "the social context and the symbolic value of languages" (Kaplan *et al.* 2000, p.3), that is, language viewed as a complex sedimentation process serving a variety of discoursal, symbolic and practical functions (Ricento 2006). Increasingly researchers working in the field of language policy and planning have come to realise the political nature of their work. That is, language policy and planning are not neutral; choices made in those areas represent power struggles enacted through language, fought between dominant and dominated languages (from a political and social point of view), and no longer confined to the national arenas.

Of particular interest to this study are the concepts of cultural propaganda, cultural diplomacy and cultural relations that Mitchell (1986, p.28) presents in a progression "from the use of culture as a force to advance national ends, through the association of culture with current diplomatic aims, to an open collaborative relationship". Mitchell highlights the fact that at any point on the scale there may be an element of propaganda. It could be argued that this element of propaganda is fundamentally self-interest (any perceived positive outcome obtained

43

from the engagement) and is always present in the relationship. The awareness and willingness to respond/satisfy the needs/interests/objectives of the '*Other*' (state/people) engaging in the relationship is what distinguishes the concepts. However, a lesser degree of 'selfishness' in state relations does not imply more equal relations, since the parameters of the relationship may rest in different power positions anyway – as those defined by hegemonic processes in the case of colonialism, postcolonialism or in the contemporary pervasiveness of American culture. The notion of cultural propaganda has somewhat fallen in disuse and, in the study area of cultural diplomacy and relations, the concept of soft power (power as an indirect influence) has become increasingly popular. The concept of soft power is defined as an ability to entice and attract, co-opting rather than coercing people (Nye 2002, p.8-9) and "associated with intangible power resources such as an attractive culture, ideology and institutions" (Nye 2002, p.9), soft power is hegemonic and is not new. It is intrinsic to the imperialist project (as in the use of language and culture in India and Sub Saharan Africa discussed in Rassool 2007).

With the increasing interconnectedness of the world, new dimensions have been added to the relations between national states and foreign states and peoples. Besides the traditional state-to-state relations, the relations have been broadened to national state-to-foreign people relations, people-to-people relations and also foreign people-to-state relations. The increasing use of the concept of public diplomacy (Leonard et al 2002, Bound et al 2007, Melissen 2007) denotes some of those changes. The term, coined in 1965 by Edmund Gullian of the Fletcher School of Law and Diplomacy (Malone 1988, p.12), is described as "a diverse array of activities whose only common bond is that they are intended to affect people's attitudes and that they support the foreign policy interest of the nation" (Malone 1988, p.3). Its underlying idea is "that by communicating directly with the people of other countries we may be able to affect their thinking in ways beneficial to ourselves and even to them as well. The objective, in most cases, is "to influence the behavior of a foreign government by influencing the attitudes of its citizens" (Malone 1988, p.2-3).

The concept of public diplomacy has become particularly important in the United Kingdom (UK). In 2005, British cultural diplomacy underwent a major review conducted by Lord Carter of Coles. The review led to the establishment of the Public Diplomacy Board. One of its specific objectives is to agree among the main public diplomacy partners, "a list of 25 (or so) priority countries for public diplomacy" and another to agree on "geographical priorities, target audience, priority themes, action planes and measurable outcomes" (Foreign and Commonwealth Office 2006a, p.1). Overall, the British Council now operates within the strategic framework set by the Public Diplomacy Board. Its aim is "to inform and engage individuals and organisations overseas, in order to improve understanding of and influence for the UK in a manner consistent with governmental medium and long term goals" (British Council 2006, p.5). According to a Demos report (Bound *et al.* 2007, p.23): "The review marked an important shift in approaches in the UK, because it moved away from the idea that public diplomacy aims merely to change *perceptions*, to the notion that it should also seek to change *behaviour*, in line with the government's international priorities."

Alternative or closely related expressions to public diplomacy are overseas information policy, national self-advertisement (Taylor 1997, p.79); public oratory (Dovring 1997, p.44); popular diplomacy (Fox 1999, p.3); cultural branding (Tomalin 2004, p.1); and nation branding and competitive identity (Anholt 2009). The development of this increasing number of terms tries to encapsulate the multidimensionality in which cultural relations and cultural diplomacy are developed and the increasing difficulty of the state to secure its role as the main architect of international cultural relations. However, within that multiplicity, the state still has an important role in the development of cultural relations in the practice of its foreign or external cultural policy, in which I include external LSP. External LSP, the spread of a national language abroad, is regarded for the purposes of this study as a part of foreign or external cultural policy.

Foreign policy includes specific policies in the cultural area, a sub-area that can be named foreign cultural policy or external cultural policy. Regardless of subdivisions, the overall objectives of foreign policy have an impact on external cultural policy, for instance in the choice and prioritisation of countries with which to interact (as seen earlier in the UK example). Mitchell (1986, p.78, 226-227) defines external cultural policy as a product and a component of foreign policy, insofar as this is seen as the national concept in relation to the world and individual countries. This concept of foreign policy is in line with the observation of the national interest, given a country's geopolitical and economic aims. External cultural policy is also connected with internal cultural policy, given that foreign policy is developed and mediates between the internal environment of a state and the global context (Evans and Newnham 1998, p.179).

Seeking to clarify the terms cultural relations and cultural diplomacy some authors make differentiations based on agents and/or objectives (for example Mitchell 1986). I propose to use the concept of cultural relations as a general term to describe the relations in the area of culture between collective identities, that is, regardless of type of agents, means or objectives - cultural relations can be conducted for mutual and/or unilateral benefits, that is, something that needs to be determined case by case. A definition of cultural diplomacy should be restricted to governments and their agents that focus on exchange of cultural ideas and goods, where the 'mutual understanding' has as, direct or indirect, objective the pursuit of soft power. Phillipson (1992, p.58) considers cultural diplomacy to be one of the means of cultural imperialism. It could be argued that this position dismisses any positive aspects of cultural diplomacy (presenting yourself and knowing the '*Other*') and also underestimates the capacity of the '*Other*' to receive and reason whatever is presented. Nevertheless some activities of cultural diplomacy can contribute to cultural imperialism, defined as "the sum of processes by which a society is brought into the modern world system and how its dominating stratum is attracted, pressured, forced, and sometimes bribed into shaping social institutions to correspond to, or even promote, the values and structures of the dominating center of the system" (Schiller 1976, p.9 cited in Phillipson, 1992, p.58).

The development of cultural diplomacy encompasses a broad area that does not depend intrinsically upon the diffusion of language (Mitchell 1986, p.161). However language is very important; it is the basis of most communication and is seen by many states as a symbol of their national identity. Wyszomirski (2003, p. 3 and 12) in her comparison of cultural diplomacy programs identifies a common repertoire that specifically includes language related activities:

- the exchange of individuals for educational and cultural purposes
- sending exhibitions and performances abroad
- sponsoring seminars and conferences both in-country and abroad that include international participants
- support for language studies programs and institutions
- support for infrastructure in the form of cultural institutes/centres/forum abroad
- resources in the form of staff and personnel (both at home and abroad)
- support for country studies programs (e.g., American studies, Austrian studies, etc.)
- international cooperation on cultural programs and projects
- activities that are related to trade in cultural products and services.

This study focuses on language teaching and the model of the national cultural institute/centre, which are often tied together, but not exclusively. The breakdown of the concept of external LSP in the following subsection will help structure the analysis presented in the findings.

2.1.3.4 External Language Spread Policy

'External language spread policy' is not an expression used in political discourse. The terms normally used are, in English, *language promotion and development*; in French, *diffusion* and *promotion linguistique, rayonnement de la langue*; in Portuguese, *difusão* or *divulgação da língua, promover* or *valorizar a língua, afirmação da língua*. Ammon testifies that in Germany, the term preferred is 'language promotion'/ *Sprachförderung* (1992b, p.33). Language spread policy (LSP) is defined as comprising "all endeavors, directed or supported by institutions of a state, which aim either at spreading a language beyond its present area and domains or at preventing the retraction of a language from its present area and domains" (Ammon 1992a, p.7). The distinguishing feature of LSP is, according to Ammon (1992b, p.33) the intentionality of spreading language. External language spread refers to the development of those policies abroad that is outside of the territory of the state developing the policy.

In the 1992 volume 95 of the *International Journal of the Sociology of Language* dedicated to LSP, Ammon (1992a, p.6) observed the need to develop a critical view of the activities of language spreading, in order to become fully aware of the interests involved in the policy, both of the side that spreads it as well as of the recipients - since "(a)ny kind of language-spread policy is typically justified, upon questioning, by some noble motives, which, however, upon close examination prove to camouflage more earthly interests".

A strong current of authors classifies LSP activities as linguistic imperialism (this theory is explored in section 2.2.3.1). Authors such as Ammon (1992b, p.48) consider a general condemnation of LSP as inadequate, although recognising that LSP "seems to be more or less intricately connected with a number of attitudes towards language", such as preference for one's language, monolingual state, mother-tongue advantage, power or market view of language, refutation of artificial language (Ammon 1997, p.56).

Interesting to this study is also the clarification Pennycook (2000, p.107-108) makes of the two different meanings of ideology in the context of global language spread (he refers to English but his words can be generalized to other international languages). Pennycook (2000, p.107-108) differentiates two concepts of the ideological; first, ideological in a general sense to mean "political": "ideological implications refer to a critical and political analysis of the effects of the global spread of English" - analysis of the "structural power" of English. A second "sense of ideological seems to imply that the spread of English has ideological effects on people, that is to say, English is the purveyor of thoughts, cultures and ideologies that affect the ways in which people think and behave" - analysis of the "discursive effects" of English (Pennycook 2000, p.107-108). This second sense regards the view of language as a discourse.

Language as discourse is an embodiment of meaning, a particular voice (Luke et al. 1990). Discourse, in this sense, is a particular way of representing some part or aspect of the world, as in ideology, as a system of ideas whose hold depends "not only on its expression of the interests of a ruling class but also on its acceptance as 'normal reality' or 'common sense' by those in practice subordinated to it" (Williams 1988, p. 157 and 145). Discourse is independent of which language is used, it relates to ways of thinking and how any language can be used to perpetuate conscious and unconsciously (unequal) relations of power. Although this study is mostly concerned with the structural power of international languages, in particular how external LSPs are contributing to the creation, maintenance and expansion of a hegemonic political and linguistic space for Portuguese language and its agents, I am also interested in exploring language as discourse, that is, exposing the ideological underpinnings of the external LSPs activities and discourse. The real motives for LSP are often not clear. Ammon (1992b, p.34) assumes that motives can be inferred from the reasons given for LSP – and for the general justifications given for cultural diplomacy - but warns about problems of such an inference: "The declared interests are not necessarily identical with the real ones. It seems helpful to perceive such declarations generally as *rhetoric*, which deserve to be analysed critically" (Ammon 1997, p.54). In the field of cultural relations, Mitchell (1986, p.12-21) outlines four main arguments in their support that ultimately can also justify the pursuit of LSP: as an instrument of peace, creating a favourable atmosphere; as a support for conventional diplomacy whereby the activities of cultural agencies create a favourable impression on foreigners; as a vehicle for international understanding, it connects with the first argument, since cultural relations are seen to further positive understanding; and as a lubricant for trade, cultural relations favour the circumstances of a country. The public justifications for external LSP synthesised by Ammon (1997, pp.54-55) as gaining advantage for a country are:

1. The native-language or near-native-language advantage in communication: "asymmetry in language skills can very much affect the weight of arguments."
2. A channel for spreading one's view of the world, one's values or ideology.
3. Improved conditions for developing economic ties: "People prefer, as a rule, doing business with countries whose language is familiar to them to doing business with others."
4. Revenues from foreign-language studies of the country's language and from selling language-related products: People also spend less in learning other languages when international communication takes place in their language.
5. Preservation of national identity or, rather, national pride.

Underlying the above list of motives and reasons is a range of justifications that highlights values of a global identity and moral (mutual understanding, peace) to a longer list of "selfish" interests (reinforcement of national identity,

48

advantage in communication, cultural acculturation, lubricant of activities of the source country in the target country). This is not surprising as historically pervasive social, economic and political theories stress the divisiveness of humankind. These are general arguments and justifications that will be examined in the practice of the case studies. However to better understand some of the nuances of the concept of external LSP in practise I analyse briefly the French case.

Historically, France has evidenced a political historical determination to internally spread French (and to defend its usage in particular from English) and a strong, consistent and clear commitment to maintain the international status of French language abroad. In order to advance their project, incentives that stretch the factual truth are often used, a recent example is a title from the 2009 brochure of the French Ministry of Foreign and European Affairs, *Promoting French Around the World*, that reads: "French, the only language other than English that is spoken on all five continents" (Ministère des Affaires étrangères et européennes 2009, p.3). *Francophonie* is a hallmark of French foreign policy, meaning "all the measures to promote French and the values that it conveys" (OECD/DAC 2004, p.22). The official justification for French external LSP has shifted in the 1980s, and especially the 1990s, from the greatness of French culture and the beauty of French language to stressing the defense of language diversity and cultural pluralism through the continual promotion of the teaching of French worldwide and its use in international organisations, along with supporting other languages also present in Francophone countries. The 2008 White Paper on France's Foreign and European Policy (Juppé and Schweitzer 2008, p.63) advances practical measures, for instance, to intensify the stress on the principle of cultural diversity - French diplomats should lead by example and learn the language of the country in which he/she is serving; by indicating that Francophony is not fighting the global vehicular language, that is the English language; by advising to accept the idea that French officials can and should work in other languages in order to defend the interests of their country (particularly in English, German, Spanish and Arabic). The French Ministry of Foreign Affairs (Ministère des Affaires étrangères et européennes 2007c) justifies: "The policy of spreading and promoting the French language implemented by the Ministry of Foreign Affairs is at the exact conjunction of two priorities that underpin France's international co-operation action: the requirement of solidarity and influence strategies". Solidarity is defined as regarding "the partner countries where France is the language of education" and with which educational cooperation is developed; and influence "as a dialogue with other languages and cultures in the world in order to promote cultural diversity". The same document also uses the expression "external linguistic policy", a first use in the governmental documents reviewed for this study. It reads: "our external linguistic policy is organised around three main areas of work: promoting multilingualism, which notably involves maintaining the place of the French language in international organisations, in particular in Europe; enhancing the status of the French language as a development aid tool in the countries in the priority solidarity zones and redefining our language offer in the major emerging countries in order to attract new interest in the French language" (Ministère des Affaires étrangères et européennes 2007c). It can be argued that "solidarity", "dialogue", "cultural diversity", "multilingualism", "cooperation", "development aid" are used to invoke positive meanings to mask or disguise the straightforward more nationalistic and selfish interests: "influence", "maintaining the place of French", "enhancing the status" of French, "attract new interest in the French language".

The typical agents of LSP, as of language policy and planning in general, are governments, although churches and private organisations can play a significant role (Ammon 1992b, p.33). Historically, and in particular in the colonising enterprise that underpins the case studies, the work of missionaries in the area of language was particularly important. They played a crucial role in the definition of what a language was (and is). The different missionary groups, differentiated by their own national origin, faith and other characteristics, identified, named and codified different languages that from a view of the speakers, and/or by using linguistic criteria, were the same language. They also worked with the states in the dissemination of the European languages. At present the influence of the missionaries is still very important. In the case studies presented later, now as in the past, they are important disseminators and producers of linguistic resources. Internationally, the work of the Summer Institute of Linguistics, a faith-based NGO, for capacity building in sustainable language development and research (Ethnologue) is widely recognised and reflects the continuous importance of the work of missionaries in the area of language, internationally.

Governments can develop LSP directly or through executing agencies that "are dependent on the government only with respect to basic policy lines but quite autonomous in the details of policy implementation" (Ammon 1997, p.51). Government approach to cultural diplomacy and LSP is often related to the way central government is organised: policy definition and activities can be centralised or devolved by means of arm's length institutions. However, pure models tend to exist only in theoretical exercises. Governments use a variety of approaches and means.

For instance, traditionally the French government conducts its cultural diplomacy through the Ministry of Foreign Affairs. The Direction Générale de la Cooperation Internationale et du Développement (DGCID), is responsible for cultural co-operation and promotion of the French language. In 2009 the

Direction Générale de la Mondialisation, du Développement et des Partenariats, DGM, was created in response to the challenges of globalisation and is now responsible for the promotion of French language and culture, with the involvement of other bodies. However, the relations of the case study countries with France were managed by the French Ministry of Cooperation until the end of the 1990s. Cahen (1998) saw the fact that the PALOP (African countries with Portuguese as Official Language) were dependent on the French Ministry of Cooperation and not on the Ministry of Foreign Affairs as an indication that France always wanted to extend its influence to Portuguese Africa.

Here it is worth noting an important current of criticism to French policies in Africa. During the 1980s and 1990s, personal links between French and African political élites were often criticized for extending colonial rule, as regimes where supported in exchange for political and financial favours. One of the most prolific but also controversial writers on the subject was François-Xavier Verschave. In his books, *La Françafrique* (1998) and *Noir Silence* (2000) he accused some of the actors of French African policy of exploiting the natural and geopolitical resources of the Francophone countries. He demonstrated how corruption, murder, manipulation of war and arms traffic were used as tools in a number of different countries, mostly Francophone, such as Rwanda, Congo, Cameroon, but also in Lusophone countries, such as Guinea-Bissau and Angola. The *Françafrique* allegations have been difficult and time consuming to prove. For instance, in 1993 the son of former President François Mitterrand, Jean-Christophe Mitterrand had to face justice over an illegal deal to sell arms to Angola: the process, concluded in 2006, confirmed fiscal fraud.

Prior to 1998, the Ministry of Cooperation handled French relations with former colonies, and other, mostly African, countries, collectively known as *le champ*. In February 1998 the French development system underwent extensive reform that included among other changes the extinction of the Ministry of Co-operation and the fusion of its services with the Ministry of Foreign Affairs. The merger embodied the idea of a unique diplomatic corps, with the objective to give greater unity to the exterior action of the state in terms of cooperation. This change of organisational structure in France had great impact on the work developed in Africa. Up to 1999 only the Ministère de la Coopération had responsibility over Africa. The French cultural centres in Africa were under their jurisdiction and their mission was cultural cooperation (Belorgey, Director of the Centro Cultural Franco Moçambicano, 2002 interview). After 1999, according to Belorgey (2002 interview), that merger of institutions, also mixed two different institutional cultures: on one hand, the culture of the Ministère de la Coopération which was one of development (people that knew the ground), and on the other hand, there was the culture of the Ministère des Affaires Étrangères, a culture of cultural diplomacy (promotion of France's image). Belorgey (2002 interview) commented that this prompted the arrival, in Africa, of Cultural and Co-operation attachés and directors of cultural centres with no experience of Africa - that purely transplanted what they had been doing in Europe to Africa, without proper consideration for local realities.

The issue of the influence of organisational changes affecting policies will be referred to in the findings of this study. For the moment I would like to establish that there are different organisational cultures and ideologies that have a direct impact in the definition, planning and implementation of policies, and in the study's particular area of external LSPs.

In terms of the overall structure in place for cultural diplomacy and external language spread, it is also interesting to note the case of France. Unlike the UK with the British Council or Germany with the Goethe Institute, France has not delegated its cultural action to one main institution; instead it operates through a multitude of specialized agencies. French cultural policy, which includes a policy of promotion of French language, makes use of a network of cooperation and cultural action services operating at embassies, cultural centres and institutes, Alliances Françaises and French *lycées*. Although not under the aegis of one single entity, those various organisations resemble a family engaging in external French cultural action (Alliance Française de Paris 2002, p.5). However, there has been a progressive rethinking of the French cultural network abroad. In 2004, the Duvernois Report outlined a new cultural influence strategy to help France defend its national interest and deal with the decline of prestige it has suffered in the hierarchy of nations (Duvernois 2004, p.7). As a consequence two new bodies, inspired by UK models, were introduced, in 2006, into France's cultural relations portfolio: Campus France (similar to Education UK) and CulturesFrance (sharing similarities with the British Council). In the launch, the then French Foreign Minister, Phillipe Douste-Blazy, said "I would like to make the trade mark of France more visible, in just the way the British Council does for Britain" (British Council 2006a, p.4). CulturesFrance allows France to have a *signature labellisée* (Duvernois in Legendre 2007), in the same way the British Council and the Goethe Institute, function for the UK and Germany. However, in November 2006, the Cour des Comptes (National Audit Office) accused the new arts body of deviating from its main mission of promoting French culture abroad, to become a cultural operator in France. This prompted a new report, by Adrien Gouteyron (2008), advising an overall change of strategy, in the sense of diplomacy at the service of culture (aiding in the internationalisation of cultural operators – particularly relevant in developed countries) instead of culture at the service of diplomacy. New legislation was approved by the French senate on 22nd February 2010 and it was later adopted by the French National Assembly in

July, establishing two new agencies, the Institut français and the Agence Française pour l'Expertise et la Mobilité Internationales to replace respectively CulturesFrance and CampusFrance The decision to connect the French cultural centres abroad and the embassies' services for cooperation and cultural action (SCAC) to the new Institut français is expected to be decided in 2013, although experimental connections will be tried out. The changes follow the process of reform launched by French Foreign Affairs Minister, Bernard Kouchner in March 2009 to respond to the French *diplomatie culturelle en crise* and having as main objective to shift from a "*logic of diffusion* trapped in its own historical heritage, to *a diplomacy of influence*, based on the dissemination and enrichment of French culture by contact with other cultures while adapting to local realities"[5] (Kergueris 2010, p.11).

The above lengthy examination of the French case, illustrates how organizational structures change, adapting to internal (shared roles of ministries, economic efficiency) and external challenges (public diplomacy, nation branding), to maintain optimal systems of culture and language spread. In the specific field of cultural diplomacy and external LSPs, policies are defined and conducted differently according to the target although using the same organizational structure. Developed countries and developing countries seem to be treated differently.

The structure of the international system, historical conditions and the different capabilities of each state have an influence in the motives, strategies, organisation, activities and resources (human, material, financial) each country is able to devote to LSP and also on how a country is able to reason being the target of LSP. The international system is not a system of equal states. Although formally it can be said that states are equal (e.g. formal sovereignty recognised by other and acceptance as members of the UN), their different capabilities (at social, political, economic and military level) are different. Therefore, some states are more equal than others - just like in Orwell's fable *Animal Farm* -, some states have more power and resources than others; some states are weaker than others. Rhetorical discourse about the democratic and universalistic spirit of international cultural relations can make us overlook the intrinsic inequality of states in the international system: in particular, between the Western nation-states creators of the system and a few handful of other countries successful in fitting the modernization frameworks and developmental paths set by the West,

---

5   "logique de rayonement, prisonnière de son heritage historique, à une diplomatie d'influence, s'appuyant sur une culture Française qui ne cherche pas seulement à de diffuser, mais également à s'enrichir au contact des autres cultures en s'adaptant aux realités locales"

which are the gatekeepers of the same international system (through systems such as the UN Security Council or the G20), and the developing nations, weaker and exploited states, issued mainly from the decolonisation processes of the 1950s, 1960s and 1970s in Africa and Asia.

The discussion so far has examined how language and nation-state relate, how states act on languages, and paid particular attention to the concept of external LSP. I will now analyse the legacies of colonialism in the area of language in sub-Saharan Africa, exploring the linguistic situation, the language policies and the general issue of interpretation of language relations.

2.2 Language, Colonialism and Postcolonialism

With the sea voyages of the 15th Century, Europeans encountered lands and people that they used for their own benefit. Their worldwide presence had a major impact in the area of language and transformed the political and economic structure of the world. For languages it was "the beginning of the end for very small languages, and the start of the era of big languages" (Janson 2002, p.200). For the world system it signalled the start of colonial relations. As Europeans established relations with the different peoples, language contact resulted in some languages being wiped out and replaced and new ones emerging. Europeans imposed their own political and economic systems and explored the territories and their people to their advantage.

The European legacies of colonial language, models of state organisation and structural economic dependency lingered into the postcolonial world, as the modern European assembly of nation-states - idealised as a group with one leadership and one spoken and written language, in perpetual competition in the arenas of politics, culture, and language - became the model for much of the world (Janson 2002). An ideal and illusionary equal model, as the new states of the postcolonial world are different in terms of history and social, economic and political structures from the nation-states of the West they try to emulate. These territorial states are weaker states, in the sense that many are still today developing "efficient political institutions, a solid economic basis and a substantial degree of national unity" (Jackson and Sørensen 2007, p.20).

Language relations, defined and established in the colonial encounter, were transferred to postcolonial societies by continuation and reproduction of structures and discourses from the colonial masters to assimilated (consciously or not) strata of the population that became the elite of the new states. The colonial and the postcolonial state, through language-in-education policies, engineer the distribution of linguistic and cultural capital (Bourdieu 1991), revealing the instrumental role of language in the production, maintenance and change of power relations in society (Skutnabb-Kangas 1988, 1998, Rassool 1998, Fairclough 2001).

2.2.1 Legacies of Colonialism

Africa is a continent carved up by European colonialism. The Scramble for Africa is a major event in the politico-cultural history of Africa: within a period of 20 years (1880-1900) only Liberia (run by ex-African-American slaves) and Ethiopia were free of European control. Up to 1880 European presence in Africa was limited to coastal areas and along major rivers, such as the Niger and the Congo. However a series of factors caused a race of the European powers in the colonization of Africa. Those factors - which are not discussed in this study - included: enforcing the end of the slave trade and finding economic alternatives for the European markets (legitimate trade), which were also suffering in the Long Depression (1873-1896); increase exploration of the interior of the African continent that resulted in the discovery of new resources (markets, labour and materials), supported by advances in medicine (treatment of tropical diseases) and technology (weaponry, iron hulled boats and steam engines); new outlet for the rivalry of European powers (also unified Germany and unified Italy wanted to expand, which was no longer possible in Europe).

The Agreement of the Berlin Conference of 1884-85, signed by the UK, France, Germany, Austria, Belgium, Denmark, Spain, USA, Italy, the Netherlands, Portugal, Russia, Sweden-Norway, and Turkey (Ottoman Empire), laid down the rules for the partitioning of Africa. The powers seeking colonies agreed to the development of trade and civilization in Africa, ruled by several principles, the main ones being the notification of other powers and the principle of effective occupation. As the European powers divided up Africa at the Berlin Conference, relying on the hegemonic concept of terra nullius, they fractured existing political and cultural boundaries (Rassool 2007) and replaced them with economic and politically driven divisions, reinforced later by cultural colonialism. European languages dominated state administration, teaching and written transactions. The language inequalities that emerged in the process of colonisation would have long-term sociocultural, economic and political effects throughout sub-Saharan Africa (Rassool 2007). This Scramble for Africa and the historical rivalries of metropolitan colonisers can be seen as a framework in which to interpret some contemporary discourses on the 'war' of languages. Laitin (1992, p.85) presents a synthetic depiction of the Portuguese colonialist case:

The Portuguese government, in ruling Angola and Mozambique, felt more threatened by English and French - disseminated by traders and missionaries -than by the vernaculars. In 1903, the colonial government forbade the use of English in Angolan schools. Most of the Catholic Mission Society schools were run by the French, but to assuage government fears the French catholic fathers presented themselves in Lisbon pretending to be Portuguese.

Once English and French were marginalized, however, Portugal challenged the growth of the vernaculars. Overriding the missionary tribal divisions that gave each denomination the right to a specific language group, Portuguese-government education, once it got under way, emphasized immersion in Portuguese. Decree no.77, published in 1921, prohibited the use of native languages in all schools and prohibited the publication of anything in the vernacular, except as a parallel text to Portuguese. As in the French colonies, knowledge of the colonial language was the key criterion for citizenship. After the Second World War, the government took greater control over education, and in 1950 Portuguese was established as the medium of instruction in all schools (Henderson, 1979; Newitt, 1987).

This depiction by Laitin (1992, p.85) encapsulates a number of issues that are relevant to this study. First, the perception of threat to Portuguese from English and French spread by traders and missionaries (respectively the first economic agents of globalisation and of cultural colonisation - culture here understood in a broad sense to include religion) - that will linger in certain postcolonial/neocolonialist discourses, with particular relevance for the 1990s, regarding the case studies in this research. Secondly, local languages were not perceived as representing a threat in line with dismissive colonial attitudes towards the African languages - in some colonial Portuguese discourses derogatively labelled *língua de cão* (dog's tongue) or *língua de preto* (black's tongue). These attitudes were assimilated and are still present in the postcolonial societies (Saiete (2008) provides a contemporary example of similar language attitudes in Mozambique). Thirdly, Laitin alludes to "the missionary tribal divisions that gave each denomination the right to a specific language group". This relates to the power that European agents (in particular missionaries) had of naming, standardising and developing languages, according to their own standards and not those of the speakers of the languages. Fourthly, Laitin notes the immersion in Portuguese and how the language became a criterion for citizenship. The population in the Portuguese colonies, clearly seen as African (Cape Verde's population was seen as miscegenated) such as Angola, Guinea-Bissau and Mozambique, was divided into three legal categories: "citizens, i.e. the Portuguese; indigenous or native; and "assimilated". The assimilated were indigenous people who had to undergo a probation period and exams in order to prove that they were Christian, that they dressed in European fashion, that they were monogamous, and that they spoke Portuguese" (De Almeida 2008, p.6).

Returning to the issue of competition between LSPs it is also relevant to the understanding of the rivalry between colonial powers involving Portugal to note the historical episode of the Pink Map. At the Berlin Conference (1884-1885) the European powers decided that only effective occupation should justify claims to territory in Africa. This undermined Portuguese ambitions to unite the two coasts of Africa, joining Angola and Mozambique, producing a corridor between the West and the East of Africa. A 'Pink Map' (1886) was drawn showing a Portuguese Meridian Africa, right on the way of the British ambitions to unite Cairo to Cape Town along a North-South axis. An ultimatum demanding retreat from the disputed areas was issued by the UK in 1890; the matter was later settled by treaties in 1890 and 1891 (De Magalhães 1990). The ultimatum episode forced Portugal to give up its ambitions, straining the relations between the two countries, and leaving in Portuguese historical memory the ghostly presence of a threatening England. At the time, as De Almeida (2008, p.5) notes, Portugal, given the demise of its empire in India and the East in the 16th and 17th centuries, and in Brazil in the 17th and 18th centuries, had no economic, military or demographic power to effectively occupy its historical territories in Africa. Only with Salazar's dictatorial regime (1926-1974) was it possible to set up a proper colonial enterprise in Africa (De Almeida 2008, p.5). European powers endeavour to negotiate amongst themselves the limits of their spheres of influence, sometimes behind each other's back; therefore similar episodes to the mentioned just above were not uncommon.

The weakening of the major European powers after the two world wars, allowed most colonies to attain political independence. Moreover the spread of European theories of freedom and equality, especially the right of people to self-determination, and the spread of Marxist ideas, provided colonised nations a theoretical structure to oppose white colonialism and develop a 'third alternative' to the West and to Eastern socialist countries. The colonial disconnection between the European and African countries would lead, in the case of British and French possessions to formal independences in the 1950s and 1960s, but retaining dependence through economic development aid and the debt crisis of the 1970s and 1980s. In the British case the relations with many of its former colonies were formally maintained through the Commonwealth of Nations. The Arab countries have not joined the Commonwealth - and the UK retained sovereignty over 14 Overseas Territories. In the case of France, President De Gaulle started, in 1958, an autonomy process through a *Communauté*, linking the metropole to a series of overseas territories that split two years later in a multitude of independent states (Breton 2003, p.207). Some states continued under French sovereignty, they are collectively known by the acronym DOM-TOM (*departments d'outre-mer - territorires d'outre-mer*). The independent states remained connected to France through the Franc zone, the *Francophonie* and military alliances, which, according to Breton (2003, p.207), allow "French diplomacy to have at its disposal on the international scene – and notably at the UN - the support of faithful African client-states" and to play "the role of a sub-hegemonic power on the international scene, including allowing itself to police this part of Africa." I have already mentioned the *Françafrique* critiques to French policy in Africa (perceived to seek the maintenance of a neocolonialist relationship), drawing on the notional affiliation to France implicit in the colonial policies followed by France.

In the case of Portugal, despite the international pressure and the guerrilla wars for independence started in the 1960s, the dictatorial regime, given its isolated position in the international system, was able to maintain the colonies until it was overthrown by a bloodless military coup in 1974 - when automatically all five colonies were able to negotiate independence. It is worth noting that while Portuguese colonialism lasted longer, effective colonisation of Portuguese Africa would only take place under Salazar's dictatorial regime, mainly during the 1940s and 1950s. During the dictatorship "the African colonies were to occupy a major and central role not only in the economy but also in the official representations of national identity" (De Almeida 2008, p.5). This use of the colonies was tied to the development and use by the Portuguese government of a positive interpretation of Portuguese colonialism that embodied the ideology of *Lusotropicalismo* - Portuguese colonialism as different from other types of colonialism, with "less violence, with more miscegenation, with more dialogue" (De Almeida 2008, p.6/7). Brazilian writer Gilberto Freyre, proposing an historical interpretation of Brazil's formation in which the Portuguese played a major role, developed in the 1950s the notion of Lusotropicalism as "a special kind of inclination or capacity for miscegenation that the Portuguese were supposed to have" (De Almeida 2008, p.1). In the early 1960s, Freyre's Lusotropicalism became official in Portugal and "(t)he colonial forced-labour laws were abolished as well as the special statute that excluded indigenous populations from citizenship. All were now legally considered Portuguese, and the colonies were renamed as Provinces" (De Almeida 2008, p.7). This colonial discourse has stood the test of time and still underlies most discourses regarding the relationship between Portugal and the independent African countries as will be seen in the findings of this study.

Africa's decolonisation did not stop European involvement, or that of other emerging powers, at military, political, economical and humanitarian levels. As pointed out by Schraeder (2004, p.272), at the beginning of the 21st Century, "the four Great Powers", France, the USA, Germany and Japan, "remain heavily involved throughout Africa". China is also becoming involved in Africa, mainly through a proactive outreach development strategy that includes: aid packages, forgiveness of debt, and funds for vast infrastructure projects (Thurston 2008).

During the Cold War era there was major involvement of the communist bloc in Africa, which coincided with a waning of interest by Britain. Other "middle powers" played various roles in Africa: "Canada and the Nordic countries, most notably Sweden, demonstrate a strong humanitarian interest" (Schraeder 2004, p.273). Meanwhile, American leadership encouraged the European allies to take the lead in their former colonial territories to contain the ideological interest of the former Soviet Union and communist allies (Schraeder 2004, p.274). This led in the postcolonial area to the constitution of spheres of influence and control, *domaine reservé* (natural preserve) or *chasse gardée* (private hunting ground), by the ex-colonial powers, that mirrored those established at the Berlin Conference, which were quite evident in the case of France (Schraeder 2004, p.275). A cold peace would replace the Cold War, "in which the major northern industrialized democracies struggled for economic supremacy in the highly competitive economic environment of the 1990s" (Schraeder 2004, p.272). In the background of international affairs, the ongoing African struggle for development would continue into the new century still at the mercy of the developed world. I will discuss the contemporary trends in the last section of this chapter.

Thus the domination of Africa by the developed world continued despite formal independence after the Second World War. This implied the perpetuation of the colonial language policies, resulting in the continuation of linguistic and cultural dependency in sub-Saharan Africa (Adegbija 1994, p.22) in the post-colonial world:

> Past colonial attachments have also occasionally served, in contemporary times, as an excuse for the former colonial masters to feel concerned about anything going on in their former colonies. Thus, Portugal has been very concerned about Angola and France about Algeria and Togo. Occasionally, such concern, which sometimes wears the garment of very welcome and easily accepted 'Foreign Aid', has often resulted in the funding of language related projects, which intentionally or unintentionally, further deepen the dominance of the former colonial languages.

Breton (2003, p.206) further refers to the elaboration by European countries of "post-colonial or neo-colonial policy, including certain forms of cultural and linguistic domination". Besides continuous influence through language and culture, economy is flagged as a main area for continual dependency. For example, Wardhaugh (1987, p.9) is adamant that the old colonial masters continue to promote and encourage the dependency on their languages, and stresses the linkage of aid to the sustaining of dependencies between former colonial masters and colonies. Stiglitz (2002, p.7), in a broader outlook, accuses the developed world, working through the international organisations regulating economic flows, of driving the globalisation agenda and "ensuring that it garners a disproportionate share of the benefits, at the expense of the developing world". This situation of clear linkage between colonialism and post-colonialism, and defending the existence of theories of continuing domination, led Breton (2003, p.204) to argue that the cultural tripartition resulting form the linguistic areas formed by English, French and Portuguese in sub-Saharan Africa as having "such heavy geopolitical implications that it may be qualified as a politicolinguistic divide, that is, one with deep political and linguistic implications." A form of that divide is the politico linguistic blocs that have been constituted including most African countries, and which will be examined later in 2.3.1.

Dismissed by some as associated with "monoglossal ideas of linguistic areas of influence" (Lüdi 2006), these blocs are founded on several determining forces. Mazrui and Mazrui (1998c, p.81), for example state that "behind the apparent predominance of political and economic factors in Africa's foreign relations, there are the cultural forces of language and religion." Mazrui and Mazrui believe that "language has been a greater determinant of foreign policy", for the following reasons (1998c, p.82):

- Élite formulation of foreign policy is bound somewhat by their linguistic assimilation;
- An élite that is competent in Portuguese alone is likely to learn more about the Portuguese-speaking world than about the French- or English-speaking worlds. Through these linguistically-based constraints on the flow of information, then, Western languages continue to exercise their influence on the foreign policies of the individual African states;
- Language is important not only in orienting the élite, in foreign policy formulation, toward particular Western countries, but also in the formulation of the future élite, who study in the universities of the Western countries whose language they know;
- Finally, within Africa itself birds of the same linguistic feather are more likely to stick together than birds of the same religious feather …cooperation between African states has often followed these divisions based on Western languages.

The examination of this type of affinities is very relevant for this study. It provides interesting insights for the analysis of the case studies, that I am interested in verifying. But first it is necessary to provide adequate context for the examination of the linguistic linkages between the colonial and the post-colonial moment, and how this can be interpreted for the purpose of this study.

2.2.2 Languages and the Postcolonial State in Africa

The artificial frontiers of the new African states led to the building of unity through elements inherited from their former colonial masters. The use of European languages in the development of national identity in Africa has been highlighted as a significant area of social integration and development (Tengan 1994, p.129). However, we should not forget that national language policies constitute "an act of governance which legitimizes specific economic, cultural and political projects of particular interest groups within the arena of the state" (Rassool 1998, p.89).

It is sometimes argued that African countries chose European language as their official languages of their own free will. One can argue that the adoption of the language of the coloniser by the former colonies, now independent countries, in Africa, has a political explanation. The elites, formed within the colonial habitus, now responsible for their own language policies and linguistic choices, followed existing models of state, nationhood and language policy. As Rassool (forthcoming) argues colonial domination displaced the cultural heritage of previously relatively cohesive socio-political entities and the emerging postcolonial societies throughout Sub-Saharan Africa were defined by discursive collective memories and the habitus of subjectification. The integration of colonial languages into the structures of the colonies associated them with upward social mobility, increased economic currency and political status. This potent cultural, linguistic and symbolic capital placed them in a dominant and hegemonic position in the linguistic market. The free will argument can thus be challenged on the grounds of the hegemonic consciousness developed under colonialism, further enhanced by the precarious situation of the new territorial states and their extreme dependence on bilateral and multilateral aid. Additionally, at international level, the countries are subjected to the general constraints of systems such as globalisation, bilateral or multilateral alliances, issues of international communication and participation, general dependency of the country towards the exterior.

African aspirations of development following independence have been largely unfulfilled. This has been caused mainly by a power imbalance of the international system, in which despite the closer (and progressive) integration of countries and peoples, Western countries still hold the capability to set the economic, political and cultural international agendas to their own benefit. African countries have been forced to open their markets and to undergo structural reforms, while the Western countries keep their markets protected and change the rules of the international engagement as they see fit (Stiglitz 2001, 2002, 2006). Language, and specifically the predominant use of ex-colonial languages in education in Africa, is also seen as a major factor in the underdevelopment of Africa.

The rest of this section explores this issue (and again in 2.3.2.3 in relation to globalisation) by examining the situation regarding policies and ideologies affecting European and African languages, and analysing how relations of power can be read off language relations, within the linguistic panorama of Sub-Saharan Africa in which Guinea-Bissau and Mozambique, the country case studies targeted for external LSPs, are situated.

As stated Africa's history is indelibly marked by European colonisation; the political, ethnic and cultural cohesiveness of the continent was carved up by the political and economic driven ambitions of the European powers, dispersing people and their languages across boundaries arbitrarily drawn in 1885. The effect on the linguistic situation of the continent has been extremely powerful, determining attitudes into the present. Languages originating in Africa were counted at 2,110 in the 2009 edition of the Ethnologue (Lewis 2009). This represents roughly a third of the world's languages, although it is a variable number: "as some languages are still being 'discovered', while others with few speakers are being eliminated" (Heine and Nurse 2000, p.1). To these large numbers of endogenous languages, Arabic and European languages must be added to understand Africa's complex linguistic pattern.

The transition from the colonial period to independence brought little change in the language policies developed in Africa. Most African countries "retained the overall structure of the language policies which they inherited from the respective colonial power" (Heine 1992, p.23) and virtually all states of Black Africa "have declared a foreign language as their national official language, which is the only medium of government controlled national communication in the domains of administration or education, with the possible exception of the first years of primary education where local languages may be used" (Heine 1992, p.25). Therefore, some academic writers believe that, in postcolonial Africa, "the problems of de-colonisation amidst the continuance of colonial power structures may be read off from the linguistic relations" (Weiβ and Schwietring 2006, p.4 and Rassool forthcoming).

Colonialism, as a particular discourse, attributes different values to the different languages involved in its process, and consequently to the individuals that use them (and also how they use them). European languages were, and for many still are, the most valued linguistic asset given a complex set of reasons (economic social and political rewards, reach to wider number of speakers/ audience, subjective cultural values, access to particular cultural contents, etc). I return briefly to the notion of language as discourse and evoke Fairclough's (2001) views of discourse as a place where relations of power are exercised, enacted and fought and powerful participants control and constrain the contributions of non-powerful participants. In the context of this study, it can be argued that the colonial masters and later the elite of the new states control the discourses (both the content and the means, that is, what is important and the language to use) in society. Their power in the society is mediated through language – having or not having the right language and linguistic skills contributes to the definition of the position of the individual and of the group. Language thus is a mechanism of power, it empowers or disempowers the individual in social relations. In general, full awareness of this role of language is not widespread – nevertheless most of us are aware that, within our social arenas, how we speak a language, or which language we speak, is likely to place us in a particular rank of the social scale, in a particular position in a scale of power (less or more empowering).

Despite the importance of language in the positioning of an individual - in particular during colonialism - we need to be careful not to overrate it. The positioning of the individual is not unidimensional, it does not depend on a single characteristic. Analysing the social world, Bourdieu (1991) positions individuals in a multi-dimensional social space. The positioning is determined by the quantities of different types of capital individuals possess, such as social, cultural or symbolic capital. The language that individuals speak (power relying on the group who speak that language) and how they speak it (linguistic competences within a social arena), contributes to the accumulation of cultural capital (Bourdieu 1991, Rassool 2008). Cultural capital (as values, beliefs, norms, attitudes, experiences, competencies, skills or qualifications) is passed on from generation to generation by the individuals themselves (on a class basis) and by formal education (general set of dominant state approved and engineered "capital") and can be traded within the labour market (Rassool 2008). Thus language is not purely an instrument or method of communication it is a sign of wealth and authority (Bourdieu 1991). The state, through national language policies, controls the distribution of cultural/linguistic capital.

The imposition of European languages and the discourses backing them have, then, been identified as a major determining factor of language attitudes in sub-Saharan Africa. These language attitudes include the perception of European languages "as languages of the master, of power, of high position, of prestige, and of status", legitimised and enhanced by legal and constitutional provisions, and negative attitudes towards African languages through colonial and postcolonial language and educational policies that discourages or limit their use, creating a language and social gap (Adegbija 1994, p.30-47). These attitudes are reinforced by the introduction of western type media as opposed to oral spread of information, and by the idiosyncratic sociohistorical ecology of language (status and corpus development, association with nationhood, number of speakers, amount of literature possessed, the political and economic stamina of speakers, geographical spread) (Adegbija 1994).

From the description above, linguistic neocolonialism seems to be the situation in Africa. The language scenario in sub-Saharan Africa countries (based on Alexandre 1971, p.660 cited in Adegbija 1994, p.14) is characterised by:

- A western and modern orientated elite group using a European (ex-colonial) language, which is also the official language of the country;
- Large multilingual groups using local languages plus an African lingua franca of national or regional extension;
- Traditional orientated groups, monolingual or not, at a strictly local level.

However more recently there are successful cases where African languages are being used formally both as official languages and/or as primary medium of education, such as in Ethiopia, Somalia and South Africa (Brann 1985, Obondo 2008, Heugh 2009). As Obondo (2008, p,154) points out "The disastrous consequences of the use of ex-colonial languages for the education of the majority of African nations" (ineffective communication, poor literacy rate, high drop out rate, ineffective education, negative impact on social and economic development), "has led to a growing demand for an alternative concept for language and education in Africa, based on multilingualism" and where extended mother-tongue (or in a language the learners know well) education must play a fundamental role. However, as Heugh (2009, p.105 information in brackets added) notes "there has been a convergence towards an early transition from MTM [Mother Tongue Medium] education to a second language (L2) [normally a European language] education system across most sub-Saharan African countries, even though this is not compatible with contemporary education research". This indicates that there has been a change in the policies followed by some governments, however not in a scale that would be recommended by research or would be beneficial to building meaningful indigenous linguistic capital.

Moreover, languages are dynamic and the 'empire strikes back': the European languages, in a first stage forced in and imposed to the local intelligentsias and to those (few) attending the education systems, are in the process of being assimilated, appropriated, transformed to a degree into local varieties of those European languages. This issue is re-examined further into the chapter. For now I would like to establish that the situation cannot be read by a simple dichotomy of European versus African languages, in a negative/positive balance. The linguistic future of Africa must embrace a multilingual repertoire reflecting the multilingual and multicultural character of the communities in the context of an increasing interdependent and interconnected world.

2.2.2.1 European Languages as Official Languages

As pointed out by Breton (1991, p.155 information in brackets added): "In the colonial situation, the official languages of the [English, French, Belgian, Portuguese, Italian, Spanish, German] ruling powers were *ipso facto*, and without any contest, the paramount and nearly sole means of administration and the vehicle of culture recognized in each territory". However in the territories under British rule primary education was provided in African languages (Rassool, 2007; Heugh 2009) thus it was based on a transitional model of bilingualism as English became the main language in secondary school. The continuation of similar policies in postcolonial Africa led to the ex-colonial languages becoming the national official languages, used in government, schooling, print media, and key for social and political mobility. That 'choice' was made by the African elites in postcolonial countries upon independence:

> This often western-orientated élite class controls, shapes and almost creates the economic and political destinies of most countries in sub-Saharan Africa, since it holds the key to power. It keeps a tight reign on each country by virtue of its political power, partly acquired due to competence in the European language. Moreover, it is this group that has to fend for each country in international relations and diplomacy. In essence, the western-orientated élite is the voice of each sub-Saharan African nation, especially at the international level. Its dominance in national affairs naturally continues to perpetuate the dominance of ex-colonial languages in contemporary Africa. (Adegbija 1994, p.18)

The elites were socially, politically and economically a product of the colonial education system, they embodied colonial hegemony by assimilating cultural imperialism and perpetuating the political, social and economic inequalities of colonialism - there is also, obviously, the opportunity to build counter-hegemonies. Calvet (2002b, p.178) comments that "the pseudo-independences put in place in the neo-colonialism setting have multiple interests in the permanence of an economic and cultural domination, and the maintenance of the dominant language is then a necessity."[6] He points an accusing finger to the African elites, specially to the intellectuals, *bâtards culturels* (Calvet (2002b, p.182): "The language of these former colonies, which are theoretically independent, is an important social key, giving extraordinary powers, and those who profit from

---

6   "les pseudo-indépendences mises en place dans le cadre du néo-colonialisme ont de multiples intérêts à la permanence d'une domination économique et culturelle, et que le maintien de la langue dominante est alors une nécessité."

these opportunities have no interest in losing them."[7] For Calvet (2002b, p.192) the struggle for national liberation should also integrate liberation in the linguistic area, otherwise colonialism only becomes neocolonialism. Trudell (2010, p.337) argues that "organized, intentional action by concerned members of the African elite can have a significant impact on language-in-education choices". However, she notes the ambivalence of their positioning: at the same time, they are agents of Western assimilation (perpetuating, for instance, exclusion through language-in-education choice); they also have a growing sense of responsibility about developing local languages.

The choice of an exoglossic policy - use of foreign language as the primary media of communication at national level (Heine 1992, p.23) - is also explained by authors such as Myers-Scotton (1982, p.68) by the fact that not many African countries have lingua francas wide enough spread to accomplish national integration.

Several other justifications have been suggested for the adoption of European languages. The four most commonly given reasons why colonial European languages should be used in primary African schools (but which can be applied in a wider sense) have been identified by Ansre (1979) as:

1. The cost of producing educational material in indigenous languages is excessive in both money and human effort.
2. The World is 'shrinking' and pupils need an international language to be able to have dealings with people from different countries and large groups.
3. With so many languages and tribes, there are tendencies towards tribalism and divisiveness and, therefore, it is better to use a neutral foreign language to achieve national unity.
4. Since Africans need rapid technological development and yet none of the language is 'developed' enough for use in giving modern technology education, they must teach in the languages which have a highly developed technical and scientific terminology and concepts.

Ansre (1979, p.12-15) rejects the arguments highlighting the role education plays in economic, technological and social development; that its focus should be the national context, considering the importance of mother tongue; that importance should be given to the development of multilingual nations; that languages can be developed. The arguments described by Ansre, above, are clearly

---

7   "La langue dans ces anciennes colonies théoriquement indépendantes, est une importante clef sociale, confère des pouvoirs exorbitants, et ceux qui profitent de ces potentialités n'ont bien entendu aucune envie de les perdre."

neocolonialist and can be connected to the ideologies of linguistic nationalism, monolingual reductionism and linguistic imperialism, as they sustain the rationale for the hegemony of European languages in Africa and have been shown in practise to be invalid (Heugh 2007 and 2009). As Heugh (2009, p.103) points out, the systematic revisionism of the history of Africa – implying loss of memory regarding the use of African languages in written form and as primary mediums of education, practice of mother tongue medium education during the colonial period and in the postcolonial period, recognition that dynamic multilingualism is the African lingua franca, and the misuse of discourse, terminology and theory regarding mother tongue education – has been a "necessary instrument of the political partition and the creation of new identities after 1885 and it continued as an integral component of political and economic control by the colonial and post-colonial state structures as well as neo-colonial agencies concerned with global influence from the second half of the twentieth century onwards".

The dependency of Africa on the developed world is another factor that Breton (2003, p.213) calls the "linguistic non-development of Black Africa":

> The general African reliance on external verdicts on their economic situation, which are conditional for any international aid - either from the former colonial powers or from international organisations requiring structural adjustments – does not favour cultural considerations. The grouping of states into blocs according to politicolinguistic areas, the inclusion of many of them inside international or even planetary feudal client systems, tied to far away strategies and dependencies, does not pay much attention to the plea of field researchers, Africanists, linguists or UNESCO in favour of a future for Africa in harmony with its traditions.

Despite being at the top of the linguistic hierarchy as official languages, the fact is that European official languages are known by still small percentages of the population (e.g. Gadelli 1999, p.9, Heine 1992, p.27, Myers-Scotton 1982, p.68). Wolff (2000, p.317) estimates that at least 50% of the people living in Africa are multilingual, and that European languages are "often only understood and actively used by less than 10 per cent of the national population as in most 'Francophone' states, and somewhat higher (maybe up to 25 per cent) in 'Anglophone' countries".

This linguistic gap between the elites and the masses is seen as widening (Pattanayak 1991, p.32-33). However, in Mozambique and Guinea-Bissau there has been an increase in the spread of the official language to the masses in the postcolonial period through schooling, as the independent countries reinforce their state and nation building processes tied to the official languages. Breton (1991, p.172) reflecting on this "general situation of conscious and voluntarily chosen diglossia", states that "(w)ithout any strong political decision to reverse

67

this process and implement resolute language planning measures in favour of African mother tongues with efficient budgetary efforts, the competition with official languages can only lead to a growing *de facto* supremacy of the latter." The process of diffusion of the official languages can be read as a 'glottophagic' / language cannibalism process, whereby, over time, there is a transfer of speakers from the languages perceived to confer less prestige to the ones perceived to have more status and to be a gateway to economic benefits, the official languages.

According to Calvet (2002b) colonialism at different stages produces diverse effects in the linguistic area. As colonialism is getting settled, *colonialisme naissant*, the dominant language is adopted by those representing, near or in some way dealing with power. These speakers will be bilingual, as the rest of the population remains monolingual. In this first stage the situation is the result of an economic situation and the linguistic split coincides with social differences. In a second stage, once colonialism is installed, *colonialisme triomphant*, the linguistic split will also take a geographical dimension: city versus countryside. Moreover bilingualism will be transformed in monolinguism and vice versa: meaning that the upper classes will tend to abandon the dominated language entirely, becoming monolingual in the dominant language, and the lower city classes will tend to acquire the dominant language, becoming bilingual, the countryside will remain monolingual in the dominated language. Eventually, a third and last stage will be reached, that of the death of the dominated language, that Calvet calls *glottophagie*. In the postcolonial world the linguistic cannibalism has continued. However the process described by Calvet is a simplification - nevertheless a possibility - of the complex linguistic processes that characterise the multicultural and multilingual African landscape. A similar process is described by Lopes AJ (2001) in the suburban regions of Greater Maputo (Mozambique). However, he notes that despite Portuguese being the language most often transferred intergenerationally among the urban elite, the dominant communication role is still played by African languages, in this case Xironga and Xichangana. Language planning and policies to support African languages are tentatively being developed and they may, it is hoped, in the long term, be able to challenge the lingering colonial linguistic and cultural hegemony.

Regarding the predominance of European languages, it is important to note Ngugi wa Thiong'o's (1986 p.16) argument that colonialism's "most important area of domination was the mental universe of the colonised, the control through culture, of how people perceive themselves and their relationship to the world", in which language domination was crucial. Language then is a major determinant in mediating reality, influencing our sense of identity and the perception of our affiliations. African languages and cultures therefore must be given their right place in their societies, the hegemonic position of European languages must be broken, so that language(s) mediating the relationship of the individual with the different levels of his/her reality are relevant and do not threaten individual and collective human/cultural/linguistic rights.

Other authors, such as Pieterse and Parekh (1995, p. 2) deproblematize the introduction of European languages in Africa, arguing that "colonialism introduced no more than one new idiom, one new strand, in the complex mosaic of the societies subjected to it". Pieterse and Parekh (1995, p.3) add "Colonialism evolved a new consciousness out of a subtle mixture of the old and new; decolonisation has to follow the same route". In my view they fail in their analysis by underestimating the Western ideological predominance and effective exploitation that lead to the underdevelopment of Africa in all levels. Pieterse and Parekh (1995) do not take into account the issue of power and the cultural inheritance of colonialism.

In this ideological debate about European languages, Portuguese language African writers are viewed by Mata (2002, p.61-62) as following Nigerian writer Chinua Achebe, who argues that an African writer does not need to learn English as a native:

> The price a world language must be prepared to pay is submission to different kinds of use. The African writer should aim to use English in a way that brings out his message best without altering the language to the extent that its value as a medium of international exchange will be lost. He should aim at fashioning out an English which is at once universal and able to carry his peculiar experience. (Achebe, 1975, p. 433).

Achebe (1975, p.434) calls for a new English to carry these new cultural experiences, an English in his case, adapted to its new African surroundings. However, localisation, appropriation of the European languages, is not a simple straightforward process. As Pennycook (1998, p.198) argues, although resistance and change to the continual reproduction of colonialist discourses is possible, the task to find cultural alternatives to these constructs is hard work. In the findings of this study there will be occasion to explore the thoughts of the Mozambican writer Mia Couto on the subject that confirms Mata's (2002) interpretation.

Two ideological poles surround the role of European languages as official languages in Africa, on one side their rejection and the defence of African languages and their re-centralisation, on the other side the acceptance and appropriation of European languages also as African languages. The following subsection discusses the situation of African languages and the importance of their inclusion in the educational system.

2.2.2.2 Local Languages and Cultures

Many authors have criticised the propagation of European languages in Africa and the consequent marginalisation of African languages. Breton (2003, p.209) states:

> With the former colonial languages enjoying official status in independent states – and dominating in essential areas such as politics, economy, education and science – African populations never ceased to be mainly taught in these languages, and through them, in exogenous cultures. Increasingly, through extension of schooling, not only have the dominant languages continued to be the vehicle of expression of African elites, but they could also penetrate the masses far more deeply than during the colonial period. This certainly assures the opening of Africa to the rest of the world, but, at the same time, this general reliance on colonial languages could be criticised as leading to neglect and repudiation of the autochthonous cultural heritage represented by ancestral African languages.

As mentioned previously, the European languages have continued to be reproduced in postcolonial societies associated with social, economic and political currency and status (Rassool forthcoming). The inefficiency of the education system has somewhat limited their spread, but the majority of African governments, with Western backing, continue to fuel language spread. However it is not acceptable, from a human rights point of view that the majority of the population of a country is kept from fully participating in its own cultural, social, political and economical context. Therefore it is important that African languages are given their right place in the national/regional/local education systems and that their status is recognised.

Other authors, such as Obeng and Adegbija (1999, p.356), have put forward the argument that given the development of local varieties of European languages in Africa, "the European languages can indeed be taken to have an African aura around them and so may not be as ethnically neutral as one might think." However, even if it is accepted the appropriation (which as pointed out is a complex process) of European languages to identify with an ethnie (taken here in a figurative sense - the urban group of the population and/or as symbol of the emerging nationhood in the African countries), that does not override the importance of African languages in the construction of the African nation-state, necessarily multilingual and multicultural.

The influence between colonial policies and the present status of European and local languages in Africa is undeniable. Breton (1991, p.155), for example, highlights a certain Latin attitude (influenced by the colonisation of Portugal, Spain, France and Italy) in terms of linguistic uses as:

more inclined to use deep "assimilationist" discourse, attitude and even policy. Here a certain elite among the autochthonous dominated elements had theoretically a vocation to be promoted ... to the level of the dominating ones ...This stand, that allowed many well-considered matrimonial alliances, placed the ruler's language in the position of a gift to the masses that the potential elites of "educated" should be worthy to use or, even, really master according to their talent. This "evolved" part of the population could also ...receive full citizenship of those dominating and then participate in their political game up to the Parliament. ...Consequently, in "Latin" areas, the colonial language had a vocation to fill alone every possible public mission, either in education or in administration.

In contrast, Breton (1991, p.156) groups the Germanic and Anglo-Saxon behaviours that "convinced of the innate superiority of their languages as of their culture and way of life" did not share it with the natives: "African languages were recognized as indispensable marks of an African-ness destined to persist and to be carefully preserved as part of the divided world". Rassool (2007, p.44) points out, that in the case of the Germans they did not believe in educating the colonized. Rassool (2007) presents an ideological divide between the 'associationists' (British, Belgians and Germans) and the 'assimilationists' (French and Portuguese).

Ngugi wa Thiong'O (1986, p.19) observes:

In history books and popular commentaries on Africa, too much has been made of the supposed differences in the policies of the various colonial powers, the British indirect rule (or the pragmatism of the British in their lack of a cultural programme!) and the French and Portuguese conscious programme of cultural assimilation. These are a matter of detail and emphasis. The final effect was the same.

The present linguistic balance in favour of European languages in Africa has allowed little room for the development of African languages. The African languages, object of corpus and status development policies, are often designated in official documents as national languages. The concept is sometimes used more in the sense of languages contributing for national identity, not necessarily languages of the majority. Heine (1992, p.23) believes:

An active endoglossic policy serves above all to promote socio-cultural independence from the outside world, especially independence from western culture and ideology. It aims at either restoring a traditional structure of social organisation and government or else at creating a new structure based on traditional values, or both. In most cases it is associated with a political philosophy promoting maximum participation of the people in the governing process.

Safran (1999, p.88) also points out that "because "language is a symbol of domination" (Horowitz 1985: 219-224), the glorification of the idiom spoken by

71

an indigenous population has been part of that population's cultural and national legitimation." As seen, language is an important element used in the construction of national identities, besides being a marker of identity.

The development of African languages has been slow in moving on. Besides national and regional projects, the African Academy of Languages (ACALAN) has been active since 2001 in the promotion and development of African languages throughout the continent. However Breton (2003) remarks most states have not gone beyond the level of political discourse in the safeguarding of African language. Breton (2003) highlights three major constraints, the first, financial, as in Africa the priority sector for development are economics, thus limiting the amount of money available for language planning; the second, related with the potential electoral consequences of favouring, even temporarily, particular autochthonous languages; and finally the fact that real cultural development remains the monopoly of the official ex-colonial language.

Although old hegemonies remain resistant (Rassool, forthcoming), the importance of local language and cultures has increasingly been recognised internationally, and, in areas of Sub-Saharan Africa, the influence of ideas on the importance of mother-tongue education in multicultural/multilingual setting has produced results. Some countries (including one of the case studies, Mozambique) are developing large bilingual education programmes, progressing in the development of the corpus of local languages and formally recognising the importance of African languages in the construction of nationhood, as national languages (status planning). These experiences of multilingual education are, at the same time developing new directions for research and practice (Benson 2010). The fact that the World Bank has recognised the importance of mother tongue in learning to become literate and advocates its use in primary education is very positive and encouraging for the defence of African languages - I will return to the role of the World Bank when discussing globalisation.

Despite this support, at least from a theoretical point of view, the fact is that colonial languages still dominate the classrooms in Africa. Alidou (2004, p.195) notes that, in Africa, "the retention of colonial language policies in education contributes significantly to ineffective communication and lack of student participation in classroom activities. Moreover, it explains to a large extent the low academic achievement of African students at every level of the educational systems". The importance of language in education must be highlighted. Language plays a fundamental role in the development and socialisation of the individual. Initially through the family group and immediate social structures, language exercises a controlling role of the individual. That role is intensified by language in education as "the transmitter of culture through the literary cannons and knowledge base sanctioned by educational policy" (Rassool, 2004 p.2). In this study, one of the fundamental ways in which the exercise of power through language is witnessed is precisely in education, and particularly through the choice of language/s for use in education.

The social group controlling access to language/s, a dominant bloc or elite group in a society will more easily reproduce a particular system of relations. As Fairclough (2001, p.33) points out "education, along with all the other social institutions, has its 'hidden agenda' the reproduction of class relations and other higher-level social structures, in addition to its overt educational agenda." However, the important role of the state in setting the educational agenda and language medium should not exclude other stakeholders. For example, in the case of the postcolonial societies discussed in this study, other very important agents are teachers and the agents delivering development aid (not just representing foreign governments and international organisations, but also interest groups such as NGOs and churches). Additionally, students cannot be seen as empty, docile vessels for education. Bruner's (Olson 2007, p.6 and 14) work in cognition highlights the role of the mind "not as a receptacle for impressions", but an active, strategic, idea forming, thinking organ", and viewing knowledge as making aspects of the world visible. Although Bruner infers, as do Vygotsky and Luria, that the models and representation of the world that the mind constructs are taken over from the larger culture (Olson 2007, p.17).

The opposition of European and African languages can obscure a more fundamental problem, that of general hegemony. The problem is not if the language is originally foreign, local or native but the ideology, the discourse behind the language, the domination of some by others, the negation of different possibilities for the construction of the self and of group identity. Authors, such as Giroux (1987), Pennycook (1998) and Rassool (2008), believe that access to language (a cornerstone in the linguistic human rights discourse) does not guarantee its use, participation in dialogue or access to certain discourses. Pennycook (1998, p.81) criticises the dominant paradigm of language planning theory, applied linguistics and sociolinguistics, where "language is all too often understood as an objective system that can either be given to or withheld from people". This objective, undifferentiated view sees language learning as the acquisition of a system instead of as a process of socialization into a cultural world, and literacy is understood in terms of reading and writing the world rather than deciphering and creating the world (Pennycook 1998, p.83). Pennycook (1998, p.82) points out that "literacy and language education need to be understood as potential tools for social control rather than automatically as a means to social emancipation" or of understanding. It is important to ask "who is providing what to whom and for what purposes" (Pennycook 1998, p.83). Rassool (1995, p.423) argues that "if language thus mediates social reality, then it follows that literacy

73

defined as a social practice cannot be really addressed as a reified, neutral activity but that it should take account of the social, cultural and political processes in which literacy practices are embedded". Giroux (1987, p.1) advocates a Gramscian view of literacy, as political and ideological: having "less to do with the task of teaching people how to read and write than with producing and legitimating oppressive and exploitative social relations". The concept is dual as it can serve the purpose of self and social empowerment (as social movement) or of repression and domination (as ideology) (Giroux 1987). The question of hegemony also raises the question of the possibility to escape social control. It could be argued that it is incorrect to oversimplify power relations by overemphasizing the question of language. Fairclough's (2001, p.24 and 26) argues that the social constrainment (determined by relationships of power in particular social institutions, and in the society as a whole) of discoursal action or practice (to talk or write) does not preclude being creative. This raises the question of awareness, or using Freire's (1970) term *conscientização*. Therefore, even if, like Fairclough (2001, p.30), it is accepted that discourse is the favoured vehicle of ideology, and therefore of control (exercise of power) by consent as opposed to coercion, or, as Skutnabb-Kangas (1998, p.16) suggests, it is accepted that colonisation of consciousness of the dominated through the dominant group's ideas is done through language, it can be admitted that awareness of authority and power, and voluntarism, may elicit liberation. The hegemonic position of European language in Africa should address not just the question of 'which language' but also 'what discourse'. The importance of the role to be played by the education system in the *conscientização* of the individual must be stressed as a way to resist hegemonies.

Concerns over the decrease in the number of languages spoken today are widespread, despite different estimates for the number of languages disappearing. This is also an important backdrop to discussions about African languages, as the continent is perceived to be an important storehouse of linguistic diversity. Janson (2002, p.243) reports that from the perhaps 2,000 languages on the African continent, most of them small, around 200 are acutely threatened or are not actually in use any more. The picture is not clear. UNESCO (2006, p.1) reports that, despite many positive developments with many African languages, "the threat to linguistic diversity in Africa remains strong, only a restricted number of African languages are being extensively used in the public domain; worse, hundreds of languages - both large and small - are endangered and with them the oral traditions and expressions of hundreds of communities and peoples."

As mentioned previously, African languages are commonly seen to be threatened of disappearance by European ex-colonial languages reproduced in the formal educational system. Breton (1991, p.172), for instance, wrote that "most African languages may completely disappear before three generations". That is to say language choices can shift totally in the space of three generations (grandparents monolingual in indigenous language/ parents bilingual in indigenous and European language/ children monolingual in European language) (Bjeljac and Breton 1997). This is a very important point that highlights the precariousness of language sustainability and the potential language death in face of hegemonic processes.

Some authors contend that African languages are more threatened by other African indigenous languages than by European ones. Mufwene (2005, p.40) argues that the indigenous languages are being endangered by the "expansion of the indigenous lingua francas that also function as urban vernaculars", "which are associated with an aspect of modernity that is more tangible, being closer to indigenous cultures" (Mufwene 2005, p.32). These urban vernaculars not only spread "at the expense of traditional ethnic languages", but "apparently also of the colonial European languages which continue to function as official languages" (Mufwene 2005, p.40). A similar opinion is shared by Mazrui, A.M. (2004, p.3) and Janson (2002, p.243/4). For example, Rassool (forthcoming) reports the emergence of Sheng in Kenya, a sub-cultural code drawing on English, Kiswahili and local ethnic languages developed amongst urban youth.

The uniqueness of the African cultural system, whose open structures allow adaptation of incoming cultural systems, which sometimes lead to the development of new languages, such as the Creoles or sub-cultural codes mentioned above, is highlighted by Tengan (1994, p.129). Tengan (1994, p.129) points out that "languages in Africa tend to reflect such an immense variety and to change so rapidly that they often reveal a very complex multilingual and diglossic situation." Tengan (1994, p.136) admits however "It might be true that, due to unbalanced power relations, European societies sometimes make an attempt to monitor cultural transformations in Africa much to the dissatisfaction of the local community. This, however, will not affect the historical movement towards a new authentic African culture." Whilst I share Tengan's positive outlook, I fear that the intervention of the developed states in Africa, does more than monitor cultural transformation in Africa. It interferes in the businesses of the states, as often economic investments are also met by opportunities of cultural and linguistic spread with hegemonic intentions - as will be discussed in the findings of the case studies research. Unless African countries can overcome their external political and economic dependencies, external pressures (not just the ones issuing from globalisation, but in particular the ones originating from specific bilateral partners that tie in aid) can also affect the cultural definitions of the nation.

This section discussed how language functions as a mechanism of power in the context of the legacies of colonialism. The following section addresses awareness of language and power issues and examines selective approaches regarding the relationship of language systems and their speakers.

2.2.3 Language Relations

One of the main recurring themes in this study is the analysis of the role of the state in the question of language choice, as the structuring agent of the language system in the social context. In particular, the study examines the influences of external LSPs in the development of national language policies. In that context it is important to stress some points about the awareness of linguistic issues at individual level. Maurais (2003, p.28) observes that:

> The expansion and retraction of languages is a social phenomenon, which reflects a position of power. The disappearance of a language always has non-linguistic causes, which are a result of a balance of forces. As a result of a constant media bombardment, the man in the street is well aware of the threat that hangs not only over the environment, but also over all the animal and plant species of the planet. But most people have never heard about the threat to a large portion of the languages presently spoken on earth: indeed it has been estimated that 90% of all languages will disappear or will be near extinction in the twenty-first century.

The unawareness of language issues, is also stressed by Skutnabb-Kangas (2000, p.25): "Despite 'knowing' that we live in an information society ... and that language plays a major role in mediating information, the role of language in maintaining and reproducing (unequal) power relations and in colonising people's consciousness may not even occur to people." Unawareness of language issues is here placed at two levels: What we do to language and what language does to us. Regarding what we do to language, if we change the language we speak, if we add to or remove languages from our linguistic repertoire that will have a cumulative impact on the number of speakers. Depending on the field of inquiry, the factors for individual decision on language choices differ. However the controlling role of the state in engineering linguistic repertoires through language policies, and in particular through the education system, is undeniable. The linguistic choices of the speakers can be very limited or even predetermined (although linguistic resistance can be a possibility); such was the case of most colonial language policies or Stalin's policy of Russification of the USSR during the 1920s and 1930s. The long tradition of research in language policy (since the 1960s) has, however, according to Ricento (2000, p.23), been unable to answer the question "Why do individuals opt to use (or cease to use) particular languages and varieties for specified functions in different domains, and how do those choices influence - and how are they influenced by - institutional language policy decision-making (local to national and supranational)?" Overall the general unawareness of the speakers regarding linguistic issues allows for a (mainly) silent war of languages:

> The war of languages knows no truce. It is conducted by states that promote their own languages, spoken within their frontiers, at the expense of the one of their neighbours, of their internal minorities as of their external dependencies. ... Perpetually, in the brain of individuals, as in the practice of groups, the erosion and the abandonment of certain languages is done with the profit for the spread of others"[8] (Bijeljac and Breton 1997, p.71).

The war of languages is not just between states it is also between the state and the individual in the imposition of language through, mainly, the education system.

To support the analysis of the linguistic spaces discussed in the study I will briefly examine the work of selected authors on models of the relationships of languages at world level. Their approaches to language spread and shift vary in a continuum from a neutral stance of pure linguistic description to charged economic and political explanations. The five approaches referred to are: Wardhaugh's biological metaphor (1987) Calvet's gravitational model (1974, 2000), De Swaan's galactic metaphor (1998, 2000), Laitin's enriched game theory (1992), and Robert Phillipson's linguistic imperialism (1992).

Several authors find biological metaphors useful in visualizing linguistic phenomena. Wardhaugh (1987, p.1), for instance, sees languages as being born and dying, ascending and declining. Languages are viewed as living organisms, having a natural cycle of life. Wardhaugh (1987) ties in language with the state, nation and identity, while viewing languages as having a life of their own, and in this he fails to highlight the hidden agency behind language spread. He lists as factors for language spread: geographical opportunity (a factor that today has lost its importance as relations are increasingly enacted in a virtual, communicational, non-physical space); military conquest (again a factor that had application more historically then particular relevance at present); political control (language is certainly a mediator and an instrument of power relations); religious factors; historic factors; economic factors; neocolonialism; attitudes of speakers; 'openness' of language (Wardhaugh (1987, p.15) sees as possible that language

---

8   La guerre des langue ne connaît pas de trêve. Elle est menée par les Etats qui promeuvent leur expression propre, à leurs frontières, aus dépens de celle de leurs voisins, de leurs minorités internes comme de leurs dépendences extérieures. ... Perpétuellement, dans le cerveau des individus, comme dans la pratique des groupes, l'érosion et l'abandon de certains parlers s'effectuent au profit de l'extension de certains autres."

is neutral: "no cultural requirements are tied to the learning of English"). Although Wardhaugh's (1987) analysis is useful picking out factors of language spread, some of which may have a more historical application, his liberal approach and neutral biological vision of language ignores the role of speakers, the underlying power struggles that envelope their choices, and the influence of social systems in which the language operates and is constructed.

In his 1974 book *Linguistique et colonialisme*, Calvet presented the *modèle gravitationnel*, a hierarchical system of languages connected by bilinguals and determined by power relations. Calvet (2002b, p.16, information in brackets added) describes the gravitational model as:

> a representation of language connections among the languages of the world in terms of gravitations built around pivots languages in different levels. We have, at the centre, a hypercentral language, English, pivot of the entire system, which speakers manifest a strong tendency to monolinguism. Around this hypercentral language gravitate a dozen of supercentral languages (Spanish, French, Hindi, Arab, Malay, etc. [Further ahead in the text, he adds the examples of Chinese and Portuguese]), which speakers, as soon as they acquire a second language, learn either English, either a language of the same level, meaning another supercentral language. They are in their turn gravitational pivots of hundred to two hundred central languages around which gravitate then five to six thousand peripheral languages.[9]

Calvet (2000, p.36) emphasises the dynamic nature of his mode, as languages spoken by few people die out, others appear. The languages and their functions evolve and are able to change place in the system, since "(l)ike history itself, the history of languages does not stand still. It moves on, constantly changing and being shaped by the practices of users" (Calvet 2000, p.36).

Calvet's work presents a vision of relations between languages based on power, dominance and inequality. He views the relations between languages as power relations, and he (1998) speaks of dominated and dominant languages:

> The linguistic theories of previous centuries had constructed a model of the relations between peoples, which was founded on the principle of inequality. The peoples of the 'civilized' West were superior to the 'savage' peoples, and their languages

---

9   "Une représentation des rapports entre les langues du monde en termes de gravitations étagées autor de langues pivots de niveaux différents. Nous avons, au centre, une langue hypercentrale, l'anglais, pivot de l'ensemble du système, dont les locuteurs manifestent une forte tendance au monolinguisme. Autour de cette langue hypercentrale gravitent une dizaine de langues supercentrales (espagnol, français, hindi, arabe, malais, etc.), dont les locuteurs, lorsqu'ils acquièrent une seconde langue, apprennet soit l'anglais soit une langue de même niveau, c'est-à-dire une autre langue supercentrale. Elles sont à leur tour pivots de la gravitation de cent à deux cents langues centrales autour desquelles gravitent enfin cinq à six milles langues périphériques."

('clearer', 'more logical', 'more developed') were, in the same way, superior to the languages of those who had been colonised. In practice, this theory of inequality gave birth to an organisation of the relations between languages that was based on dominance, the dominance of one people by another, of course, but at the same time, dominance of one culture by another, and of one language by another. (Calvet 1998, p.ix)

In Calvet's (1998, p.xiii) work the linguistic phenomena "are deeper translations of deeper social movements", language translates power relations, power and negotiation. However, Calvet (2000, p.35) sees the power relying on the speakers, as they ultimately choose which language to speak. He (2002a, p.94-95) sees man as an actor in the existence of languages:

Vanishing languages are the sign of situations where the convergence of political, social, economic and psychological factors push their speakers to use them less and less, and only use them with people their age and not with the young, in situations more and more private, more and more vernacular and less and less vehicular. The speakers are also responsible by the fact they choose not to speak a language, even if this desertion is in part explained by sociological and historical factors.[10]

Calvet treats the issue of speakers' choice and how it translates power relations superficially. Choice may be extremely reduced in the face of national language policies and the economic capital of particular languages (language favoured by the labour market (Rassool 2007)).

Overall, Calvet's is an appealing model, it recognises agency behind and in language and the unequal relations between languages. However, its extreme simplicity and under-theorisation fail to assist in a deeper analysis of external LSPs, in the context of the structuring of power relations within a hybrid global and national environment.

De Swaan (1998, p.63) proposes a model very similar to Calvet's. He also regards the languages of the world as a dynamic "global system held together by multilingual people who can communicate with several language groups." He uses a metaphor based on solar systems, in which national languages occupy the place of planets, and local or tribal languages are moons, with one language in the galactic centre, English. This multiple nested system presents an order resulting from demographic distribution and patterns of foreign language acquisi-

---

10   "Les langues qui disparaissent sont le signe de situations dans lesquelles la convergence de facteurs politiques, sociaux, économiques et psychologiques poussent leurs locuterus è les utiliser de moins en moins, et è ne les utiliser qu'avec des gens de leur âge et non pas avec les jeunes, dans des situations de plus en plus privée, de plus en plus vernaculaires et de moins en moins véhiculaires. Les locuteurs sont aussi responsables du fait qu'ils choisissent de ne plus parler une langue, même si cet abandon est en partie explicable par des facteurs sociologiques et historiques."

tion, dictated by political authorities and imposed through the school curriculum. De Swaan explains language choices based on political economy and sociology. He defines languages as "hypercollective goods" (De Swaan 1998, p.68-70). Languages are considered free goods, not produced or owned by anyone, from whose use no one can be excluded and that need the collaboration of many to survive, increasing its utility with the number of speakers. Examining language competition, De Swaan views the commitment for one language as depending on the expected net benefits of that option, minus the expected net benefits of the next-best option, plus the costs of switching to that alternative. He sees the spread of languages, indirectly, creating economies of scale. A person by learning a certain language will increase its utility for all other speakers. In a competition situation, people will opt for the alternative that is most likely to survive. Nevertheless, the costs of language acquisition and feelings of language loyalty are also specific factors that may prevent language desertion. In De Swaan's analysis, language is seen from a biological perspective, having a life of its own, as did Wardhaugh (1987). However the liberal vision is now replaced by a free market (neoliberal) view, as choice of language is seen as an individual matter being regulated by the laws of a linguistic market. This neoliberal market vision does not stress enough the linguistic interventionism of states, and the influence of international organisations, transnational corporations and media on the speakers' choices.

The use of decision and game theory is suggested by Calvet (2002a) for the analysis of linguistic policies:

> In all situations (political, diplomatic, military...) in which «players» have different interests, we have to consider two factors, *cooperation* and *conflict*, that will combine, according to their converging or diverging interests, in games of cooperation, of conflict or of cooperation and conflict. In cooperative games, the players have converging interest in the face of a single foe, they can adopt a common strategy leading to a common objective. In conflict games, on the contrary, players do not have any convergent interest, any common objective, and are engaged in duels. In conflict and cooperation games, players have interests at the same time convergent and divergent.[11]

---

11 "Dans toutes les situations (politiques, diplomatiques, militaires...) dans lesquelles les «joueurs» ont des intérêts différents, il nous faut considerer deux facteurs, la cooperation et la lutte, qui vont se conjuger pour donner, selon que leurs intérêts convergent ou divergent, des jeux de cooperation, de lutte ou de cooperation et de lutte.. Dans les jeux de coopération les joueurs ont des intérêts convergent face à un adversaire unique, ils peuvent adopter une stratégie commune menant à un but commun. Dans les jeux de lutte, au contraire, les joueurs n'on aucun intérêt convergent, aucun but commun et se trouvent engages dans des duels. Dans les jeux de lutte et de coopération enfin, les joueurs ont des intérêts à la fois convergents et divergents."

However the artificiality of game theory in language choice is in my view validly criticised by Cox (1981, p.129) since "the notion of substance at the level of human nature is presented as a rationality assumed to be common to the competing actors who appraise the stakes at issue, the alternative strategies, and the respective pay-offs in a similar manner". This idea of a common rationality reinforces the non-historical mode of thinking (Cox 1981). Cox (1981, p.126) sees theory as "always *for* someone and *for* some purpose. All theories have a perspective. Perspectives derive from a position in social and political time and space, and from ideological and power positions.

Laitin (1992) analysing language choice in Africa, from a political science point of view, uses game theory applied to cultural politics. Laitin (1992) couples the rational-choice foundations of game theory with independent data on language preferences and choices in Africa to allow for the analysis of the reciprocal impact of structural constraints, individual purposes and strategies in actor choice. In his analysis, Laitin (1992, p. xi/xii) also uses historical context, state-building outcomes and historical evidence to highlight "the attempt by states to influence the language repertoires of their citizens". He (1992, p.x) further justifies his choice of approach by saying it allows to go beyond primordialism and cybernetic theory: "Primordialism, which conceives of ethnic identity as rooted in blood, has no grasp on cultural change at all. And cybernetic theory, which portrays individuals as nodes in communication networks, cannot appreciate the manipulation of social networks by political forces." Laitin (1992) is able to provide a concise and comprehensive analysis of multilingualism in Africa that stresses that comparisons with European cases are inadequate given the complexity of the local language repertoires and the history and context of nation-building. Laitin's perspective is able to give the adequate relevance to the effects of power in language choices, while at the same time incorporating elements of historical sociology to adequately explain specific situations. However, Laitin's overall concern with a model constrains the analysis to a script that would be too narrow for the purposes of this study.

For this study I will use as framework Robert Phillipson's theory of linguistic imperialism. In the following section I explain the theory, point out the critiques and justify my choice.

2.2.3.1 Linguistic Imperialism

Phillipson's (1992) controversial and influential book, *Linguistic Imperialism,* examines how and why English is a world language. The influence of English Language Teaching (ELT) ideology in Third World countries and the perpetuation of North-South inequalities are of special concern to him. He exposes and analyses the UK and USA governments' involvement since the 1950s in the international spread of English language and Anglo-Saxon culture worldwide (Rothkopf 1997, Saunders 1999). Central to his theory is Gramsci's concept of hegemony, whereby "(h)egemonic ideas tend to be internalized by the dominated, even though they are not objectively in their interest" (Gramsci 1970 cited in Phillipson 1992, p.8). Phillipson (1992, p.53) also alludes to a use of language that recalls Nye's soft power concept (section 2.1.3.3), whereby power is exerted increasingly by means of ideas (persuasion) and not sticks (impositional force) or carrots (bargaining). Dominating Phillipson's (1992, p.52) view of the international system is Galtung's division of the world into "a dominant Centre (the powerful western countries and interests), and dominated Peripheries (the underdeveloped countries)". The centres of power in the Centre and in the Periphery exploit their respective peripheries, and their elites are linked by shared interests. Phillipson (1992, p.52) claims that they are also connected by language, in sum: "The norms, whether economic, military, or linguistic, are dictated by the dominant Centre and have been internalised by those in power in the Periphery." However, Phillipson (1992, p.63) qualifies that by recognising that "Periphery decision-makers have some freedom of manoeuvre in negotiating with the Centre": "A conspiracy theory is, therefore, inadequate as a means of grasping the role of the key actors in Centre or Periphery." Phillipson (1992, p.53) establishes linguistic imperialism as a distinct type of imperialism, since it permeates all the types of imperialism. First because language is the primary medium of communication for links in all fields, and secondly because linguistic imperialism dovetails with other types of imperialism and is an integral part of them. Linguistic imperialism is a possible explanation for LSP according to Phillipson (1994, p.20) - linguicism being a key concept: "Linguicism is defined as "ideologies, structures and practices which are used to legitimate, effectuate and reproduce an unequal division of power and resources (both material and immaterial) between groups which are defined on the basis of language (Skutnabb-Kangas 1988:13)." English linguistic imperialism is an example of linguicism, since "(t)he continued advance of English involves the suppression (displacement and replacement) of other languages and the defeat of competing imperialist languages" (Phillipson 1992, p.36):

> the dominance of English is asserted and maintained by the establishment and continuous reconstitution of structural and cultural inequalities between English and other languages. Here structural refers broadly to material properties (for example, institutions, financial allocations) and cultural to immaterial or ideological properties (for example, attitudes, pedagogic principles). (Phillipson, 1992, p.47)

Phillipson (1992, p.48) believes in the relationship between global language promotion and economic and political interests on the one hand, and English linguistic imperialism in educational language planning and in the classroom on the other. He argues that "English as a "universal" lingua franca conceals the fact that the use of English serves the interests of some much better than others. Its use includes some and excludes others" (2000, p.89). Recently, Phillipson (2008) has also written about English becoming neoimperial, that is, English language in all its variants, Global Englishes, is central to ideological control in the global linguistic market:

> Linguistic neoimperialism entails the maintenance of inequalities between speakers of English and other languages, within a framework of exploitative dominance. As in earlier linguistic imperialism, this is achieved through penetration, fragmentation, marginalisation, and supremacist ideologies in discourse. (Phillipson 2008, p.23)

In the case of African and Asian periphery-countries, Phillipson (1992, p.30) sees English as having a twofold importance:

> English has a dominant role *internally*, occupying space that other languages could possibly fill. English is also the key *external* link, in politics, commerce, science, technology, military alliances, entertainment, and tourism. The relationship between English and other languages is an unequal one, and this has important consequences in almost all spheres of life.

This unequal relation does not preclude reaction. As Phillipson (2007, p.382) points out: "speakers of languages that are subject to linguistic imperialism are not helpless victims, but in a more complex relationship with the forces propelling a language forward". However he (2008a, p.3) warns that "(t)he power of English as a symbolic system in the global market is such that its legitimacy tends to be uncritically accepted". Phillipson (1992, pp.173-222) examines closely linguistic educational imperialism. He distinguishes five tenets that he sees underlying the doctrine for the teaching of English worldwide:

1. the monolingual fallacy: reflects the belief that other languages, including the mother tongue, are a hindrance in foreign language learning;
2. the native speaker fallacy; the ideal teacher is a native speaker, who can serve as a model for the pupils;
3. the early start fallacy: exploits the capacity young children have to learn foreign languages informally;
4. the maximum exposure fallacy: the more a language is taught, the better the results;
5. the subtractive fallacy: if other languages are used much, standards of the language intended to be promoted will drop.

The falsity of each tenet is examined by Phillipson regarding English Language Teaching (ELT). Phillipson (2009b, p.4) finds that they still underlie today the pedagogy of global English and contribute to the failure of African education systems. I will verify if and how these apply to the case studies.

Other authors, such as Ngugi wa Thiong'o (1986, p.20), Mazruis (1998d), Breton (2000, p.23), Alexander (2007) and Rassool (2007) have connected the use of English to the logic of imperialism. Mühlhäusler (1996, p.18), in his account of linguistic ecology in the Pacific, also uses the concept of linguistic imperialism to "attempt to dispel the myth that the loss of linguistic diversity is a natural process (a view found throughout the relevant literature)", and makes a case for "a historical 'accident' brought about by deliberate human agency." Wardhaugh (1987, p.9) labels as neo-imperialist the fact that "ideologies compete with one another and languages find themselves used as weapons of considerable importance in the world-wide competition for minds and power." It is also relevant to point out Hamel's (2005, p.29) insight about the disappearance of the term imperialism from political and scientific debate, and in particular its application to language, in favour of globalisation:

> The world language system (de Swaan 1993, 2001) and the future of threatened languages (Maffi 2001), English as a global language (Crystal 1997), geolinguistic dynamics (Maurais 2003), the fate of languages (Mackey 2003), an ecology of the languages of the world (Calvet 1999), the linguistic market and the linguistic effects of "mondialisation" (Calvet 2002) are but a few of the most common concepts and metaphors used to describe the recent processes of language spread and shift, and of the changing power relations between ethno-linguistic groups and their communicative practices. Only a few scholars refer explicitly to *language empire* or *imperialism*. ... Many of those involved in exploring the possibilities of counteracting language domination would agree with the facts used by Mühlhäusler, i. e. "the expansion of a small number of languages at the cost of a large number of others" to define linguistic imperialism (1994, 122), but would rather adhere to more popular terms like globalisation.

Since it was published in 1992, Robert Phillipson's book *Linguistic Imperialism* received both praise and criticism, becoming a fundamental mark in the thinking about issues of language spread. Twenty years after the publication of *Linguistic Imperialism*, it should be asked if the theory is still relevant. Phillipson himself revalidated the issue in 2009 with the publication of *Linguistic Imperialism Continued.*

2.2.3.1.1 Critiques

Phillipson's *Linguistic Imperialism* has been the target of much outrage. Numerous book reviews and articles have been written criticising the excessive politicization of the linguistic processes analysed and his views on the role of ELT. In terms of the sources used, the reduced number of interviews (eight interviews with ELT policy makers) carried out by Phillipson in his assessment can be pointed as a weak base for insight into the policy-making process, even if balanced by a wealth of written information. The series of official reports connected with ELT and its agents, with the British Council featuring heavily, can also be seen as providing a too unilateral view of the issues discussed. I will now deal with selective critiques to linguistic imperialism theory deemed important for this study, as my interest in Robert Phillipson's work is centred on his development of a general theory that explains the structural power behind the spread of international languages.

Many of the critiques to Phillipson's (1992) are, in my view, due to a misunderstanding of his general theory. For instance, Graddol (2006, p.112) believes that "(t)he concept of linguistic imperialism ... does not wholly explain the current enthusiasm for English which seems driven by parental and governmental demand, rather than promotion by Anglophone countries". Graddol fails to grasp the essence of Phillipson's theory, which should not be reduced to an Anglophone conspiracy, and fails to reflect on why the demand for English occurs, which is precisely what Phillipson tries to explain. The demand for English cannot be viewed has having no ideological charge. Language operates in a social arena, and holds intrinsic and extrinsic power. However, despite, the volume of research backing that view (Phillipson 2006, Hornberger 2008), some still defend a neutral view of language (a tool used for good or for evil, Fishman 2006) and a neutral view of the spread of English. Fishman (1996a, p.8), for example, argues:

> Perhaps English should be reconceptualized, from being an imperialist tool to being a multinational tool. ...English may well be the *lingua franca* of capitalist exploitation without being the vehicle of imperialism or even neo-imperialism *per se*. ...English may need to be re-examined precisely from the point of view of being post-imperial (... that is in the sense of not directly serving purely Anglo-American territorial, economic, or cultural expansion) without being post-capitalist in any way?

Fishman (2006, p.323) shields this neutral view of English spread justifying it with the notion of "globalization of material and non-material culture in the twentieth and twenty-first century", which he views as a modern phenomenon. It is also interesting to note here the earlier remark by Hamel (2005) about the use of 'globalisation' instead of 'linguistic imperialism'. Fishman, also presumably sees globalisation only as a phenomenon and not as rhetoric - the ideological discourse of globalisation that Fairclough (2006) points to. Fishman, like Graddol above, fails to grasp the essence of Phillipson's theory, which as he (2006, p.348) explains "entails unequal exchange and unequal communicative rights between people or groups defined in terms of their competence in specific languages, with unequal benefits as a result, in a system that legitimates and naturalizes such exploitation".

Other critics, although acknowledging that Phillipson's description of the imbalance between languages is correct, do not validate his conclusions. Davies (1996, p.490) argues that "What RP [Robert Phillipson] ignores is (a) that the choice of English (or other imperial language) has values of openness, access to and connection with modernism; and (b) the possibility that oppressed groups' common sense is active enough for them to reject English if they so wish." However, after giving examples of countries that rejected English (Burma, Bangladesh, Pakistan, Nepal, Sri Lanka, Malaysia), Davies mentions that all restored English as a local/national language…

Pennycook (1999) sees Phillipson's theory as a general theory, concerned with structural power, and connected with the threat to linguistic human rights. He (1999, p.8) believes that Phillipson (1992) lacks "a view of how English is taken up, how people use English, why people choose to use English", therefore not being able to show the effects of the spread of English on the people that use it. A similar criticism is voiced by Canagarajah (1999, p.43/4):

> In considering how social, economic, governmental, and cultural institutions affect inequality, his perspective becomes rather too impersonal and global. What is sorely missed is the individual, the particular. It is important to find out how linguistic hegemony is experienced in the day-to-day life of the people and communities in the periphery. How does English compete for dominance with other languages in the streets, markets, homes, schools, and villages of periphery communities?

Intending to safeguard extremes between acculturation and appropriation, Pennycook (1999, p.10) devised the concept of postcolonial performativity to reconcile "a political understanding of the global role of English and a means to understand contextuality how English is used, taken up, changed", viewed against the processes of globalisation (in particular capital and media), and understand the response to cultural spread. As Pennycook (1999, p.8) I find Phillipson's theory useful to map out ways in which international languages (in my case studies, not just English, but also Portuguese and French) are deliberately spread, and "show how such policies and practices are connected to larger forces".

Phillipson's theory connects with the defence of ethical human rights principles, and in particular with linguistic human rights (1992, 2008). Phillipson and Tove Skutnabb-Kangas (1995, 2008) have extensively campaigned for the rights of speakers of dominated languages. The field of language rights has become increasingly important and visible since the middle of the 20th century (Skutnabb-Kangas 2000, De Varennes 1997), when language rights were included in the Universal Declaration of Human Rights. This has given place to a particular discourse around language that is criticised by some.

Calvet (2002a, p.91-101) criticises, what he calls, a tendency for political correctness in linguistic discourse. The *discours linguistico-politiquement correct*, defined as a set of frequent rhetorical statements and procedures in the dominant discourses, includes principles as:

- all languages are equal;
- all languages can convey in the same way all human knowledge;
- all languages should be written;
- speakers have a right to be taught in their first language;
- minority languages have a right to be officially recognised;
- languages, part of heritage or threatened species, should be protected;
- to lose one's language is to lose one's roots, one's culture.

Although Calvet does not dismiss them as untrue, he classifies them as "false evidences" when applied to real situations. He exemplifies with the case of African countries, where, given the large number of languages, the propositions "all languages should be written" and "speakers have a right to be taught in their first language" are, according to him, inapplicable. Instead, in this case, he suggests, criteria highlighting the importance of languages in development should be used. Calvet goes on further in his critique questioning whether the politically correct speech is not a form of imperialism disguised by good intentions - in the way all world languages are expected to fulfil the same functions as European ones. Hamel (2005, p.27) comments on Calvet's critique of the political correct discourse that "(h)ere Calvet, like many others who use these arguments, ignores ... the force of colonial ideological domination which he had clearly identified and criticised in his previous work (e.g. Calvet 1974, 1987)". Which is precisely what Phillipson (2009, p.8) acknowledges in his argument that: "(t)here is a conflict between the rhetoric of supporting all languages and the realities of linguistic hierarchies and marginalisation".

This politically correct discourse that Calvet refers to encompasses the discourses of linguistic human rights and the defence of linguistic and cultural diversity. I do not agree that politically correct speech is a disguised form of imperialism. I see it as an attempt to secure the acknowledgement of basic human rights (e.g. mother tongue education) by the international society and a struggle to maintain education as a human right and not as a commodity (Rassool 2007, Phillipson 2009), despite the need of a thorough discussion about what universal language rights are (Rassool 1998, Pennycook 1998, 1999, Coulmas 1998).

2.3 Language and Globalisation

In the previous section particular attention was paid to defining relations between languages, which provides an important framework for the analysis of the findings in this study. The next final section explores the constitution of politico linguistic blocs and issues of language in the context of globalisation, which also envelop the case studies.

2.3.1 Political Blocs based on Culture and Language

The sharing of language and culture between countries has been an important factor in the creation of political organisations geared towards their defence and promotion. A situation easily understood as "(t)hose who speak the same language not only can make themselves understood to each other; the capacity of being able to make oneself understood also founds a feeling of belonging and belonging together" (Weiβ and Schwietring 2006, p.3). However, this should not make us overlook the importance of the political factor and the engineering of culture.

The constitution of language blocs has occurred in a postcolonial period organising mainly the relations of the formerly colonised amongst themselves or/and of those with the former colonisers. Brann (1985, p.2) speaks of the "Arabic, French, English or Portuguese-speaking block" and Calvet (2002a, p.190) identifies five big linguistic groups - Arabic, French, Spanish, English and Portuguese - he designates by *Xphonies,* linguistic-political realities that correspond to organisations such as the Organisation International de la Francophonie (OIF), the Comunidade de Países de Língua Portuguesa (CPLP) or the Arab League.

From the selected literature review undertaken for this study I conclude that the study of these groupings is disparate and that there is no particular widely accepted designation. Before introducing the relevant international blocs to this study, I would like to state my position regarding language and culture, and univocal views of humankind.

Language is an element of culture, that may be or not a fundamental element, and culture is an aggregate of elements with which individuals can identify. In their lives, individuals develop numerous affiliations (the different categories of the self mentioned in 2.1.1) that give them a particular identity, however "(n)one of them can be taken to be the person's only identity or singular membership category" (Sen 2006, p.5). For instance, the Swiss, define themselves as such, despite the fact that they have large language communities organised in different cantons. Those plural identities are chosen by the individual, consciously or not, and the relative importance of each one is decided in particular contexts, subject to the influence of the social *milieu* and individual characteristics (Sen 2006). Nevertheless, despite our choice on how we want to see ourselves, it may be difficult to "persuade *others* to see us in just that way" (Sen 2006, p.6).

I find this question of perception fundamental, and in the case of this study, I am most interest in it from a collective outlook. That is how perceptions of collective identities (implicitly solitarist definitions) can obscure the individual and group multiple identities (multiple affiliations). The breakdown of the world into collective cultural identities results in multiple diverse groupings. Different weighting given to different elements of the identity will result in different arrangements. For instance, Huntington (1993) presents a view of the post-Cold War world politics as competing cultures, and labels the different cultural groupings 'civilizations', under discussable criteria that at times appears to equate civilization/culture with religion. Bennett (2003) develops the concepts of network civilization and commonwealth based on the argument of the kinship of social, political and cultural values. He overtly campaigns for a closer union of the English-speaking nations, the Anglosphere, claiming that what distinguishes it are customs and values, namely freedom, rule of law and honouring contracts (Bennett 2002, 2003). These represent potentially dangerous exclusivist and univocal views of human beings (Sen 2006, p. 176/7).

Before proceeding with the presentation of the politico linguistic blocs that are present in Lusophone Africa, and which involve transnational associations, I would like to stress that the linguistic and cultural solidarities are also important phenomena within the national arena. As Anderson (1991) reminds us, languages should not be seen as symbols of nationness, they build particular solidarities. Linguistic and cultural solidarities are present at regional and local level and can present or not a challenge to the national project. Linguistic struggles are not particular to the developing world, they are also present in the developed world. That is the case, for instance, in the re-assertion of Welsh, Gaelic, Scottish and Cornish language rights in the UK, the case of the nationalisms with very active linguistic struggles in Spain, such as Catalonia and the Basque Country (also affecting France) or the conflict of linguistic standards in Norway.

2.3.1.1 Multiple Connections in Lusophone Africa

The politico linguistic blocs, that the countries in this study are part of, illustrate the importance of the relations between language and power. In these blocs, the communality of language and/or culture (real, perceived or simple wishful thinking) is used politically to foster an alliance of countries, from which each member (although some more than others) can extract benefits (political and economical). Calvet's (2002a, 1998) analyses these linguistic situations in Africa under the *configuration politique* principle:

> The *political configuration* reveals another organisation [he refers to the gravitational/linguistic configuration] of the continent into arabophone, francophone, anglophone and lusophone zones, politically organised zones (francophony, Arab League, PALOP and CPLP for the Portuguese language countries, etc.) and compelled to different attractions, different solidarities, different oppositions.[12] (Calvet 2002a, p.30)

These configurations are identified by Calvet (2002a) as being changeable and in constant interaction. He classifies their relations into four kinds (production, conflict, contradiction and convergence) and highlights multiple memberships that are of great interest to this study.

Lusophone African countries share connections with distinct politico linguistic blocs. The different memberships are shown in the following table:

Table 2.1   The Multiple Memberships of Lusophone Africa (multiple sources[13])

	Angola	Cape Verde	Guinea-Bissau	Mozambique	São Tomé and Príncipe
CPLP	1996	1996	1996	1996	1996
OIF		1996	1979	2006 (Obser.)	1999
Commonwealth				1995	
Latin Union (UL)	1997	1992	1990	1994	1992
Org.Islamic Conf.			1974	1994	

12   "- La configuration politique fait apparaître une autre organisation du continent en zones arabophone, francophone et lusophone, zones organisés politiquement (francophonie, ligue arabe, PALOP et CPLP pour les pays de langue portugaise, etc.) et soumises à des différentes attractions, à différentes solidarités, à différentes oppositions."

13   Multiple sources: http://www.cplp.org [11.11.2006]; http://www.thecommonwealth.org/YearbookHomeInternal/138810/ [11.11.2006]; http://www.francophonie.org/oif/ [11.11.2006]; http://www.unilat.org/SG/Organisation/Presentation/EtatsMembres/index.es.asp [11.11.2006]; http://www.oic.oci.org/english/main/member-States.htm [11.11.2006].

Literature regarding the multiple memberships of international politico linguistic blocs is scarce. Breton (2003, p.208) has briefly written about it. He observes the postcolonial maintenance and reciprocal influences of the linguistic Luso-Anglo-Francophone tripartition in Africa:

> Lusophone Cape Verde Islands, Guinea-Bissau and Sao Tome-Principe participating in Francophone summits or Hispanophone Equatorial Guinea entering the Franc zone. For their part, Anglophone countries felt the need for some alignment with the surrounding Francophonie. ...Nigeria...adopted the right-hand drive system of all its neighbours, and took the decision in the 1990s to make French its second language .... In an opposite direction, the awkward support by French diplomacy and military forces of the Rwanda genocide against their opponents coming from Kenya and Uganda, motivated, after liberation, the proclamation of a bilingual Rwanda where English was supposed to reach equality with French.

Breton (2003, p.208) also notes the diffusion of Arabic:

> There has also been a certain diffusion of Arabic, as an official language, outside the Arabophone countries, at least on the margins of Black Africa, with states – such as Djibouti, Somalia and Comoros – becoming members of the Arab League. There has also been a diffusion of Arabic in Chad, where a strong Arab minority lives.

Additionally Breton concludes that the politico-linguistic situation of Black Africa has not been affected to a great extend by the penetration of new international actors: "Soviet Union, China and Japan slipped easily through the new net with their already multilingual experienced teams" (2003, p.208).

As far as Lusophone Africa is concerned, all the countries are members of the Latin Union and, with the exception of Angola, are members of the OIF (although Mozambique only has observer status). Mozambique is the only country affiliated with the Commonwealth, and along with Guinea-Bissau, is a member of the Organisation of the Islamic Conference (OIC).

The importance of this multiple belonging is always relative. For instance, when Mozambique in 2006 became observer of the Francophonie, the reasons put forward by the then Mozambican Foreign Minister, Henrique M'banze were: the possibility of Mozambique to exchange experience, potential gains in the domains of education, research, politics and economy, ability to contribute in conflict resolution (BBC para Africa 2006). Questioned on which criteria had to be met he said that Mozambique is committed to the promotion of the French language as well as being committed to the values of peace, democracy and the respect of human rights (BBC para Africa 2006). These justifications can in fact be applied to any of the countries and organisations. They denote a pragmatic approach to these blocs. The membership is used to gain voice in the international arena, to build skills and opportunities for development. Language is here seen as purely utilitarian.

For the Lusophone countries, linguistic likeness might be a facilitating factor when seeking help. The former coloniser Portugal and Brazil, the other Portuguese-speaking country that is in a position to assist, are naturally (historically and economically determined) first ports of call, since their elites share a language and historically close relations. However language is not a barrier in seeking and providing developmental assistance, most development partners will have multilingual teams or are in a position to hire the right staff. After independence, given the ideological alignment, many members of the intelligentsia of these countries studied in communist countries during the Cold War, this produced a close connection to the Soviet Union and its allies. Later in the 1980s, the Western aid replaced that linkage. Moreover, the countries are increasingly integrating in their regional areas. Overwhelmingly the opportunity to develop oneself when in a situation of underdevelopment will be taken regardless of language or culture.

Undeniably, these blocs offer great opportunities to stand out in a world of 'equal' states. They provide, in particular for the stronger countries, political and economic opportunities, enhancement of their power and prestige, diversification of investments, and enlargement of markets.

In the examination of the findings I will discuss how these connections are experienced in the case studies, which discourses are used by the different intervenients, and why. To provide a base for that discussion the next section summarily introduces the linguistic blocs more relevant to the study.

2.3.1.2 Anglophone, Francophone, Lusophone and Latin Bloc

This section includes a short mention of the Anglophone and Francophone bloc, followed by a lengthier discussion of the Lusophone bloc, since it is the least known in English medium academic circles and the one most relevant to my analysis. This section also introduces the Latin forum created in 2001, Three Linguistic Spaces, that gathers Lusophony, Francophony and Hispanophony.

I start with a remark on terminology. The term 'Anglophone bloc' is used here in the sense that English language creates a bond between countries, nurtured by political, economical and cultural links. However, it does not correspond to a developed and settled theoretical content. The term Anglophony that could be carved by contrast with Francophony or Lusophony, does not exist in English language. This can be seen to indicate different degrees of political (and academic) concern that each group of countries dedicates to the subject and different national perceptions on the subject of cultural and linguistic association.

Within the focus of this study the most important formal political association gathering English-speaking nations is the Commonwealth of Nations. The modern Commonwealth (1949) evolved from the UK's colonial empire. Today it gathers 54 states that through a common language, English, and a series of wide-ranging intergovernmental and non-governmental associations consult and co-operate "in the common interests of their peoples and in the promotion of international understanding and world peace" (Commonwealth Secretariat 2008).

The Commonwealth of Nations does not gather all the English-speaking nations. Many important former British colonies have not joined the Commonwealth, such as the USA and the Arab countries. Mazrui and Mazrui (1998a, p.207) call attention to that phenomenon. They advance ideological/religious reasons (British monarchy as head of state), potential power shifts (Washington displacing London), organisational rivalry (Commonwealth versus League of Arab States), political reasons (British policies viewed as pro-Israeli tarnished the Commonwealth). Mazrui and Mazrui's analysis hints at a neo-colonial character of the organisation, the implicit continuation of Britain, the former colonial power, as the leading country. The USA inclusion would definitely change the balance of power given the status of the country as a world power. And if neither Britain nor other countries desired those changes, neither the USA needed the organisation. In terms of the Arab countries the ideological, political and religious stances conflicted directly with those of the Commonwealth. The relations between the countries seem to denote a clientelist nature that is shared by the other politico linguistic blocs. The Commonwealth of Nations also includes Mozambique - a member since 1995 and the first never to have been associated with British colonial rule. Mozambique, from the mid-1970s, had been associated with the Commonwealth in imposing sanctions to Rhodesia and struggling against South Africa's apartheid regime (Commonwealth Secretariat 1995, p.36). Mozambique became in 1987 an observer at Commonwealth meetings, and in order to help Mozambique and as recognition for the support, the Commonwealth set up special programmes for Mozambique that included scholarships.

The Commonwealth includes in its organisational family many organisations that through their activity directly promote English language, they are, for instance: the Association for Commonwealth Literature and Language Studies, and the English-Speaking Union of the Commonwealth. However the explicit spread of the English language is not their concern. Nor does it need to be, given the status and spread of English in the contemporary world.

The francophone bloc of countries corresponds to the movement usually denominated *La Francophonie*. Under this broad denomination are included several structures of which the most important is the Organisation Internationale de la Francophonie (OIF), gathering 56 member states and 14 observers.

French language is official language, on its own or with other languages, in 32 of the 68 countries (including 13 observers) party to the OIF. Membership depends on the overall place the French language has in the country, which allows a flexible and inclusive membership - quite adequate given the linguistic ambition of France.

The OIF aims to develop multilateral cooperation to assist developing and transitional countries to acquire the means to master their own development process and enable them to generate their own dynamic towards a durable and equitable form of human and social development (OIF 2008). The promotion of French language has always been paramount in the context of the defence of cultural and linguistic diversity:

> La Francophonie seeks the reinforcement of French as a tool of communication and cultural vector and, by extension, as a language of international communication, teaching and support to an intellectual, scientific and cultural innovative dynamism. It associates this action with a commitment in favour of plurilingualism in symbiosis with the big linguistic communities of the world.
>
> In the national arena, the promotion of French language is set in a cohabitation issue involving French and other partner or international languages[14]
> (OIF 2008).

It is widely recognised that Francophony has been a clear priority of French policy throughout the 1990s and before. Although Francophone African countries initiated the movement of *La Francophonie*, France has been the main investor, given its interest in ensuring that French language maintains and, if possible expands, its influence worldwide.

France has been accused of using Francophony to develop neocolonialist policies - I have already mentioned the *Françafrique* critiques. Blamangin (2000, p.188 quoting Leymarie) alluding to French political support for African dictatorial and corrupt regimes through *Francophonie*, finds this movement often structured on the idea of a cultural and political front, of a frontier of influence, to be guarded against enemy powers (as in the time of the empires or of the Cold War) and operating in the fashion of a medieval feudal system.

---

14   "La Francophonie veille au renforcement du français comme outil de communication et vecteur culturel et, par extension, comme langue de communication internationale, d'enseignment et de support à un dynamisme intellectuel, scientifique et culturel novateur. Elle associe cette action à son engagement en faveur du plurilinguisme en symbiose avec les grandes communautés linguistiques dans le monde.
Au plan national, la promotion de la langue française s'inscrit dans une problemátique de cohabitation du français avec d'autres langues partenaires ou internationales."

France's attempts to influence postcolonial Africa are part of a wider strategy to defend the status quo of France in the international system. Linguistic concerns are also present, as Africa is seen often as instrumental in the future of French language: continual spread and maintenance of French language there would assure or contribute greatly to the maintenance of international language status. French language spread in Africa has been questioned. Some authors, such as Mazrui and Mazrui (1998a, p.198) comment "France is unsure whether to try and remain a major cultural and economic presence in Black Africa, in the face of competing opportunities opening up in Eastern and Central Europe". Other authors, such as Blamangin (2000), also highlight the fact that Francophony is changing towards an asserting of governmental status. In the findings of this study I try to determine if the changes reflect on the case studies.

The Commonwealth of Nations and the OIF have 11 members in common. The Secretaries-General of the organisations meet every year to discuss issues of joint concern. The first Memorandum of Understanding between the Common-wealth and *La Francophonie* was signed in 1992 and outlined modalities of col-laboration in the areas of economic and social development. One of the most important current collaboration projects is "Hub and Spokes", financed by the European Union, helping the 79 ACP states with high-level expertise to formu-late, negotiate and set trade policies (Commonwealth Secretariat 2003, 2007). The Commonwealth has reported contacts in 2006 with the Organisation of American States and Secretariat of the Lusophone grouping of countries.

The Lusophone bloc is, in comparison with the Anglophone and the Franco-phone, the most recent formal association. That is not surprising, considering that these blocs have formed in the postcolonial era, and that Portugal had the longest lived of the European colonial empires. The PALOP, despite their guer-rilla wars for independence, had to await the overthrow of dictatorship in main-land Portugal in 1974, and Macau was only returned to China in 1999. The idea of a Lusophone movement takes inspiration from similar ones, especially Fran-cophony. This study takes the view that the movement came about more by the imitation of similar phenomena than by an intrinsic force. This stand must be taken as an assumption, since the origins of the idea of Lusophony or the history of its political organisation are not discussed in depth in this study.

The basic tenet of the movement of Lusophony is the spread of Portuguese language internationally. Portuguese speakers are spread worldwide and Portu-guese language is the official language in several international organisations (CPLP, OEI, SADC) and regional blocs (EU, Mercosul, UA), and a working language in some international organisations, such as the World Intellectual Property Organisation. Portuguese language is also the official language in eight countries: Portugal, Brazil, Timor-Leste, Angola, Cabo Verde, Guinea-Bissau,

Mozambique, São Tomé and Príncipe. In all of these countries, Portuguese shares the linguistic space with other languages - and only in Portugal and Brazil does Portuguese occupy the top place for the number of speakers. *Lusofonia* has been defined as the idea of language as cultural homeland (Coelho 1986, p.63)[15]. This philosophical definition contrasts sharply with the Portuguese government's apparently practical definition of the concept of *Lusofonia* as the ensemble of Portuguese language communities in the world (República Portuguesa 2007). However, Lusophony, as a transnational community of Portuguese speakers, is the embodiment of a discourse that places language as "the main symbol, resource and fetish" in the reconstruction of a post-colonial Portuguese national identity (De Almeida 2008, p.8). Mozambican writer Mia Couto (1995) comments:

> There are ties that history has created. There is still a long way to weave those ties in a family web. That project cannot be built on illusions, misunderstandings and benefits that some intend to establish. The first of those misunderstandings: we are not really 200 million speakers. In Mozambique, the Portuguese language is the second language of just a meager slice of the population. The same happens in Guinea-Bissau and, in a lesser degree, in Angola. Second misunderstanding: cultural proximity. Portuguese language does not provide that familiarity. A Mozambican speaker is closer, from the cultural point of view, to a South-African or Zimbabwean than to a Portuguese, Brazilian or Cape-Verdian.
>
> Another illusion: friendship ties. Even recognising the strength of friendship, it is not the motor of communion these days. We speak of countries, governments, national interests. Any of the seven (or eight) thinking of Timor) nations is integrated in different regional interests. We are peripheries of different centres.[16]

The fact that the member countries of Lusophony are peripheries of different centres, therefore, subject to different centripetal forces, does not stop authors,

---

15 "ideia de língua como pátria cultural".

16 "Existem laços que a história criou. Falta ainda um longo caminho para tecer esses laços em rede familiar. Esse projecto não pode ser erguido sobre ilusões, equívocos e facilidades que alguns pretendem estabelecer. O primeiro desses equívocos: não somos realmente 200 milhões de falantes. Em Moçambique, o idioma português é a segunda língua de apenas uma magra fatia da população. O mesmo se passa na Guiné-Bissau e, em menor grau, em Angola. Segundo equívoco: a proximidade cultural. A língua portuguesa não confere essa familiaridade. Um falante moçambicano tem mais a ver com, do ponto de vista cultural, com um sul africano ou zimbabweano do que com um português, brasileiro ou cabo-verdiano.
Outra ilusão: os laços de afecto. Mesmo reconhecendo a força da afectividade, ela não é o motor de comunhão nos dias de hoje. Estamos falando de países, governos, interesses nacionais. Qualquer uma das sete (ou oito) pensando em Timor) nações se integra em interesses regionais diferentes. Somos periferia de diferentes centros."

such as Palmeira (2006, p.11), from viewing Portuguese language as a potential strategic element in a geopolitical project for Portugal given the number of speakers around the world and the fact that it is the official language in eight states. Cultural branding (Tomalin 2004) is thus proposed by Palmeira (2006, p.14) as a possibility for the Lusophone area: "The "Lusophone space" has the potential to be a "brand" (of Portuguese origin) in the international system's global market, if the (eight) States that represent it manage to converge on policies that, beyond defence and promotion of the common language, imply the institutionalisation of a cooperation extended to other mutual interest domains."[17] I will try to determine in the context of this study how that type of initiative is being perceived and adhered to.

The two major political organisations of Lusophony are the Community of Portuguese Language Countries (Comunidade dos Países de Língua Portuguesa, CPLP) and the International Institute of Portuguese Language (Instituto Internacional da Língua Portuguesa, IILP).

CPLP is a multilateral forum gathering all the Portuguese language countries. Its main aims are political and diplomatic coordination concerning international relations, cooperation in all domains and the promotion and diffusion of Portuguese language. The process was initiated in 1989, by Brazil's initiative, and continued to mature in the 1990s. The organisation was finally set up in 1996, gathering Portugal, Brazil and the five PALOP, the African Portuguese-speaking countries (Angola, Cape Verde, Guinea Bissau, Mozambique and São Tomé and Príncipe). Six years later, in 2002, the newly independent Timor-Leste became the eighth member. CPLP has from the beginning limited its membership to countries, although pressure has been present since the beginning, particularly from the Spanish region of Galicia, where Galego, a 'sister' language of Portuguese, is spoken. In July 2006, CPLP amended membership rules and opened up the organisation to new members, and, at the Bissau summit, Equatorial Guinea and Mauritius were admitted as observers. In 2008 Senegal was also admitted as an observer. 44 NGOs have also been admitted since 2006 as consultant observer members (CPLP website www.cplp.org 2010), which can be seen to denote an increasing relevance and visibility of the organisation in the political space of Lusophony and in the international arena. In 2010 at the Luanda Summit, Morroco, Ucrain and Suaziland presented requests to

---

17 "O "espazo lusófono" ten potencialidades para ser unha "marca" (de orixe portuguesa) no mercado global do sistema internacional, así os (oito) Estados que o representan consigan converxer en políticas que, para alén da defensa e promoción da lingua común, pasen pola institucionalización dunha cooperación ampliada a outros dominios de interese mutuo."

become observers. It is rumoured that also Australia, Indonesia and Luxemburg are interested in acquiring that status in the organisation.

At the same meeting in S. Luís do Maranhão, Brazil, where the CPLP process was initiated in 1989, the Instituto Internacional da Língua Portuguesa (IILP) was created. The IILP had been the idea at the origin of the CPLP, and was intended to become one of its corner stones. However, its creation would only materialise in 2005. The mission of the IILP is to "plan and execute programmes for the promotion, defence, enrichment and diffusion of the Portuguese language as a vehicle of culture, education, information and access to technological and scientific knowledge and of use in international forums" (CPLP 2007). Up to the present the institution has had limited activities (http://www.iilp.org.cv).

CPLP has been described as a "poor's man club"[18] (non-attributable source[19]). The member countries are required to make financial contributions, which are limited and often late. Also CPLP still lacks a language policy and strategy of its own, despite its mission to promote and diffuse Portuguese language. This is a potentially sensitive issue, since, within CPLP, there are those who believe that promoting Portuguese language in the context of the PALOP could come across as a "neocolonialist attitude" (non-attributable source). It is evident that some issues regarding the colonial past have not been fully resolved between Portugal and the PALOP. However, despite all the problems of this fairly recent political project, membership is coveted. In July 2007, President Teodoro Obiang Nguema Mbasogo announced the predisposition of his government to make Portuguese the third official language of Equatorial Guinea, in order to meet the full membership requirement of the CPLP – Portuguese became official language of the country on the 20th July 2010, three days before Equatorial Guinea formally presented its request to become a member of CPLP at the Luanda Summit. Although controversy has surrounded the issue, negotiations are underway. Equatorial Guinea is the only Spanish-speaking country in Africa that also has French as an official language. It is strategically placed in the Gulf of Guinea and has oil reserves that make it an ally not to be despised, despite the bad democratic record – the President has been in power since 1979 following a coup (Notícias Lusófonas, 2007).

This concludes the presentation of the politico linguistic blocs relevant for the understanding of this study. The following section, the final of the theoretical framework, develops some of the themes developed in the previous sections and analyses them in the context of a globalising world.

---

18   "clube de pobres".
19   It is unwise to disclose the speaker's identity for strategic reasons.

2.3.2 Africa, Languages and States in a Globalising World

In this section I discuss language, culture and national identity in relation to globalisation, with particular attention to what is happening in Africa. The section is divided in three main areas. As a starting point, I define globalisation and look at the inherent tensions between the dual poles of homogeneity/ heterogeneity and pluralism / universalism by looking at globalised languages, politico linguistic blocs and linguistic and cultural imperialism. In the second subsection, I analyse the challenges faced by the state with increased globalisation, particularly in the areas of identity and culture. In the final section attention is focused on Africa and I briefly analyse the continent's struggle for independence and development in an increasingly globalised world, having in mind the main concerns of the study, language and culture.

2.3.2.1 Language and Culture in a Globalising World

Globalisation, in this study, is defined as a set of processes and discourses relating to the worldwide interconnection and integration of a multitude of areas (economy, technology, biology, society and culture) through globe-spanning networks. As contextual background, I should say that I favour the view of a deep historical origin of globalisation, as in Andre Gunter Frank's (Frank and Gills 1995/2001) world system continuity thesis where the guiding idea is the continuous history and development of a single world system in Afro-Eurasia for at least 5,000 years. I do not see globalisation as a distinct modern phenomenon.

My definition of globalisation is influenced by Fairclough (2001, 2006) as I acknowledge the importance of both the real processes of globalisation and the representations of those processes in discourse. However, like Fairclough (2006, p.4/5), I note that, although distinguishing between actual processes and discourses, these cannot actually be separated, since the representation of the real processes inevitably draw upon chosen discourses - that decision becomes another problem.

Many of the strands of discussion that run through this study relate to discourses of globalisation that dually discuss the roles of language and culture in globalisation as a process leading to homogeneity and globalisation fostering diversity and localisation.

Language is a key element of our essence as human beings; it allows us to communicate with others, to create affiliations, to build societies. These societies are diversely constructed, in time and space, by different groups of individuals, creating particular cultures. The processes of globalisation, through easiness of communication and transport, have enabled individuals to developed more connections between different societies; consequently their boundaries became more fluid. This causes a dynamic tension between cultural homogeneisation and cultural heterogenisation, that Appadurai (1990, p.295) has identified as the central problem of globalisation. Language and power negotiate the struggles brought by globalisation. These struggles are "partly struggles over language, both over new ways of using language, and over linguistic representations of change" (Fairclough 2001, p.204). Language mediates the struggles and the discourses it embodies seek hegemonic positions in the linguistic and intellectual social markets. Hegemony is here taken in the sense of commonsense, naturalized rationalization of structural, social and cultural control (Gramsci 1971) - thus 'soft' forms of control.

Within the framework of this study regarding the topics of culture and language, I focus on the globalisation discourses stressing homogeneity that include discussions on: the dominance of some languages and cultures over others impacting on the decrease of linguistic and cultural diversity worldwide; the loss of languages and cultures; the hegemony of English language (as the most used language for communication between people speaking different languages) and of Western (particularly American) culture in the world (spread of American cultural content in cultural products, not necessarily made in the USA, given the homogenisation of discourses); the narrowing of ways of using language (as a form of communication) and the loss of the range of discourses for representing the world in different domains of social life and across different countries (Fairclough 2001); the need to defend the inherent diversity of humankind by increasing the awareness of concepts of multiculturalism and multilingualism, and the need to formalise and therefore protect human rights including cultural and linguistic rights. These discourses highlight negative effects of the potential homogenising effects of globalisation.

Other strands of the same discourse stressing homogeneity through globalisation, offer positive views. That is the case of the perception of the use of international lingua franca, namely English, as a neutral tool, that gives access to universal objectives and values, such as modernity, development, freedom and democracy. However, culture and language are inherently diverse and the processes of globalisation are not changing that.

As I see it, the world experiences at the same time the pulls of universalism and particularlism. A world that still maintains many of the characteristics of a system of competing national cultures seeking to improve the ranking of their states (Featherstone 1990), but that has to coexists with: different political/economic/cultural co-operating arenas and blocs of countries; a mass of international organisations building the basis of an international society, namely the UN system, despite eventual bias in its definition towards the West; an increasingly powerful civil society organised in NGOs and other informal groups and populated by influential individuals; transnational corporations that are able to operate on their own terms given the process of economic and financial globalisation.

In this setting, global cultural flows are composed of complex, overlapping and disjunctive orders that do not allow for any homogenised perspective, determined in great measure by mass migration and electronic media (Appadurai 1990). This diversity however harbours in itself homogeneity and hegemonic processes. Appadurai (1990) identifies a dialogic process within globalisation, whereby diverse and inherently complex cultural flows, also integrate processes of homogenisation through hegemony within the different strands of diversity, transforming the diversity within them in an homogeneity that make them unique and different from others.

A parallel can be drawn with language. The inherent diversity of language incorporates processes of homogeneisation for linguistic reasons (need to communicate) but also for political and ideological reasons (processes of standardisation, linguistic nationalism). With the increase of the processes of globalisation, the concept of language homogeneity was able to go beyond the nation-state, and languages are perceived as global entities, e.g. English/Spanish/Portuguese/French etc as world languages - that is languages spread through migration fluxes and foreign language learning throughout the planet. Therefore topics such as the rank of the top languages spoken in the world, the loss of languages worldwide or the domination of English as an international lingua franca have emerged as important in an international linguistic agenda.

This idea of global languages has been particularly used by the countries associated with the international or world languages (spoken in different countries and continents) named above to enhance their image and ultimately their prestige and power. Many of those countries collaborate with each other in the institutionalisation of politico linguistic blocs, mentioned in section 2.3.1. In those cases, the notion of speaker of a language is often (incorrectly) equated to nationality. For instance, not all citizens of Guinea-Bissau or Mozambique speak Portuguese, but because the countries are part of the Lusophone bloc (colonial legacy, political affiliation with CPLP) their populations are included in the calculation of the often advertised over 200 million Portuguese speakers worldwide. For globalised languages, the notion of a speaker is rather fluid: I mentioned association with nationality, but in other cases the number of speakers may also include estimations based on fluency (but at what level?), particularly if the speaker in question has a nationality not usually related with the language in question.

101

The idea that I would like to stress is that global languages are used by the different states that identify with them as political tools to enhance their capacities to operate in the international system. But they are only able to do so by employing co-operation strategies, that may involve or not hegemonic processes. If globalised languages exemplify the dual pull of universalism and particularism in the contemporary world, it should be asked if the politico-linguistic blocs are the embryos of new imagined communities, of another level of imagined identity between the nation-state and humankind.

Official political discourses on politico-linguistic blocs often stress the communalities (the 'common' language) and forget about the differences in a pattern that perpetuates the unidimensionality of identity of individuals and societies. This obviously reflects ingrained ideas about the bonds between individuals, societies and states that I discuss in section 2.3.2. Thus if tension between homogeneisation and heterogeneity is also visible in the construction of politico-linguistic spaces, it is then pertinent to ask, as Tardif (2004c, p.1) does, "if, in the present world dynamics, the linguistic-cultural areas have a reason to be, enough consistency, the capacity and the will to mobilise around significant common projects to face the present challenges"[20]. It could be argued that the cultural/linguistic blocs can create a new affiliation, that of Lusophone, Francophone, Hispanophone, Anglophone, etc, as long as that is viewed as part of the chosen multidimensionality of the individual and of the group, in the spirit of cultural and linguistic diversity. Yet, at the same time, account needs to be taken of asymmetries of power between the cultural/linguistic blocs and the developing countries involved in the external language spread.

At this point I would like to restate that I advocate a view of the international system as a world system continuity (Frank and Gills 1995/2001). In this view the world system is composed of an inter-linked set of center-periphery complexes (including 'hinterlands', surrounding areas). In this approach, distinct regional, imperial, or market mediated center-periphery complexes are all part of a single whole with systemic links to one another. However this multicentricity does not mean equality among the various centers or between different center-periphery complexes, rather there is a complex hierarchical chain of metropole-satellite relations. Also peripheral and hegemonic positions are not static; the world historical process will make them change over time. Hegemony at the scale of the entire world system is thus perhaps not possible; instead we have 'inter-linked hegemonies'.

---

20   "si, en la dinámica mundial actual, las áreas lingüístico-culturales tienen una razón de
       ser propia, una consistencia suficiente, la capacidad y la voluntad de movilizarse alre-
       dedor de proyectos comunes significativos frente a los desaíos actuales."

Having discussed how globalisation is viewed in this study and how that view affects my perspective on cultural and linguistic diversity, I analyse in the following section the new challenges to the state presented by increased globalisation processes.

2.3.2.2 State, Identity and Culture: New Challenges

Many authors argue that globalisation has dispossessed states of their central role in the international system. The dimension of many activities nowadays is bypassing the considered traditional domain of the state (a sovereign territorial entity providing security, freedom, order, justice and welfare to a population). These include:

> ever-increasing international trade and investment, expanding multinational business activity, enlarged NGO (non-governmental organization) activities, increasing regional and global communications, the growth of the Internet, expanding and ever-extending transport networks, exploding travel and tourism, massive human migration, cumulative environmental pollution, expanded regional integration, the growth of trading communities, the global expansion of science and technology, continuous downsizing of government, increased privatization and other activities which have the effect of increasing interdependence across borders. (Jackson and Sørensen 2007, p.24)

However the world we live in is still a world of sovereign states, albeit one where sovereignty has changed due to more intense cooperation: "countries bargain about influence on each other's internal affairs" (Jackson and Sørensen 2007, p.269). The states do form numerous associations, some of which are integrating them quite closely, as is the case of the European Union (EU) (a political and economic union of 27 countries), but sovereignty, as the supreme power of a collectivity to decide its destiny, has been preserved.

At the same time globalisation has eroded the concept of sovereignty, it has also devalued national identity, by increasing de-spatialisation and deterritorialisation of identities. National borders may be less relevant for a whole range of people: intellectuals, scientists, arms and drug dealers, footballers or financiers. For instance some people, such as activists of the ecological movement may see themselves as owing their main allegiance to the defence of Planet Earth rather than any national identity, international terrorists, such as the British nationals that perpetrated the London bombings in 7/7/2005, were also motivated by their own religious causes, regardless of national identity.

Citizenship of the world is created by a global consciousness that runs through a variety of issues: the perils facing humanity and the environment (overpopulation, global warming), a global consumer society, the international finance flows and economic markets, international labour market, cyber communication, transnational media, migration. At the same time, since national identity is no longer constrained by territory, diasporic communities create with their original homelands, through transnational media (television, internet) and communicative social spaces. Appadurai (1996) calls these diasporic public spheres or translocal communities. These imagined communities create new ways of living national identity.

Globalisation besides freeing national identity from territorial boundaries, has freed other individual attributes, other individual affiliations, such as gender, religion, skin colour, etc, of localisation. They are now lived in a global space through the transnational networks of money, travel and communication. As Billig (1995, p.133) notes, national identity must compete on a free market of identities. Supra and sub-national identities are challenging the state and the very definition of national identity has been affected. As Rassool (1995, p.95) points out, "the [relative] homogeneity of national cultures is increasingly being challenged by the large scale social displacement of large groups of people across the world". The inescapable reality of linguistic and cultural diversity in the world, reinforced by the processes of globalisation, has forced major changes on the state and in the ideas about nationhood, consequently common languages as symbols of national identity will have to be renegotiated. The freeing of the attributes of the self with globalisation and the bypassing of the state in many activities has also had important consequences in the traditional representation of 'national' culture and in the relations between 'national' cultures.

Changes in the way cultural relations operate are certainly underway, given the simple fact that they cannot escape the processes of globalisation. The popularisation of the concept of public diplomacy clearly marks the shift from a formal government-to-government approach to one that identifies the foreign public as the target audience for foreign policy. Additionally, besides states and their agents (in which I include the national cultural institutes even if at arms' length as is the case with the British Council), other actors have acquired a significant role in cultural relations ranging from arts organisations themselves and the individual practitioners, international organisations, transnational corporations sponsoring or getting directly involved in cultural relations, to a variety of groups and organisations (including private foundations and NGOs) that work transnationally.

A shift in paradigm from cultural diplomacy to a "more genuine" cultural cooperation has been tentatively advanced by Fisher (2009, p.2). He identified a series of challenges that impact in the development of 'traditional' cultural diplomacy: globalisation; geopolitical change; migration flows raising questions about whose culture is being represented in the international promotion of culture by nation states; the exponential growth of non-state actors sharing the 'cultural space' traditionally occupied by Foreign Ministries and national cultural institutes; conflicting government objectives (diplomacy / cooperation / international market development of culture); difficulty in some cultural diplomatic communities to adapt to the new environment (communication with foreign publics rather than peers) and territorial tension (EU/state/region/local); conflicting agendas between the national agents - Ministry of Foreign Affairs and Ministries of Culture - delivering foreign cultural policy; research into the foreign policy objectives and geographical priorities of some states suggest that they are more aspirational rather than realistic; foreign policy objectives and priorities are not always matched by sufficient resources to deliver the ambitions stated, and the economic crisis was beginning to have a serious impact on international cultural relations budgets.

Fisher (2009) in his analysis of policy shifts in international cultural relations claims that cultural diplomacy policies are showing signs of being less encumbered by foreign policy agendas. He (2009) identified Austria, Germany and Slovenia as some of the countries where the paradigm shift had taken place. In others, such as the UK, Finland and the Netherlands both currents - traditional cultural diplomacy and the cultural cooperation policies - seemed to be present. In France, for instance, there was an active discussion of policy. It should be mentioned that Fisher's (2009) research, in which I was personally involved supporting and collecting data, was a general exercise, mainly based on the stated policy objectives and selected projects and it was mostly concerned with the relation between European Union countries and developed economies in Asia and Americas as well as the EU's immediate neighbours to the East.

The relations that most concern this study, those between developed and developing countries, were not covered by Fisher's (2009) study, but some of the research conclusions are relevant because they give an idea of what is happening in the source countries of external LSPs covered in our study - I will come back to these in more detail in the findings. In general the study concluded that there were mixed messages, with some countries showing clear signs of policy shifts and others just good intentions; it was also evident in research that there was some convergence of policy interest between foreign affairs, culture, trade (creative industries) and development involving the need to develop transversal governmental strategies; cultural policy was becoming more structurally integrated in foreign policy objectives; cultural organisations, in particular the larger ones, were developing their own international networks, with or without government support - the same was happening with other actors, such as regions (for instance in Spain) and cities.

However there is one particular conclusion in Fisher (2009, p.3, information in square brackets added) that I find of extreme relevance to this study and that provides a good context for all the above observations:

> Among other conclusions were that co-operation between NCIs [national cultural institutes] was likely to increase in third countries [non-European Union countries], whether on economic grounds or to demonstrate 'European' credentials, but this was less likely in the BRIC (Brazil, Russia, India and China) countries because individual governments were keen to have a cultural stake in potentially large markets.

This shows the continuing importance of the export of culture in national terms, particularly in contexts where economic and political competition is important. Governments still very much use culture as a way to advance their national identity and interests - although state action and the definition of their identity and interests and the measure in which they are acted upon may vary with influence "by "structure" (anarchy and the distribution of power) versus "process" (interaction and learning) and institutions [collective stable set of identities and interests often codified in rules and norms]" (Wendt 1992, p.393, information in square brackets added).

Additionally the trends tentatively indicated by Fisher's (2009) research towards cooperation, common interest projects, sharing of premises, mutuality and multilateral relations have to be interpreted in a particular context of relations between EU countries and particular developed economies. That does not mean that they cannot be taken as an indication of change affecting the whole spectrum of international cultural relations. A paradigmatic example is the work developed by the Goethe Institute. This national cultural institute, besides the teaching of German, has diversified its action to encompass all the arts, society, knowledge and development. It has become a powerhouse for the dissemination of German language, culture and society while increasingly serving as a channel for foreign cultures in their own countries and abroad (see case studies in Chapter 4).

However, changes in terms of how the relations are enacted in cultural diplomacy, such as the diversity of areas in which they operate or the opening up to mutuality of relations, still do not change the direction of the majority of the flows and their purpose. The equality of cultural relations still depends on the relative power and interests of the actors intervening. For instance, in the case of relations between developed and developing countries, although desirability for mutuality in relations is often expressed in official discourse, and marginally practised, I do not see the relations becoming equitable.

As I have pointed out in section 2.1.3.3, cultural relations are moving away from a national base. Apart from the participation in cultural relations of an increasing number of actors, the media plays nowadays a fundamental role in the mediation of relations between societies. Tardif (2004d, p.4) maintains that "Cultural industries are now largely created by media detached from territorial constraints and in trade in cultural goods and services. This is why, as with all oligopolies, large inequalities in cultural exchanges are unacceptable."

In this section I have briefly analysed the impact of globalisation on the role of states and in the development of cultural diplomacy. The next section discusses Africa's struggle towards independence and development in the light of some globalisation processes.

2.3.2.3 African Struggle for Development

The postcolonial state in Africa was built upon the territorial demarcation of the colonial state. The countries of Africa have attempted to create "'territorial nations' within the historical framework of western-imposed bureaucratic states, by a political intelligentsia to whose needs and interests the postcolonial state-nations minister" (Smith 1983). Smith (1991, p.120/1) identifies the intelligentsia (the professionals: lawyers, doctors, engineers, journalists, teachers, etc), followed (some way behind) by the entrepreneurs, managers and traders, as a group playing a prominent role in early territorial nationalisms, disseminating the idea and realizing it in political institutions and activities. That intelligentsia has been created by the colonial state, being constituted by those few that had had access to the education system and had been able to progress in it (with higher education being often ministered at the metropole) and often served within the colonial structures. There was then a transposition of structure and ideology between the colonial and the postcolonial state.

The African states emerged in a fight against colonialism. As Hobsbawm (1990, p.67) argues African states were not issued from feelings around ethnicity and race, but "formed out of former European colonies whose only internal cohesion came from a few decades of colonial administration" - regardless of the fact that later a "dominant *ethnie* model" or a "civic territorial nation" would lead the process of nation-building (Smith 1991, p.110-116), or if ethnicity played a role in the construction of rival forms of nationalism or national identity. Ethnicity is only marginally relevant for this study although it has played a part, for instance, through the political use by nationalist movements of ethnic divides in Guinea-Bissau (Smith 1983, pp.120/1). I will not deal in this study with the rise and nature of African nationalism (Smith 1983). I will generally assume it as consequence of a multitude of factors with relevance for the demise of European colonialism.

Regarding the independence of the African country case studies, and that of the other Lusophone African countries, their late decolonisation in the early 1970s occurred in special circumstances following a revolutionary coup in the metropole. Portugal struggled with 40 years of dictatorship that was taking its toll both in the development of the metropole and of the colonies, in a decisive anti-colonial international climate. The USA and the USSR divided world hegemony and were against the European countries keeping colonies. Communist ideology was at the time a powerful ideal that captured the imagination of the Third world intelligentsias seeking to free themselves from the shackles of colonialism. Angola, Mozambique and Guinea-Bissau thus became some of the few 'pure' Marxist regimes in the Third World (Smith 1983, p.97).

Third world countries emerged as independent states in a world divided by the Cold War and were many times used as pawns in that same war. With the fall of the Berlin Wall in 1989 and the subsequent collapse of the USSR, the East-West polarisation of world politics came to an end. The end of apartheid in the Republic of South Africa (1994) allowed the country to become a regional leader. Africa became free from communist ideological constraints (Schraeder 2004, p.272) and embarked on a political route to democracy and on an economic path to regeneration and development set in an increasingly globalised world.

The processes of globalisation, particularly those of economic nature, have advanced the dependency of Africa on the developed world, the predominance of Western discourses in development, as well as the dominance of their languages, with particular importance for English. Africa, as is the case with many other regions, of the world, is strongly dependent on the developed world, victim of history (colonialist exploitation of material and human resources) and of the structure, processes and institutions of the international system (enduring political interference, markets dependency, cultural colonisation), is involved in a struggle to 'modernise'. This discourse of modernisation, now in the process of being replaced by one of sustainable development, is present on both sides of the inequality divide as it is in the words of a variety of actors. Similarly developed and underdeveloped/developing countries use it to justify the offer and acceptance of aid to development, as also do the range of non-state actors (international organisations, NGOs, intellectuals, etc) that participate in the processes. However the terms of engagement seem to still be related to dependency.

A particularly critical role regarding Africa is that of the World Bank and the International Monetary Fund (IMF). These organisations have been a major instrument to structure the global economy (via structuring the national economies of developing countries) and have been criticized for the social and economic impact of their policies in the population of the countries where they intervene.

The 1981 World Bank study, *Accelerated Development in Sub-Saharan Africa: An Agenda for Action* concluded that "misguided decisions of the first generation of African leaders were responsible for the mounting economic crisis of the 1980s. To resolve this crisis, the World Bank and the IMF proposed linking all future flows of Western financial help to the willingness of African leaders to sign and implement the Structural Adjustment Programmes (SAPs): "economic blueprints designed to radically restructure African economies" (Schraeder 2004, p.288). These programmes resulted in further dependency of African states on the World Bank and the IMF, signalled by authors such as Harrison (1998, p.250), Mazrui and Mazrui (1998a, p.199) and Schraeder (2004, p.288).

Critically, Schraeder (2004, p.288) describes the SAPs as embodying "the liberal economic consensus of the northern industrialized democracies that Africa's future economic success depended on the pursuit of an export-orientated strategy of economic growth that systematically dismantled all forms of governmental intervention in national economies." The programmes included a series of conditionalities focusing on liberalisation, deregulation and privatisation along with political conditionalities that included "the promotion of good governance, the creation of transparent, accountable, and efficient political systems patterned after those of the northern industrialized democracies" (Schraeder 2004, p.288-9). These political conditionalities only emerged in the 1989 World Bank report, *Sub-Saharan Africa: From Crisis to Sustainable Growth: A Long Term Perspective Study* (Schraeder 2004, p.288).

Overall the work of the World Band and the IMF has been criticized for causing further debt and poverty in the countries where they intervene, benefiting the already wealthy countries and the transnational corporations. These critics emanate both from those external to the organisations, but particularly interesting by defective elements of those organisations, such as Joseph Stiglitz (2002 and 2006), former Chief Economist of the World Bank. Stiglitz (2002) partially blames the IMF and the World Bank for the failed development of sub-Saharan Africa. Also Buchmann (1999) in her study on poverty and educational equality in sub-Saharan Africa concludes that in the last two decades of the 20th century many Africans experienced decline or stagnation in the quality of their lives.

Regarding the specific focus of this study, the World Bank and the IMF have been accused of culturally obliterating the countries receptacles of their policies and of ignoring the voices defending cultural and linguistic diversity. Mazrui and Mazrui (1998a, p.199) believe that "SAPs [structural adjustment programmes] are – in their consequences - also cultural adjustment programmes. The economic changes unleashed by SAPs have repercussions in the field of values, lifestyles and modes of communication. In other words, SAPs have linguistic consequences as well." Mazrui and Mazrui (1998a, p.203) contend that the prescriptions of the World Bank and the IMF "essentially function in favour of European languages, in general, and the English language in particular." SAPs, by encouraging a reduction of government subsidies, have according to them, lead to a reduction of investment in the development of materials in local African languages and contributed to make universities more elitist (Mazrui and Mazrui 1998a, p. 203/4).

At the turn of the century the World Bank started making efforts to include cultural concerns in its policies. However the extend to which these formal actions have practical impact is debatable. In 1999 the World Bank published the report "Culture and Sustainable Development: A Framework for Action". In this report the World Bank considers the cultural implications of its lending policies.

The World Bank did not begin to focus on the cultural impacts of its work until the Bank's Social Development Task concluded in 1998 that culture was an essential dimension of development, in the sequence of a profound change in the development thinking during the 1990s. The World Bank proposes to finance culture-based activities in response to needs expressed by client governments and validated by their own diagnoses and priorities, through the Country Assistance Strategies (CAS) (Duer 1999, p.8). The Bank has continued to explore its potential in the area of culture and in "The Kimberley Consultative Workshop on Culture in Africa" (Taboroff 2001) it explored how arts and culture can contribute to the economic development of sub-Saharan Africa. The report admits the ad-hoc nature of the work of the Bank and the need for a more strategic approach.

Discussions on the influence the World Bank and the other institutions pillars of economic globalisations, such as the IMF or the World Trade Organisation, are, in Africa, an important area of discussion that unfortunately needs to be limited given the scope of this study. It should be retained that the agency of the African countries has in many cases been removed or limited by the conditionalities imposed by the mentioned organisations and that the work of those organisations is geared to integrate states in an international financial, economic and labour market.

Returning to the main issue of this study, language, I note that the activities, policies and ideologies of these international agents have a major influence in the national governments decisions and local attitudes towards language.

The African postcolonial state, built in the likeness of the Western nation-state model, also tried emulating its model of one nation, one language, by adopting the colonial language as official language, the one language of the emerging nation. The other languages were often, in a first postcolonial moment ignored, devalued or seem as pernicious to the development of the national spirit

110

of the new African state. The international languages, and in particular English, with dominant positions in the international arenas, and their agents were in privileged positions to influence official and foreign language choices in developing countries. These options were often associated with certain dominant concepts of modernisation and development that connected them closely with European languages.

The importance of the role of language in the development process has been highlighted by authors such as Robinson (1996, p.5), recognising languages as the basis of communication:

> At the heart of the development process are relationships, the cultural context, the parameters of communication. Language is one such parameter, an obvious one, though not the only one. It is a parameter which both reflects other social realities and structures them. At the end of the day Africa faces more pressing problems than its languages, but that must not be an excuse for ignoring their role and effect on the development process. Wherever people are put at the centre of the development process, issues of language will always be close to the surface – good communication require it.

Others, operating in a neocolonialist ideology, ignore they role, seeing the providers of aid as influential mediators, therefore keeping the developing countries agents at bay in a passive receiver role. That is the case of Mitchell (1986, p.90) highlighting the cultural dimension of aid:

> The cultural dimension for aid-giving countries consists in mediating between their own culture and values and those of developing countries. Inevitably, there will be a flow of influence from a dominant to a receptive society; this has happened in all periods of human history. The task of cultural agencies is to make this process beneficient and to modulate its effects. We might call this exercise of influence – in the anthropologist's term, acculturation. It is a prerequisite of cultural relations work that it should be founded on an understanding of the social configuration of the host country.

The linguistic influence of international organisations and NGOs has added to the internal dysfunction in relation to languages, that many authors believe Africa already suffers. Heine (1992, p.28) observes that the expectations of language planners that equated the association of European languages and economic progress were disappointed and suggests that the lack of an adequate linguistic communication system on the national level has significantly contributed to the present economic situation of African countries. The work of the Bretton Woods organisations, and of other international organisations, has reinforced the use of English in Africa and the dissemination of certain discourses concerning development and modernisation.

111

African leaders have tried developing alternative frameworks of development; the most important being NEPAD, New Partnership for Africa's Development, an integrated socio-economic development framework for Africa adopted in July 2001 by the Organisation of African Unity. Under NEPAD, African leaders seek grant aid and foreign investment and trade in the context of economic and political reforms monitored by peer review mechanisms (Schraeder 2004, p.290). NEPAD, along with the reformulation of the African Union, or the establishment of ACALAN, are a sign that political leadership in Africa is recognising the need for "a regional closing of ranks in order to acquire the strength and the sense of unity of purpose that will make it possible to bargain for a better deal for the continent at the global tables of plenty" (Alexander 2007, p.17). As Alexander (2007, p.19) points out Africa must "initiate a counter-hegemonic trend in the distribution of symbolic power and cultural capital implicit in the prevailing language dispensation in Africa's education systems".

The increasing attention given to international discourses relating to the importance of mother tongue education (e.g. UNESCO), the need to defend linguistic and cultural diversity, the enforcement of the reality of multiculturalism and multiculturalism in all the states of the world (due to migratory fluxes, easiness of travel, tourism, international labour markets, etc), is providing a new framework for the development of strategies of statehood based on cultural and linguistic diversity. I return to these issues again later in my discussion of the case studies.

In this chapter I provided the theoretical background in which this study is based: language, state, colonialism, postcolonialism and globalisation. This mass of intersecting issues forms the basis on which I will explore the findings regarding the external LSPs developed in Mozambique and Guinea-Bissau.

Chapter 3 Methodology

This chapter details the research design and describes how the inquiry process was approached, developed and implemented. The sections are structured as follows: research questions and objectives; assumptions; design; methodology; data sources, collection methods and analysis; and ethical issues and practical constraints.

3.1 Research Questions and Objectives

This study, the questions it asks and the objectives it purposes to achieve, derives from the author's interest in the subject of external LSPs. I perceive those policies as instruments for the gain, maintenance and expansion of power and influence in interstate relations. In the context of postcolonial relations, I find it is important to expose them as a contemporary continuation of colonialist practices. Additionally, in the wider context of the promotion of cultural and linguistic diversity, I perceive those policies as potentially leading to language subtraction and cultural homogenisation of postcolonial societies in Western terms. My perception does not exclude positive uses of those policies for the mutual understanding of people around the world.

This study aims to contribute to the development of knowledge in the area of postcolonial sociolinguistics and international relations and to bring the topic of Portuguese language spread into the mainstream of politico-linguistic issues. The main research question of the study is: Are languages at war in Lusophone Africa? The answer to this question will reveal if, how and why ex-colonial countries compete in postcolonial Lusophone Africa, by examining external language spread policies (LSPs) in the context of the two case studies, Guinea-Bissau and Mozambique.

The overarching questions guiding the research are:

1. How and why did Portuguese become and how and why has it been sustained as official language in Mozambique and Guinea-Bissau? Why is this important in the context of the case studies? Is the Portuguese language being threatened in Mozambique and Guinea-Bissau? If yes, by which languages, how and why? If no, why has that perception occurred?
2. Are competitive external LSPs being developed in Mozambique and Guinea-Bissau? If yes, by which countries, how and why? How are the policies perceived? What are the implications for the countries involved? If no, why has that perception occurred?

3. Is the language spread policy of ex-colonial countries a good or bad thing for postcolonial societies?
4. What is the place of European languages in postcolonial African societies?

A detailed list of research questions, some adapted from Ammon (1992a, p.8-9), were used to guide the task of data collection:

1. What and how are languages used in the country?
2. What is the national language policy in the country?
3. What is the national language-in-education policy?
4. Which national policies have implications for language and how do they affect language use? What is the rationale behind the language policy?
5. Do external LSPs operate in the country? If so, what are they? Are they officially declared?
6. Which reasons or motives have been given for this language policy by its protagonists? Do these reasons or motives prove to be valid on close scrutiny, or are there presumably others that have not been openly declared; that is, is there an ideology of LSP?
7. Do the European countries have strategies for external LSP? What is their importance for the source country? How do the country case studies fit into these strategies? To which domains or institutions is it aimed?
8. How is the European countries' external language spread organised in the case study? Which organisations, personnel and resources are engaged in this policy? Which is the highest authority that directs it?
9. Which languages are seen as, or actually are, 'competitors' of the language intended to be spread? In which respect, and in which regions and domains, are these languages seen as or actually are such competitors?
10. What is done to win that competition?
11. Which countries or other actors cooperate, directly or indirectly, willingly or not, in taking parallel or supportive action in the promotion of the language in question? How is that done?
12. What is the position of the country target of the LSP? Are the government and the population aware of the fact that the country is a source of competition? Does the country take advantage of that?
13. Do the African countries also engage in external LSP of their own initiative? How, and why?
14. Are there special relationships between the source and target country, for example alliances, economic dependencies (e.g. former colonies) or traditional connections that are of relevance for language spread policy?

These questions will be examined through the following objectives:

1. To find out what position Portuguese and other European languages occupy in the linguistic panorama of Mozambique and Guinea-Bissau and why.
2. To find out how the language policy-making process in those countries is developed and if it is influenced externally.
3. To find out which European countries develop external LSPs in Mozambique and Guinea-Bissau, why and how they develop them.
4. To find out how Mozambique and Guinea-Bissau perceive and react to the development of these policies and why.

The next section identifies the assumptions of the research in terms of ontological, epistemological and methodological choices.

3.2 Research Assumptions

The choice of research subject was closely connected with my academic background and personal life. Since my teenage years, in Portugal, my home country, I had been in contact with external LSPs: learning French at the Alliance Française; Italian at the Istituto Italiano di Cultura in Portogallo; German at the Göethe Institut; taking translation courses at the Institut Franco-Portugais; getting a Certificate of Proficiency in English through the British Council; and by receiving a Chevening Scholarship from the Foreign and Commonwealth Office for a Master's degree. During my first degree in International Relations, with a specialisation in Political and Cultural Relations, I became more aware and knowledgeable of the potential use of language as an instrument of national state power. At that time (1986-1990), I became interested in the diffusion of the Portuguese language worldwide and from then on maintained an interest in the subject.

Being a researcher from the West and specifically from Portugal, and having attained my degree at the Instituto Superior de Ciências Sociais e Políticas (founded in 1906 to train civil servants for colonial posts), my initial research assumptions were very influenced by a milieu that perpetuated the romantic image of a uniform Portuguese language being well accepted and diffused throughout the so called Lusophone world. Drawing on mythological utopias of Portuguese history, such as Pessoa's *Quinto Império* and Freyre's *Lusotropicalismo* (Cristóvão 2002, De Almeida 2008) - the cultural and linguistic linkage of Portugal to Brazil, to the PALOP, to Timor-Leste, to Macau and India and to the Portuguese-speaking communities worldwide hide a very different reality: that of linguistic variation and political interest.

During the 1980s and 1990s, the Portuguese press cyclically published articles pertaining to the Portuguese language being threatened in Africa, especially by English in Mozambique and French in Guinea-Bissau. A change in career from cultural management to international relations and a want to deepen my understanding of the discourses surrounding Portuguese language spread abroad prompted my research. The opportunity of conducting research at PhD level on this subject was made possible in 2000 by a scholarship from the Fundação para a Ciência e a Tecnologia (Portuguese Science, Technology and Higher Education Ministry) and the European Social Fund (EU). The process initially was very much influenced by the realist theory of international relations, seeing the state as the main actor in the international political system, having as a main focus the furthering of its own power (in this case, by spreading the language associated with the nation). As my research progressed, other theories of international relations came to the fore and the disciplines of linguistics and sociolinguistics became increasingly important, enriching the analysis of the case studies.

When I embarked in this research I assumed that I would be able to access language policies, official documents and activity reports in order to be able to draw a picture over time. That was not the case, language policies were not always written down and often annual reports were non-existent or their information content was very poor. This apparent widespread lack of planning, monitoring, evaluation and accountability reflected, in my opinion, the immediate nature of the organisations' activity and the enduring bad habits of heavy bureaucratic apparels.

Research *in situ* assumed access to a number of resources and people. That access was, at times, made difficult for logistical reasons, such as lack of telephone lines to contact them, resulting in not being able to go ahead with the interviews. Bissau, Guinea-Bissau's capital, took me by surprise, as I was not prepared for the lack of lighting in the streets, or the lack of pavements - I quickly learned that making interviews at dusk was not a good or safe enterprise. In Maputo (Mozambique) figuring out how to return from the Eduardo Mondlane University campus to the centre of town made me realise how much I took public transportation for granted and how organised I had to be managing transfers between interviews. These and other minor culture shocks I overcame with an open mind and the help of my contact people and of all the other anonymous people that crossed my path and stopped to help.

As mentioned, I started the process of this research from a quite narrow theoretical basis, namely international relations and cultural diplomacy and therefore I anticipated the process of research and its findings to be also quite confined. As my research progressed an increasing number of important crosscutting issues emerged, and, at times, it was difficult to refocus on the main objective of the study, the competition of external (European) language spread policies.

Additionally I did not appreciate the personal and academic challenges that I would go through in the process of the study. While carrying out the research, my personal life also brought me closer to multicultural and multilingual issues, as I became engaged in raising a bilingual English/Portuguese family of two boys with my British (pretty much) monolingual husband. That personal process, although a cause for serious delays, was an unexpected source of inspiration and reflection on the processes of language acquisition and maintenance and issues of personal identity and language. After long delays, the end of the academic process would also not be straightforward. Having submitted the study in 2008, I had to resubmit the thesis with major amendments in 2010, when all ended with the best of results.

3.2.1 Ontology and Epistemology

The study adopts a constructivist approach (Guba and Lincoln 1994) to the nature of social reality and the character of knowledge. 'Society' is taken as a social construct built from the perceptions and actions of social actors (Bryman 2004, p.16; Flick *et al.* 2005a, p.7). 'Research' is then a twofold construction of reality, guided by the choices of the researcher, and based on his/her perceptions and actions and of those observed. 'Knowledge' originates from that "interaction of inquirer and phenomenon (which, in the social sciences, is usually people)" (Guba and Lincoln 1994, p.107) and is value dependent. This approach leads to a close connection between the nature of social reality and what is knowledge: our knowledge is bound by our perceptions of the world. The researcher constructs his/her view of the research topic, based on his/her perceptions of the world. These are theory-laden, influenced by the researcher's worldview, values and beliefs. Therefore, perceptions are inherently imperfect and our knowledge fallible, if we think in terms of the positivist paradigm of science, which focuses on an objective reality, independent from the researcher. The building of knowledge, by understanding reality and achieving (ultimately unattainable positivist) objectivity, is viewed as a social enterprise. It is amassed as theories and interpretations presented by researchers stand the test of time and of peer reviewing. Individually researchers should always seek some validity for their work, and in this study that is achieved by way of triangulation. This is discussed in greater detail later in this chapter.

3.2.2 Methodology

The exact model of the natural sciences has traditionally supplied principles that guide research with the following purposes: "to clearly isolate causes and effects, to properly operationalize theoretical relations, to measure and quantify phenomena, to create research designs allowing the *generalization* of the findings, and to formulate general laws" (Flick 2009, p.13). However, the perception of social reality as a complex phenomenon has shown that science does not produces 'absolute truths' (term borrowed from Bock and Bonβ (1989, p.31) in Flick 2009, p.13). Only qualitative research can analyse that complexity in its fullness, capture the 'pluralization of life worlds' (Flick 2009, p.13), and provide the necessary rich insight into human behaviour, by analysing the meanings and purposes human actors attach to their activities (Guba and Lincoln 1994 p.106). Qualitative research is viewed in this study as an encompassing inquiry across disciplines, paradigms and methods, where researchers are "committed to the naturalistic perspective, and to the interpretative understanding of human experience" (Nelson *et al.* 1994, p.4, cited in Denzin and Lincoln 1998, p.6).

I agree with Robson's (2002, p.23) view that "(p)eople, unlike the objects of the natural world, are conscious, purposive actors who have ideas about their world and attach meaning to what is going on around them. In particular, their behaviour depends crucially on these ideas and meanings", therefore "(t)heir behaviour, what they actually do, has to be interpreted in the light of these underlying ideas, meanings and motivations". This analysis is paramount for this study. Further, being a predominantly political topic, individual actors are constrained by systems of meaning socially engineered by political stakeholders. By this I mean that each country, each society, each government has created different predominant perceptions on the deployment and/or acceptance of transnational LSPs. Therefore, the need was felt to conduct the research of the social actors perceptions in their 'natural setting', leading - with additional reasons later discussed - to the choice of *in situ* inquiry of the cases studies.

To guarantee the credibility of the qualitative analysis was a concern from the start, although given the constructivist approach of the study, this thesis is clearly assumed as a perspective on the topic. The robustness of the qualitative research undertaken was determined by criteria for evaluating qualitative research, which was taken into consideration during the process of inquiry. Lincoln and Guba (1985 cited in Bryman 2004, p.30) propose 'trustworthiness' as a criterion of how good a qualitative study is, and it should have the following characteristics, which are paralleled with quantitative research criteria:

"- *Credibility*, which parallels internal validity – i.e. how believable are the findings?
- *Transferability*, which parallels external validity – i.e. do the findings apply to other contexts?
- *Dependability*, which parallels reliability – i.e. are the findings likely to apply at other times?
- *Confirmability*, which parallels objectivity – i.e. has the investigator allowed his or her values to intrude to a high degree?"

To insure 'credibility', Bryman (2004, p.275) advises two techniques, respondent or member validation and triangulation. Member validation entails the good practice of research and "submitting research findings to the members of the social world who were studied for confirmation that the investigator has correctly understood that social world." Member validation was not applied to this study given administrative difficulties in sending and receiving information from the 83 interviewees in five countries. Internal validity of the research was achieved by triangulation. Triangulation, as the use of different sources of data, methods, theories and perspectives in the research (Denzin and Lincoln 1998, pp.3-4; and Patton cited in Yin 2003, p.98), was used to find meaning and to validate data. Triangulation is also envisaged as "a strategy leading to a deeper understanding of the issue under investigation, and thereby as a step on the road to greater knowledge" (Denzin cited in Flick, 2005b, p.178). Data triangulation was used to check the results of the research by cross-examination of people and organisations. For instance, by interviewing people belonging to the same organisation and comparing the information provided, or checking different interpretations of the same event. Methodological triangulation involved the comparison of the results of research provided by the elite-interviews with the qualitative analysis of newspaper articles and government official documents and with the quantitative and statistical information available. The triangulation of theories from international relations and sociolinguistics and the triangulation of individual perspectives of our interviewees were developed with the main aim of producing an account that translated accurately the richness and the complexity of the topic, proving also the necessary credibility to the study. Triangulation of investigators was not envisaged, as this thesis is the work of a single researcher.

'Transferability' is achieved by the use of 'thick descriptions' as a "database for making judgements about the possible transferability of findings to other milieux" (Guba and Lincoln cited in Bryman 2004, p.275). 'Thick descriptions' can be defined as "rich accounts of the details of a culture." (Geertz 1974 cited in Bryman 2004, p.275). In this study, the case studies work as thick descriptions of the perceptions involving the subject of external LSPs. Their transferability to other settings is achievable in the measure that certain patterns that occur in the cases examined can be observed in other countries and therefore can reinforce analytical theorisations. Transferability in this study is only attempted to the area of Lusophone Africa.

Concerning 'dependability', Bryman considers that researchers should adopt an auditing approach: "This entails that complete records are kept in all phases of the research process ... in an accessible manner. Peers would then act as auditors, possibly during the course of the research and certainly at the end to establish how far proper procedures are being and have been followed" (2004, p.275). During the course of research, research diaries were kept and the whole process of research and writing was followed by supervisors, who can be said to act as auditors of the process. Additionally, the present chapter depicts and justifies the methodological choices made and the course of research, making the auditing process accessible to a wider audience.

With regard to 'confirmability', Bryman (2004, p.276), while "recognizing that complete objectivity is impossible in social research", notes that "the researcher can be shown to act in good faith; in other words, it should be apparent that he or she has not overtly allowed personal values or theoretical inclinations manifestly to sway the conduct of the research and findings deriving from it". The process of triangulation mentioned previously is also applicable to the validation of the confirmability criteria.

3.3 Research Design

The study analyses and compares external LSPs developed in Mozambique and Guinea-Bissau, in the context of a number of issues in the area of sociolinguistics and international relations. The key concepts, discussed in the theoretical framework outlined in Chapter 2, include: globalisation, foreign relations, language relations, cultural capital, economy, power, identity, nationhood, colonialism and postcolonialism. This study is simultaneously exploratory (Are there languages at war?), descriptive and explanatory (How and why is war waged amongst languages?) in nature.

A case study approach was deemed to be the most appropriate to deal with the research subject as it was the researcher's desire to "(a) define topics broadly and not narrowly, (b) cover contextual conditions and not just the phenomenon of study, and (c) rely on multiple and not singular sources of evidence" (Yin 1993, p.3).

The research design draws on a cross-national, sectional, comparative, multiple-case study (Bryman 2004, p.53-56; Hantrais and Mangen 1996, p.1-2; Flick 2005a, p.147). The technical definition of case study is:

"A case study is an empirical inquiry that
- investigates a contemporary phenomenon within its real-life context, especially when
- the boundaries between phenomenon and context are not clearly evident."
(Yin 2003, p.13)

The sectional case study design is an in-depth study of a particular area – in this case, of external LSPs, defined as governmental policies aimed at spreading the language of a state abroad. This study emerged in response to my perception of neocolonial attitudes in the area of language in Lusophone Africa. The intensive study of an area allows for the topic to be convincingly reinterpreted through both a descriptive and critical approach. The primary unit of analysis of this study are the different foreign governments developing LSPs in the country case studies. These units are embedded in national, transnational and international contexts and their operation is affected by a number of issues previously referred to.

Generalizability of case studies may be, as pointed by Guba (1978, p.29), a holy grail - to be pursued but never quite attained. The fact that, in case study design "explanations and generalizations are limited to the particular case study at the particular time of investigation" (Burnham, 2004, p.55), can be mitigated by the choice of multiple cases, which provide a more compelling and stronger test for theory testing and building (Burnham, 2004, p.55; Bryman 2004, p.55; Herriott and Firestone 1983 cited in Yin 2003, p.46). This was a reason to present two case studies. Nevertheless, case studies are always generalizable to theoretical propositions – not to populations or universes (Yin 2003, p.10). That is to say that "the case study, like the experiment, does not represent a "sample", and in doing a case study, your goal will be to expand and generalize theories (analytic generalization) and not to enumerate frequencies (statistical generalization)". This study presents a contextualised narrative around the motivations, perceptions and consequences of external LSPs, based on the discourses of the actors involved, deconstructing its meaning and attempting analytical generalisation relying on the theory - described in Chapter 2 - that shaped the problem being studied, as viewed by the researcher.

The comparative method is applied to the case studies. 'Comparative' design is used as a broad method to discover empirical relationships among variables between comparable cases (Lijphard 1971, p.682-683). These are:

"similar in a large number of important characteristics (variables) which one wants to treat as constants, but dissimilar as far as those variables are concerned which one wants to relate to each other. If such comparable cases can be found, they offer particularly good opportunities for the application of the comparative method because they allow the establishment of relationships among a few variables while many other variables are constant." (Lijphard 1971, p.687)

However as Rustow states "comparability is a quality that is not inherent in any given set of objects; rather it is a quality imparted to them by the observer's perspective" (Lijphard 1971, p.688). The main observer in this study is the researcher, but she is not the only one. Given that this study uses a constructivist approach – the researcher constructs the 'story' of the study as her perceptions interact with the perceptions of those she observes. Regarding the comparability of cases for the purpose of this study, there are a number of geopolitical, socio-linguistic, and economic variables, which may influence the processes surrounding external LSPs. These will be discussed in the following section.

The similarities provide a common background for the case studies. The dissimilarities represent potential causal factors to be investigated. For Bryman (2004, p.55) these are the key to the comparative design, as they "act as a springboard for theoretical reflections about contrasting findings." The comparative method has its limitations. Burnham et al. (2004, p.70-71) and Lijphart (1971, p.685) have pointed out the following limitations to the comparative method: 'too many variables, not enough cases'; the fallacy of attaching too much significance to negative findings; the 'travelling problem' (neither theoretical concepts nor empirical measurements are consistent across temporal and/or special settings); the issue of value-free interpretations (misinterpretation of values in unfamiliar political systems); and 'Galton's problem' (political outcomes are due to external or global process, therefore are not independent from each other). During the course of this study, for instance, the concept of 'Lusophony' emerged during the research in Africa as quite controversial. The different connotations were determined in the different contexts. This is discussed in Chapter 4.

However, despite limitations, the comparative method helps understand the motives of the actors and the meaning of their acts and provides a sounder base to make generalisations about the practices and processes. The comparative method here is used as triangulation of data, using sectional data across countries, comparing the development of external LSP in Guinea-Bissau and in Mozambique. As Burnham et al. (2004, p.56) point out "Political events and processes are often clarified and illuminated by comparison with similar events and processes in other contexts." Issues related to comparability in this research are discussed below in the section on research methodology.

The research of the case studies in situ was intended to familiarise the author with the social world being researched. Qualitative grounding was seen as the most adequate way to uncover the view of the 'other'. By interviewing the participants in their social and physical world, and experiencing them, the research-er gained a new insight into the subject. As McCracken (1998, p.9) states "Every social scientific study is improved by a clearer understanding of beliefs and ex-perience of the actors in question". The study trips also aimed at preventing cri-tiques similar to those made to Phillipson (1992), in particular by Canagarajah (1998, p.405), who believed the latter's thesis of linguistic imperialism was wanting in complexity, partially because of his "inability to directly observe or study how the politics of ELT is played out in third world communities."

3.4 Research Methodology

Research for this study used an iterative grounded strategy, as it was constructed weaving back and forth between data and theory (Bryman 2004, p.10), and where data is also a source of theory (Glaser and Strauss 1967). The research derives from observations of reality, insights from semi-structured interviews and documentary sources, informed by the theoretical concepts, explored in Chapter 2. There is, then, "an interplay between interpretation and theorizing, on the one hand, and data collection, on the other" (Glaser and Strauss 1967, p.270). For example, the first interviews, carried out in Europe, were useful in uncovering new threads of research: interviewing M. Lemos (2002) raised the possibility of language competition between Portuguese and Arabic in Guinea-Bissau. This topic was followed up in the study trips by interviewing local reli-gious leaders and resources people knowledgeable about or belonging to Islamic organisations.

The starting point of the research originated in a perception of a problem by the researcher - neocolonialist language attitudes and competing external poli-cies in Lusophone Africa - influenced by her international relations background. As Guba (1978, p.44) notes "(p)roblems do not exist in nature but in the *minds of people*". From that initial problem, research progressed lead by the data, gen-erating the need to look into other areas of knowledge besides international rela-tions, namely sociolinguistics. As such, my initial broad idea of a comparative study on external cultural policies concerned with issues of power and influence became synthesised in the concept of external LSP, as defined by Ammon (1997, p.52), opening up the theoretical framework to multidisciplinarity and to a whole new range of implicating issues, such as linguicism and language ecol-ogy.

Within Lusophone Africa, Mozambique and Guinea-Bissau were chosen as case studies because they represent two contrasting settings in terms of geopolit-ical location, political stability and economic development, relative importance in the international community ranking and linguistic situation and policies. Mozambique, on the eastern coast of southern Africa, is surrounded by countries having English as an official language and maintaining strong ties with the UK; the country is considered an example of success among the developing countries; Portuguese is the official language and is widely used as a lingua franca by the multilingual population. Guinea-Bissau, located in the coast of western Africa, is a troubled country set in a Francophone region, where Portuguese despite being the official language competes with Crioulo as lingua franca of a multilingual population. Regarding movements for mother tongue education and the building of local language infrastructure, Mozambique has officially acknowledged the importance of mother tongue (African languages) and has been experimenting with transitional models of bilingual education since 1992. In Guinea-Bissau, Crioulo and ethnic languages have been used for transitional literacy programmes, but the projects are severely hindered by a lack of continuity and at present are very limited.

To include all the five countries of Lusophone Africa as case studies was considered impractical for both time and financial reasons. Nevertheless, evidence of external LSPs in action on all of those countries is referred to as appropriate. Additionally, Angola was not envisaged as an option for the case studies due to the civil war that only officially ended in April 2002 - the year the research trips to Africa took place. The other two countries of Lusophone Africa, Cape Verde and São Tomé and Príncipe, given their less diverse linguistic composition (Portuguese language and Portuguese based Creoles), insular situation, smaller size and perceived less political and economic importance in the international community were not considered a better option in relation to the chosen case studies.

As identified above, the countries chosen for our study share similarities and dissimilarities that can be identified as variables influencing the development of external LSPs. Burnham et al. (2004, p.62) present a triple category of variables:

> "Variables (or factors) can be divided into three categories: dependent variables, independent variables, and other variables, which we can call spurious or intervening variables. Dependent variables are the phenomena that we want to explain in the research. Independent variables are the things we suspect influence the dependent variable. Everything else (that is, everything else that makes up the social, economic and political context and backdrop of the dependent and independent variables) fits into the third category. Such variables might be spurious (that is, falsely appear to have some bearing on the relationship between the dependent and independent variables) or intervening (that is, actually having some bearing on the relationship between the dependent and independent variables)."

According to this typology this study uses the 'most similar research design' to compare cases:

"that are as different as possible in terms of the independent variable(s) and as similar as possible on all the spurious and intervening variables ('backdrop variables')... [and] that by a basic process of elimination all the variables in the 'other' category can be ruled out of the research. If they do not have an effect on the dependent variable, they have the same effect on the dependent variable across all cases. This leaves the independent variable, which has a differential effect on the dependent variable in the two or more cases (which is the reason why the cases were selected in the first place). This means that any observed differences between cases with respect to the dependent variable can be associated with the only variable that makes the cases different: the independent variable." (Burnham et al. 2004, p.63)

Following this rationale, Mozambique and Guinea-Bissau are similar in the way that both are coastal Sub-Saharan African multilingual countries, former colonies of Portugal, occupying lower ranks in the Human Development Index (backdrop variables). However they are different in terms of language relations and policies, political stability, economical development, regional context, donor interest – the independent variables that may explain different situations regarding being the object of external LSPs (the dependent variable). Also the European countries initially identified as developing external language policies in the case studies (Portugal, France, and the UK), shared similarities and dissimilarities. The former colonial European countries, although on a league of their own in terms of human development in relation to the African ones, have amongst themselves substantial differences that range from overall capacity and economic development, foreign policy range and objectives (e.g. historical interests in particular geographical areas), strategy and investment in the areas of development aid and external LSPs, and participation of civil society in areas relevant to external LSP, that may explain the differences in the deployment of external LSPs.

The investigation of variables in this study has remained conscious of the limitations of the comparative method, in particular, the influence of external processes affecting language spread. For instance, the spread of English as the most used contemporary international lingua franca impacts, with different intensities, in both case studies at governmental (language in education policies) and individual level (choice of foreign language to learn). The importance of such process is acknowledged and investigated within the case studies, but the investigation of the basis of external process (why is English spreading as a lingua franca) is beyond the scope of this study.

3.4.1 Research Population

The general research population for this study includes those that define, implement and assess governmental language policies in Mozambique and Guinea-Bissau and in the countries that target them for external LSPs. Those countries were initially identified as being Portugal, UK and France. Other countries identified in the process were the United States, Australia, Brazil and Germany. The last two countries were object of further research given the relevance of their policies in the context of the case studies.

Given that the primary unit of analysis of this study are the different foreign governments developing LSPs in the country case studies, the specific research population could be reduced to a more manageable scope to include politicians and senior government officials, directly and indirectly, involved in the definition, development and implementation of external LSPs both from a source and target point of view.

The study focuses mainly in the governmental level; nevertheless the relevance of other actors in the area of study is acknowledged. That is the case of international organisations and other development partners in the country case studies, the officials and consultants of those organisations and countries that can prove influential in the policy definition process that serves as a context for external LSPs.

At the implementation level, there is an indeterminate number of governmental, non-governmental (consultants, NGO workers), national and foreign officials and practitioners (teachers) that are relevant to the execution of policy decisions. The information they provide and their perceptions are very important as they allow the researcher to determine how the reality of the implementation of language policy matches the formal decision and how that policy is understood at grassroots' level.

In terms of the assessment of the language policies - which ultimately feeds back into the definition stage -, consultants commissioned by governments and international organisations undertake influential evaluations, often available through published reports. The analysis of that process is also interesting for this study. The informal assessment of the development of language policies is also important. To be able to register and analyse the perceptions of the wider society on the topic of external LSPs, through the comments of intellectuals, journalists, researchers and all those involved in the linguistic system is also a valued point of view in this study.

This research was not designed to follow the complete cycle of policy making. The ultimate target of language policy, the population, was not considered directly as part of the research population for this study. However it is a perma-

126

nent background element represented both by the available statistical data on numbers of speakers and by examples of individual language attitudes used to convey insights on existing general language attitudes.

Given that this study was undertaken by a single researcher working with different geographical locations - with limited physical and temporal access to the research population - the research population had to be accessed through sampling. The decisions and the processes surrounding that decision are discussed on the following section.

3.4.1.1 Sampling

Sampling creates limits to the creation of general knowledge. In this study the foreseen frontier of knowledge creation is dual: specific knowledge in terms of the analysis of the case studies and their comparison, and extended knowledge to similar cases in Africa, in particular in the area of Lusophone Africa.

The criteria for good qualitative research and the trustworthiness of this study are important concerns for the researcher. Therefore how strong should a sample be to provide an adequate base for inferences? Burnham *et al.* (2004, p. 145) note:

"Since it is never possible to collect and analyse all pieces of information about any political phenomenon, virtually all general knowledge in political science has emerged through inference-making. We know what we (think we) know about the political world because we have studied a few cases, and from these cases we hopefully extrapolate general knowledge about other, similar cases, and try to determine under what conditions our research conclusions apply to them, too. In this manner inference making serves to enhance the potential magnitude of the contribution a piece of research can make to theory building and refining hypotheses. Most things that political scientists study are simultaneously unique cases and parts of general patterns, which means that case studies, even ones that cover only one or two cases, always need to address the questions: to what extent are these conclusions valid beyond the cases from which they were drawn? And to what extent are the conclusions due to the unique features of these cases?"

So how to assess uncertainty of inferences? Through awareness of the inadequacies and strengths of a sample, which allows "to 'compensate' intelligently in the interpretation", according to Burnham *et al.* (2004, p.161-162). Glaser and Strauss (1967, p.30) point out that the job of the social scientist is not

"to "know the whole field" or to have all the facts "from a careful random sample". His job is not to provide a perfect description of an area, but to develop a theory that accounts for much of the relevant behavior. The sociologist with theoretical generation as his major aim need not know the concrete situation better than the people involved in it (an impossible task anyway). His job and his training are to do what these laymen cannot do – generate general categories and their properties for general and specific situations and problems. These can provide theoretical guides to the to the layman's actions".

This is an expectation I will try to live up to, by discerning patterns and regularities in the data, which can lead to the formulation of some tentative hypotheses that can be explored.

Table 3.1 presents a categorisation of the 83 semi-structured interviews conducted during research. The detailed lists of interviewees are available in Appendix 1.

Table 3.1 Elite Interviewing: categorisation by country[21]

	Portugal	UK	France	Mozambique	Guinea-Bissau
Researchers	-	-	-	4	4
Government officials	12	4	1	5	6
Foreign government Officials – Portugal	-	-	-	5	4
Foreign Government officials –UK	-	-	-	2	-
Foreign Government officials – France	-	-	-	3	1
Foreign Government officials – Brazil	-	-	-	1	3
Language teachers	1	-	-	4	-
NGOs members	2	-	-	8	5
Writers, journalists and editors	1	-	-	3	1
Religious leaders	-	-	-	3	-
Total interviews	16	4	1	38	24

These interviews were mainly conducted in 2002. In June 2010 a further batch of 14 interviews (out of 22 contacts made) (Appendix 2) was undertaken by phone and email to provide an update on the situation of the case studies. The interviews targeted a sample of the previous interviewees: in same case the same person was still in the position (or at least in the same institution), in other cases there was a new occupier of the post that became the resources person.

Given the topic is the development of external language spread policies, in the interviews sample, government officials predominate, from the different for-

---

[21]   Note: Some interviewees holding positions in more than one organisation or in consequence of their experience and knowledge could be placed in a double category. To simplify presentation the interviewee was classified under the category considered predominant in the interview.

eign governments developing LSPs in the country case studies and from the national governments connected with language and educational issues.

Having decided on an iterative grounded strategy, allowing data on the field to be a guide in the research process, the decision on whom to interview was taken using the 'snowball' or 'referral' sampling technique (Burnham *et al.* 2004, p.207). A first batch of interviewees was identified from an initial conceptual list based on literature search and suggestions of some specialists in the field. In the second stage, the interviewees were asked to name other relevant experts in the field of study identifying subsequent batches. Since it was not possible to follow all and pursue each string of referrals, a decisive question was: Will the interview provide enough potentially important information to make it worth spending time and effort on it? As Burnham et al. (2004, p.208) note: "A point is reached where each additional interview yields diminishing returns. One needs to recognize when the 'saturation point' is reached in a series of interviews where each interview is adding relatively little to the stock of information or understanding". This saturation point had also to be considered in terms of the categories of informants being interviewed. The number of interviews is also inevitably justified from a pragmatic point of view, accessibility of the interviewee, and constraints of time, money and logistics. This matter is further discussed on the section Interviews in Practice.

3.5 Data Sources, Collection Methods and Analysis

A combination of data sources was used to provide and verify data to answer the research questions. The sources used in this study include primary, secondary and tertiary data. Primary data, as data the researcher collected from elite-interviewing: the replies provided by interviewees to the questions of the researcher; and, in some cases, the way the interviewee reacted to the questions and the way he/she answered constituted also data, as it help to identify extreme cases of 'political speak'; materials authored by the interviewees, such as articles. Secondary data, as data others had collected: for instance, statistics on numbers of speakers, budgets and, in general, governmental and organisational reports. Tertiary data, as data analysed by others: mainly books and articles by individuals or organisations pertaining the topic.

The research for this study was carried out in London, UK, and Lisbon, Portugal - both residential basis for the researcher - in addition to research trips to Paris, France, (01.12.2001 to 07.12.2001 and 13.05.2002 to 19.05.2002) to Mozambique (04.10.2002 to 19.10.2002), and to Guinea-Bissau (23.11.2002 to 07.12.2002). The reason for the research in Europe was to obtain contextual information into the external LSPs of ex-colonial countries. Research in Africa explored the practice of external LSPs and the perceptions of the actors involved. The research trips took place in 2002 but the data collection span from 2000 to 2010. The time span between the study trips and the final publication of the study does not affect its validity since updated information was collected and the objective of the study is the development of external LSPs during the 1990s and into the new century. The interviews and material collected in the research trips provided a good stock of material regarding what happened in the 1990s, the decade when the perception of competition of external language spread policies was most voiced. The case study trips data provided a reflection on what and why that perception had emerged and evidenced new perceptions regarding the phenomenon. The documentary sources help understand the interviews and vice versa, providing an anchorage or backdrop for the analysis.

Research in Europe comprised literature surveys and interviews. Research in Africa was mainly centred on elite-interviewing, because the researcher wanted to privilege the acquisition of primary source data that allowed her to have an insight into the perceptions of the actors and into the policy processes. Whenever possible, written, published, and non-published material, were obtained from libraries, bookshops, organisations and interviewees (both at the time of the interviews and subsequently by email).

Serendipity inevitably had a place in the discovery of documentary sources and interviewees, especially during study trips. Documentary sources originating in the African countries were at times difficult to obtain. In the case of Guinea-Bissau, many important documents relevant to the political history of the country had been destroyed in the sequence of conflicts. In other cases, that difficulty was related with information management. For example, many of the foreign embassies and/or cultural services approached did not reference, collect or synthesize data pertinent to language spread policy as such - the information was often diluted under other activities. Serendipity helped in the discovery of some information and data in that area. In terms of interviewees, serendipity worked to obviate administrative difficulties arranging appointments of interviews.

3.5.1 Elite Interviewing

Elite interviewing is defined in Burnham et al. (2004, p.205) "both in terms of the *target group* being studied, an 'elite' of some kind, and the *research technique* used, most characteristically what is known as semi-structured interviewing." Elite interviewing is "used whenever it is appropriate to treat a respondent as an expert about the topic at hand" (Leech 2002, p.663).

Being politics one the most sensitive areas for research, getting access to certain individuals, institutions and documents was at times very difficult or almost impossible. This fact hinders the use of certain research techniques, including observation. McCracken notes that "time scarcity and concern for privacy, stand as important impediments to the qualitative study of modern life" (1998, p.11). Therefore the interview becomes invaluable since "It allows us to capture the data needed for penetrating qualitative analysis without participant observation, unobtrusive observation, or prolonged contact. ... to achieve crucial qualitative objectives within a manageable methodological context" (McCracken 1998, p.11).

The purpose of conducting elite interviews for this study was to obtain first hand knowledge about the perceptions and motives of those that make, execute and evaluate external LSPs and access additional data on such policies. The interview data is seen as a narrative through which people describe their worlds (Silverman 2003, p.343). As Burnham *et al.* (2004, p.219) observe: "The reality of modern democracy is that many political decisions are taken by small groups of highly qualified and knowledgeable individuals. ...The shared assumptions and meanings which inform these private worlds still require exploration, and elite interviewing remains the most appropriate technique." In an iterative or recursive process, the interviews ground the theory and the theory guided the interviews, in order to obtain a picture of reality - although this is not necessarily the only valid one. As McCracken (1998, p.9) observes, the interview is "one of the most powerful methods in the qualitative armoury...The method can take us into the mental world of the individual, to glimpse the categories and logic by which he or she sees the world... gives us the opportunity... to see and experience the world as they do themselves".

Other researchers have used similar techniques in their work. Phillipson (1992) and Ager (1996b), for example, used library research and interviews as research techniques in their studies of language policies. Phillipson interviewed eight British ELT (English Language Teaching) experts and Ager acknowledges the use of ten interviews granted by organizations and by an undetermined number of individuals.

3.5.1.1 Interviews in Practice

Establishing contact with potential interviewees required persistence that most times would pay off. Contact was normally made first by sending a letter, either by post, fax or email: introducing the researcher, the supervisor and the home university; giving information on the research; and requesting the interview and/or information, explicitly stating to be used on a PhD thesis. The letter was followed by one or more phone calls, until an interview of an hour was set. Nevertheless, some of the potential interviewees still were impossible to reach and, even with careful preparation, interviews were cancelled. This could be due to their demanding schedules and the fact that being interviewed by a researcher did not come top of their priority list.

Trying to obtain information from organisations was at times a complex business. Contact was initiated either by letter or directly in person going to their headquarters. In some big organisations, such as the Gulbenkian Foundation in Lisbon or the Ministère des Affairs Etrangères in Paris, contact was impossible. The examples can be described, respectively as a wall of silence and a bunker! In other organisations it was difficult to identify suitable respondents, which lead to the researcher being passed around less important officials, which at times represented a significant loss of time, although it provided a good insight on how the organisations worked.

Interviews were semi-structured and conducted in a flexible manner. The task research questions were used as topics to be covered - reminders of the ideas to be touch upon during the interviews or of information needed, providing a framework to ensure cross-case comparability (Bryman 2004, p.234). Bryman (2004, p.321) highlights the flexibility of the lists of questions or interview guides: "the interviewee has a great deal of leeway in how to reply. Questions may not follow on exactly in the way outlined on the schedule. Questions that are not included in the guide may be asked as the interviewer picks up on things said by interviewees". In the case of this study the precise questions and topics would vary according to the person being interviewed, dictated by their area of expertise. Interviewees were always asked if there was anything else she/he would like to add, in the hope of new issues being raised that could be taken into consideration in the development of the research. Upon return to Europe thank you letters were sent to all interviewees.

The interviews took place mostly in the interviewees' offices, some in their houses or in restaurants. The offices provided, generally, the most disturbance free environment, and also predisposed the interviewees to disclose written information more readily and easily. The duration of the interviews ranged from 20 minutes to four hours, the average being an hour. Most of the interviews were recorded on tape and transcribed. Permission to record and use the information was always asked at the beginning of the interview. Notes were taken of all the interviews, to help any memory lapse or allow for technical problems. These were invaluable even in the recorded interviews because most times the interviewee would actually provide interesting information after the interview had ended and the tape recorder was switched off. The transcripts of the interviews and of the notes taken helped the analysis of data as it made them permanently available.

Interviews were analysed manually, relating concepts, themes and events relevant to the study. The coded data was then critically analysed by formulating descriptions and making comparisons across interviews (Rubin and Rubin 2005, Aberbach and Rockman 2002) - see Chapter 4.

With regard to the interviews undertaken as information updates (by phone and email), it was at times difficult to find the person intended to be contacted, as contact details had changed. Additionally, in some cases, the person contacted ended up by not providing information. In the case of Guinea-Bissau the information update was more difficult given the increased mobility of people in official positions and difficulties in the communication networks. Overall the information obtained was less rich than the one provided in face-to-face contacts.

3.5.1.1.1 Mozambique

This study trip took place in October 2002. Intensive previous research, using documentary sources and contextual interviews, allowed the identification of a significant number of interviewees and some interviews were set before arrival in the country. However in other cases the researcher only had names, not even contacts, and it was only after arrival that interviews were arranged. That was never problematic and the researcher was always well received.

Mozambique was a very busy and fruitful research trip, see schedule in Appendix 3. During the two weeks spent there 38 formal interviews were conducted (See categorization in Table 3.1). Of those interviews initially previewed only one - Virgílio Juvane, Director of Planning at MINED - did not take place due to his busy schedule. Interestingly I was able to interview him in July 2010, in London, in his position of Education adviser at the Commonwealth of Nations.

Most interviews took place in Maputo, the capital of Mozambique, where national government services and foreign representatives are based. Interviews in the North of Mozambique, Nampula and Ilha de Moçambique, allowed the researcher to have a broader view of Mozambique, as a country of contrasts: ethnic, religious, linguistic, economic, geographic.

3.5.1.1.2 Guinea-Bissau

The research trip to Guinea-Bissau followed the one to Mozambique, in November/December 2002. The preparation followed the same lines of the previous one. Some interviewees were contacted and interviews set, others were only arranged after being in the country. However, in Guinea-Bissau arranging interviews on location was more difficult given problems discussed further.

The study trip was overall very successful (see schedule in Appendix 4), although the geographical scope, and consequently the interviews, had to be restricted. Planned interviews with religious leaders in Gabú did not take place because the insecurity and irregularity of public transportation advised against it.

The 25 formal interviews (See Table 3.1 for categorization) and several informal contacts, with groups of children, radio broadcasters, teachers and the catholic clergy, made Guinea-Bissau a very interesting and rich field of study. As in the case of Mozambique, some of these interviews were set up through referral. Of the initial planned interviews it was particularly regretted not being able to get an interview with someone in the Foreign Affairs Ministry: unfortunately the initial contact did not honour his appointment and a substitute contact could not be located.

In the case of Guinea-Bissau, difficulty in arranging some interviews was due to a series of factors:

- Political instability: two weeks prior to the research trip the parliament had been dissolved by the then President Kumba Yalá. Changes in political positions were in the process of happening. Elections were scheduled for 2003.
- Teachers' strike: the academic year had not yet started. Faulty payments to teachers caused withholding of last year's grades and a strike on the beginning of the new academic year.
- Timetable of most public services: officially 8am to 2pm, but less in practice. In some places the service would resume after 4pm until 6pm. Apart from climatic reasons (intense heat, always around 30° Celsius), most people have a second job since one is not enough to secure one's living - this is especially true at state level. Although the state secures many jobs, pay is often late, sometimes taking several months.
- Last minute holiday on Friday the 6th of December, the end of the Ramadan. Announced informally the afternoon before.
- Guinea-Bissau is one of the 10 poorest countries in the world, where communications and transportation are difficult. Bissau, the capital, has deficient supply of water and electricity – only a few hours per day, but it may lack for days. A phone is something difficult to have access to and not always lines are operational. Internet: then there were only two places in Bissau where it worked reasonably well.

The instability of the political environment originating a rapid turnover of government officials and the lack of a reliable communications network really made it difficult to locate interviewees and arrange interviews. To overcome that problem, luck and personal affiliations were crucial. A used strategy was to appear unannounced at the organisations and try to locate a good interviewee. This worked most times and with outstanding results. I believe this is possible due to the fact that elites are much smaller and more concentrated than in European countries and also to the fact that maybe the researcher was perceived as a 'not so foreign' researcher. In terms of nationality, being Portuguese had the advantage of having a historical and linguistic connection. In terms of age and gender, being a young looking woman removed the negative connotation of the "old coloniser". In terms of status, being affiliated with a British university brought prestige. These observations on how the researcher might have been perceived also apply to Mozambique.

Most of the interviews took place in the capital, Bissau, where the state bureaucracy is concentrated. Research in Guinea-Bissau was enriched by a weekend visit to Bubaque, in the Bijagós Archipelago, where a project of mother tongue education in Creole operates thanks to the persistence and passion of an individual, the Catholic priest, Father Luigi Scantamburlo. In a country with so many needs, distance highlights the asymmetries of development.

3.5.2 Documentary Sources

The documentary sources researched range from non-published materials provided by interviewees, published materials provided by state organisations and non-governmental organisations, books, theses, journals and newspaper articles (collected from libraries or directly from the press, in paper and electronic form). As Burnham *et al.* (2004, p.188) testify, a "careful use of a wide range of documentary material is one of the most reliable methods open to the political researcher and provides an opportunity for the production of authoritative studies, even if the 'definitive account' remains just out of reach".

Given the sensitiveness of politics as a research area, documentary sources represent a main tool of investigation into the policy-making process. Policy documents, published political interviews, and declarations can be successfully contrasted with the realities of the implementation of the language policies, accessed by interviews to government officials and other practitioners and mediators of language policies, providing an interesting insight into the process. In terms of investigating reactions and perceptions regarding language policies, both documentary sources and interviews are useful techniques that provide: the former, a more thought through statement and, the latter, a more immediate, visceral response. However one cannot underestimate the skill of some types of interviewees, particularly in the area of politics: being careful about what they say and how they say it, and in controlling the events and their meaning (Ball 1994, p.96).

The statistical information available for number of speakers of each language provides the possible scientific positivist background for the policy-making process. Definition problems, accurateness and time delays are some of the limitations that need to be taken into account when using language statistics.

3.5.3 Data Analysis

This study analyses discourses on language policy and relations by interpreting the data retrieved using qualitative content analysis as defined by Burnham *et al.* (2004, p.236):

> "Content analysis is a technique for analysing the content of communications. Whenever somebody reads, or listens to, the content of a body of communication and then summarizes and interprets what is there, then content analysis can be said to have taken place. ... [In] qualitative methods of analysis, ... the importance of the content is determined by the researcher's judgement. The researcher decides on the intrinsic value, interest and originality of the material. S/he decides on a topic or hypothesis to investigate, determines which documents or other communications are appropriate sources of evidence, and then selects a sample of texts to investigate and analyse. This process results in a subjective assessment of the content and value of the material. It relies heavily on the judgement and expertise of the researcher".

The data analysis in this study extracts, from the different sources of data, descriptions of the situations, examines their different readings by the actors and interprets the processes observed, in relation to the research questions, relying on the theories informing the study and on the evidence gathered.

The data was validated by triangulation, as explained before. In the case of the interviews, the interview guide was flexible enough to accommodate the confirmation of assertions by extra questions, and in some cases, where the need was felt to seek more information or to establish a better rapport with the interviewee, the person was meet more than once.

3.6 Ethical Issues and Practical Constraints

I share Mann's point when he "argues that research is a seamless web without a clear order and without a defined beginning or end" (1981 cited in Burnham *et al.*, 2004, p.45). The researcher creates the story. Although aware that the researcher effect should be minimised, that consequential presence cannot be foreclosed. During the process of research, the researcher has to make choices. Flick (2002, p.62 cited in Merken, 2005, p.165) places selection at three levels: data collection (case selection, case-group selection), interpretation (selection of and within material), and presentation of results (presentation of material). He argues further that criteria to guide those decisions are essential to the rational criticism of the outcome. It is hoped that the present document makes clear the decisions taken by the researcher in this PhD process.

External factors also pose limits to the choices of a researcher. Time, money, confidentiality of data, and personal constraints were the major limitations faced in this particular study. These are general limitations and to some degree felt by all researchers.

However the research-in-practice for this particular study highlighted interesting limitations according to physical location. For instance, interviews in Europe were more difficult to arrange and conduct than in Africa, in particular those with government officials or related with larger organisations. A series of factors is advanced as a possible explanation: elites are possibly larger and more disperse in Europe, making it more difficult to identify the 'right' person; they could also be more aware and concerned with the consequences of disclosing potentially sensitive information, therefore spending time talking to a researcher was low on their priorities - also the greater availability of documentary sources made it easier to redirect the researcher to 'safer' forms of releasing information; the hierarchical structure of the organisations in Europe had more historical time to organize the channels of communication with the outside world making the contacts between their members and the outside world more structured and less flexible; cultural factors, African elites were friendlier and more open than European ones.

Documentary sources were more difficult to obtain in Africa, either because they did not exist or because interviewees saw it as sensitive and were not willing to part with it. In the case of Guinea-Bissau, the country was (and still is) in an unstable political situation. The 1998 civil war destroyed part of the Instituto Nacional de Estudos e Pesquisa and the French Cultural Centre, and these and other institutions lost irreplaceable archives that documented the history of Guinea-Bissau. This instability has also had a negative impact on acquiring additional information from outside the country.

Other limitations, with ethical implications, are the ones arising from the interactions between the researcher and the people she used as source of data. As Ball (1994, p.97) argues an interview is a confrontation and a joint construction. Who the researcher is or is perceived to be (visual and non-visual cues or status differences) can have a major impact in what information is disclosed. I felt that I had been able to establish an emphatic relationship with the interviewees that led most to talk happily and help. Because of that empathy, extra information or a referral to see some else was obtained. In some cases, I saw the interviewees more than once, which facilitated the disclosure of additional information.

Another ethical issue relating to the interviews is the frankness of the inter-viewees. It is assumed that most interviewees were frank. However, as advised by Ball (1994, p.96/7), the researcher paid attention to the form of the inter-views, and to the significance of the interviewees' attitude: careful choice of words, limits to the disclosure of information, control of the meaning of the words.

Anonymity of interviewees was not envisaged for this study. However, there were occasions in which 'off the record' was requested for a comment or docu-ments were released under that condition – in the cases of comments, when rele-vant, they were used without disclosing the identity of the speaker, and the doc-uments were only used for information of the researcher. In the case of contro-versial statements during the interviews, the request to quote and attribute them in the PhD thesis was restated and confirmed verbally.

Regarding translation: *"Traduttore, traditore!"* It is sometimes said that the translator is a traitor. This study involved sources in five languages, English, French, Galician, Portuguese and Spanish. I hope the translations, done in good faith and with the best of my knowledge - I am a certified Portu-guese/French/English translator - have not done a disservice to the originals, which are always given in the footnotes.

This chapter describes the constructivist character of the study. The re-searcher's perspective on external LSPs in Lusophone Africa is built in an ongo-ing process of interaction between her perceptions and the data she uncovers in the research inquiry. This stand does not impede the pursuit of validity follow-ing criteria for qualitative analysis. The following chapter, where the data for both case studies is analysed, uses the variables identified here to concretize the findings, in addition to drawing on the theoretical framework to highlight the different perceptions on the topic.

Chapter 4 Country Case Studies: Mozambique and Guinea-Bissau

This chapter presents the two country case studies that form the basis of my research. Each case study includes an introduction to the countries, an examination of the role of language in the polities, including the linguistic legacies of colonialism and their impact on the present language policies of the country, a discussion of the external language spread policies deployed in the country, and finally an analysis of perceptions and discourses about policies and language(s) relevant to this study. The aim is to provide a contextualised analysis of external language spread policies that takes into account the complex environment in which they are deployed. For the purpose of this study the latter includes the construction and maintenance of national identity, the hegemonic construction nationally and internationally of political and cultural power as well as the need to account for the linguistic human rights of individuals and thus the maintenance and fostering of linguistic and cultural diversity.

4.1 Mozambique: A Country Case Study

4.1.1 Country Profile

Mozambique stretches 2,500km along the Indian Ocean in the east coast of southern Africa, opposite Madagascar.

For five centuries a Portuguese colony, the country was mainly use as a transit country involved in the development of its landlocked neighbours. Mozambique acquired independence in 1975, following a guerrilla war (1962-1974). Independence led to the departure of most settlers to Portugal (98% according to AJ Lopes 2002 interview) this caused serious problems in the organisation of Mozambique as an independent country, since administration and economic management had been mostly in the hands of those who left. The chaos of the prolonged civil war that ensued (1976-1992) destroyed most of the country's economic and social structures. The Mozambique National Resistance (Resistência Nacional de Moçambique, RENAMO) fuelled by the neighbouring white Rhodesian regime (now Zimbabwe) and later by the apartheid regime in South Africa, fought Mozambique's Liberation Front (Frente de Libertação de Moçambique, FRELIMO), the party ruling the post-independence communist regime in Mozambique, until the signature of Peace agreements in 1992. Natural disasters, such as drought, cyclones and floods have also seriously affected Mozambique's development. In 1989, the ruling FRELIMO party abandoned Marxism and made way for democratic elections and a free market economy. However Mozambique is still dominated by a party-state (Sumich and Honwana 2007). FRELIMO has won all national and local elections held in Mozambique - only in 2008 an independent candidate won an election and became the mayor of Beira (Mozambique's second largest city).

The 1990s were for Mozambique a decade of hope and renewal. The implementation of World Bank structural adjustment macro-economic stabilisation programs to achieve economic growth and reduce poverty levels led the country to become an example of success in the area of international development aid in Africa, registering average economic growth rates of 8% between 1994 and 2007 (2010 World Bank www.worldbank.org, Mozambique Country Brief). Nevertheless, it is still one of the poorest countries in the world, ranking 172nd out of 182 countries in the Human Development Index (UNDP 2009). The Human Poverty Index indicates that 46.8% of people are below certain threshold levels in each of the dimensions of the human development index that is living a long and healthy life, having access to education, and a decent standard of living; it ranks Mozambique at 127th among 135 countries for which the index has been calculated (UNDP 2009). The country has received a steady volume of aid throughout the years and is very dependent on foreign aid and investment - around half of the state budget was dependent on international donors in 2009. The main donors, between 1997 and 2007 were: The World Bank (International Development Association), The European Commission, UK, USA and France (Bartholomew et al. 2009).

Mozambique is closely connected to its immediate neighbours through formal associations. The most prominent is the Southern African Development Community (SADC), of which Mozambique is a founding member (1980). Most of the SADC countries are also members of the Commonwealth of Nations, although Zimbabwe withdrew from the organization in 2003. The other exceptions are Angola that with Mozambique is one of the eight members of the Communidade dos Países de Língua Portuguesa (CPLP), and Congo and Madagascar, members of the Organisation Internationale de la Francophonie (OIF), of which Mozambique is an observer.

4.1.1.1 Language Situation

Mozambique ranks among the 15 most linguistically diverse countries in Africa (Lopes AJ 1999, p.92). The Ethnologue (Lewis 2009) lists for the country 43 languages, all living languages - although there are discrepancies regarding the names and the exact numbers depending on source of information and dialect/language classification (Matsinhe 2005, Liphola 2009). Given that Mozambique has Portuguese as its official language, the country is sometimes described as a Portuguese-speaking island in an Anglophone sea. All of Mozambique's land neighbours have English as their official language (in some cases the status is shared with African languages). The Portuguese-speaking population in Mozambique still represents a minority within the context of the overall population. According to the Mozambican population census of 1997, Portuguese language is spoken by 39.6% of the population, is the mother tongue of 6.5% (up from 1.2% according to the Mozambican population census of 1980), and concentrated in the urban areas (Instituto Nacional de Estatística 1999). The available results of the 2007 census indicate an increase in the spread of Portuguese language in Mozambique.

4.1.2 Languages and the State in Mozambique

The status of Portuguese as the official language in Mozambique is recognized in both the 1990 and the 2004 National Constitutions. Portuguese is used throughout the state and education system, and the media. Constitutionally, African languages are recognized as national languages forming part of the country's cultural and educational heritage. Despite the official recognition of the status of African languages their official use is limited. Although used extensively in the radio and in some TV programs, the use of African languages in the education system is restricted. Apart from literacy and non-formal education, 16 African languages are mediums of education in the first three years of primary education in schools participating in a transitional bilingual project (examined in section 4.1.2.2). Additionally, they are also used as auxiliary languages in the teaching of Portuguese and in health awareness campaigns.

This section will analyse the positioning of the different languages in Mozambique, starting by examining the importance of Portuguese language, and how this is linked with the colonial legacy. It can be argued, from a point of view of linguistic imperialism, that the adoption of the colonial language by the former colony is a continuation of an external language spread policy - that of the colonial power (autonomous polity) to its colonies (non autonomous territories). The colonial legacy is considered to be the main determining factor in the development of national language policies but other factors, namely the association of certain languages with access to aid for development, and the interest of their spreading agents in acting in Mozambique, are crucial to understanding Mozambique's situation.

Portuguese was brought to the now Mozambican coastline during the 16th Century. However it remained confined to particular points where soldiers, missionaries, merchants, estate-holders and government officials were located (Ribeiro 1993, p.2, Newitt 1995). The Portuguese colonial enterprise was for a long time focused on Brazil and Portuguese occupation of the Mozambican territory would only really start after the Berlin Conference had established the principle of 'effective' occupation. The systematic occupation of Mozambique in 1918, with the end of the military campaigns of 'pacification', marked a new period in the colonisation of the territory.

In the 1930 Colonial Act, Portugal formally regulated its relationship with the colonies and it was the year in which indigenous education was established. Colonial education was organised in two distinct strands: *oficial* for Portuguese settlers (*colonos*) and *assimilados* (with potential to progress to higher education), and *indígena* (mostly vocational and supplied through Catholic missions from 1941). Portuguese was the teaching language and African languages were allowed only in religious teaching (Mazula 1995). In 1964 the education system was restructured in an attempt to improve the results and to become more inclusive of the African indigenous population. The educational situation in Portuguese Africa in the 1950s was reported as one of the worst in Africa (Mazula 1995). At the time Portugal's dictatorial regime was increasingly isolated and needed efficient exploration of the colonies, it therefore needed the development of a local elite that would be able to supervise the economic development of the territories. At the time pressures for change were present internally in the colonial system (wars in Angola, Mozambique and Guinea Bissau) and externally (international movement for decolonisation and self determination). The apparent restructuration of the educational system included the incorporation of the *indígena* strand of education by the state and its removal from the Catholic Church, now under the title of *ensino oficializado*. There was also an apparent acknowledgment of the value of African languages. Mazula (1995) cites two laws from the early 1960s that allow their use: one in primary education as a means to teach the Portuguese language and the second in the context of colonial administration courses. However, education in Mozambique under colonial rule was limited, and at the time of independence illiteracy was between 93 and 97%, and only 44 black people attended university (Navarro, responsible for the editorial services and cofounder of the Mozambican Writers Association, 2002 interview). Portuguese colonial policy regarded Africans as inferior; some of those racist attitudes are still present amongst some white people in Mozambique as I had occasion to witness during field research. Portuguese colonialism was, not just racist, but also fascist - with no interest in culture - and that affected both the colonised and the (white) settlers (Navarro 2002 interview). The

Portuguese colonial administration was limited to aspects serving colonial objectives and not to the needs of the populations (Monteiro 2006, p.3). However the basis for the future hegemony of Portuguese in the Mozambican linguistic space had been established: Portuguese had become the language of the emerging Mozambican elite. Postcolonial Mozambique in its decision to make the former colonial language the official language is in line with similar decisions of most African countries, which must be read in the context of the legacies of colonialism (impact of political, cultural and linguistic hegemonies) including the centrality of a common language as a central principle of the nation state, an idea that prevailed in Europe during the eighteenth and nineteenth centuries. Portuguese was chosen to symbolise the national unity of the new country and to function as the lingua franca.

Commitment to the Portuguese language dates from the struggle for independence against colonial Portugal. Portuguese, as the operational language of FRELIMO, was seen as the common language, a link that would enable to maintain unity among the different ethnical and linguistic groups (Mondlane 1995, p.107 and 138), as well as a useful tool to know the enemy and a more efficient method in the military domain (Ribeiro 1993 and Miguel 1994, p.50). The then FRELIMO leader Eduardo Mondlane justified it thus: "Portuguese was maintained as the official language mainly for reasons of convenience, since no African language had such an ample spread"[22] (Mondlane 1995, p.107). FRELIMO was based on the alliance of southern *assimilados* and rural aspiring elites, that in the early years (1962-1969), was riddled with factionalism and purges, as the party leadership became increasingly preoccupied with the idea of unity (Sumich and Honwana 2007, p.6/7). Rejection of Portuguese, as an official language, was defended at the II FRELIMO Congress, in 1968, by the perceived reactionary line of Simango–Nkhavandame. The reasons have been reported by Couto (1981, p.4) as echoing individual political ambitions: individuals who did not become proficient in the Portuguese language saw it as an impediment to progression into higher political positions. This cleavage in the liberation movement, later the ruling party, will be echoed later in Mozambican society, in a divide between those who speak and those who do not speak Portuguese, a divide that has been overshadowed by an apparent national consensus around Portuguese. Still at present there are members of the Mozambican parliament that do not participate in debates or present their ideas due to lack of mastery of Portuguese language (non-attributable source).

---

22 "O português foi mantido como língua oficial sobretudo por razões de conveniência, porque nenhuma língua africana tinha uma divulgação tão ampla"

In the aftermath of independence, with the guerrilla war and the exodus of the Portuguese settlers, Mozambique was adrift. FRELIMO was the dominant social force and when they assumed power in 1975, "they became both the state and the nation" (Sumich and Honwana 2007, p.2). In 1977, FRELIMO chose the ideology of Marxism-Leninism to steer the construction of national unity, which led to central control and a suppression of local traditions. Tribalization was feared as well as any divisions based on cultural factors, such as religion, ethnicity or regional identity (Meneses 2007 p.21), as the emerging elite attempted to create a *Homem Novo* (New Man) on the basis of the dismantling of the colonial state. This *Homem Novo* "would be both a universal subject and the embodiment of the emerging Mozambican personality and model of citizenship" (Sumich and Honwana 2007, p.9). As Meneses (2007 p.19) states "(f)or the sake of national unity, so it was widely agreed, sacrifices had to be made. At its most extreme, the tendency was fundamentally against legal pluralism. The nation-state would be a centralized state, and it would extend basic rights to citizens equally." The nation building process in Mozambique thus follows the tradition of Western European nationalism, in which nationhood is achieved by hegemony of a part claiming to represent the whole nation and national essence (Billig 1995).

It is possible to argue here that there appears to have been continuity between the Portuguese colonialist discourse and FRELIMO's Marxist Leninist discourse of civilizing nationalism (Meneses 2007, p.21). As Fry (2000, p.129 cited in Sumich and Honwana 2007, p.8) notes, the Marxist-Leninist period in Mozambique (1977-1983) follows an *assimilado* logic, that is:

> Structurally speaking there was little difference between an authoritarian capitalist state run by a small body of "illuminated" Portuguese and assimilados and an authoritarian socialist state run by an equally diminutive and equally enlightened vanguard party.

A similar continuity can be argued to have taken place in terms of language and language policies: Portuguese, the language of the ruling elite - mainly constituted by urban *assimilados* - becomes official language, and African languages, seen as a potentially divisive factor, remain ignored. However, the role of the Portuguese language is now perceived to have changed from civilizing mission of the African in the image of the Portuguese master, to be the common language of Mozambican citizens, the language as a vehicle to building national unity and identity. Here, as elsewhere in Africa, it perpetuated the logic of the hegemonic role of common languages in nationhood (Billig 1995) and that of modernization, that is the 'need' of a common language to integrate discrete groups into one nation (as discussed in 2.2.2.1).

A common remark found during my field research pointed to the perception of an ideological liberation of Portuguese language with independence: Portuguese is a war trophy (expression attributed to Angolan writer Luandino Vieira). Matusse (1997, p.541) explains that the independence of the country "liberated the language from its racial and class trappings". In the interview, Matusse, then Secretary General and Co-ordinator for Culture, Information and Sport of SADC in Maputo (2002 interview) added: "our independence has freed the Portuguese language – Portuguese was only spoken by one class, the *assimilados*, the colonial leaders and the Portuguese elites in Mozambique. After independence Portuguese is used by the masses."[23] These comments highlight a perception of a shift in the ownership of the language. However, despite that change, the use of the language followed the 19th century European conventions of forming a nation-state, as previously mentioned. Additionally, the idea of the 'liberation' of Portuguese expressed by Matusse pointing to a neutral view of language (section 2.2.3.1.1), fails to acknowledge the inherent ideological charge of a language, and the complexity of the processes of appropriation (section 2.2.2.1).

The consensus around the role of Portuguese language as official language and language of national unity in Mozambique has been reaffirmed throughout the years in different policy documents regarding language, culture and development, as I describe next.

In that sense it is important to note that the constitution of the elite group in Mozambique has remained stable. FRELIMO has been able to dominate the political scene in Mozambique, throughout the political shifts from Marxism Leninism and socialism to liberal democracy, and one party system to a multiparty system. They can be seen as representing a continuity in their perceived role as "engine of modernization" (Sumich and Honwana 2007, p.18). It can be argued also that the external dependencies in Mozambique have reinforced the gap between the elite and the population. Sumich and Honwana (2007, p.21) defend the view that the ruling elite has "relatively little interest or need" on the rest of society, since they gain legitimacy for the transformation of the country from foreign funding. Thus, Sumich and Honwana (2007, p.21) describe Mozambique as having "a state with a tightly interlinked elite who have densely intertwined material interests, but large sections of the population remain weakly incorporated in this framework". This has obvious consequences

---

23   Matusse (2002 interview) said in Portuguese: "a nossa independência libertou o português – o português era uma língua falada apenas por uma classe, portanto, a classe dos assimilados, e os próprios dirigentes coloniais e as élites portuguesas que estavam aqui em Moçambique. Depois da independência é que se verifica o uso do português pelas massas em geral."

for language, thus I argue that the external dependencies will enhance external influences on language policy and diminish the importance of the internal definition of language policies.

However, as the Mozambican state furthers the process of democratisation and political participation (Meneses and Santos 2008), the decentralising of the role of the state will give more opportunity for other political forces and other voices in civil society to be heard and to make their opinions count. This, in my view, will have a major impact in how linguistic policies are to be conceived in the future - that is, in a way that further favours local languages. It should be noted that some changes have already taken place regarding the recognition of African languages, which can be connected to the adoption of liberal democratic ideology and to external pressures, as will be seen ahead - however the external influences sustain the hegemony of Portuguese in Mozambique. Regarding voice and the expression of alternative opinions in Mozambique, it is worth noticing that the country is being assisted by the World Bank, however the result of their action is not predictable. For instance, it is interesting observing that one of the objectives of the 2008-2011 World Bank's Country Partnerships Strategy for Mozambique is to "Strengthen civil society, academia, think tanks and media and their capacity to enhance voice and monitor governance", in alignment with the country's development strategy to increase capability and public voice (PARPA II), nevertheless the issue of which language is not raised (World Bank 2007, p.27). Unfortunately, language is a basic human right that is often over-looked.

Returning to the main point of this section, languages and the state in Mozambique, I would like to examine the latest official document currently stating that vision, *Agenda 2025*. The document drafted by an extensive list of governmental and civil society participants, published in 2003, establishes a national consensus and vision on the development of Mozambique for 2025 - the year when the country celebrates 50 years. The main strategic axis of the document is the reinforcement of the Mozambican Nation and the increasing in pace of the process of national integration, while respecting ethnic, cultural and linguistic diversity (República de Moçambique/Comité de Conselheiros 2003, p.102).

In linguistic terms, *Agenda 2025* reaffirms Portuguese language as the official language, while coexisting with the (African) national languages. The document reinforces the vision of Mozambique as a multicultural country, recognising the ethnic, cultural, linguistic and religious diversity of the country as an asset to reinforce the social capital of the country, perceived as the basis for national cohesion and conscience. *Agenda 2025* nevertheless recognises the existence of fault lines in Mozambican society, being one of them the asymmetry between those who speak Portuguese and those who do not, that is stated to be

146

felt as "result of a deliberate policy of exclusion, which leads to the reanimation of ghosts of divisions and discriminations"[24] (República de Moçambique/Comité de Conselheiros 2003, p.42) - this can be interpreted as an indication that the fear of tribalism is still present in Mozambique. The authors of Agenda 2025 thus highlight the need to establish a social and cultural pact in Mozambique for the preservation and consolidation of *moçambicanidade* (Mozambiqueness). The social pact is defined as equity, solidarity and economic security and the cultural pact - which interests me the most - regards the issue of unity in diversity and reaching an equilibrium between the belonging to the nation and the belonging to a specific cultural identity (República de Moçambique/Comité de Conselheiros 2003, p. 144). The solution implies the "integrative capacity of the nation" establishing a relationship between the political project and the ethnic and social characteristics of the populations (*ibid.*). Part of the solution is the creation of a language policy regarding the national languages, the absence of which is highlighted by the experts drafting *Agenda 2025*. This concern reveals awareness, at least from part of the Mozambican elite, of the need to search for a model of nationhood that does not rely on a single language. However, it is also a concern that has been met with very limited action, although a national policy is reported as being in the process of drafting (Sendela 2010 email). *Agenda 2025* also mentions other languages besides Portuguese and the African languages. The reinforcement of international languages, such as English and French, is advanced as being indispensable to the participation in the global market.

Agenda 2025 sets the broad national context for the exploration of the linguistic situation and the various policies affecting language in Mozambique. In line with this study's focus on external language spread policies I will now examine the policies and contexts affecting each of the languages that I found relevant for this study. This includes Portuguese, the language spread in colonialism and adopted as the official language and the language in which education is delivered, despite it being a minority language; the African languages, the national languages, as the languages of the majority of the population, recognized as an important part of nationality, and important in the delivery of education, but that are constrained in education (three years transitional bilingual education project); and French and English as the foreign languages taught in the national education system, that are object of contemporary external language spread policies.

---

24   "resultado de uma política deliberada de exclusão, o que leva a reanimar fantasmas de divisões e discriminações"

4.1.2.1 Portuguese Language and Education in Mozambique

As stated earlier, Portuguese was regarded as "the neutral or conventional choice between and among Mozambicans", as "(l)ocal languages were perceived to signal local identities alone, not a national commitment and loyalty" (Matusse 1997, p.545/6). Being adopted as language of national unity, Portuguese was spread by the Mozambican government in a very successful literacy campaign (1975-1983), supported by Sweden and Norway (Navarro 2002 interview). The norm adopted was that of European Portuguese - deviation from the European variety has occurred since the end of the 1970s (Gonçalves 2000, p.2) and has led to a new variety, Mozambican Portuguese, which is still in the process of standardisation.

The literacy campaign in the aftermath of independence led the country in 1981 to being close to reaching universal primary school attendance, with most children aged 7-10 years at school (UNDP 2006, p.40). The 1983 National Education System Law (*Lei do Sistema Nacional de Educação*) emphasised access to education for all. The document also included concerns with the diffusion of Portuguese language in relation to the consolidation of national identity (article 4, no. 2, paragraph g), and with the study and promotion of the Mozambican languages as part of the national heritage (article 5). The literacy campaign, started in 1975, had to stop in 1984 given the escalation in the civil war. Education was one of the areas most affected by the war: 58% of the existing schools, mainly located in the rural areas, were destroyed (Christie 1996, p.90). This has been recovering since only in the late 1990s.

With the end of the civil war and the country's conversion to democracy and capitalism at the beginning of the 1990s, a new law, *Lei n.º 6/92 de Maio*, was issued in 1992, readjusting the national education system to the new ideas. The document, stripped of its former socialist bias, included in its aims the introduction of national languages in the education system (article 4). This coincides with the launch of the experimental phase of the bilingual project in primary education that has been implemented since. This is discussed in section 4.1.2.2.

In 1995, a National Education Policy (*Política Nacional de Educação*, PNE) was drafted with regard to the five-year governmental programme (1995-1999). The policy maintained, as an objective, achieving universal primary education (spreading the network of schools, improving the quality of education) and the solid command of Portuguese language (República de Moçambique 1995, p.180). To put this policy into in practice, an Education Sector Strategic Plan for 1999-2003 was approved in 1998. The plan (República de Moçambique, Ministério da Educação 1998) embodied ideas that translated in the bilingual education project in the first years of primary education with transition to Portuguese language, mentioned the use of mother tongue in the classroom as an auxiliary in the improvement of the quality of education. This validated a practice already taking place in the education system and in particular undertaken by NGOs working in education (for instance Progresso) -, and advocated the development of curriculum and materials for literacy in adult and non-formal education in national languages. This plan was set within a new approach to development relations, a sector-wide approach (SWAp), that pools and channels external funds from different donors to education, via the Mozambican's government budget, which is responsible and accountable for its management.

Beside the internal documents that define national policies and planning, policy-making process in the case studies must be examined in the light of the dependency of these countries towards the (mostly) external frameworks that determine their developmental paths. The Mozambican government defines its priorities according to a range of agreements, including the Millennium Development Goals (MDGs), New Partnership for the Development of Africa (NEPAD) and the Southern African Development Community (SADC) (Republic of Mozambique 2006, p.7). The goals are broken down into a series of targets and measured against indicators developed by specialists from the international multilateral agencies (UN Secretariat, the International Monetary Fund (IMF), the Organisation of Economic Cooperation and Development (OECD) and the World Bank) (UNDP 2006, p.iii). The international donor community pools the resources that will enable Mozambique to implement the policies to achieve those targets. Mozambique's General State Budget is heavily dependent on donor support. Massingue (1995, p.14) states that "In the education sector, external support covers about 70 percent of costs, and the extent of political influence mirrors the level of this contribution". Regarding donor influence, Massingue's (1995, p.14) research notes that "most people [at the Ministry of Education] do not feel that donors have a negative influence", however "they see a tendency among donors to want to support the areas of greatest interest to themselves".

Thus Mozambique national education policies follow the main lines of international thinking about education - in particular UNESCO's - set in the broader context of Mozambican government's priority in the reduction of absolute poverty and the relaunch of economic and social development. At present, in terms of education, Mozambique's purpose is to attain the MDGs, in particular the goal of achieving universal primary education for all (Education for All, EFA) by 2015. One of the main problems identified in Mozambique is the high rates of children repeating grades and dropping out of school. This has been partially attributed to the fact that Portuguese language, the medium of teaching, is not the mother tongue of most of the children (UNESCO 2004) - but this factor is not given the importance it deserves and is generally overlooked or subtly stated/subsumed under the general heading of improvement of quality of education. The UNDP data indicates promising progress in improving access to basic education (in Portuguese). In Mozambique, the net school attendance rate in the lower cycle of primary education EP1, recorded in 2004, was 75.6%, from about 43.6% in 1999. Nevertheless, repetition rates remain high, reaching 21% in 2004 (UNDP 2006, p.5). However, the goal of universal primary education for all reinforces the spread of Portuguese in Mozambique, given that it is status of official language and teaching language in the education system. Thus, it can be argued, that the whole of the donor community supports and reinforces the dominant position of Portuguese language in Mozambique.

The 2006-2010/11 strategic educational development plan maintained the educational concerns indicated in the previous plan with emphasis given to tackling the issue of the quality of education in primary education. In this report, the question of teaching language is mentioned as affecting the quality of education, as is the need to reinforce bilingual education with educational resources, "when applicable" (República de Moçambique, Ministério da Educação e Cultura 2006, p.22, 25 and 27). This may signal potential restrictions in the implementation of the bilingual education project (section 4.1.2.2). The 2006-2010/11 plan has a broader remit than the previous one, as it includes culture and transversal issues - the Ministries of Education and Culture merged in 2005 (a strategic option aiming at reinforcing education and culture as complementary areas) (República de Moçambique, Ministério da Educação e Cultural 2006, p.110). In terms of the cultural policy, the cultural strategic plan states the need for more research into all aspects of Mozambican culture, including languages. Previous cultural policies similarly emphasised the duality of asserting the role of Portuguese language and defending at the same time the important role of national/African languages. The Mozambican Cultural Policy, Ministerial Resolution of 1997, (*Resolução* 12/97, *Política Cultural de Moçambique*) restated the development and expansion of the Portuguese language, as the official language of Mozambique, through the education system, and at the same time safeguarded the national languages, as the main repository of national traditions and the main means of communication for most Mozambicans. The second National Conference on Culture (República de Moçambique, Ministério da Educação e Cultura 2009), that took place in May 2009, continues to highlight diversity by stressing the multiplicity of the actors involved and the importance of the participation of civil society in culture. Additionally there is recognition of the importance of the role of culture in development, economy and in society and a need for the professionalisation of the cultural actors.

Is it clear in the analysis of Mozambican policy documents that Portuguese has been systematically sustained as official language, which can be seen to reflect the stable composition of the elite in Mozambique, as was discussed previously. That commitment has been translated into the almost exclusive use of Portuguese as teaching language in the education system. The Portuguese language has thus spread with the widening of the school network and the increase in enrolments, in the connection of this language with social, professional and economic mobility (Lopes AJ 1999, p.120) and urbanisation and mixed marriages. The documents also provide evidence of an increasing concern with the status of African languages. In the following section I examine how this has translated into practice.

4.1.2.2 African Languages and the Transitional Bilingual Education Project

Mozambique is a multicultural, multilingual country. The 20 recognised national languages and many more dialects (according to the Centro de Estudo de Línguas Moçambicanas, NELIMO, at UEM – the Ethnologue, as mentioned in 4.1.1.1, lists more than double the number) are scattered throughout the country according to ethnic boundaries. The urban agglomerates where Portuguese thrives are, however, points of convergence for all ethnicities. The relationship between the African languages and Portuguese has been described as dichotomised between modernity and tradition: "Portuguese is the language of public life, covering the administration, the education system and the mass media, while the bantu languages are generally restricted to the domains of family life, traditional social life, religious rituals etc" (Juvane and Buendia 2000, p.52); or associated with the divides urban/elite for Portuguese and rural/masses for the African Bantu languages (Liphola, 1988, p.14).

Language policy regarding African languages is described as status planning without corpus planning by Matusse (2002 interview), since the Mozambican government gave those languages a formal role (status of national languages) but has been slow to provide, for instance, measures to develop their corpus. Efforts to study and standardise the local languages have been made since 1978, through the Núcleo (now Centro) de Estudo de Línguas Moçambicanas (NELIMO). However the scope of the work has been too big for the resources of that organisation. Recent scholarship in the area is in favour of devising and implementing common linguistic policies regarding the 17 African languages shared with neighbouring countries, thus overcoming a 'nationalizing view' of the common linguistic heritage (Liphola 2009) and providing efficiency of resources. Critics often target the discrepancies between the declared policy and the daily linguistic practices. Ngunga (2001, p.98) reports that politicians, he describes as "brainwashed *assimilados*, are unable to realise the importance of the use of (African) mother tongues in education" - they see African languages as "tools to be employed only when they need them", that is, used in the political rallies to win election votes. Matusse (1998, p.3) also mentions that Mozambican citizens successful in ascending the social ladder only exceptionally use their African languages: to demonstrate cultural and ethnical identity when asking for a favour or, mostly, to advertise themselves as eligible for public positions. This reflects the legacies of colonial discourses that did not ascribe African languages their value, reflecting the power positions in society.

Only in the 1990s, after the country acquired some stability and adopted liberal democracy, have Mozambican authorities started pilot experiments to introduce African languages in the national education system. Jona (2008) and Benson (2004, p.4) advance educational development objectives as a main justification for the bilingual experimentation programs in Mozambique: "experimentation in Mozambique began following a conference on how to reduce the high repetition, failure and dropout rates plaguing basic education". Benson (2004, p.4) also highlights the fact that "Such initiatives have received more attention and support in recent years from donor agencies interested in improving educational quality and equity while promoting democracy (see e.g. Sida [Swedish Cooperation] 2001)". Noticeable here is the linkage between the international educational agenda, donors' interests and the bilingual program developed in Mozambique. Moreover the work of religious missionaries remains fairly important regarding African languages in Mozambique. As reported by Nsiku (2008, p.15), INDE experts, Bible Translators of Mozambique, experts in NELIMO and experts at the Summer Institute of Linguistics in Mozambique have been working together. He claims this is not done out of religious motives arguing that those working with language "become co-creators of bilingual education and 'co-verifiers' of the impact of the implementation of this process" of revitalisation of African languages. The value of the missionaries' work is undeniable; however the extent of their influence in the communities is something to be determined.

From 1992 to 1997, INDE undertook the experimentation of bilingual education in Nyanja/Portuguese and Tsonga/Portuguese, respectively in two and three schools in the provinces of Gaza and Tete, with UNDP and World Bank financing (Guirrugo 2009). The results were encouraging and the Ministry of Education decided to extend the experiment. Of the 20 languages that in Mozambique have been developed to a certain standard, 16 were selected to be used in the project, starting with the most linguistically homogenous areas (Sendela, from the Mozambican Languages Department at INDE 2002 interview). In 2003, a new basic education curriculum was set up to introduce local languages in early primary grades. The implementation of the project was initiated that year with 23 primary schools and in 2010 it included 75 schools around the country, with a total count of 15000 students (Sendela 2007, Benson 2010).

The bilingual education project is not without its critics. Jona (2008, p.10) notes the existence in Mozambican society of dissident voices in the praise of bilingual education (democracy and social inclusion, cultural and educational benefits) that stress mainly the costs of resources and the lack of access that it provides to participation in the global terrain. These arguments although proven wrong by research (Heugh 2007, 2009) continue to be popular in mainstream discourses. Ribeiro (2007) believes this bilingual education model is not sustainable given the poor state of education in Mozambique. She describes a gloomy picture where, despite a great increase in the number of children attending school, nearly one million were still out of the system; where the quality of the teaching and of the infrastructures have not been able to keep up the pace. Ribeiro (2007, p.2) mainly questions the strategy of the Mozambican government: she wonders how the goal of bilingual education can be reached, if the government is still getting to grips with the overall objective of education for all (EFA), and issues such as gender imbalance and HIV awareness. It can be argued that by centring her argument in the general benefits of being provided education, Ribeiro does not give enough importance to the issue of linguistic human rights and the crucial benefits of education in a language that is familiar to the student. As Benson (2004, p.16) notes:

> What EFA means for people in developing countries is access to basic literacy and numeracy as well as other skills that will improve their lives. Mother tongue-based bilingual education not only increases access to skills but also raises the quality of basic education by facilitating classroom interaction and integration of prior knowledge and experiences with new learning.

Seemingly then Ribeiro is overlooking the underlying reason for mother tongue education, which is the valorisation and empowerment of the individual by being able to use a familiar language to learn to further explore the world. In this sense, Nsiku (2008, p.13) presenting an evaluation of the bilingual project, highlights positive changes in the relation between children and teachers "from vertical and asymmetric to horizontal and symmetric". He adds that the dialogue also involves the parents, which means a greater connection with the community, thus interpreting the changes as producing a new environmental context for schooling. This is a crucial change that could make all the difference in the educational success in Africa. Moreover, Benson (2010, p.331) reports better results in bilingual schooling than all-Portuguese schooling in terms of "classroom participation, student achievement in all subject areas, including Portuguese, student self-esteem, parent participation and many other aspects of primary education".

Mozambique is currently negotiating a critical stage between experimentation and implementation of bilingual schooling (Benson 2005, p.249). According to Benson (2005, p.258), who was closely involved in the project as external adviser, the question seems to be whether or not a growing body of scholars and practitioners can inform the public and influence policy so that more widespread implementation can begin.

In Mozambican society, some are sceptical regarding the future of African languages in Mozambique, since government policy, although recognising them, attributes them no official function. Many, especially black élites (represented by intellectuals such as Simbine, Matusse and Ngunga), believe that the situation is a consequence of Mozambican élites having an inferiority complex regarding their African mother tongues, resulting from the colonial stance of promoting Portuguese only. Others, as the Mozambican poet José Craveirinha (Saúte 1990, p.45), keep their faith in the power of the options of the speakers, as highlighted by Calvet (2000, p.35). Craveirinha (*ibid.*) believed: "there is no cultural aspect, that is preserved through agreements between Heads of State. That will be the work of the anonymous people. It is the people that make the language that transforms culture."[25] As previously observed, the options of the person in the street can be very limited by the linguistic policies of the state.

There are additional positive signs regarding the use of African languages in Mozambique. The national languages, besides being used as a teaching language in bilingual education are also being introduced in the education system as a subject and have been "authorised" to be used as auxiliary in the teaching of Portuguese (Sendela in Sambo 2007). They are also used as a vehicle to disseminate information about important issues such as awareness in HIV/AIDS campaigns. Another positive development, in terms of declared policy, is the use of African languages in local government. In September 2000, the Municipality of Maputo adopted Xironga, the main language of the region, and other local languages, as working languages in plenary sessions and commissions, meaning that any citizen of Maputo who wishes to conduct business with the Municipality can do so in her/his language (Lopes AJ 2001, p.263). This was classed as a "genuine local turnaround with a national impact in respect to the sociolinguistic context of the country" (Lopes AJ 2001, p.263).

---

25   "não há nenhum aspecto cultural, que seja preservado a partir de acordos entre chefes de Estado. Isso vai ser obra do povo anónimo. É ele que faz a língua que a transforma."

From the above, one can argue that the Mozambican government was encouraged to introduce the national languages in the education system mainly by external pressures from international organisations (solution to failure of the education system) and by interest of certain donors that were keen to contribute funds (Sida). Also, from the policy documents analysed in the previous section and the considerations made earlier regarding the Mozambican elite, it can be argued that there is a consensus regarding the role of Portuguese as the language of national unity and national communication and that in parallel with that the role of African languages has slowly been recognised. There is thus potential for a coherent and broader support for bilingual education in Mozambique if those for whom African languages are important are able to voice their opinions and participate in the political process.

Mozambique was preparing in 2010 a national linguistic policy, signalling a strong political will to manage language (Sendela 2010 email). Nevertheless, the extent to which African languages are going to be able to play a role in the recognised multicultural and multilingual Mozambique is still an open question in Mozambican society. Mozambique's most renowned author Mia Couto sees it as a challenge to "create diversity, without hegemony"[26] (Radio Moçambique 2010). But is that possible? I will return to this in Chapter 5.

4.1.2.3 English Language, Development, Regional and Global Links

Portuguese and English are the languages most used for Mozambique's external communication: Portuguese as the official language and English due both to the geopolitical context in which the country is set (in most SADC countries English is the official language) and to the fact that English is perceived as 'the international lingua franca' and 'the language of globalisation'.

In this section I will look into the historical and contemporary spread of English in Mozambique and evaluate its present situation.

The initial presence of English language in Mozambique was mainly connected with trade and economic interests. First, in a colonial setting, Mozambique was mainly used to provide services and human resources to the surrounding territories that formed part of the British Empire (latter independent countries that adopted English as official languages); additionally there was a strong hold of foreign capital (mainly British) in the private companies that had concessions to operate in colonial Mozambique. Secondly, in post independent Mozambique, a multitude of factors has sustained that presence: continuous political and economic support from the United Kingdom and the Commonwealth (initially in the context of sanctions against the Rhodesian regime) increased

---

26 "o desafio é criar diversidade, sem hegemonia"

relations and integration with neighbouring countries (SADC), influence of external organisations (international and NGOs) operating in Mozambique, processes of globalisation (access to regional/international labour market, further education).

Historically, British interests in the Mozambican area have always been strong. Lopes, AJ (1998, p.39-40) identified migrant labour in Southern Africa as the principal element through which British influence in Mozambique was extended since the 19th Century. To that, Lopes (1998, p.40) adds "the concession by Portuguese authorities of vast areas of land, as well the utilisation of transport networks, particularly the railway lines to and from the hinterland". Linguistic traces of that influence are visible in English words borrowed by African languages (Lopes, AJ 1998, p.41), particularly in the local languages in southern Mozambique: *spuna*/spoon; *tafula*/table; *watcha*/watch (Matusse 2002 interview). However, in the immediate post-independence, given Mozambique's option for Marxist-Leninism, the country was fairly closed, maintaining privileged relations with the Socialist countries of Eastern Europe. At this point, "Mozambique did not feel the need for English" (Juvane 2010 interview).

In terms of recent spread, English in the early 1980s was linked to the opening up of Mozambique to liberal democracy and the influx of external aid, since Mozambique joined the World Bank and the IMF in 1984 and many NGOs also started operating in the country at that time and later to support the pacification process and the return of the refugees (Juvane 2010 interview). The end of Apartheid in South Africa, 1991/2, the lifting of sanctions and the consequent opening up of the country, also led to a greater demand for English in Mozambique as the two countries developed partnerships. Esselmont, English Language Teaching Co-ordinator at the British Council, (2002 interview) gave as an example her experience at the Eduardo Mondlane University, where the money injected by the World Bank for capacity-building created an increase in the need of English to develop links in southern Africa. That perception of the importance of English and the surge in demand led "to rumours and worries that a death warrant was soon to be signed on Portuguese" (Matusse 1997, p.547) - I further analyse some perceptions of language relations in Mozambique in section 4.1.4. The demand created in the 1980s a quite profitable market for English language teaching in Mozambique, causing, around 1986, a proliferation of clandestine private schools (Macaringue 1990) - at the time private education was forbidden - the law was only changed in 1990. Matusse (1997, p.547-548) explains that the two factors that "frustrated the initial surge in the spread of Portuguese" in Mozambique after independence - the civil war and the difficult economy situation of Mozambique -, in 1980, had "compelled the elite and professionals to learn English". Matusse (1997, p.547-548) presents a detailed analysis of the factors that include: the disruption of schools by the war, including the fact that many agents of Portuguese language spread (teachers, nurses, government officials) were forced to relocate; the war caused a reduction in internal movement of the population and a diminishing need to communicate in languages other than the ethnic one; the depreciation of the local currency due to the war and other economic and political factors led to the search for "dollar-paying jobs" mainly offered by foreign NGO with which proficiency in English was normally associated; proficiency in English was also sought after by government institutions given their foreign-funded projects; the increasing importance of English language at university level (access to information, studies abroad, publishing); exposure to English through technology. Matusse (1997, p.552) concluded that English was being pragmatically adopted as a complementary language, a trend also visible in many other countries.

The spread of English in Mozambique is intimately associated with a certain discourse of globalisation - English as gatekeeper to more money, information, better education, technology and, ultimately, development. The arrival in Mozambique of international and non-governmental organisations - that mainly operate in English as the language of communication presently sustained by the international system - to support the country to achieve (internationally set) developmental goals represented a defining factor in the power of attraction of English language to a certain layer of the population already involved or in perspective of acquiring employment in the business of the state, those who were interested in furthering their education (studying abroad) and increasing their earning power (better jobs in and out of the country). However the 'pragmatic' adoption of English as complementary language in Mozambique harbours consequences. This includes further reinforcing of European languages and discourses and the continual undermining of African languages and cultures. A policy aimed at the promotion of African languages and cultures (that includes economic benefits arising from its use), which also implies the raising of individual awareness regarding language rights, the widening of participation of civil society in the definition of the state and the consideration of alternative strategies of development is therefore imperative.

The spread of English in Mozambique has taken place also via migration flows (refugees, trade and labour) and public and private education. In this study I focus on education as this strand is considered the most important in my subsequent exploration of external language spread policies.

The presence of English in Mozambique before independence was limited and spread through work fluxes and business interests. During colonial times, French was the first foreign language to be learned in secondary school and the second, with fewer years of teaching, was English. However as described previously, education was accessible to only a small part of the population. Portuguese legislation (such as the *Portaria 3602* of 23.11. 1938 and the *Diploma Legislativo 724* of 11.09.1940) would also control the use of foreign languages, for instance by forbidding its use in public advertisement (Matusse 1991, p.32). After independence and during the civil war, due to a shortage of teachers, the teaching of French stopped (Eduardo, Director of VSO Mozambique, 2002 interview). English continued to be taught for 3 years at the upper levels of secondary school, although in patches, in reduced time, and affected by lack of teachers (and lack of teachers with adequate training) and materials (Eduardo 2002 interview). Esselmont (2002 interview) indicated that, during the civil war, "in the cities, you could find some experience of English [teaching] going on. And in fact a lot of the NGOs that were here at the time did have English teachers in particular schools throughout the country".

Since independence, the policy to train all first and second university years in English was maintained. However, a noted lack of sufficient mastery of the English language prompted the conclusion that the 3 years of English language teaching in upper secondary school was not sufficient (Ussene, English Teacher at Nampula's Secondary School, and Eduardo 2002 interviews) - in 2002 90% of the bibliography available at Universidade Eduardo Mondlane was in English. In 1989, there was a reformulation of the educational system that extended the teaching of English, from 1990 onwards, to the pre-university years - English was now to be taught for the full 5 years of secondary school (Ussene 2002 interview). However, many secondary schools did not have English language teachers, and the existing ones often lacked specific training - the teachers at the time were mainly people that had lived during the war in neighbouring 'English-speaking' countries with no specific qualifications for the teaching of English. With the end of the civil war in 1992, the government identified the need for more English language teachers, and for better training of the existing ones. Thus the first National Conference on English Language Teaching in 1994 highlighted the need for a sustainable institutional capacity to deliver quality ELT (Eduardo and Uprichard 1995), something the country lacked, according to numerous 1980s reports (Murray 2001, p.13). The problems identified in English at Secondary level were, among others: shortage of teachers, poor quality of teacher training, existence of many untrained teachers, poor teaching/learning conditions/resources, weak student assessment and a examination system (Murray, 2001). To improve the situation, the Ministry of Education approached the British Department for International Development (DFID) to support Secondary English in Mozambique, and that led to the STEP project (*ibid.*) examined in section 4.1.3.2. Since 2003/4, a new basic education curriculum has been set up that includes the introduction of English in later primary school grades, namely the 6th and 7th (UNESCO 2004 and Domingos, at the English Department of the Ministry of Education, 2010 interview).

It is noticeable, from my above description, an increasing demand/offer of English language courses associated with the development of regional links and Mozambique developmental efforts; English language has also been taught at increasing earlier stages in the education system, a trend that is visible in many countries and is justified as equipping the population to be able to access the increasing globalised markets. There still remains a concern about the quality of the teaching of the language (adequate qualification of teachers). Justifications collected during fieldwork associate the spread of English in Mozambique with the global and regional status of English (Ussene and Esselmont 2002 interviews, Juvane 2010 interview); its use by international organisations (English as work language in the World Bank, IMF, European Union); and with the influence (especially economic impact) some countries (mainly South Africa, but the USA was also mentioned as economic world power) have in Mozambique (Navarro, Costa, Simbine and Amaro 2002 interviews).

The official discourse justifies the use of English in the pursuit of mainly economic objectives. In the mentioned first National Conference on English Language Teaching, that took place in Mozambique, in September 1994 (Eduardo and Uprichard 1995, p.13), the role of English was defined as:

- contributing to economic growth and poverty reduction;
- assisting in the transition from a command economy to a market economy;
- a command of English will help medium and high level manpower to promote and manage economic growth and poverty reduction measures and programmes;
- being particularly relevant in the areas of commerce and trade, accessing aid, regional and international partnerships, higher education and research, information technology, skills and technology transfer and tourism.

Most recently, the Strategic Plan for Education and Culture (2006-2010/11), entitled *Fazer da escola um polo de desenvolvimento consolidando a Moçambicanidade.* (Make School a Beacon of Development Consolidating Mozambiqueness), refers to the relevance of English language in the secondary school curriculum in connection with the skills perceived as needed to perform well in the labour market (República de Moçambique, Ministério da Educação e Cultural 2006, p.22). All these arguments stress the functional advantages of English (Phillipson 1992, p.271), advantages built on the structural power English language has been accumulating thanks to its spreading agents (countries, organisations, and individuals). There is therefore a continuity in the justification for the use and spread of English overwhelmingly centered in development, an argument that obscures the structural spread of English.

4.1.2.4 French Language, the Power of Francophony

Up to 1975, when independence took place, French had been the first foreign language taught in Mozambique - following the same principle as the continental Portuguese education system. After independence the fragile state of the Mozambican educational system, the regional context and the international environment, contributed to the French language position becoming weaker and English rising in importance (Belorgey 2002 interview). After a 20 year gap, French was slowly reintroduced in the national education system in 1996, as the second foreign language (after English), taught as a mandatory subject in the 11th and 12th grades - the last grades of the secondary school -, and, since 2009/10, optionally, in the 9th and 10th grades. The close involvement of France in relation to the reintroduction of French is analysed in section 4.1.3.3.

Beside French being taught as a foreign language in secondary schools, higher education institutions, and private and semi-private schools (such as the Instituto de Línguas), there are French departments in some universities, of which the most important of is at Universidade Pedagógica (Maputo, Nampula, Beira and Pemba) that train the new French teachers. The Centro Cultural Franco-Moçambicano has increasingly developed its offer of French language courses. There is also a French school in Maputo to which Mozambican and other nationals can be admitted.

4.1.3 External Language Spread Policies in Mozambique

As defined in Chapter 2, external language spread policy is the government promotion of a language abroad. I have also previously established that in the historical process of nationalism, language became in some countries a symbol of nationhood. Additionally I argued that external language policies could be used as tool for a country to create and sustain influence in another and that they would bring political and economical advantages. This influence is achieved by attracting the elites of the target countries and promoting a positive and appealing image of the country. Teaching them the language, offering scholarships, maintaining contact networks, builds a bond that predisposes people to develop positive attitudes. It is a policy that works in the long term and its results are not obvious.

At the beginning of the Mozambican case study I discussed how Portuguese language became an official language in Mozambique and a basis for national unity, noting the importance of the colonial legacy, and interpreting it as the result of the language spread policies of the colonial power in the non-autonomous territory. Further I noted the spread of English and French tied with the discourses of development and, in particular English, related to the structure of the international system and processes of regional integration. I will now analyse specific contemporary external language spread policies in Mozambique. In my analysis I do not focus strictly on linguistic activities (such as language courses). I take a broader approach that includes cultural activities, since as explained in section 2.1.3.3, I see language spread policies as part of cultural diplomacy. Thus, in the case studies, I look into the model of the cultural centre as a privileged instrument of cultural diplomacy, that associates the spread of culture and language (which includes the offer of language courses, associated with the work of the cultural centre); and at activities the source government develops to spread its language through the target country's education system.

This study focuses on the 1990s to 2010. Three external language spread policies stand out in Mozambique, namely, Portugal, United Kingdom and France aimed at spreading and/or reinforcing, respectively, the use of Portuguese, English and French. Besides the governments of those countries, there are other governments and other organisations that participate in that spread. I will only briefly note their role, since the focus of this study is on government policies. Beside the mentioned three main external language spread policies, I will briefly examine, in the context of Mozambique, those of Brazil and Germany, the first given its association with Portuguese language, and the second to represent a new player with a potentially different approach to language spread.

An initial note is required regarding the particularity of Portuguese external language spread policy in the case studies. As former colonial power, and given that Portuguese was adopted as the official language in the PALOP (*Países Africanos de Língua Oficial Portuguesa*, African Countries with Portuguese as Official Language), the development of specific cooperation in the area of education is part of the Portuguese government's strategy. Overall Portugal assists in the initial and in-service training of teachers and supports the development of educational materials. There is also specialist support for the Portuguese language training of translators, members of parliament and other professionals.

4.1.3.1 The External Language Spread Policy of Portugal in Mozambique

Mozambique, as a colony, was viewed as a distant land from Portugal, both in a geographical and psychological sense. The distance would continue after independence, although often masked by the supposed strength of the historical cultural and linguistic links. In 1998 the then Mozambican President Joaquim

Chissano, awaiting the visit of the then Portuguese Prime Minister António Guterres commented (Avillez 1998):

> It is a Head of Government that comes to find out about Mozambique's situation, what will allow him to take more grounded decisions. I normally tell people that one of the difficulties we have here is to explain Mozambique. The terms of reference are different... When they arrive here, they then understand many of the things we tried to explain.[27]

This comment indicates the lingering of the strain caused by the colonial bond, the conflict in the perceived images of the *Self* and of the *Other* and the need to readjust the relation. The ambiguity in the relations is also clear in this comment reported by a Portuguese teacher in Maputo when someone was introducing her: "Here in Mozambique, there are Mozambicans, foreigners and Portuguese"[28] (Siopa 2002 interview). The use of the same language provides opportunity for easier communication and understanding, albeit important to note that 'speaking the same language does not imply that we mean the same thing or that we have the same culture' (Skutnabb-Kangas 2000, p.253).

Up to 1974, Portugal concentrated its efforts on cultural relations in Europe. Following the overthrow of the dictatorship in April 1974 and the process of decolonisation, the relations between Portugal and the ex-colonies in Africa went through a difficult phase. This distancing was reinforced by the shift in Portuguese political strategy to get closer to Europe - a process that would culminate with the accession to the European Union, then the European Economic Community, in 1986. This shift from a so-called 'Atlantic vocation' (implying the close connections not just to Brazil and Africa, but also to England and the USA) to a 'European vocation' was a much debated political topic dividing the country, as it represented a break with the concept of Portugal as a nation based on the glorification of the 'Discoveries' and the country's 'projection in the world' - not just political, but also cultural and linguistic. Since then, Portugal has been able to integrate the European and the World vocations into its national strategy and concept by a continuous commitment to the European Union and by rebuilding links with the former colonies both bilaterally and multilaterally, through the CPLP, and the cultivation of concepts such as Lusophony (to in-

---

27 "É um chefe de Governo que vem inteirar-se da situação em Moçambique, o que lhe permitirá tomar decisões mais fundamentadas. Costumo dizer às pessoas que uma das dificuldades que temos aqui é explicar Moçambique. Os pontos de referência são diferentes...Quando aqui chegam, compreendem então muitas das coisas que nós tentávamos explicar."

28 "Aqui em Moçambique, há os moçambicanos, os estrangeiros e os portugueses."

clude diaspora communities, former colonies, and in general any Portuguese-speaker).

Political relations between Portugal and Mozambique are good, although at times can be considered complex. The impact of issues, such as the ownership of the Cahora Bassa hydroelectric plant (only settled in 2006), debt relief or different views on the Lusophone citizen status (within CPLP), have taken their toll on the relations between the two countries. In terms of commercial relations, the overall weight of those relations between Portugal and the PALOP is reduced. In the total of the Portuguese external commerce exports with those countries (and East-Timor) represented, in 2008, 7.07% of exports and 0.76% of imports (Banco de Portugal 2008). Portuguese direct investment in the PALOP and East-Timor represents only 6.2% of the total, and of that 92.5% is absorbed by Angola; Mozambique follows with a distant 5.1% (Banco de Portugal 2008). In terms of the PALOP's export and imports, most countries, and in particular those that concern the case studies, show a growing regional integration. Portugal, although present in their economies, is not always the major partner. South Africa and China have grown to be major commercial partners in Angola, India and Senegal in Guinea-Bissau, and South Africa and the Netherlands in Mozambique (Banco de Portugal 2008). However statistics should be used with care. For instance, in Maputo, the Portuguese Cultural attaché (Braga 2002 interview) was adamant that Portugal was the third major donor in Mozambique, but that data was not visible in the statistics, since many projects were not quantified. Nevertheless, it could be argued that although direct economic benefits are one of the most important factors in the relations between countries, they do not appear to be the major determinant for the commitment of Portugal to maintain and increase the spread of Portuguese language in the PALOP. There is a clear political commitment of Portugal in relation to the PALOP that is intrinsically linked to the construction of Portuguese national identity and to the building of a politico linguistic bloc that can offer benefits in the international system (a subject to which I will return).

Political, societal and cultural ties between the countries are prolific, and new avenues for relations have intensified with the establishment of the CPLP in 1996, although, it should be noted, the visibility of Portuguese culture in Mozambique is more evident than the reverse; thus mutuality remains an issue. The connections between the two countries are maintained by a diversity of formal and informal channels such as those established by the Mozambicans that immigrated to Portugal and those that study there and by the return to Mozambique of former settlers or their descendants to work and invest in Mozambique; the development of arts, educational and other exchanges and co-operation projects both through governmental and civil society partners; the increasing diffusion of international Portuguese-speaking media (Internet - Sapo search engine - RTP International and RTP Africa), tourism and business.

Portuguese external language spread policy aiming to spread the European variety of Portuguese language (a Brazilian variety is standardised and others from the PALOP are in the process of developing) has been undertaken, since 1992, by the Instituto Camões (IC), a body dependent from the Portuguese Ministry of Foreign Affairs. Portuguese external LSP can be traced back to the 15th century 'Discoveries'; however since I focus on the contemporary period, the formal shaping of Portuguese external cultural policy can be placed in 1929, with the creation of the Junta de Educação Nacional (JEN, National Education Board) under the dictatorship, aimed at integrating Portugal into contemporary intellectual trends by addressing the issues of teaching and culture (Trindade 1986, p.7). This precursor of the IC was under the aegis of the Ministry of Education - latter this body would develop dependent organisations that through successive transformations and changes of tutelage would lead to the IC. At present, IC implements external LSP through three main networks including *leitorados* (lectureships) and chairs in universities, Portuguese cultural centres closely connected to the embassies and, from 1998, a network of Portuguese language centres especially created to assist teachers in their task of teaching Portuguese language and promoting Portuguese culture at higher education institutions. From 2010, IC is also responsible for the teaching of Portuguese at primary and secondary level abroad, which until then was the responsibility of the Ministry of Education.

Analysis of the successive government programmes (available at http://www.portugal.gov.pt) reveals that the 'defence', 'valorisation', 'expansion', 'affirmation', 'diffusion' and 'promotion' of Portuguese language in the world, with special reference to the Portuguese communities abroad and the Portuguese-speaking countries, are a constant policy objective of Portuguese cultural diplomacy. The justification for this objective is the statement and reinforcement of national identity 'in face of globalisation and European and Peninsular integration' (e.g. XV Government Programme, 2002-2004). The identification between Portugal as a nation-state and Portuguese language is strong and ancient (Portugal has arguably the most ancient borders in Europe, dating from the 13th century), given first the formation and sustaining of the state constantly battling centripetal forces of Spanish kingdoms and later, the dilution into European and global identities.

Support of Lusophone Africa, along with the consolidation of Portugal's position in Europe, the review of relationships with Brazil, and the maintenance of historical links with the Orient were the main strategic axes of Portuguese external LSP declared in the 1980s (ICALP 1984, p.1). There is a clear connection

164

between these and the loss of empire (Brazil at the beginning of the 19th Century, the African colonies in the 1970s, and Macau, the last of the Oriental possessions in 1999). These are still valid today, with additional emphasis on asserting the status of Portuguese as an international language: "Portuguese language as Language of Work - in diplomacy, commerce, banking, Internet - Language of Science and Multiculturalism" (IC 2005b). There is then a reinforcement of the strategy for the promotion of Portuguese beyond the historical ties and linguistic legacy, by emphasising the communicational use of the language, that leads to the increasing the number of speakers, and number of countries that have it as official language as well as the number of organisations that use it.

During field research, Portuguese officials in Mozambique avoided answering direct questions regarding justifications of external LSP. Answers would generally point to a lead by the Mozambican government that the Portuguese government was happy to assist, given that the independent PALOP had assumed Portuguese as their own language, thus connecting directly Portuguese actions to support or aid to development. The Portuguese Cultural attaché and also Director of the Instituto Camões' Cultural Centre, when asked to describe Portuguese external cultural policy regarding Mozambique, reversed the question saying that what should be inquired was: what were the expectations of the Mozambican government regarding cooperation with Portugal - since in international cooperation it is expected that the receivers draw projects and apply for international funds (Braga 2002 interview). The Portuguese cultural attaché presented Portuguese cultural cooperation strategy as relying on the development of projects suggested by the Mozambican Ministry of Culture, and described how he had periodic contacts with the Mozambican Culture Minister, who would transmit his concerns and then, in turn, Portuguese authorities would decide in what ways they could be of assistance (Braga 2002 interview). Braga (2002 interview) thus described Portuguese cooperation as "non-affirmative" - justifying that the reverse would be quite problematic politically. The operational mode described is in line with the rules of engagement between independent countries. However it masks the inherent dependency of the African countries in relation to donors, the contemporary policy objectives of the European countries and the political and historical background that contextualises those relationships. Additionally the above comment prompted in many of the interviewees in Mozambique a characterisation of Portuguese government's action as reactive. That is, of not having a clear strategy in place.

However, as mentioned, successive Portuguese governments have been very clear in their objectives to spread Portuguese, and the development of policies in the PALOP is a stated strategy. The XVIII Constitutional Government program (2009-2013) states that the Portuguese Government: "Will seek, with all the

CPLP countries, that Portuguese language is taught as language of instruction and expression in these countries and in the diaspora"[29]. Portuguese language and its worldwide presence is central to Portugal's concept as a nation and also part of the national project of the PALOP that are now co-partners in the spread and internationalisation of Portuguese language. Portugal willingly and to the maximum of its capacity cooperates with them, as Portuguese language is considered its compared advantage or valued added in relation to other countries offering aid (although that advantage may be decreasing in non-linguistic areas, as both from the side of the aid providers and aid receivers there is a general rise in multilingual teams). Portuguese language spread brings multiple benefits to Portugal, of which the political seem to be the most prominent, since as examined earlier increasingly the regionalisation of economies and the diversification of partners take place. However, the push for the internationalisation of Portuguese aims at trying to unlock the economic potential of the language.

Further to the critiques of the Portuguese reactive action in Mozambique, Braga (2002 interview) noted that, often, local politicians would describe the way Portuguese cooperation operated as too spontaneous. He believed that this characteristic had some positive outcomes: given that there was so much to do in the country, a lot could be done without extensive planning (or as he put it, without the NGOs saying what needed to be done) and explaining: "Because there is a vocation for Portugal and for many Portuguese to cooperate with Africa", "many projects happen in Mozambique thanks to those people with a mission in life: cooperation"[30]. The above critiques and comments about the operation of Portuguese structures in Mozambique leads to two main issues: the overall structure and operation of Portuguese cooperation and the 'special relationship' between Portugal and Africa. Criticisms of Portuguese cooperation policy are present in reports by the OECD's Development Assistance Committee (DAC) in 1991, 2001 and 2006 (in 2010 another evaluation is taking place). The DAC (OCDE/DAC 1997) described the initial stages of the Portuguese efforts to engage in cooperation with the PALOP in the early 1990s as based on a "traditional set of activities dispersed among different ministries in their respective fields, in particular education (with an emphasis on scholarships and universities) and health (especially hospitals)". Those activities and *modus operandi* did not change much during the 1990s and Portugal was criticised by the DAC, in

---

29   "Procurará, com todos os países da CPLP, que a Língua Portuguesa seja ensinada como língua de instrução e de expressão nestes países e na diáspora"

30   Braga (2002 interview) said in Portuguese: "Porque há uma vocação por parte de Portugal e de muitos portugueses para a cooperação com África", "muitos dos projectos que acontecem em Moçambique é graças a essa gente que tem uma missão na vida, que é a cooperação".

both 1997 and 2001 evaluation reports, for failing to contribute to poverty reduction and development of the partner countries as it was "not clear that these programmes have a strong foundation in the development strategies of the developing partner countries". Moreover that "A considerable portion of the aid provided in these areas is expended in Portugal itself, through scholarships and other Portugal-based training and services". Throughout the years, the Portuguese government acknowledged these critiques (for instance, Instituto da Cooperação Portuguesa 1999a, p.16 and Instituto da Cooperação Portuguesa 2002f, p.7), and responded by establishing new programmes and setting up several bodies and reformulating others.

Undoubtedly, activities at country level, although adapted to the local environment are set in an overall structure and policy strategy originating in the source country of external language spread policies and are limited by that. The Cooperation attaché of the Portuguese embassy in Maputo believed government changes in Portugal would always have consequences, although not too strong, given the fact that cooperation was done having in mind the local needs (Costa 2002 interview). In terms of Portuguese external language spread, the politicization of the Instituto Camões (IC) is evident in the choices of President, closely connected with governmental changes, and in the successive change of ministerial tutelage despite its short history. Created in 1992 under the dependency of the Ministry of Education, IC was in 1994 transferred to be the political responsibility of the Ministry of Foreign Affairs (while the Ministry of Education kept responsibility for the teaching of Portuguese abroad at secondary and primary level until 2010). Then in 2006, a shared responsibility with the Ministry of Culture in the definition of strategic objectives was established. According to inside views, the government defines the priority areas, the president of the IC defines the strategies, and the heads of service, within IC, propose initiatives (Ramos 2002 interview). This arguably leaves little manoeuvring room for the structures in the countries themselves.

In 2002, the Portuguese Cultural attaché (Braga 2002 interview) in Mozambique criticised the inward, politicised view of the IC. He highlighted the tension between the perception of IC's mission as 'to support Portuguese cultural agents' and IC as 'an arm of the Foreign Affairs Ministry for external cultural relations'[31]. I interpret this as denoting a lack of political consensus in the deployment of external cultural policy. Although there is agreement on the overall

---

31 Braga (2002 interview) words in Portuguese were: "O Instituto Camões é o braço do Ministério dos Negócios Estrangeiros para a relação cultural externa e é uma instituição que em Portugal tem vivido muito em função dos desafios internos e eles lá devem viver atrofiados com isso."

objective to promote Portuguese language and culture abroad, the integration of the political, linguistic and cultural action has not been properly clarified and articulated, operating along traditional divides, such as politics / culture, domestic / abroad, developing / developed countries, diaspora / former colonies. Therefore I link this matter to the increasing globalization that has extended cultural action beyond traditional compartmentalised areas and government relations. Faced with broader definitions and uses of cultural relations and action and an increased importance of non-governmental agency, the Portuguese traditional structure appears to struggle with the expanded realm of cultural diplomacy, public diplomacy - which leads to more diffuse forms of soft power - and how to integrate this into its national strategy. Additionally, given the concentration of Portuguese language spread efforts in the PALOP and in Timor-Leste, there has been an increasing linkage of the external LSP activities with support to development. For example, Portuguese as the official language is the officially accepted medium for development - I will further explore this in Chapter 5 in relation to the international 'Education for All' project. The 2006 prescription of the involvement of the Ministry of Culture in the definition of the IC strategic objectives may indicate a potential paradigm shift in the way external cultural action is devised, potentially accentuated by the concentration of the responsibility for all education action abroad in IC from 2010 (previously only responsible for higher education).

Portuguese external LSP in Africa has been and will most likely continue to be of great importance to Portugal. Portugal, in the measure of its financial capacity, by cooperating with the Mozambican government, supports the Mozambican efforts in terms of development at the same time that it develops its own objective of reinforcing the status of Portuguese worldwide. In Mozambique, education has been and is a priority in the relations between the two countries and is the sector most invested in by Portuguese cooperation (IPAD 2008). The promotion of Portuguese language as a vehicle for education and training is a main objective of Portuguese cooperation (IPAD 2007). The centrality of education follows strategic options of the Mozambican government - in this case, Education For All - nevertheless it is a choice that is matched with the objectives, financial and human capacity and the "advantages" in specific areas of Portuguese cooperation (IPAD 2007, p.45). As highlighted in the 2007 edition of the Indicative Cooperation Programme between Mozambique and Portugal (IPAD 2007, p.14/5):

> Resources are limited, and as such they have to be concentrated in which Portugal's comparative advantages are greater – language and history. Thus geographically they are concentrated in Portuguese-speaking countries, and in sectoral terms they

focus on education and training, as well as on providing support for judicial and public-administration systems.

Language is at the core of Portuguese cooperation. Education and culture in Mozambique are coordinated by the Portuguese Embassy based in Maputo. Education is coordinated by a career diplomat, directly responsible to the Ambassador and to the Foreign Affairs Ministry; and culture is coordinated by a dual capacity officer that incorporates the post of Cultural attaché (directly connected with the Foreign Affairs Ministry) and that of representative of the IC in Maputo (he is also the Director of the local IC's cultural centre). This organisation of responsibilities mirrors the different ministerial responsibilities (in the process of change during 2010): the teaching in primary and secondary schools abroad as a responsibility of the Ministry of Education and the teaching of Portuguese in higher education establishments and cultural action as being the responsibility of the IC (a split to end in 2010, but that at the time of my information update in June 2010 had yet to produce changes at local level).

Regarding the cultural action network, Instituto Camões (IC) has a cultural centre in Maputo (1996), with an extension in Beira (1998). Cultural action is also developed through the higher education network for which IC is responsible, which includes beside five *leitorados* (lectureships), six Portuguese Language Centres (Centros de Língua Portuguesa) throughout the country - these are resources centres created since 1998 to assist the lecturers in the their task of teaching Portuguese and promoting Portuguese culture. Since 2005, the IC in cooperation with the Universidade Pedagógica (UP) has provided a network for secondary school teacher training based in seven cities throughout the country. Cultural and linguistic spread is thus tied, in the sense that the *leitorados* and language centres besides teaching Portuguese and supporting training also develop cultural activities. However the public they reach can be restricted - this is in some cases overcome by outreach activities but depends on the particular dynamic of the *leitorados*/language centres.

The IC Centro Cultural Português de Maputo (IC-CCPM), the main Portuguese cultural centre in Mozambique is the hub of Portuguese cultural activities in the country. As stated earlier there is an extension of the centre in Beira. Cultural activities, under the aegis of the IC, are developed in all artistic areas mixing components of local and Portuguese culture. The planning of cultural activities was reported to be undertaken within a spirit of fusion. Braga (2002 interview) noted that if a Portuguese group was invited to Mozambique, he would try, for instance, to arrange a workshop including local musicians, or that Mozambican musicians could be integrated in European tours. The main objective of these activities, coinciding with IC's general aim, is to promote Portuguese language and culture, and in Africa, also to promote the cultures of Portuguese expression[32]. Other objectives include: diversification of content and public; devolution of cultural action; support of creativity; support of education; and strengthening friendship and cooperation ties between Portugal and Mozambique (Braga 2002 interview). These objectives have been maintained since 2002 with slight alterations and a few additions. The additions relate mainly to supporting the cultural activities of the IC educational network in Mozambique, to encourage the building of audiences for cultural activities, and to contribute cultural projects to the affirmation and promotion of the CPLP and to support training and aid to development projects (Braga 2010, p.4/5). The last two additions to the strategic objectives of IC-CCPM bring it in line with some of the latest developments that affect external cultural policies: the multilateralisation of policies (in the case of Portugal through the CPLP), and the link between these policies and aid for development.

In 2010, Braga (2010, p.2) explained how IC-CCPM included in its programs activities that promote Mozambican culture and that of other PALOP, by describing them as "(i)nitiatives whose scope goes beyond the promotion of a Portuguese cultural and educational matrix to project the promotion of Mozambique and of other Portuguese language countries"[33]. This remark can be interpreted in the context of a neutral view of language. That is, the promotion of Portuguese language, although promoting Portugal (as he says "goes beyond",) also promotes the PALOP, because they chose Portuguese to be their official language (which he refers to as "Portuguese language countries" - probably a slip in terminology, as in terms of political correctness, 'countries having Portuguese as official language' would be more acceptable and accurate). The examples of activities he provides are: the change of title of the "Course on Portuguese Literature History" (*Curso de História da Literatura Portuguesa*) to "Course on Portuguese Language Literatures" (*Curso de Literaturas de Língua Portuguesa*), the "Portuguese and Portuguese Language Cinema Festival" (*Ciclo de Cinema Português e de Língua Portuguesa*), and other activities based on Portuguese language such as History conferences and awards for Mozambicans in the areas of Poetry, Fiction, Essay and Theatre (Braga 2010, p.2). I would argue that this represents the overall stand of Portuguese cultural diplomacy discourse and policy, that is, Portuguese language as effectively the only accepted medium to develop cultural activities, even in a multicultural, multilingual envi-

---

32   The literal expression used by Braga (2002 interview) was: "promoção da língua e das culturas de expressão portuguesa".

33   "iniciativas cujo escopo ultrapassa a promoção da matriz portuguesa cultural e educacional para se projectar na promoção de Moçambique e de outros países de língua portuguesa"

ronment. There are no mentions or apparent concerns with the African languages that all are numerically predominant in Mozambique, and also a major part of their linguistic and cultural heritage. Seemingly then the external language spread policies of Portugal in Mozambique reinforce the position of Portuguese as the official language of Mozambique.

Portuguese cultural action, and general cooperation, can thus be said to be in tune with Mozambique's policies, favouring the spread of Portuguese language. Braga (2010, p.3) advances as validation for the Portuguese cultural action, the public recognition of the contribution of the Camões Institute in the development of culture and education in Mozambique by numerous (mainly institutional) partners. Braga (2002 interview and 2010) also notes that Portuguese cooperation is requested for all cultural activities, given the language connection - therefore, operating widely in the Mozambican society. Although I would point out that activities take place mainly in urban educated areas, and in the case of the IC-CCPM focusing on the capital Maputo (with an extension in Beira, the second city of Mozambique). Portuguese external cultural policy is thus restricted to a particular kind of public, literate urban population. Braga (2010, p.8) considers the opening of cultural centres in the provinces not to be pertinent: "There are certainly other strategies that may at this stage of development, be a better contribution to a more harmonious and sustainable growth of educational and cultural life of the people"[34]. This position is not surprising, as Portuguese language is concentrated in urban areas. Supporting Mozambican efforts to spread and improve the quality of teaching of Portuguese language in the provinces, IC is investing in a long-term project with the Universidade Pedagógica to provide training for Portuguese language teaching with no formal qualifications through the mentioned network of Language Centres.

The close connection between the cultural services of the Portuguese embassy and sectors of Mozambican society can be exemplified by the work developed with the Associação Moçambicana da Língua Portuguesa (AMOLP Mozambican Association of Portuguese Language). The idea of this association dates back to 1987, within a group of teachers and students of Portuguese Literature courses organised by UEM and the Portuguese Embassy. The Portuguese Embassy was from the start very supportive of the creation and activities of AMOLP, in particular a previous cultural attaché, Soares Martins (Angius, Librarian at IC-CCPM, and Miguel, co-founder of AMOLP, 2002 interviews). The support has been maintained through the availability of infrastructures and re-

---

34 "Há seguramente outras estratégias que podem neste estádio de desenvolvimento, melhor contribuir para um crescimento harmonioso e sustentado da vida educativa e cultural das populações".

sources and also by financial inputs. The close connection between AMOLP and the Portuguese services have in the past been detrimental to AMOLP's support by local entities, since it was perceived to be an extension of the Portuguese cultural services (Angius 2002 interview). This can be argued to be a manifestation of fracture lines in Mozambican society between Portuguese and African languages, between the *assimilados* and the *indigenas*, between the colonial past and the independent present, that still brew in the social and political process of the construction of the Mozambican national project regarding the status of languages.

Focusing on education, I have already pointed out that Portugal extensively assists the Mozambican government in achieving the objective of Education for All. In that, the language centres and teacher training centres that are part of IC's cultural action network are fundamental points of Portuguese language spread that emphasise the dominance of the European Portuguese standard and the monolingual and native speaker fallacies - the teachers come from Portugal and work and train Mozambican colleagues. IC has made major investments in steadily increasing the number of those centres since the 1990s. Educational projects developed by Portugal also involve other partners such as private foundations, as is the case with the Gulbenkian and the Bissaya Barreto foundations. Additionally, the embassy maintains a scholarship programme that enables Mozambicans to study at higher education level in Portugal. The number of scholarships provided in 2002 was 14 - the number had been decreasing, since Portugal was starting an internal scholarships scheme - a new trend guiding the operations of donors, maintained into the present. The scholarship scheme was changed to try to build local capacity and avoid brain drain. Scholarships to study in Portugal are now preferentially given to masters and doctoral levels – other levels will be still considered if they are priority areas for Mozambique that are not available in the country. Other important projects that were starting in 2002 have now developed and increased their importance. The Portuguese School of Maputo (Escola Portuguesa de Maputo), opened in 1999, has helped the IC in the promotion of Portuguese and has become an important educational resources centre. The experience of the pilot project in the area of technical education for the development of Arts and Crafts schools in Mozambique, being developed in four schools by the Portuguese Ministry of Education, the Portuguese NGO Fundação Portugal-África and the Portuguese development agency (APAD), was integrated in the 15 years Integrated Programme for the Reform of the Vocational Education, whose first phase (2006-2011) is financed by the World Bank and bilateral partners.

Overall, Portuguese external language spread policy in Mozambique has worked in support of Mozambique's own official policy and by reinforcing its

172

place as a privileged partner for the training of teachers, allows it to perpetuate the predominance of the European standard. However, recent developments regarding the implementation of the Portuguese language orthographic agreement between the CPLP countries and the increased visibility of multilateral structures, which have been developing strategic plans for the promotion of Portuguese language, may have some impact on the political legitimisation of the different standards of Portuguese. Further evidence of a potential shift is indicated by IC's collaboration with the Universidade Eduardo Mondlane (Mozambique) in a project that may contribute to the characterisation of the Mozambican variety of Portuguese by defining the linguistic competence of the university students and creating resources to deal with "recurrent mistakes"[35] (Encarte Jornal de Letras 2010b). I find the choice of terminology quite elucidating regarding the Portuguese approach - apparently torn between the political correctness of accepting other ways to speak Portuguese and being unable to leave the mindset that European Portuguese is the way to do it... Regarding the indigenous national languages, Portugal's action is limited to sponsoring bilingual dictionaries, grammars and other educational materials. As the education officer responsible at the Portuguese embassy mentioned, in 2002, the introduction of African languages in the Mozambican educational system, although not dismissed as important, is taken as "facilitating the learning of Portuguese and other disciplines, but in Portuguese" (Martins S 2002 interview).

Initial research into the spread of Portuguese language in Mozambique preempted the possibility of the existence of concurrent external LSP between Portugal and Brazil. However, findings pointed to no concerted policy or collaboration between the embassies. The Portuguese Cooperation official responsible stated that each country did its own thing (Costa 2002 interview). The Cultural attaché mentioned that he would welcome collaboration with Brazil, but observed that Brazil did not have many resources (Braga 2002 interview). Portugal and the European variety of Portuguese, in relation to Brazil and its variety of Portuguese, have in Mozambique (and in the other PALOP), the advantage given by the colonial matrix and the relatively closer geographical proximity. However given Brazil's economic potential that situation could change in the future. In the next section, I will briefly examine selected activities of Brazilian cultural diplomacy in Mozambique with a focus on the cultural centre.

---

35   "erros recorrentes"

4.1.3.2 The External Language Spread Policy of Brazil in Mozambique

Brazil is the largest Lusophone country in the world and one of the emerging world economies, and, like Mozambique, is one of the eight CPLP members. Brazil was the first country to recognise the independence of Mozambique (De Souza e Silva, Director of Centro de Estudos Brasileiros, 2002 interview) and the two countries were during that first period very close. However, after the election of President Fernando Collor de Mello in the 1980s, Brazilian diplomacy shifted its focus from the Third World to Europe and the United States (De Souza e Silva 2002 interview). Additionally, articulation problems related to the federal nature of the Brazilian state - namely in the relation between the central government and the states' government - have been pointed out as making external cooperation extremely complex (Do Rosário, President of the Bibliographic Fund for the Portuguese Language, 2002 interview).

Brazil understands cultural relations as international understanding and closeness between the peoples, and uses cultural diplomacy to promote the image of an inclusive, tolerant, ethnically diverse society in a process of constant renovation (Ministério das Relações Exteriores - Brasil 2010). The Cultural Centres are the main instruments of external cultural policy of Brazil. In Africa there are six centres covering all of PALOP (which highlights the 'lusophone' connection), plus one in South Africa - the majority of the centres are in the Americas (13 centres) and three others in Europe (Ministério das Relações Exteriores - Brasil 2010). The Centro Cultural Brasil - Moçambique (CCBM) was created in 1989 (then entitled Centro de Estudos Brasileiros, CEB, Brazilian Study Centre) as a cultural representation of Brazil in Mozambique, a bridge between the two countries, reinforcing the strong presence of Brazilians in Mozambique since independence, given the common language (De Souza e Silva 2002 interview). From September 2008, the Brazilian Ministry of External Relations changed the name of the CEBs to Centros Culturais (Cultural Centres). It states that:

traditionally the Centros de Estudos Brasileiros (CEBs) prioritised in their activities the teaching of Portuguese language. In the last years, those activities have intensified and expanded to include also the diffusion of Brazilian culture in its different forms. The denomination 'Centro de Estudos' ['Study Centre'] thus, no longer conceptually embodies the broad sphere of action of those units. Today the CEBs offer cinema sessions, dance and capoeira performances, gastronomic events, visual arts exhibitions, theatre performances, photography displays and music concerts, far beyond the promotion of Portuguese language. Furthermore, they promote the diffusion of local artistic and cultural manifestations, having transformed themselves in genuine cultural centres. It is thus justified that its denomination reflects this new reality. From now on, the CEBs will be named 'Centro Cultural Brasil-XXX (name of the country).[36] (Brazilian Ministry of External Affairs instructions to the CEBs cited in Grando 2009)

This association of the names of the target and source countries in the denomination of the external cultural policy structures is a significant trend in both case studies, denoting a concern in moulding a positive perception of their activities by using an inclusive title. I will return to this issue in Chapter 5.

In 2002, the Director of the then CEB, De Souza e Silva (2002 interview) described the activities of the centre as strongly based on the exchange of cultural activities between Brazil and Mozambique's arts (music, visual arts, literature) using the galleries and multifunctional spaces of its down-town prime location in Maputo along with a library service, and providing internet service at symbolic cost. The Director of the CCBM in 2010, Raúl Calane da Silva, (2010 interview) a well-known Mozambican journalist and writer, describes the centre as a "centre of local interaction"[37], building a bridge between Mozambique and Brazil. It is interesting to note that the present director of CCBM is Mozambican. This is a unique situation that although it may have been a pragmatic response to a localised problem, in terms of human resources, can create a precedent for change in thinking about external cultural policy managers. According to Calane da Silva (2010 interview), his predecessor did not want to return to her position and given that no Brazilian candidates applied, the Brazilian government opened up the vacancy to other nationals. Calane da Silva, who is a cultural personality in Mozambique, had always been a close collaborator of the CEB and had previously also been a journalist in Brazil, got the position. He considers his appointment a gigantic step in the change of attitudes towards external cultural policy in the Brazilian Ministry of Foreign Affairs, within "a new spirit

---

36   "tradicionalmente os Centros de Estudos Brasileiros (CEBs) focalizavam prioritariamente suas atividades no ensino da língua portuguesa. Ao longo dos últimos anos, essas atividades têm-se intensificado e expandido passando a abarcar também a divulgação da cultura brasileira nas suas diversas manifestações. A denominação 'Centro de Estudos' deixou, assim, de alcançar conceitualmente a ampla esfera de atuação dessas unidades. Hoje os CEBs oferecem sessões de cinema, exibições de dança e capoeira, encontros gastronômicos, mostras de artes plásticas, cênicas e fotografia, e concertos musicais, muito além da promoção da língua portuguesa. Ademais, promovem a divulgação de manifestações artísticas e culturais locais, tendo se transformado em genuínos centros culturais. Justifica-se, assim, fazer refletir em sua denominação essa nova realidade. A partir de agora, os CEBs passarão a intitular-se 'Centro Cultural Brasil-XXX (nome do país)'".

37   "centro de interacção local"

of CPLP"[38]. This reference to the CPLP, the international organisation of countries having Portuguese as official language, could also indicate a perception of reinforcement of the multilateral management of culture and language between those countries.

Persistent financial issues in the development of their activities have limited the CCFM, and its former incarnation, the CEB. In 2002, the Director of the then CEB, De Souza e Silva (2002 interview) stated that the CEB struggled with financial limitations. He commented that he had to complain frequently and pointed out that, for instance, the local CEB in Angola was the 'rich cousin', getting much more support for their activities. The reasons, according to De Souza e Silva, pointed to the transportation costs between Angola and Brazil being less expensive given the smaller geographical distance, but foremost, the fact that Brazil had a huge volume of trade with Angola, thus hinting at the use of external cultural policies to pave the way for and reinforce links at other levels. Overall he criticised the poor investment by the Brazilian government in the cultural centres in Africa and claimed for a more pragmatic attitude to maintaining the centres open and working on exchanges. Nevertheless, he acknowledged that both Brazil and Mozambique were in a difficult financial situation, which was an obstacle to the materialisation of the *país-irmão* (brother country) discourse - an allusion to an expression often used in Portuguese to refer to the assumed close relationship to another Portuguese-speaking country. The Director of the CCBM in 2010, Calane da Silva, (2010 interview) further noted that, since four years before, all the commercial profit made by the centre is required to be sent back to Brazil - as part of a corruption tackling program – which restricts the centre's budget to the Brazilian government's grant and discourages the centre to become profitable. Overall, the financial limitations of the CEB/CCBM can be explained by the lower priority of Africa for Brazilian foreign policy as indicated at the beginning of the section and the unavailability of funds and interest for the development of external cultural policy in Brazil.

This lack of interest and/or financial funds for the development of external cultural policy can be confirmed by the short-lived activities to create a Brazilian external cultural policy agency. In 2004, at the first meeting of the Comissão para a Definição de Ensino-Aprendizagem, Pesquisa e Promoção da Língua Portuguesa (COLIP, Commission for the Definition of the Teaching-Learning, Research and Promotion of Portuguese Language) activities were detailed for the "internationalisation of Brazilian Portuguese"[39] (Ministério de Educação do Brasil 2004). In 2005, Brazilian President, Luís Inácio Lula da Silva, announced the

---

38   "um novo espírito da CPLP".
39   "internationalização do português do Brasil"

creation of the Instituto Machado de Assis (IMA) to promote Portuguese language and Lusophone culture. The same year a study mission to the Camões Institute in Portugal took place within the context of an announced partnership with Portugal (Instituto Camões 2005a). In 2006, IMA had its own section in the Brazilian Ministry of External Affairs website that stated this body's responsibility for internal and external Portuguese language spread and related cultural activities. The mission statement describes its function thus:

> Devise and coordinate the promotion of policies of Portuguese language in Brazil and in the world; induce catalyse and organise research in Portuguese language; be a Portuguese Language reference for teaching and qualification of teachers; promote scientific and cultural activities, in Brazil and in the world, aiming for the promotion and diffusion of Portuguese language. (Ministério de Educação do Brasil 2006c)

Faraco, a Brazilian academic (2009 email), who was part of the Commission in charge of the pre-project for the Instituto Machado de Assis states that there was a conflict within the government and the project was buried. The Brazilian Ministry of Foreign Affairs was supposed to continue the project but nothing else was done since the Commissions ended its work in 2008.

Regarding specific external language spread activities, CCBM runs Portuguese language for foreigners, Brazilian literature and creative writing courses and also runs an annual seminar on Portuguese language. Portuguese language courses started around 1992, after the Peace negotiations, when several international organisations came to the country. The then CEB was the first foreign cultural centre in Mozambique and the first to have such courses. In the beginning they had up to 70 students; in 2002 they reduced to 10, and in 2010 there were 100 students per year. These foreign students are mostly connected with diplomatic circles, economic missions and NGOs. The centre also administers the *Programa Estudante Convénio* (Student Covenant Program) that offers vacancies to Mozambican students to study for bachelor and post-graduation courses in Brazil - the tendency has been for a decrease of the bachelor places, since in Mozambique the offer has been increasing (Calane da Silva, Director of CCBM, 2010 interview). It is not a scholarship programme, given the scarce resources of Brazil. The students are offered a vacancy and the course is free, but there is no maintenance allowance. The students attend the course in Brazil and only once back in Mozambique will they receive their diploma. This programme started in 1986 and is renewed periodically. This programme is used by Brazil also with other countries, including Guinea-Bissau.

On the basis on the information collected in this study, the specific external language spread activities of Brazil in Mozambique are limited to Maputo and its scale is limited, in proportion of their limited financial means and administrative procedures. Admittedly the scholarships programme maintains an enduring link between the Mozambican elite and Brazil. However the cultural and linguistic influence of Brazilian Portuguese cannot be underestimated, and goes far beyond the reach of any government policy, since Brazilian *telenovelas* (soap operas) are a huge cultural and linguistic influence in the Lusophone world (Agência Brasil 2010 and Brookes 2009).

4.1.3.3 The External Language Spread Policy of the United Kingdom in Mozambique

British cultural diplomacy has been the remit of the British Council since its establishment in 1934. The promotion of a wider knowledge of the UK and of English language abroad and the development of closer relations with other countries for the purpose of benefiting the British Commonwealth of Nations is the broader purpose of the British Council as set out in its Royal Charter of 1940. External language spread, namely the activities of English language teaching and examinations abroad, have been important elements of its activity that provide a means to influence and secure important financial resources, being closely associated to the establishment of English as an international language (Phillipson 1992). English language teaching in the 1990s is seen as a main pillar of the work of the BC:

> The global spread of the English language is fundamental to Britain's trade, culture and development. English language teaching (ELT) is therefore one of the main pillars of the Council's overseas operations. It is closely integrated with other elements of our work, particularly the promotion of British arts and education, and is a significant element of Britain's aid programme in many Third World Countries. It also brings major earnings to British publishers and suppliers of ELT materials and to British institutions involved in the teaching of English, both in the public and private sectors, and to British examining boards. (British Council 1993, p.12)

In 1995, Martin Jacomb, the then Chairman of the British Council, observed "(w)e are seeking to protect and promote the position of English, and thereby expand Britain's role as a supplier of English language goods and services, and enhance Britain's position in every field where English is important" (Jacomb, 1995, p.137). And that is exactly what was done in Mozambique.

At the end of the Cold War, the shifting pattern of international relations highlighted South Africa as a major centre for British investment, given its potential for economic growth (British Council 1990, p.24). In that context the British Council in 1989 opened offices in Mozambique and Namibia, within the biggest expansion of the Council's overseas network in over twenty-five years (British Council 1991, p.6). Before that, the Council operated with scholarships programmes for key people in government through their office in Zimbabwe, within the context of the work developed by the British development cooperation, ODA (latter DFID) that had been present in Mozambique since independence.

Regarding language, throughout the 1990s ODA operated in many English language projects in Mozambique. ODA supported the English Department of MINED in capacity-building for leaders - in practice, making scholarships in England available (Eduardo, Director of VSO Mozambique, 2002 interview) -, and also by enabling English Language Teaching (ELT) through the services of the British Council - mainly in the areas of staff development, provision of advisers and material (textbooks) production and provision (Eduardo and Uprichard 1995, p.55). ODA also promoted the quality of English teaching at the Universidade Eduardo Mondlane (UEM) - the main institution of higher education of the country by funding the Service English Project (1993-1997). However, the main British supported project regarding English language in Mozambique is the Secondary and Technical English Project (STEP) (1997-2001). This followed an ODA recommendation to the Mozambican Ministry of Education (MINED) to present a proposal for more structured support. The proposal was presented with the support of an ELT adviser in coordination with the University of London. The proposal presented and discussed with ODA, was approved in 1996 and implementation started, in 1997, already under DFID (the new incarnation of ODA after the election of the Labour Government in Britain), with a duration of four and a half years. The project was financially managed by the British Council and implemented by MINED with the following partners: University of London/IOE (in-service training), VSO (volunteer support teachers and also planning and implementation) and several private consultants (Murray 2001, p.18). The principal objective of STEP was to improve the quality of ELT provided in Mozambican secondary schools (Murray 2001, p.12), which in practical terms meant qualifying the teachers that were already teaching English but did not have appropriate academic preparation (Ussane 2002 interview).

The effect of foreign advisers and consultants on the definition of policies in developing countries is a contentious issue alluded before. In preparation for STEP, and given the lack of a formal approach to language policy in Mozambique at the time, the British advisers dedicated part of their time to help MINED to "formulate and execute its long term policy-making role" (Flavell 1993, p.2). Flavell (1993, p.2) visiting post-civil war Mozambique in preparation for the project, recognised that it was inevitable that in such a situation "there will be many gaps and only the stirrings of an articulated policy":

there does appear to be a policy vacuum in the areas of language and teacher education. There is no Language Planning Policy into which English fits; it happens to be the first foreign language largely on pragmatic, utilitarian grounds. There appears to be no specific targeting of groups to learn English; it is simply felt that it will be generally useful to all Secondary learners.

The input of the external advisers is extremely important as their opinions carry significant weight in the definition of policy. This is part of the overall situation of dependency in which the African countries are in relation to the West. Mozambique is no exception, therefore it is important to note Cunguara and Hanlon's (2010, p.22) observation that "Mozambique has been a donor darling because of a combination of two factors – subservience to donor policy combined with apparently dramatic falls in poverty". This implies that Mozambique is subservient to donor interest, that is, submitting to the field of external LSP: Mozambique's policies are influenced by which language the donors are interested in spreading. I will return to this discussion in Chapter 5.

At the end of the 1990s, British aid priority changed from ELT to poverty alleviation. The 1997 Labour government would bring a fundamental change regarding the place of language in development aid. As testified by Clare Short, in reply (on 17th August 1998) to a parliamentary question from Sir Geoffrey Johnson Smith MP (on 29th July 1998) related to ELT and development projects:

> I agree that there are circumstances in which English Language Training (ELT) has an important role within development projects. However it should be seen within the context of a country's overall language and education policy, especially those parts which concern the role of different languages within formal and non-formal education. We are always conscious when considering ELT within development projects that we should not seek to strengthen English language training at the expense of local indigenous languages. With that proviso we are supporting ELT in many of our projects particularly in countries where English is the medium of instruction and where its use can provide opportunities for poorer sectors of the community to participate on a more equal basis. (Ronnie Micallef, Director of British Council Malta, formerly stationed in Mozambique, personal email, 2002).

However, this radical change in discourse is only partially reflected in practice in this case study. In Mozambique, at the time, the STEP project was being implemented and continued until the foreseen closure in 2001. As explained by the BC Director, DFID, as opposed to ODA, "has not focused on English language teaching because of its focus on poverty reduction and they have taken the view over the years, which may be less strong now [2002] than it was, but anyway, certainly in the late 90s, that English language was elitist" (Ingram-Hill 2002, Director of British Council Mozambique, interview). This perception may reflect two different visions about English language in the conduction of British foreign policy – not unlike the one observed by Belorgey, the Director of the CCFM, (2002 interview) regarding France (section 2.1.3.4). DFID representing the 'development' view, in which English is seen as elitist, and the British Council representing the 'foreign affairs' perspective viewing English as a neutral and useful tool for development and public diplomacy. Nevertheless, with STEP, English language was being spread to the 'masses' (within the still restrict universe of those attending secondary school) through the Mozambican education system with the support of the British government. Since the end of STEP in 2001, British cooperation stopped its direct support to the teaching of English in the Mozambican education system, which is now supported, at secondary school level, by the Peace Corps' English native teachers in two year commissions (Domingos, officer at the English Department of the Ministry of Education, 2010 email). In Mozambique, ELT continued to be for the British Council a very important part of their work. By 2002, according to Ingram-Hill (2002 interview) within the Southern African Directorate of the British Council, Mauritius and Mozambique were the two countries where the major focus was the English language, since they were the only contexts where English was not the official language.

Thus at the turn of the century the work of the British Council in Mozambique was increasingly identified with the teaching of English directly and with the management of English language exams that enabled people to further study in Britain, Australia or New Zealand (Ingram-Hill 2002 interview). The British Council still provides today in Mozambique English language teaching to groups and to individuals in different formats. The teaching is funded through their grant, but in 2002 funds increasingly originated in their corporation work. As pointed out by Ingram-Hill (2002 interviews) "that it is now [in 2002] a big business, or an increasing business". However the trend seems to have reversed sharply: While the total budget for 2001/2 was GB £800,000 of which GB £294,000 was grant in aid, in 2009 the turnover decreased to GB £600,000, of which GB £500,000 were grant in aid (British Council Mozambique 2002 and McManus 2010). Also at the time of the study trip in 2002, there were plans to expand the activities of the BC to Beira and Nampula, based on existing ELT networks (Ingram-Hill 2002, p.2), that did not materialise. This appears to be related to the BC's adoption of Strategy 2010 concerned with finding the most efficient ways to generate a maximum impact in the Council's work. This new practice impacted on the teaching operation in Mozambique:

> The teaching operation in Mozambique is the most successful in the region. For security and space reasons, we needed new premises but the only ones available would have been costly to maintain and so would have threatened the financial viability of the teaching centre. This forced us to rethink our strategy and look at different ways

of working. The option we have chosen is to deliver our teaching with partner institutions. This will enable us to be more flexible, extend our outreach and divert resources into programmes rather than use them for the upkeep of large premises. This
is a model that could be explored for use in other countries. (British Council 2006a,
p.37)

Unfortunately it was not possible to obtain much updated information or
explanations from British Council Mozambique regarding changes - the Director
of the BC in 2010, Lisa McManus stated they were now a "much smaller team",
therefore not always having the time to reply to requests such as mine (Lisa
McManus 2010 email) and sent a document with some information.

Despite the patchiness of some of the information obtained, it is enough to
formulate a picture of the evolution of the work of the BC regarding language
spread. From 1997 to 2001, the British Council managed the STEP project
aimed at enhancing Mozambique's capacity to teach English at secondary
school level. In 1999, the BC starts teaching English to corporations. However
this was not a planned policy, it resulted from a response to a request from a
company (Esselmont, English Language Teaching Co-ordinator at the British
Council, 2002 interview). In 2002 when I visited Mozambique, the British
Council was at the top of the exclusive end of the English language teaching
market with the Lyndon Language School. Both offered native language teachers and for that could ask premium pay (the enduring native-speaker fallacy
(Phillipson 1992)), which was not the case with other English language schools,
both private and public (such as the Instituto de Línguas), operating since the
1980s, which only offered Mozambican teachers (Esselmont 2002 interview).
Also in 2002, the then Director reported that the area of young learners was
emerging as an important priority for the Mozambican branch of the BC since
there were plans to introduce English language at primary level in 2004 (Ingram-Hill 2002 interview) – which effectively happened as mentioned in section
4.1.2.3. This arguably resulted in an important line of action since, the British
Council website advertised in 2007 Saturday workshops for children from six to
ten years old and regular afternoon courses for eight to thirteen years old (British Council Mozambique 2007). The BC Mozambique website in 2010, which
was now a small (and difficult to find) section of the main BC Africa website,
advertises the usual English language exams and adult courses at the Teaching
centre and the availability for tailored courses for corporate individuals and
business (British Council 2010). The website also made reference to four full
time teachers in the Teaching Centre. However it is uncertain if this information
was up to date, since the document sent by the Director in 2010, in reply to my
request of updated information, mentions that they employ Mozambican teachers on an hourly basis (Could this be a reversal of the native-speaker predomi-

nance?). The same document mentions the intention of the organisation of collaboration with the Mozambican Ministry of Public Services "to develop English language (EL) learning programmes, design and implement courses and establish appropriate training to be relevant and applicable across all ministries", in the contest of the Global Strategy for Public Sector Reform launched by the Mozambique government in 2001 "to improve the performance of public officials" (McManus 2010, p.3). In Mozambique, the BC has also managed the Peacekeeping English project since 2005 (British Council 2006a, McManus 2010). In this project the BC works with the British Foreign and Commonwealth Office and the Ministry of Defence to improve the English language skills of military personnel assigned to international peacekeeping duties.

The rationale for the spread of English language in Mozambique rests mainly on functional arguments (Phillipson 1992), where the assertion is made that the status of English as a global reaching language provides immediate access to the biggest pool of resources (e.g. information, training) in comparison with Portuguese. This justification was used by Simon Ingram-Hill (2002 interview, Appendix 5), the then Director of the British Council Mozambique, to demonstrate the importance of English to DFID. Additional arguments are the links with the English-speaking regional neighbours and arguments revolving around the potential of English language to be a means for development, governance, capacity-building and poverty reduction. At present, the argument for the learning of English in Mozambique, according to the BC, is still associated with the international and regional status of the language: "Knowledge of English [in Mozambique] is seen as important in order to function effectively within SADC and on the wider global stage, and there is as a result a strong and growing interest in learning" (McManus 2010).

Piecing together the collected information, I would argue that the British Government's external language spread action in Mozambique, through the support provided by ODA/DFID to the STEP project, the supervision of the British Council and the input of the British partner institutions in the project, were able to implement and transfer the necessary structures and skills to allow English Language Teaching to be managed and implemented by the Mozambican themselves. The Ministry of Education has since reformed the English language curriculum at secondary level and redesigned teacher training. The maintenance of the system is not without difficulties, noted in my study trip in 2002 and confirmed in 2010, since the country does not have the financial resources to maintain some of the structures associated with the project (resources centres and distance learning training), particularly in face of increasing demand (Domingos 2010 email). The project targeted the masses through the education system (although it can be noted that the system still does not reach everyone) to increasingly younger audiences (now including the last two years of primary school). Thus the specific ELT work of the BC concentrated on target groups, namely, emerging leaders, middle and senior managers, young professionals (Ingram-Hill 2002). According to Renato Matusse (2002 interview), then the Mozambican SADC Co-ordinator for Culture, the United Kingdom was the leading country in terms of language cooperation with Mozambique. Many Mozambican cadres that have political and administrative leadership roles have studied in the UK for, at least, one year. A similar role, he foresaw, for Brazil, which was seeing some of their cooperation exchange students reaching top jobs at the head of universities. In his opinion, this, in the future, would strengthen the ties with Brazil. I see this as additional evidence of Mazrui and Mazrui (1998c, p.81) argument about the impact of language on elites and their action. Although no official comment was obtained regarding the present targeted groups by the BC Mozambique, from the programmes available (which I briefly refer ahead), youth and leaders are still prominently targeted audiences. Overall the changes regarding audiences and programmes relate, in my view, with changes in political discourse and policy that in the UK define the work of the BC as public diplomacy.

At this point, to understand the BC's present use of non-specific ELT projects, it is useful to note that the official discourses and policies regarding British cultural relations have, since the late 1990s, started to place an emphasis on public diplomacy. In the 1997/98 BC report, that coincides with the government change from Conservative to the Labour Party, discussions on the role of public diplomacy and the export of creative Britain underlie Sir Martin Jacomb's final statement as Chairman of the British Council:

> In order to exert a positive influence in the world, and promote the UK's interests, we cannot depend on military or economic strength. We must as a nation, reach beyond formal government-to-government dealings and, through cultural activities, foster relationships directly with peoples overseas. Governments have come more and more to recognize this.
>
> The present government has made clear its belief in the importance of spreading knowledge of Britain's cultural creativity. This is our role and we welcome this new enthusiasm (British Council 1998, p.4)

1998 was a year of great change for the BC. Pushed to find new sources of funding, streamline its network, and increase efficiency, the Council targeted younger audiences (not just the traditional opinion and decision makers), invested in information technology and communications to reach a wider audience (moving away from physical sites) and worked on building partnerships with other organisations (Fotheringham, Director of Planning at the British Council in London, interview 2002). Some impact of this shift can be observed in the

BC's work in Mozambique as the 2001-02 British Council Mozambique's Country Plan (Woods 2001) mentioned one of the strategic objectives was "(t)o promote wider and more effective learning of the English language in Mozambique, especially as a means of influencing young people's views of the UK".

In 2005, British cultural diplomacy underwent a major review, as mentioned in section 2.1.3.3, that established the Public Diplomacy Board and set as mission for the British Council to influence the change of behaviours in line with Her Majesty's Government.

The UK's contemporary thinking and policy making in cultural relations is greatly influenced by Nye's soft power theory and associated ideas (section 2.1.3.3). Current approaches used by the British Council to develop its cultural relations work can be associated with Nye's prescriptions. Martin Davidson, the chief executive of the British Council, defends the use of the new approach to foreign diplomacy: "One which recognises the international context has changed and one which delivers influence through establishing understanding and trust between nations" (Davidson 2007, p.2). The cultural relations developed under what he calls 'new public diplomacy' are "not uniquely an instrument of Government, but a pragmatic vehicle for systematically developing engagement, understanding and trust between peoples, communities and cultures - creating a platform of influence which, in our [the British Council] case, supports the UK's long term interests" (Davidson 2007, p.2). Davidson (2007, p.9) offers a view of the BC activity as "modelling the open behaviour that we [the UK] as a nation seek from those with whom we interact". Moreover he (2007, p.12) adds: "We want to recognise that people have their own hearts and minds, and that what we want is shared understanding, not a monolithic world view or even a polarised world, one where people have to sign up to one version of the truth against another". This view implies the use of culture as a potential resource for the creation of soft power - which ultimately will depend on how it is used (Nye 2010, p. 4 and 14). It is thus critical to analyse the impact of the UK's interest in the positive context of mutuality, trust, understanding and engagement that is allegedly being built between the UK and other countries.

I would argue that the above-presented laudable view of mutuality in British cultural relations carries in itself a monolithic, one-way attitude towards language relations. Moreover I would argue that the UK's self interest has the external spread of English language as a major cornerstone and this ultimately undermines the positive benign context in which cultural relations are built, since it implies asymmetrical linguistic relations. Developing his rationale above, Davidson (2007, p.12) notes "Mutuality means what it says: a return for both parties. There is always something tangible for the other nation, and this can be summed up in a single word - access". However, the first bullet point he mentions as providing access is *"Access* to world-class training *to learn the global language of English"*, the second *"Access to globally-recognised qualifications* and through those, access to employment and trade in a globalised economy" (2007, p.12, my highlight in italics). He (2007, p.15) states further that "We offer access to skills, training, qualifications, culture and the English language. And in return we get access to young leaders and, increasingly, to wider populations too". Additionally, he (2007, p.13) comments that "We don't run the InterAction programme or Dreams and Teams [examples of programmes developed to provide access, one through leadership training, the other through sports connections, both involving Africa, and namely Mozambique] purely for altruistic reasons. We do it because we want to build networks and to develop influence for the UK". It is clear and public the strategy and intentions of the British government in the use of public diplomacy, already mentioned, to influence and do business ("Britain is a country worth doing business with" in Davidson 2007, p.18). Philllipson (1992 and 2009a) has extensively exposed English linguistic imperialism and British ELT, and how "(t)he structural power of English generates English-extrinsic resources, just as the English-extrinsic resources have consolidated the structural power of English" (Phillipson 1992, p.278). In the contemporary context of international cultural relations, that appears to show signs of paradigm shift to genuine collaboration (Fisher 2009), the issue of linguistic human rights must constitute an important debate. Incidentally, Fisher's (2009) research denies this paradigm shift in the UK in clear opposition to the official discourse.

Meanwhile the export of English language has been a growing business for the BC, pushed to find alternative sources of funding to the governmental grant-in-aid. The British Council's earned income from activities such as teaching and examinations accounted in 2008-09 for more than 48% of the total GB £644,824 million resources of the Council (British Council 2009). The steady importance of these activities in the financing of the BC will further increase as the body faces cuts in real terms given adjustments in its grant and the economic downturn. Thus the 2008-11 corporate plan stresses as solutions to "move from large number of small-scale projects to fewer, larger-scale programmes", "increase impact through expanding our earned income activity", "to work for a major stepping up of our partnerships with other organisations" (British Council 2007, p.22). Thus most of the projects now developed in Mozambique by the BC are regional programmes, large scale projects such as Power in the Voice (2005-08), a project that grew from an initiative in Mozambique, and used art forms such as slam poetry, rap and hip hop to reach large, youthful audiences; Dreams + Teams Africa (2007-08) used sport to engage young people and partners UK and African schools. International Inspiration, launched in Mozambique in 2009, aims that "By 2012 each child in Mozambican school will experience 2hrs of quality PE and each PE teacher will have access to materials and technique to support the future development of PE in school" (MacManus 2010). The above examples demonstrate in practice the public diplomacy action of the BC based on the implementation of large-scale projects. The importance of these for language spread is indirect through the reinforcement of regional and international links where English language dominates.

I would like to restate again that my critique of language spread, and in particular of English language spread, must be seen in the context of my stand in defence of a balanced linguistic societal equilibrium. I find that European countries promote and reinforce the structural advantage of their international languages and contribute to the lack of use of the other languages. While, in the contemporary world, the need for international languages is undeniable, governments actively seeking to spread them should also foster the use of other languages – in the case of Africa, part of their cultural/language spread budgets and know-how should also be applied to the local languages.

Although the UK, through the British Council maintains a predominant role in English language spread in Mozambique, many other partners reinforce that task and compete for the same 'business'. These include many NGOs, such as VSO - in Mozambique since 1996 and one of the partners in the implementation of STEP - as well as the diplomatic services of other countries such as Australia and the USA. For instance, the Peace Corps (in Mozambique since 1998) intervenes in eight of the ten provinces of the country, where volunteers provide: "*quality English* and science instruction to over 19,000 students in secondary and technical schools. They also work with Mozambican colleagues to expand the range of teaching methodologies, improve English communication skills, and provide assistance in completing certification responsibilities for the national in-service training program" (my emphasis in italics) (Peace Corps 2010). The Aga Khan Foundation has plans to build an Aga Khan Academy in Maputo, which will use English as a medium of teaching. ETL is also undertaken by Mozambican institutions, private schools and the semi-public Instituto de Línguas (Language Institute, that has been supported by the ODA, British Embassy, NORAD, AIDAB and SADC). The Instituto Superior Pedagógico has an English Department that has run a Licenciatura (bachelor's degree) in ELT, since the beginning of the 1990s.

4.1.3.4 The External Language Spread Policy of France in Mozambique

I start this section with a quote from the Document Cadre de Partenariat France-Mozambique (2006-2010):

> Although France has long been present in Mozambique, where it opened its first consulate in 1895 and its first embassy in 1976, Mozambique's membership of the Community of Portuguese Speaking Countries and its predominantly Anglophone [regional] context, with the notable exception of Madagascar, explain the relative weakness of bilateral exchanges.[40] (Ministère des Affairs Étrangères 2006)

This official description of France's positioning in Mozambique, I argue, is illustrative of the French view of international relations - one marked by European based politico linguistic and cultural divisions. Mozambique's multiple membership of politico linguistic blocs is alluded to as a reason for the historical weakness in bilateral relations. This implies, in my view, an interpretation of those memberships as channels of influence that potentially preclude or compete with each other. As I attempt to demonstrate in this case study, this stance will ultimately determine French foreign policy priorities and activities in Mozambique.

Despite the existence of a convention, regularly renewed since 1981, establishing the Agence Française de Développement's intervention in Mozambique (Ambassade de France au Mozambique 2007), cultural cooperation between France and Mozambique started truly in 1989 with the creation of a Mission de Coopération et d'Action Culturelle, today the Service de Coopération et d'Action Culturelle (SCAC) of the French Embassy. In 1995, the Centro Cultural Franco-Moçambicano (Franco-Mozambican Cultural Centre, CCFM) became the second agent for French cultural policy implementation dealing with all cultural aspects not under the umbrella of SCAC, which deals with education and French language *per se* (Belorgey, Director of CCFM, 2002 interview).

French Cooperation (Ministère des Affairs Étrangères 2000, p.21) evaluating ten years (1989-1999) of presence in Mozambique highlighted how they have followed the Mozambican government priorities (a common yet controversial assertion that all donors make and that I will discuss in Chapter 5) and described its activities as being concentrated on sanitary and social support, the reinforcement of the rule of law, support to governance and promotion of

---

40 "Bien que la France soit présente de longue date au Mozambique, où elle a ouvert son premier consulat em 1895 et sa première ambassade en 1976, l'appartenance du Mozambique à la Communauté des Pays de Langue Officielle Portugaise et son environnement majoritairement anglophone, à l'exception notable de Madagascar, expliquent la relative faiblesses des échanges bilatéraux."

private enterprise. The same document stressed the commitment to the promotion of French as a foreign language, the reinforcement of *Francophonie* and the development of cultural actions. These linguistic and cultural objectives have remained stable in the bilateral relations between the two countries. The present cultural and educational cooperation between Mozambique and France, positioning the defence of cultural diversity as a major theme for the bilateral relations, maintains a "dynamic policy in favour of the French language and of Francophony"[41] (Ministère des Affaires Étrangères 2006, p.4): "A strong linguistic activity responds today to the demand of Mozambique, influenced by Latin culture and keen to encourage the practice of French as a compulsory foreign language"[42] (Ministère des Affaires Étrangères 2006, p.2). It is interesting to note the use of the concept of cultural diversity to legitimize the spread of French - I will return to this subject in Chapter 5. It is also worth noting the expression "the demand of Mozambique". I explore the Mozambican government's willingness to reintroduce and spread French further into the section. I will now analyse the main activities developed by the SCAC and the CCFM that impact on external language spread.

The Service de Coopération et d'Action Culturelle (SCAC) concentrates its action in two areas: educational and cultural development and institutional development (reconstruction of the state at administrative, social and economic levels). I will limit my analysis to those activities directly relevant to French language spread, namely, teacher training, scholarships, language courses and liaisons with universities. The main projects of SCAC in the area of human and cultural development during the 1990s in Mozambique were:

- Support to the reintroduction of French teaching (1994)
- Construction of the Centre Culturel Franco-Mozambicain (CCFM) (1996) and support to cultural exchange
- The French School of Maputo
- Implantation of Radio France Internationale (1990)
  (Ambassade de France au Mozambique 2007)

Of the above projects I focus my attention on the reintroduction of French and the role and activities of the CCFM. Before proceeding I would like to mention that regional cooperation with the (Francophone) Indian Ocean is an important theme of French-Mozambican cooperation. This is interesting to the

---

41   The source in French reads: "une politique dynamique en faveur de la language française et de la francophonie".

42   "Une action linguistique forte répond aujourd'hui à la demande du Mozambique, influencé par la culture latine et soucieux d'encourager la pratique du français, langue étrangère obligatoire"

study because often justifications for external languages spread invoke the usefulness of a particular language in the construction of regional connections. French language usefulness in Mozambique is often stressed in those terms, as I will explain. Mauritius, Madagascar, Mayotte, and Reunion are connected to the colonial history of Mozambique and France is keen to support those connections: "Politically, the French Government is firmly committed to the valorisation of overseas regions in this area [Indian Ocean] and the promotion of exchanges with neighboring countries"[43] (Ambassade de France au Mozambique 2010a, p.1). In that sense France sponsors a cultural festival in Ilha de Moçambique, cultural links with Mayotte and Reunion and sponsors university links between Mozambican universities and universities in Reunion (Ambassade de France au Mozambique 2010a). The SCAC provides scholarships, some specifically for French language teaching, however, as is the case with other donors, these are increasingly been offered for training in the country or in the sub-region to avoid brain drain.

Throughout the 1990s and most of the 2000s, investment in the spread of French language was a top priority for French diplomacy in Mozambique. France developed several projects to support the reintroduction and extension of the teaching of French in Mozambique:

> Virtually disappeared in Mozambique, French (one of three official languages of SADC) has regained its status as 2nd mandatory living language since the end of the civil war through a strong political will.
>
> Two first projects in 1994 (900 000 euros) and 1998 (1.2 million euros) devoted to the reintroduction and expansion of the teaching of French in Mozambique resulted in an increase from 400 to over 19,000 learners.
>
> A new ongoing project (2002-2006) aims to build a team of "trainers of trainers" and secondary school teachers, the ultimate goal being the creation of a sustainable system of initial and ongoing training of over 500 secondary school teachers, which will be in charge of training 52,000 students ...
>
> Concurrently training in professional French is provided for executives in government and business wishing to open their economic and cultural activities to the surrounding francophone world (west Africa and Indian Ocean).[44] (Ambassade de France au Mozambique 2010c)

---

43 "Au plan politique, le Gouvernment français s'est engagé résolument dans la valorisa-tion des régions outre-mer dans cette zone [Indian Ocean] et la promotion des échanges avec les pays voisins"

44 "Pratiquement disparu au Mozambique, le français (une des 3 langues officielles de la SADC) a retrouvé son statut de 2éme langue vivant obligatoire depuis la fin de la guerre civile grâce à une volonté politique forte.

The above text retrieved from the French embassy's website in Mozambique illustrates the magnitude of the effort that successfully reintroduced French into the Mozambican educational system and extended its use. French language spread worked by increasing the supply of French teaching and thus, in my view, created an artificial demand for French language learning, given the inclusion of French as mandatory discipline in the last two years of secondary school. French cooperation also provided the means for the self perpetuation of the scheme (similar to the English strategy referred to in the previous section), through the creation of in-country training - Phillipson's (2006) analogy of English as a cuckoo does spring to mind, although we are talking of a different language and setting.

I would like to further illustrate my argument with the extract of an interview (FIPF 2008) to a Mozambican participant at an international conference of French teachers, that besides teaching French also works for the Mozambican Ministry of Education and Culture (which I also interviewed in 2002):

Why did you choose to teach French and not another language?

It was a bit by accident...I had finished my degree and I was selected amongst the best students to do training in France; I benefited from a scholarship. That training led to the teaching of French.

Why do your students learn French?

In Mozambique, French is a statutory discipline in the Humanities strand. In a year, French will be introduced at earlier stages (Grades 9 and 10), in which French will be optional.[45]

Deux premiers projets, en 1994 (900 000 Euros) puis 1998 (1,2 M Euros) consacrés à la réintroduction et à l'extension de l'enseignment du français au Mozambique on fait passer les effectifs de 400 à plus de 19 000 apprenants.

Un nouveau projet en cours (2002-2006) vise à constituer une équipe de "formateurs de formateurs" et de professeurs de lycée nationaux, l'objectif final étant la création d'un dispositif pérenne de formation initiale et continue de plus de 500 professeurs de lycée, qui seront en charge de la formation de 52 000 élèves...

Parallèllement sont assurées des formations en français de spécialité pour les cadres des administrations et des entreprises qui souhaitent ouvrir leurs activités économiques et culturelles au monde francophone environnant (Afrique de l'ouest et Océan Indien)."

45 *"Pourquoi avoir choisi d'enseigner le français et pas une autre langue ?*
Ça a été un peu un hasard... J'ai fini mon bac et j'ai été sélectionnée parmi les meilleurs élèves pour suivre une formation en France ; j'ai bénéficié d'une bourse. Cette formation conduisait à l'enseignement du français.
Pourquoi vos élèves apprennent-ils le français ?

The above dialogue clearly establishes how the asymmetrical position of the countries (source/target of external language spread; developed/developing) works in practice. The asymmetry of language and international relations (powerful European languages and states / powerless African languages and states) and the connection of language to access to development (scholarship/European training=better job prospects) easily open the way to language spread. It should be noted that I am not arguing against the fact that African populations acquire European languages, I argue against the fact that European countries and multilateral organisations perpetuate asymmetrical (linguistic) power relations that are detrimental to African languages and cultures.

As mentioned, French was abolished from the Mozambican education system after independence and was not taught in Mozambique's educational system from 1975 to 1996. Since 1989, French authorities had with the Mozambican Ministry of Education a joint project to expand the teaching of French language, a project that ultimately lead to its reintroduction in 1996. According to Hervé Brocard (2002 interview), the director of the French department at Universidade Pedagógica (Maputo), the (re)introduction of French was a request from the Mozambican government. However, a non-attributable source confirms that the French authorities suggested the project to the Ministry of Education. French authorities (Brocard 2002, p.1) analysing the rationale for the Mozambican political willingness to reintroduce French in the national education system arrived at the following reasons:

1. Historical: continuous presence of a small Francophile and sometimes still Francophone élite in Mozambique, formed during the pre-independence educational system, when French was taught as the first foreign language, that found renewed vitality enabling it to influence political key holders;
2. Political: Perception that French language facilitated relations with Francophone Africa and the Indian Ocean, therefore providing opportunity to diversify external relations and benefit from closer ones with France and other Francophone countries;
3. Cultural and scientific: Evolving perception of French language not just as a language of a great culture and with large diffusion, but also as a gateway to knowledge and high level training in all domains.

The above are typical arguments for the adoption of international European languages in Africa. The first can be connected to language as a determinant of

---

Au Mozambique, le français est obligatoire pour les classes de lettres. Dans un an, le français sera introduit à des niveaux inférieurs (9e et 10e), dans lesquels le français sera optionnel."

policy through the assimilation of elites as identified by Marzrui and Marzrui (1998c, p.81) (section 2.2.1). The other two sets of reasons can be interpreted in the context of Ansre (1979) - the 'shrinking' world and access to technological development arguments - and Phillipson (1992) - the functional argument explored respectively in sections 2.2.2.1 and 2.2.3.1. Thus I argue that the Mozambican government's 'demand', 'willingness' or 'strong political will' can be interpreted as being more induced than the result of free will. This inducement relates, in my view, to the conjunction of a series of factors that include: the structural power of international European languages, the legacies of colonialism that linger in Africa and allow the perpetuation of the top positioning of European languages, the political/economic/cultural interest of the European/Western countries in the maintenance of the association of development with their languages.

A remark by a French participant in a mission to Mozambique in 1990 in preparation for the project of the reintroduction of French in secondary schools (Appendix 6), adds to the previous reasons the statement of difference in relation to the Anglophone regional context:

> French is no longer taught after independence, but there is a real will of reintroducing it in education. The reasons are a will to open up to the Francophone world, a desire to facilitate access to higher and technical education in French, and also a worry of not giving into a monopole, the powerful attraction of the Anglophone world omnipresent by their frontiers. (Comté[46] 2002 interview)

Since the difference in relation to the geopolitical environment of the sub-region is already provided by the national official language, Portuguese, what is arguably provided is a diversification of the (European) languages of international communication taught in the national curriculum. This ultimately can facilitate contacts with countries and organisations using the particular language being spread, thus enabling the development of favourable economic/political relations and the sourcing of additional aid to development, since their spread is still ultimately connected to a source of economic and political power. Justifications for the spread of French in Mozambique collected during the fieldwork were: a Mozambican need, given the cooperation ties with many French-speaking countries (Comté, officer at the French Department of the Ministry of Education, and Ussene, English teacher at Nampula's Secondary School, 2002

---

46   Remarks on page 3 of a printed four-page document supplied by Comté (2002 interview, see appendix 6) and containing no direct indication of source, but clearly attributable by its content to the participants in the French Mission to Mozambique in preparation for the project of the reintroduction of French language in secondary education, 14 to 21 October 1990.

interviews), the existence of many scholarships for French-speaking countries (Ussene 2002 interview). Again these arguments relate to the usefulness of French and its ties with country and personal development.

The initial project of the reintroduction of French also had the native-speaker myth as a language ideal:

> Teaching, in its first stage, can only, according to the Ministry [MINED], be trusted to the French, as - we quote - "we would not trust the teaching of Portuguese language to Brazilians".[47] (*ibid.*)

This further reinforces my above comment regarding the linkage of language spread to a centre. As I mentioned when examining the politico linguistic blocs in Chapter 2, France was active in the establishment of a Latin bloc (section 2.3.1.2), this vision is evident in some of the perceptions found during research. The director of the French department at Universidade Pedagógica (Maputo), Hervé Brocard (2002 interview), while highlighting the importance of pluralism in the context of an agreed linguistic consensus in Mozambique, also saw French as a political flag against the English-speaking world; French as part of the Latin bloc against the extremely strong English-speaking domination. It is also worth noting the indicated preference for Portugal in relation to the support for the teaching of Portuguese in Mozambique - a preference easily understood in relation to the historical context of colonial domination.

The project of the reintroduction of French aimed at: extending the teaching of French in secondary schools across the country; establishing certified local quality training for teachers of French; allowing Mozambican cadres to pursue high level training in France or in Francophone countries; and favouring access to information in French. In Mozambique it developed Francophone hubs and allowed the development of cooperation relations between Mozambique, France and the rest of the Francophone world (Ambassade de France au Mozambique 2002, p.2). The process was developed in three stages (Brocard 2002 interview):

1. 1994 to 1998 (Re)introduction of French in Mozambique;
2. 1999 to 2001 Support to the teaching of French;
3. 2002 to 2006 Support to the training of teachers, including distance learning (Beira and Nampula).

The basis of the first stage started with the financing of a training programme for Mozambican teachers by French Cooperation in 1989. According to Comté (2002 interview) a first group of 15 or 16 Mozambican teachers went to

---

47   "Pour ce faire l'enseignement, dans sa première phase, ne pourrait, selon le Ministre, être confié qu'à des Français, de même que - nous le citons - "on ne confiait pas celui du portugais à des Brésiliens."

France in 1989, and a second group of 16 teachers went in 1990. On their return, MINED was able to reintroduce French in the pre-university years (11th and 12th grades) in some secondary schools in Maputo. In 1994/1995, also on the basis of these returning teachers, a French Department at Universidade Pedagógica was also opened to carry on in-country teacher training. In 1995, French teaching started to spread to the provinces, and, in 1998, a new project to include its teaching to all pre-university grades was initiated. Until 2002 this project was supported by French cooperation, both financially, in terms of human resources and also in the supply of equipment (e.g. IT). A transition period followed until 2006, with a reduction in the financial levels of investment from the French cooperation and new objectives. Meanwhile the teaching of French has been extended to earlier grades. In 2009 the teaching of French was expanded to the 9th grade and in 2010 to the 10th grade, in both as optional discipline. Expansion also took place geographically. The teaching of French that in 2002 was mainly centred on Maputo now covers most of the country, with the exception of a small number of schools that lack the necessary infrastructure (Comté 2002 interview, Mabunda 2010 interview).

French financial support to the project of the re-introduction of French language in Mozambique ended in 2008. In 2010 the officials at the Mozambican Ministry of Education and Culture are working with a French technical assistant in the development of new projects that will enable the relationship to continue (Mabunda 2010 interview). Meanwhile a new multilateral partner is involved in French language spread in Mozambique. Since 2008, French language in Mozambique has been supported by the Organisation Internationale de la Francophonie. The project aims to locally produce French teaching books - currently for 9th and 10th grades and subsequently for the 11 and 12th grades (Mabunda 2010 interview). This new involvement of the multilateral francophone organisation in French language spread in Mozambique appears to be connected with the missions sent to seven countries (Mozambique, Burundi, Ghana, Greece, Laos, Lebanon and Romania) in 2008 by Abdou Diouf, Secretary General of La Francophonie, to witness OIF's interest in their efforts to promote French language and to know about their "ambitions regarding the valorisation of French language in their country"[48] (OIF 2008).

A paramount symbol of French cultural diplomacy in Mozambique is undoubtedly the Centro Cultural Franco-Moçambicano (CCFM). The CCFM, opened in July 1995, in the renovated Club Hotel building in the centre of Maputo, is the largest French cultural centre in Africa, comprising a 700 place thea-

---

48   "connaître leurs ambitions en matière de valorisation de la langue française dans leur pays"

tre, a 180 places auditorium, exhibition and course rooms, press room, library, internet access, bar, offices and garden area. CCFM is *per se* an important cultural infrastructure in Maputo. CCFM is one of the five bi-national French centres in Africa, along with Guinea-Bissau (Bissau), Guinea-Conakry (Conakry), Namibia (Windhoek) and Niger (Niamey). The status and mission of the bi-national centres is different from the French Cultural Centres. These are the full-responsibility of the French government and have as their mission to be a show-case for French culture. The CCFM is the object of an agreement between the French and Mozambican governments to build a structure for cultural cooperation, whereby the Mozambican government maintains ownership of the building and the French government pays for the operational costs - in addition to having spent 40 million French Francs (over five million GBP) on its renovation and enlargement. French authorities present it as an instrument of cultural dialogue, not solely between Mozambique and France, but extending to many countries and organisations (Ministère de Affaires Étrangères 2000, p.23). The mission the Franco-Mozambican Cultural centre, as a bi-national centre, emphasises co-operation and development (Belorgey, Director of the CCFM, 2002 interview).

At the time of my study trip in 2002, the mission of the centre was according to its then director, François Belorgey (2002 interview), to promote the cultural and artistic richness of the countries through exchanges - not to import French culture. He stated that he worked mainly in a Francophone dimension, making exchanges with other Francophone African countries such as Mali and Senegal. He subscribed to a plural vision of Francophony, therefore saw his mission not in the promotion of French culture but working in exchanges between the Lusophone and Francophone spaces. The Director in 2010, Patrick Schmitt (2010 interview), although acknowledging the continuity of that mission of CCFM as a centre of promotion and exchange of the arts and culture, stressed the present vocation as also supporting the export of Mozambican cultural products and the professionalisation of Mozambican artists. This echoes the advice provided by the Gouteyron (2008) report on the crisis of French cultural diplomacy, mentioned in section 2.1.3.4, that French diplomacy should be at the service of culture, aiding in the internationalisation of cultural operators. This new aim is developed by enabling and supporting contacts between Mozambican artists and foreign cultural operators in the Indian Ocean, Europe and Latin America (Schmitt 2010 interview). Another important change in the mission of the centre is the reinforcement of the French language-teaching programme; as Schmitt (2010 interview) stressed, the CCFM is "an important centre for the teaching of French"[49]. This was justified in connection with the international use

---

49 "um importante centro de ensino da língua francesa".

of French language: "French is the third most useful language in Mozambique [after Portuguese and English] in terms of communication with the outside world"; "half of Africa speaks French"; "in the Indian Ocean everyone speaks French"[50] (Schmitt 2010 interview). This justification, relying on what Phillipson (1992, p.271) calls the functional arguments, echoes some of the predominant discourses about language in the political and public arenas, where importance is placed on the communicative role of European languages within and across countries, while African languages are (most often) totally ignored.

The broadening of the mission of the CCFM described above is underpinned by two main objectives that were set up in 2008: the opening of the CCFM to new audiences and the increase of Mozambican participation in decisions regarding the programmes of the Centre (Schmitt 2010 interview).

In the attraction of new audiences, two projects have been set up *Formação de Público* and new French language courses. In *Formação de Público* (which I liberally translate as Audience Building), the CCFM works with the older students from local secondary schools and organizes theatre plays and dance sessions that enable them to visit the Centre for the first time. This occasion is then used to explain the functioning of the Centre, stressing for instance that it is open to all and that they develop free and low cost activities. As CCFM's Director stressed, this outreach activity will bear fruits in the long term: "We invest in this sector of the population, because they are tomorrow's audiences"[51] (Schmitt 2010 interview). This early attempt to captivate the audiences of the future, at the same time that sensitises teenagers to cultural events, allows them a close contact with French culture and language spread - one, I am sure, French authorities hope will last and deepen. New courses of French are also being launched to target younger audiences. From September 2010, CCFM will offer specific courses for ages 16-20, including also preparation courses for the 12th grade exams. I find this fact interesting and ironic, in the sense that it is clearly connected to the reintroduction of French in the Mozambican education system, a process supported by the French government. The teaching of French has always been a component of the CCFM, albeit not as significant as at present. From a monthly average of 80 students, they now have 280 students attending courses in diversified times and rhythms of progression. The courses are attended by undergraduates and professionals. The centre is one of the least expensive places

---

50 The original words were "a língua francesa é a terceira língua mais útil em Moçambique em termos de comunicação com o mundo lá fora", "metade da África fala francês" and "no Oceano Índico todo o mundo fala francês".

51 "Investimos neste sector da população, porque são o público de amanhã"

to learn French - one of the reasons being because the teachers there are Mozambican - the myth of the native speaker lives on!

The second new objective of CCFM, the increase in the Mozambican participation in the decision process regarding the cultural events presented at CCFM, is being attained by the work of a project evaluation commission which comprises: CCFM, the Mozambican Ministry of Culture, relevant national cultural bodies (such as the National School of Visual Arts) and Mozambican cultural personalities. According to Schmitt (2010 interview), there is now a standard form (available at the centre and online) that allows anyone to present a project, which is then evaluated by the commission. It is apparently an effort in the democratisation of access and a sharing of responsibilities between French cultural representatives, the Mozambican authorities and the Mozambican artists. This is a positive aspect of French cultural action that nurtures the creation of a thriving, professional and democratic cultural and artistic environment in Mozambique, and at the same time a potential door for French and/or Francophone influence.

In 2002, the Director of CCFM, François Belorgey (2002 interview) said the centre was not a priority for the French government. He differentiated between the main policy objectives of the French government and their application to the realities of the different countries. He demonstrated this with the case of funds available for documentation centres on Contemporary France, which he requested and was awarded, but intended to use for a documentation centre on Lusophony and Francophony in Mozambique. He showed concern in building a policy adequate to the local conditions. In the case of Africa, he believed work should be developed on the causes of the migration fluxes to Europe, namely developing policies to foster regional integration, also at cultural level, and encourage the circulation of information and cultural products at horizontal level: South-South, instead of North-South. Since then changes have occurred. The documentation centre on Lusophony and Francophony did not go ahead, only one focused on the Francophone world and in supporting the learners of French is scheduled to open in 2011 - to exist alongside the one already in place in 2002 (Schmitt 2010 interview, Ambassade de France 2010b). It was not possible to determine why the documentation centre did not go ahead. A mix of causes can be advanced: spending cuts, changes in central policy and local management. In general, the Director in 2010, Patrick Schmitt (2010 interview) does not see the (forever ongoing) institutional changes in France, as referred in section 2.1.3.4, having an impact on the CCFM, given its bi-national status. Nevertheless, he admitted that the reduction of available monies, in the context of the present economic crisis, have forced the Centre to rethink its activities, for instance by relying more on in-country content than bringing programmes from abroad.

Overall, I see the mission and activities of the CCFM has having re-centred in the development of Mozambique's cultural and artistic *milieu*, in contrast to a previous broader regional interaction and concern due, arguably, to restrictions in financial resources and changes in local management. In addition, French language spread became an important part of the work of the Centre, the diversification of the courses allowing for additional income, but most importantly, to boost the reach of France's influence; overarching concerns and projects deployed to reach younger audiences along with the reinforcement of the Mozambican decision making in CCFM allow a legitimatised French influence to reach wider and younger audiences. As Schmitt (2010 interview) stressed the CCFM is "the first element of French cultural cooperation in Mozambique: the most visible and the most active"[52]. On this evidence the CCFM is a paradigmatic example of contemporary French cultural diplomacy, one where the logic of diffusion is sought to be replaced by a diplomacy of influence in line with the latest thinking in French cultural diplomacy (Kergueris 2010), as discussed in section 2.1.3.4.

4.1.3.5 External Language Spread Policy of Germany in Mozambique

Germany is one of the donors contributing to support the Mozambique government, and the German cooperation's priorities for Mozambique are education, decentralisation and economic and sustainable development. In 2003 Germany became the latest player in the area of external language and cultural spread to operate in Mozambique. The analysis of its strategy, if brief, is important as it brings new elements to my analysis of external LSPs.

> The Cultural Institute Mozambique – Germany (Instituto Cultural Moçambique-Alemanha ICMA) is a project of the Mozambique-Germany Friendship (Association Associação de Amizade Moçambique-Alemanha AAMA) for the promotion of the intercultural dialogue between Mozambique and Germany. (Goethe Institut/ICMA 2010)

This is how the Instituto Cultural Moçambique-Alemanha (ICMA), founded in 2003 and operating in Maputo, presents itself online. ICMA is part of the Goethe Institut network as a 'sociedade cultural' (cultural society) - these institutions work within the norms of the Goethe Institut and also offer similar programs (Goethe Institut 2008, p.2). In the case of Mozambique, the activities of the ICMA are coordinated by the regional Goethe Institut in Johannesburg.

---

52   "o primeiro elemento da cooperação cultural francesa em Moçambique: é o mais visível e o mais activo"

The German embassy in Maputo stresses the importance of the cultural policy as the third pillar of German foreign policy and highlights the importance, for German - Mozambican cultural relations, of the 26,000 Mozambicans that as students and workers lived in the former Democratic Republic of Germany and that on their return to their country maintain their fluency in the German language and organize themselves in associations: "Several ministers and vice-ministers of the Mozambican Government, as well as two governors are examples of those that returned"[53] (Embaixada da Alemanha Maputo 2010). As argued by Mazrui and Mazrui (1998c, p.81) this language linkage to the elites can be a major determining factor. In this section I explore the argument that this linkage partially explains the present strategy of German language spread, I also discuss how Germany appears to be following a similar strategy to France in terms of external language spread policy in Mozambique, although enveloped by an arguably more enlightened *modus operandi*.

In this light it is interesting to note the German embassy's more comprehensive explanation of the birth of ICMA: "born out a model cooperation between the Goethe Institut in Johannesburg, the Germany Embassy in Maputo and three organizations of Mozambicans that had lived in Germany "[54] (Embaixada da Alemanha Maputo 2010). Thus ICMA is not merely a civil society initiative, as the initial citation at the beginning of this section could lead one to believe, but also a government project.

The aim of the Goethe Institut in Africa is "achieving the classical tasks of the Goethe Institut - to transmit the German language and an up to date image of the Federal Republic of Germany, as well as encouraging international cultural cooperation - , also provide aesthetic and discursive contributions to the process of modernization and development of the region"[55] (Goethe Institut 2008, p.2) The Goethe Institut has since 2008 intensified its activity in sub-Saharan Africa to "develop stable structures for cooperation in the areas of culture and teaching"[56], within the program 'Aktion Afrika' launched by the German Federation Minister of External Affairs, Frank-Walter Steinmeier (Goethe Institut 2008, p.2). The Goethe Institut cultural projects in Africa have a marked pan-African

---

53 "Vários ministros e vice-ministros do Governo moçambicano, bem como dois governadores são exemplos de tais "regressados""

54 "nascido de uma cooperação em projecto-modelo entre o Instituto Goethe em Joanesburgo, a Embaixada Alemão em Maputo e três organizações de regressados"

55 "além de cumprir com as tarefas clássicas do Goethe-Institut – transmitir a língua alemã e uma imagem atualizada da República Federal da Alemanha, assim como fomentar a cooperação cultural internacional -, também aportar com contribuições estéticas e discursivas ao processo de modernização e desenvolvimento da região"

56 "desenvolver estruturas estáveis para a cooperação nos âmbitos da cultura e do ensino"

dimension, that is, the different bodies of the Goethe network in the different African countries join to undertake a wide variety of projects, bringing together artists and professionals of different nationalities. Exchanges of artists with Germany are also in place. In practice, this provides a rich and appealing context for the development of external language spread policies.

In terms of language spread ('linguistic work' in the Goethe's Institut terminology), the Goethe Institut has, in sub-Saharan Africa, ten Goethe Instituts and seven Goethe centers that directly offer German courses, plus three other centres that are also supported by the Goethe Institut (Goethe Institut 2008, p.7). Out of the 47 countries of sub-Saharan Africa, 14 have German being taught in their educational systems, and other countries, among which is Mozambique, are reported as beginning to be interested in introducing the German language as a foreign language in their educational systems (Goethe Institut 2008, p.7). This introduction is always supported by what the Goethe Institut calls 'educational specialists': "These specialists are advisors to the education authorities, to schools and teachers, supporting the networks of collaboration, organizing training seminars, assisting with events promoting German language and with cultural events for students"[57] (Goethe Institut 2008, p.7). As previously noted the influence of these advisors in the policy making process is undeniable but difficult to prove. I was unable to confirm the reported interest of Mozambique in introducing German in the education system, but see it as a likely possibility. It is in that sense that at the beginning of the section I hinted that Germany could be following a similar strategy to the French one: reinforce supply and encourage demand.

The Goethe Institut (2008, p.7) identifies the following reasons why in Africa there is desire to learn the German language:

- economic and tourism connection between the African countries and the German language countries;
- advantages in professional terms and in the world of business;
- interest in studying at university level in Germany (due in part to the presence of the German language in the curricula of those countries);
- new immigration laws in Germany only allow visas for husbands/wives to visit the other living in Germany if they can prove having knowledge of the German language;
- professionals that wish to work directly with Germans and Germany.

---

57 "Estes especialistas são assessores para as autoridades de educação, para escolas e professores, dão acompanhamento às redes de colaboração, organizam seminários de aperfeiçoamento, colaboram com eventos de promoção da língua alemã e em eventos culturais para alunos"

The arguments advanced by the Goethe Institut are not dissimilar to those of the other agents of external LSPs - the functional arguments, particularly connected with economic benefits (tourism, business, professional development) dominate. At the same time the perception of Germany in Africa as a center of excellence for learning is no different to that of other European countries - although in different degrees. It is interesting to note the actual acknowledgment of the fact that German being in the curricula of the countries favours interest in studying in Germany.

If German cultural diplomacy is similar to other European ones, I found in the Mozambican operation an interesting distinction. The work of ICMA in Maputo is distinct from the work of other cultural centers in the sense that besides teaching German they also have courses of Changana, the predominant African language in the area of Maputo. I find particularly significant the offer of an African language course in a foreign cultural center, as I see this as an example of good practice of what cultural relations and language spread activities should aim for: an interaction geared for cultural and linguistic balance.

4.1.4 Perceptions and Discourses about Languages and Policies in Mozambique

In this section I discuss perceptions and discourses about languages and policies in Mozambique that are important for external language spread in the context of this study. These include: language relations and competition; Portuguese and African languages; external language spread policies and politico linguistic blocs; and the cultural centre as an instrument of external cultural policy.

4.1.4.1 Language Relations and Competition

I start this section with a description of linguistic attitudes registered in the capital city of Maputo by Katupha (1991, p.11):

> Portuguese is generally regarded as a language of success, power and social prestige amongst those who speak only the local languages. Amongst those who can speak Portuguese, the great majority defends the view that the African languages ought to be used in all aspects of life as much as Portuguese. However, when it comes to comparing Portuguese and other European languages, most of those who can speak it regard English as the language for further opportunities of success, especially amongst the younger generation.

Although made in 1991, this observation is regarded as valid, given the increased profile of English as an international language, the predominance of the western model of development in Africa, and the regional context.

Within this linguistic context, as pointed out at the beginning of this study, perceptions of Portuguese language being threatened was a common topic during the 1990s - in particular from sources originating in Portugal, although not exclusively. For example[58], an article by a Mozambican journalist in one of the main Portuguese daily newspapers, reporting a Mozambican Conference on National Culture and implying Portuguese language status could be revised, had as headline: "A Portuguese Goodbye: Portuguese Language loses strength in Mozambique and there are those who think of English for "official language"" in *Público* (19.07.1993). The start of the headline is an allusion to the Portuguese film *Um Adeus Português* (1985) by João Botelho, the first to explicitly use the colonial war as the drama focus, and also transmits the main idea of the article which is the loss of influence by Portugal in Mozambique, here symbolised by the possibility of potential loss of official status in favour of English. Effectively English, as demonstrated, had been spreading in Mozambique as foreign language, not as an alternative to Portuguese as official language. As Mozambican sociolinguist Armando Jorge Lopes (1998, p.43) reports, "Mozambican administrative elites are quite keen to develop their spoken and written English", but "they have not reacted negatively against Portuguese nor have they ever indicated they would favour a substitution of the present official language" - the one substitution he saw as likely would be also affording Bantu languages official status, which "would, certainly, be normal, and a fair resolution with regard to the languages spoken in Mozambique for centuries". Thus in Mozambique, Portuguese language was not threatened; rather it is a threat to most African languages spoken in the country.

However, this perception of linguistic threat reflects political concerns about the postcolonial relationship between Portugal and Mozambique. It is worth noting that during the 1990s the concept of Lusophony was being established and the cultural/linguistic label was increasingly being used (mainly at a political level) to foster the communalities of the countries connected with Portuguese language, culminating in the constitution in 1996 of the CPLP. At the same time Mozambique was diversifying its relations and a year before, in 1995, joined the Commonwealth. Reactions in Portugal evidenced, from some sectors, an outdated colonial mindset haunted by the ghosts of the Scramble for Africa (section 2.2.1), which is exemplified in the following headline: "Portugal Chagrined": "England, our ally, will achieve now with the Commonwealth what Queen Victoria didn't"[59] in *O Diabo* (28.11.1995). These sorts of declarations were often dismissed as emotional by the Portuguese authorities. For instance, José Soares

---

58   Further examples in original transcripts are available in Appendix 7.
59   See Appendix 7 for fuller original transcripts.

Martins, Portuguese cultural attaché in Maputo from 1978 to 1997, rejected any concerns about the future of Portuguese language in Mozambique and highlighted the distortion in the reading of Mozambican society by Portugal (Bandeira 1998). British authorities in Mozambique were aware of sensitivities in relation to English language and the role of the UK, as is clear in the British Ambassador speech during the National Conference of English Language Teaching held in 1994: "Clearly, Britain, the home of English, is particularly well-placed to assist in the development of English Language Teaching in Mozambique. This is not a question, to use a German phrase, of 'Kulturkampf' or *a language war*. We are responding to a strong and rising demand" (Eduardo and Uprichard 1995, p.11, my emphasis in italics).

During the research for this study Arabic also was referenced as a threat to Portuguese in Africa, namely in Guinea-Bissau (Lemos 2002 interview), which led to the subject also being investigated in Mozambique. Mention was found of an increasing islamisation in Mozambique, highlighting the linguistic weight of the Koranic schools (Cavacas 1994, p.19). In Mozambique, the Muslim religion is embraced by 17,8% of the population, and the country is, since 1994, a member of the Organization of the Islamic Conference. Historically, the Muslim presence is concentrated in the North. At present, the situation is, as described by Vaux *et al.* (2006, p.11):

> There has been an influx of funding from the Middle East for mosques and Koranic schools but it is almost inconceivable that Islamic extremists could gain a foothold here. Islamic practice is so lax that sterner Muslims would receive no support from local people. Money may create some manifestations of religious formality but these are likely to be superficial. Tension between Christians and Moslems is remarkably absent.

This description matches what was found during the field research: peaceful cultural coexistence and the use of Arabic as a religious language (Jamú, Muslim leader at Ilha de Moçambique, 2002 interview). During field research, evidence of the importance of Koranic schools in the Mozambican system was found in the Island of Mozambique, province of Nampula, a predominantly Muslim region. There, the Madrasa Pre-School Programme (started in 2000), developed by the Aga Khan Foundation, seeks to organise communities around pre-school education, in an attempt to increase the attainment of students in primary schools, by preparing children for schooling in Portuguese (Juma interview 2002).

The threat of Arabic to Portuguese language can be framed within Huntington's (1996, p.63) influential paradigm of the Clash of Civilizations: "As the power of the West gradually declines relative to that of other civilizations, the use of English and other Western languages in other societies and for communications between societies will also slowly erode." Also the security concerns, boosted by the terrorist attacks since 9/11/2001, made their imprint in contemporary discourse on cultural coexistence, where the "Islam and the rest" dichotomy is recurrent.

In Mozambique, the main issue in the area of language relations and competition is not between Portuguese and English (or Arabic), but between Portuguese and the local African languages. The place to accord the different African languages and their relation to the official language appears more problematic. Although the inclusion of African languages in the first years of the educational system is being implemented and expanded, the results of that initiative are still unclear, as already pointed out.

4.1.4.2 Portuguese and African Languages

At the beginning of the Mozambique case study I explored the role of Portuguese as main cornerstone in the construction of Mozambican identity and the importance of the political elite in that process. As Mozambique's most renowned writer, Mia Couto (2009, p.118) observes: "Mozambique lives the logic of a centralising State, of processes of cultural and linguistic uniformisation. The negation of that domestic globalisation is, often, done through the sacralisation of what is called tradition"[60]. African languages and oral tradition are a fundamental part of the traditional African cultural space, one that is inhabited by the majority of the Mozambican population, in opposition to the minority elite(s), which Couto (2009, p.44) describes as "a nation within a nation, a nation that arrives first, that amongst itself exchanges favours, that lives in Portuguese and sleeps in the pillow of writing"[61].

Evidence from Mozambican society, although showing concerns over the role and the future of African languages, does not appear to contest the primacy of Portuguese. Some Mozambican elites see the spread of Portuguese as ideologically charged: it is felt that not enough attention and support is given to African languages. The Dean of the Faculty of the Arts at Universidade Eduardo Mondlane, Armindo Ngunga (2002 interview) believes that the elite that has Portuguese as mother tongue does everything for its spread, while viewing other languages as a threat. He defends a relation of complementarity between the

---

60 "Moçambique vive a lógica de um Estado centralizador, de processos de uniformização linguística e cultural. A negação dessa globalização doméstica é, muitas vezes, feita por via da sacralização daquilo que se chama tradição"

61 "uma nação dentro da nação, uma nação que chega primeiro, que troca entre si favores, que vive em português e dorme na almofada da escrita"

languages. He sees it as more than a purely linguistic issue and as requiring a broader political outlook - for instance, the rural population must be regarded as more than a source of votes. Intellectual Gabriel Simbine (2002 interview) attributes the defence of Portuguese language to the legacy of colonial divides that are still echoed in Mozambique society: "The sons of Portuguese, the *mulatos* [birth by Portuguese inter-marriage] and the *assimilados* [black people with a Portuguese passport] are the ones defending ferociously the Portuguese language. Their culture is Portuguese"[62]. In his opinion the complex of inferiority in relation to the African languages induced by colonialism still endures in Mozambican elites leading to the lack of political will in the development of those languages. This divide in Mozambican society was officially acknowledged in *Agenda 2025*, as mentioned earlier; however the solution still needs to be translated into feasible measures and implemented.

Mozambican writers have a de-problematised view of language akin to Achebe's new English (2.2.2.1). Mozambican writer and journalist, Calane da Silva (2010 interview), states that "Portuguese continues to be the preferential language of Mozambican writers, since that was the language in which they became literate. However as creators they search encompassing aesthetics, enriching the language with localisms"[63]. Mia Couto (2009, p.25) stresses that "There remains the idea that only African writers suffer what is called the «linguistic drama». It is true that colonization brought traumas of identity and alienation. But the truth, my friends, is that no writer has at its disposal a language already made. All of us have to find a language that reveals us as being unique and unrepeatable"[64]. Mia Couto (2002 interview) thus validates the idea of Portuguese (as a Mozambican language) as support of national unity, as long as the violence inherent in a process of linguistic unification is reduced to a minimum in the process of creation of a Mozambican nation. He also does not share Ngugi wa Thiong'o's thesis of colonisation of the mind and envisages Mozambicans as multilingual[65], using their African mother tongue, Portuguese and English.

---

62   "Os filhos de portugueses, os mulatos e os assimilados são os que defendem acerrimamente a língua portuguesa. A cultura deles é a portuguesa"

63   "o português continua a ser a preferência dos escritores moçambicanos, pois foi essa a língua em que foram alfabetizados"

64   "Subsiste a ideia de que apenas os escritores africanos sofrem aquilo que se chama o «drama linguístico». É certo que a colonização trouxe traumas de identidade e alienação. Mas a verdade, meus amigos, é que nenhum escritor tem ao seu dispor uma língua já feita. Todos nós temos de encontrar uma língua própria que nos revele como seres únicos e irrepetíveis."

65   In the interview Mia Couto used the words he created, part of the emerging variety of Mozambican Portuguese: "bidiomático" and "tridiomático".

4.1.4.3 External Language Spread Policies and Politico Linguistic Blocs

The external LSPs identified in Mozambique originated from five countries: Portugal and Brazil assisting Mozambique, in different degrees, in the spread of Portuguese, the United Kingdom assisting Mozambique to spread English as a foreign language (with other concurring countries), France assisting Mozambique to reintroduce and spread French as a foreign language, and Germany reinforcing the spread of a third European foreign language in the country.

All these languages compete for space in Mozambique's linguistic arena, although in different domains. Portuguese, the former colonial language, as official language and language most used of inter-group communication (Benson 2010) has the dominant role. However, as discussed earlier, the development of bilingual education and the impending drafting of a language policy, may improve the status and the role of African languages in Mozambican linguistic spaces. Additionally the international status of Portuguese is being developed by the CPLP, and Mozambique can, with its partners, harvest some of the political and economic benefits that come from acting as a bloc in the international system (visibility, increased prestige and power, access to a greater pool of resources). The other European languages are present in Mozambique as foreign languages, spread by the education system and by the individual external LSPs of European countries. English language has the dominant role in terms of foreign communication given its predominance in international and regional communication. English also represents for Mozambique a political and economic tool as Mozambique is economically closely integrated with its regional neighbours (SADC, in which English dominates) and is also a member of the Commonwealth of Nations. French, ranks behind English, and its importance for Mozambique relies on being the language of the Francophone politico linguistic bloc. German is also a foreign language that maintains cultural/linguistic ties of some of the elite and offers mostly economic opportunities connected with German education, aid and investment.

The fact that English and French (and potentially German) are present in the Mozambican educational system implies between them a competition for a particular slot of time in the curriculum. As described earlier, the source countries of these European languages have subsidised and invested heavily in their introduction and maintenance in the education system. Both France and the UK have now moved to stages where the system is self-sufficient, that is, Mozambique has now the capacity to train the teachers to maintain the spread of those languages – although input from the source countries and/or international donors may still be required in terms of expertise an/or financial resources. Germany if 'rumours' are confirmed may follow a similar path. Arguably the time occupied in the curriculum with the European language competes with that devoted to the African languages (and also with resources). There are discordant positions, Juvane (2010 interview) sees African languages, taught in initial classes, with limited corpus development and lack of practical use (beyond friendship/family circles) as operating in non-competing areas. I maintain that the European languages are using resources that could be used in the valorisation of African languages. With the inclusion of the European foreign languages in the official curriculum the perception of language competition appears diluted, as now their teaching is assumed as a choice of the target country (despite the context involving the choice). However the competition for influence, of which cultural and language external policies are a vehicle, is still there, and remains most evident in the activities developed by the foreign cultural centres.

Perceptions of external LSP in the country revealed a utilitarian perspective. Matusse (2002 interview) observed that he saw no problems with the external LSPs in Mozambique and rejected linguistic imperialism, he said: "Mozambican's attitude is open, any language will do, the one that can help us survive tomorrow will do. Therefore, we are a people that absorbs all those novelties that come our way."[66] Also Miguel (2002 interview) observed that Mozambique was receptive to any external LSP: given the lack of resources, the government would take all offered help from development partners. The utilitarian attitude is also confirmed by a reported (Baptista 2005) declaration of the Ministry of Culture and Education, Aires Aly, who, after a visit to China, said the Mozambican Government was going to consider the possibility of introducing the teaching of Mandarin. The reasons put forward were the worldwide number of speakers and the large Chinese investments in Mozambique. Contemporary external language spread in Mozambique is thus tightly connected with development; the languages are seen to represent opportunities to broaden relations.

Although external language spread seems to be developed mainly through bilateral channels, there are (weak) signs of its multilateralisation. Relevant to Mozambique are the CPLP, the OIF (Francophony) and the Commonwealth. During research I was only able to find evidence for the first two. OIF is since 2008 supporting the Ministry of Education in the development of educational materials. CPLP, of which Mozambique is a founding member (1996), still operates mainly as a political forum. However there is potential for future impact

---

66   Matusse (2002 interview) said in Portuguese: "Agora em relação à atitude dos moçambicanos, é aberta, qualquer língua serve, aquela que nos puder ajudar a sobreviver o amanhã serve. Portanto, nós somos um povo que absorve essas novidades todas que nos aparecem."

as the organisation has adopted a multilateral action plan to promote, diffuse and project Portuguese language internationally (including the internal space of CPLP countries), the *Plano de Ação de Brasília*, agreed in March 2010 and approved at the CPLP Luanda Summit in July 2010.

Connected to CPLP, is the concept of Lusophony (2.3.1.2), which I find interesting to briefly discuss, since it provides insight into the perceptions surrounding Portuguese language spread. Resistance to the concept of Lusophony in Mozambique was evident in the research findings during the study trip (Navarro, Couto, Matusse, Simbine, Do Rosário, Ngunga, AJ Lopes 2002 interviews). That resistance was mainly based on three objections: the concept is terminologically too close to Portugal (*luso* refers to the tribe from which Portugal originated); denies the individuality of each African country (as in 'African countries', PALOP or the Five in the context of the Lusophone group along with Portugal and Brazil); it is used in a deceiving manner[67] (Portuguese is not the majority language in the PALOP). Some, such as Lopes, AJ (2002 interview), believe that, from a Mozambican point of view, there is no particular interest in favouring discussions around the concept of Lusophony, since other priorities, other needs, exist. Others, such as Belorgey (2002 interview), acknowledged the existence of a misunderstanding, since Lusophony refers to the cultures of Portuguese expression[68]. He noted as a major turning point in the understanding of the concept in Mozambique, the representation of the Lusophone countries by the Mozambican President Joaquim Chissano at the first TEL/3ELs summit, gathering Francophone, Lusophone and Hispanophone countries, in Paris, in 2001. Nevertheless, the organisation politically representing the notion of Lusophony, CPLP, was seen in Mozambique as an empty shell, not producing enough practical results. This perception may change, as and if the organisation is able to put into practice the above mentioned plans, however that will be difficult if the question of funding - that has always relied heavily on Portugal and Brazil - is not tackled.

It is also worth noting the activities of Portuguese language spread undertaken by Mozambique. For instance, the Southern African Development Community (SADC) Windhoek treaty of August 1992, celebrating Mozambique joining the community was signed both in Portuguese and English, the then offi-

---

67   According to some, such as Matusse and Lopes, AJ (2002 interviews) the correct term to apply to Mozambique is Bantophone, since the origin of their local languages spoken by the majority of the population is Bantu.

68   In French, Belorgey (2002 interview) said: "C'est que por beaucoup lusophonie ça veut dire portugais. Alors que c'est pas ça. Francophonie ça veut pas dire français. Pour moi francophonie sont des cultures d'expression française. Et lusophonie sont des pays, des cultures d'expression portugaise."

cial languages of the organisation. According to Lopes, AJ (2002 interview) there had been previous discussions about which languages should be the official languages of the organisation, along with English: Afrikaans, Ki-swahili and Portuguese, this last one emerged as the language of two potential regional powers, Mozambique and Angola. These two countries are also reported to implement educational projects (in Portuguese) in the SADC neighbouring countries (Matusse 2002, p.2). Portuguese is also used as working language at the African Union (Lopes, AJ 2002 interview). Portuguese language has thus gone full circle in Mozambique, from being the foreign language of the coloniser, spread in the non-autonomous territory, it became the official language of the independent state of Mozambique and the language that is also used to symbolise the country in the international arena - but is contested by other ex-colonial European languages.

4.1.4.4 Cultural Centres as an Instrument of External Cultural Policy

As discussed in section 2.1.3.3, cultural centres are one of the main instruments for the development of cultural diplomacy. These flagships of foreign culture and language are arguably the major investment in terms of cultural diplomacy that the countries referred to in this study use to operate in Mozambique. They are, not surprisingly, located in the capital Maputo, as the hub of political power in the country. Also their activities are mainly centred there, with limited outreach to other cities. The Portuguese cultural attaché commented that "The main difficulties of Cultural Centres - and generally of diplomatic missions and NGOs - on cultural co-operation in Mozambique is related to the enormous needs in term of education, human resources and infrastructures in the provinces outside the cities of Maputo and Beira, which makes it very difficult to implement projects in the provinces"[69]. Cultural activities in Maputo and Beira are reported to have grown hugely in the last five years - with Maputo hosting 6/7 international events a year (Braga 2010) - a development to which the foreign cultural centres have contributed to as demonstrated in the previous sections.

The first foreign cultural centre to open in Mozambique was the Centro de Estudos Brasileiros, CEB, (now Centro Cultural Brasil - Moçambique, CCBM), in 1989, then in 1995 the Centro Cultural Franco-Moçambicano (CCFM), in 1996 the Instituto Camões - Centro Cultural Português de Maputo (IC-CCPM),

---

69   "As grandes dificuldades dos Centros Culturais - e de uma forma geral das missões diplomáticas e ONGs - em Moçambique na cooperação cultural está relacionada com as enormes carências educacionais, de recursos humanos e de equipamento nas províncias fora das cidades de Maputo e Beira, o que dificulta muito a implementação de projectos nas províncias"

and finally the Instituto Cultural Moçambique - Alemanha (ICMA) in 2003. The British Council, open in 1989, is not regarded *per se* as a foreign cultural centre, but its important cultural actions makes it part of that group. Also the United States Information Services is reported to undertake cultural activities, although not on a regular basis (Braga 2010).

In 2002, when I undertook the study trip to Mozambique, the infrastructures and financial resources of the different centres ranked their visibility and impact in Maputo's cultural life. This situation has not changed in 2010. The CCFM given its excellent infrastructures has a unique place in Maputo cultural scene. The Portuguese cultural attaché comments:

> The CCFM is not really a French cultural centre, since it rarely hosts essentially French events. CCFM presents itself as the favourite space of Mozambican cultural producers, Cultural Centres and embassies in Maputo, including the IC-CCP, which rent the premises for events in the field of cinema, theatre, dance and music.[70] Braga (2010)

The IC-CCPM and the former CEB, now CCBM, have similar infrastructures, and focus on similar activities (library, exhibitions, and conferences). However the financial limitations of CCBM impact on the dimension of the activities developed as mentioned in section 4.1.3.2. The problem is not new: CEB's director in 2002, De Souza e Silva (2002 interview) commented that although CEB was the 'oldest cousin' of all the foreign cultural centres, it was also the 'ugly' one, in the sense that it is the poorest one, the one with least financial resources. The ICMA, is smaller than the other centres, and regularly organises events outside of its premises.

In 2002, the relations between the foreign cultural centres in Maputo (at the time CEB, IC-CCPM, CCFM and BC) were described by their directors as amicable and relying heavily on their personal relationships. De Souza e Silva (2002 interview), the CEB director, confirmed that the relations amongst the foreign cultural centres were good, but in the sense of "fraternity of brothers that are far away"[71]. He reported that the CEB, the Instituto Camões and, to a point, the Centro Cultural Franco-Moçambicano had close relations, and that the USA and the British Council were a bit more distant. He commented: "The rich cousins are

---

70   "O CCFM não é propriamente um centro cultural francês, uma vez que são raros os eventos de matriz francesa. O CCFM apresenta-se como o espaço favorito dos produtores culturais moçambicanos e dos Centros Culturais e Embaixadas em Maputo, incluindo o IC-CCP, que o alugam para a realização de eventos na área do cinema, teatro, dança e música."

71   "fraternidade de irmãos que estão longe".

211

always more complicated."[72] The CCFM Director, François Belorgey (2002 interview), described the cultural centres in Mozambique, in a certain way, as complementing each other (in terms of infrastructures and activities). Belorgey (2002 interview) believed there was no point in strategies of competition between cultural centres in developing countries. The cultural centres should be together doing things for the development of the country. In the case of the CCFM, they had the infrastructure and were always available to work with the other foreign cooperations (Portuguese, Brazilian, American, English, etc.). He went as far as stating his belief in the idea of a European centre. Although the situation has not evolved as far as that, there has been a reinforcement of the informal relations between cultural centres and the inclusion of new partners. Operating since 2008/9 the informally constituted Grupo Culturando includes the directors of the CCFM, the CCBM, the ICMA, IC-ICPM, and the cultural representatives of the foreign embassies in Maputo (Brazil, France, Spain, Germany, Italy, Portugal and Belgium) that meet fortnightly or monthly to establish joint strategies of cultural action, organising events and articulating support to local cultural agents. Culturando has been focussing on the celebration of international days, exhibitions and since two years ago they initiated Maputo's Book Fair.

I interpret the setting up of Culturando as a maximisation of the resources of the different foreign cultural diplomacies to the benefit of the local cultural life, as it brings increased opportunity for the display of Mozambican arts and culture, disseminates expertise in cultural management and opens up international and regional channels to the local cultural agents, artists and publics. Nonetheless, it can be also be argued that this fostering of local cultural life occurs mainly in Western terms, that is, in a logic that gives primacy to what is culture and cultural activities in Western terms, albeit with African and Mozambican content. For instance, the presence of African languages in Maputo's first Book Fair, organized by Culturando in April 2010, was very limited although the majority of the writers invited for talks and books signatures were Mozambican (Culturando 2010). Beside the problematic of appropriation, there is in the interpretation of contemporary global cultural flows, a latent (unresolved) tension between homogenisation (and hegemonic processes) and heterogeneity (section 2.3.2.1). Within the remit of this study, I would like to note that the activities of the foreign cultural centres can be interpreted in that duality of discourses. The activities of the foreign cultural centres in Maputo have a strong connection with the local cultural agents and actively foster the production and promotion of local content (diversity of content). Thus their work can be interpreted as being in the spirit of genuine cultural co-operation, that is showing signs of being less

---

72 "Os primos ricos são sempre mais complicados."

212

encumbered by foreign policy agendas, in the sense described by Fisher (2009) and explored in 2.3.2.2. Nevertheless, these centres are representatives (despite bi-national emphases in denomination or status) of (economically, culturally) attractive centres of power. Part of the mission of the cultural centres is to influence governments and populations favourably towards, in this case, the European governments they represent, their cultures, and mostly their languages and the discourses they embody (section 2.1.3.4). As I said in section 2.1.3.3 in cultural relations there is always an element of self-interest, and in the dependency the structure of the international system positions the African countries, I see the building of an equitable relationship as a complex (if not impossible) task. There are major power asymmetries between the powerful North and the disempowered South.

4.1.5 Conclusion

Language policy in Mozambique does not reflect the linguistic situation of the country. It reflects a political and economic agenda of the elite in power, that inheriting the colonial state, 'chose' to use the same language and to continue the same linguistic policy - albeit under different justifications. After independence in 1975, the Portuguese civilizing mission was replaced by the socialist creation of a New Man (*Homen Novo*), and with the adoption of liberal democracy in the 1990s, the construction of Mozambicanity (*Moçambicanidade*) continued to give primacy to Portuguese language as a marker of national identity and unity. This view of the process of nationality has remained, as has the state structure and content (dominated by FRELIMO), almost unchanged and unchallenged.

The multicultural and multilingual reality of Mozambique is inescapable and the state (also prompted by international organisations, backed up by advisers and international NGOs working locally) has built its capacity to develop work and offer protection to the African languages that can be translated into a more equitable balance in the Mozambican linguistic landscape, providing the speakers of all languages the opportunities to value, use and develop their mother tongues. Agenda 2025 opens up the scope for a deep reflection on Mozambique as a state and a nation that embraces that vision and points to the empowerment of African languages.

The language policy that privileges Portuguese, as official language and language of national unity, but also English and French, highlighting their importance in terms of international communication, in relation to the African languages (still restrictively used and valued in practical terms) perpetuates a political, social and economic divide between those that can speak or not those languages. No doubt the issue of promotion of African languages and that of the spread of European languages by the Mozambican government (with the backing of international organisations and of bilateral partners deploying specific external language spread policies) has to be understood in a larger context of the structure of the international system, the dependency of the country towards the exterior, the objective of achieving goals and objectives externally imposed and measured (Education for All, Development) and the context of the construction of Western framed concepts of nation-state and national identity.

As argued, language policy reflects the power relations in society. If the vision in Agenda 2025 is to be achieved language policy cannot be defined unidimensionally by the governing elite but needs to be discussed and receive inputs from the wider civil society. Also if there is seriousness in the will to promote African languages and in the investment on multilingualism in Mozambique (which seems to be in doubt as noted by Benson 2005 and Dalsgaadr 2009), the Mozambican government must think beyond educational and cultural policy, as language needs to be envisaged also as a producer of wealth. I have already observed the shift that is occurring in Mozambique in the cultural area, in terms of the conceptualization of culture as cultural industry, cultural products and the professionalisation of cultural actors. Languages, although fundamental human rights, need in the increasing globalised and competing world to be able to be seen also as economic goods - to have a value for trading in the economic market, which only strong state commitment can achieve.

4.2 Guinea-Bissau: A Country Case Study

4.2.1 Country Profile

Guinea-Bissau is located in Western African, bordering the Northern Atlantic Ocean, wedged between Guinea-Conakry and Senegal.

Portuguese navigators first made contact with the area in the 15th Century and used it as a slave trading post. The area became a Portuguese colony until the declaration of independence in 1973. In its administration, the Portuguese used the *crioulo* (mixed European and African descent) population of Cape Verde (a services colony) that would have an important role in Guinea Bissau. Independence was preceded by a rebellion initiated in 1956 and lead by Amílcar Cabral, founder of the African Party for the Independence of Guinea and Cape

Verde (PAIGC). Cabral, born in Guinea-Bissau of Cape Verdian parents, became an influential ideologist and revolutionary leader that aimed for the union of Cape Verde and Guinea-Bissau. He was assassinated in 1973, a few months before independence, and his half-brother Luís Cabral became the first President of Guinea-Bissau, within a one party system - as in many other African countries at the time. Misunderstandings within PAIGC led to the split of the party between the two countries and the union plan was abandoned in 1980 when General 'Nino' Vieira (of the minority *Papel* ethnie) took over power in Guinea-Bissau. In 1991, PAIGC accepted the multi-party system, and the first elections took place in 1994. However the country has since suffered considerable political instability and administrative chaos, caused by competition for power between the executive and legislative tiers, general political oppression and recurrent military interventions on the political scene, in a context of lack of political transparency and widespread poverty (World Bank 2006).

President 'Nino' Vieira dominated the political scene since being placed in power by a military coup in November 1980, until the 1998 military mutiny ousted him in 1999. From 1986 the country had taken an economic liberalising route greatly supported by the IMF and UNDP. However in the 1990s social unrest increased due to government mismanagement and failure to deliver services (for instance struggling to pay salaries to teachers, militaries and other civil servants). The 1998 events generated a conflict between Senegalese backed government troops and a military junta that seriously hindered the country's path towards development. The civil war caused the whole system to collapse, many infrastructures were destroyed and many western countries withdrew their diplomatic services from Guinea-Bissau.

Foreign intervention led to a truce and free elections were held in 2000. The elected President Kumba Yalá (of the dominant *Balanta* ethnie) did not manage to respond to a worsening of economic, social and political conditions. At the time of my study trip in 2002 rumours of yet another coup were widespread. The country was then tentatively trying to recover from the civil war. A bloodless coup took place on the 14th September 2003. An interim government took over until new elections were held in 2005, which re-elected former President 'Nino' Vieira. However many believed political risks and ethnic tensions were building up: "Over the past 10 years there has been an increasing politicization of ethnicity, which has been conveniently used by self-serving leaders seeking to increase their legitimacy and power" (World Bank 2006). In March 2009, the situation came to another low point with the assassination of the Armed Forces Chief of General Staff and the President. The country's international credibility has been damaged by the events of the past decade and *donor fatigue* made international aid slow to return after the 1998/9 conflict. Portugal was the only country that

215

did not close its embassy during the conflict demonstrating its continued support to the country.

In the midst of chronic political instability, and despite ongoing economic support from the international community, Guinea-Bissau's economy (mainly based on the cashew nut monoculture) has remained weak and the country has become a haven for drug cartels trafficking South American cocaine into Europe - an issue that is believed to be further fuelling corruption and political/military struggles for power, prompting the labelling of the country as a narcostate. Guinea-Bissau is one of the 10 poorest countries in the world, ranking 173rd out of 182 countries (just behind Mozambique) in the Human Development Index (UNDP 2009a). The Human Poverty Index indicates that 34.9% of people are below certain threshold levels in each of the dimensions of the human development index, namely, living a long and healthy life, having access to education, and a decent standard of living, ranking Guinea Bissau at 107th among 135 countries for which the index has been calculated (UNDP, 2009a).

In order to improve its economic chances close integration with its predominantly francophone neighbours has been sought. In 1975, Guinea-Bissau was one of the 15 founding members of CEDEAO[73], in English, Economic Community of West African States (ECOWAS), joined by another Lusophone country Cap Verde in 1977. In 1997 Guinea-Bissau joined UMOA[74] renamed UEMOA[75] in 2003, in English, West African Economic and Monetary Union (WAEMU), whose members[76] are also ECOWAS members. UEMOA is a customs union between some of the countries of the ECOWAS, which recognises one monetary unit: the African Financial Community Franc (*Franc de la Communauté Financière Africaine*, F CFA), pegged to the Euro. English, French and Portuguese are the official languages of CEDEAO, and French is the work language of UEMOA. Since 2007 there has been political pressure from Guinea-Bissau for Portuguese to be added as a work language.

4.2.1.1 Language Situation

Guinea-Bissau is a culturally and linguistically diverse country, with more than 20 different ethnic groups and 22, all living, languages (Lewis 2009). The main tribes are geographically distributed: Fula (23%) and Mandinga (13%) concentrated in the north and northeast; Balanta (28%) and Papel (7%) in the southern

---

73 Communauté Economique des États de l'Afrique de l'Ouest
74 Union Monetaire Ouest-Africaine
75 Union Economique et Monetaire Ouest-Africaine
76 The 1994 founding members of UEMOA/WAEMU (then UMOA/WAMU) are Benin, Burkina Faso, Ivory Cost, Mali, Niger, Senegal and Togo.

216

coastal areas; and Manjaco (11%) and Mancanha in central and northern coastal areas. A small percentage of the population is of Portuguese and African mixed ethnic heritage (*mestiços* or *crioulos*), which includes a Cape Verdean minority; and their language is Portuguese and/or Crioulo (also known as Creolo, Kriol or lately as Guineense, the Guinean language). These are mainly concentrated in urban areas as are the Balanta and Papel (World Bank 2006). Many people in Guinea-Bissau have animist beliefs (30%) or increasingly are Muslim (45%), especially the Fula and Mandinga; a small percentage follows Christian religions (20%) mostly Roman Catholic (2006 data in BREDA-UNESCO 2009).

Portuguese is the *de facto* official language, mostly the language of writing and formal occasions, used in public administration documents and official speeches, the language of school and of most of the media. However it is estimated that only 10,4 % of the population actually speak it, with different competency levels and are concentrated in urban areas (The statistics refer to the 1991 census, the data of the 2008 census was not available at the time of writing). Recently, official sources have been reported to state that Portuguese is spoken by 40% of the population (Ferreira 2010). Regardless of the exact percentage - which is quite high in relation to other sources - the statement translates the governmental effort being undertaken since independence to spread and promote the use of Portuguese through the extension of the network of the education system and by improvements in the quality of the teaching provided. As explained, in 4.1.2, penetration of Portuguese in the colonies was very weak. However, the efforts in the spread of Portuguese have not been as successful in Guinea-Bissau as in Mozambique, as I will discuss later, and illiteracy amongst individuals above 15 years old is 65% (2005/6 indicators), while in Mozambique it is 44% (2006/7 indicators), according to BREDA-UNESCO data (Pôle de Dakar 2010).

In Guinea-Bissau there is no vehicular language covering the whole country. Crioulo, a Portuguese based Creole, is the language that most fits that role and is seen by many as the national language. This language was formed in the 16/17th century from the contact between Portuguese and African languages and is made up of 80% adapted and transformed Portuguese vocabulary (Augel MP 2007, p.84). In the modern colonial times, Crioulo acquired a negative charge, as 'badly spoken Portuguese'. This vehicular language was the language used in the armed mobilization against the Portuguese colonial power and with independence gained increasing importance in the urban areas. According to the 1991 census, Crioulo is spoken by over 50% of the population mostly concentrated in urban areas where it has become the mother language of under 20% (Lemos 1999, p.32). The linguistic landscape of Guinea-Bissau is unique and complex in relation to the other PALOP countries (Pinto-Bull 1989, p.75). In São Tomé and Príncipe and in Cape Verde, there are also Creoles and

Portuguese, but contrary to the case of Guinea-Bissau there are no African languages spoken there. In Angola and in Mozambique, there are African languages and Portuguese, but no Creole. The Guinean situation can be characterized as triglossic: "where three different types of language - indigenous, lingua franca and official - are used asymmetrically" (Benson 2010, p.325).

Guinea-Bissau is sometimes described as a Portuguese-speaking island in a Francophone ocean, since the surrounding countries have French as their official language. Migrations and the economic integration of the country in its sub-African region therefore make French the most relevant foreign language. According to the available official data, French is spoken by 1,3% of the population, mainly as third or fourth language (Lemos 1999, p.31). Guinea-Bissau since 1979 has been a member of OIF and since 1996 a member of CPLP. The belonging to Francophony has been a source of perceptions of linguistic battles, as I will examine in section 4.2.4.1; however the official commitment has always been to Lusophony. 'Nino' Vieira who was president of Guinea-Bissau for 23 years (1980 to 1999 and 2005 to 2009) has been reported to state that Guinea-Bissau "does not and will never belong to the Francophone family, despite receiving support from France and influences from neighbouring countries due to its geographical location"[77] (Diário de Notícias 14/08/1988, in Do Couto, H. 2007, p.387).

4.2.2 Languages and the State in Guinea Bissau

This section examines the importance of language in the construction of Guinea-Bissau's national project. The government's website clearly states that the official language of the country is Portuguese (http://www.gov.gw, accessed 9/07/2010). However Guinea-Bissau's constitution (dated 1996) has no mention of languages. A small reference in article 17 mentions the assurance of the cultural identity of its citizens as a duty of the State. Portuguese, as the language of the colonizer, and the creole it created in the contact with the African languages, have high status in Guinea-Bissau and in dominant places in the local linguistic hierarchy that reflect the power relations of Guinean society. Portuguese in independent Guinea-Bissau became the *de facto* official language, while Crioulo, has increasingly developed the role of vehicular language and language of national unity. African languages have no formal role and hardly any attention has been given to their status or corpus. This situation reflects the colonial division

---

77 "não é e nem nunca será da família francófona, não obstante receber diversos apoios da França e influências dos países vizinhos devido à sua situação geográfica"

between *indígenas* and *civilizado* - "those who spoke minimal Portuguese, or at least Creole, had acquired urban habits and had the privilege of a rudimentary education"[78] (Augel MP 2007, p.59), and indicates a fault line in Guinean society. The elite, now as in colonial times, is still linguistically defined by the mastery of the Portuguese/Crioulo register, even if its composition has been able to integrate new elements (the proto elite formed from the *assimilados*, who became the freedom fighters, incorporated with the development of the country and its opening up to economic liberalization, the technical cadres and entrepreneurs).

Education in Guinea-Bissau was very limited at the time of independence - the illiteracy rate was above 90% (PNUD 2006) and the first high school only opened in 1959 (Semedo 2005). Thus education and the extension of the educational system became a primary concern of the insurgent movement and later the independent government of Guinea Bissau. The ideological father of independent Guinea-Bissau, Amílcar Cabral, although placing Crioulo as the national language, considered Portuguese extremely useful with regard to international communication and access to modernity. Thus Portuguese was maintained as language of instruction, not excluding the future use of Crioulo, once it became standardized and more developed (Laranjeira 1995, p.408, Freire 1978, p.136, Costa L 2007). This attitude, not dissimilar to the one observed in Mozambique, recognizing the cultural/linguistic capital of Portuguese and denoting an instrumental view of language - in line with socialist approaches that greatly influenced the local leaderships at the time led to the pragmatic use of Portuguese in school, in the state, in the press.

In that sense it is interesting to note the work of Brazilian pedagogue Paulo Freire in the literacy campaigns in Guinea-Bissau at the time of independence. He worked with his cultural action for freedom methods to support Amílcar Cabral's vision of "reafricanize the mentalities"[79] through the "radical transformation of the education system inherited from the colonizer"[80] (Freire 1978, p.16). That revolution of the education system was not linguistic - the Guinean government, against Freire's philosophy, had opted for Portuguese as language of instruction - it was ideological. It concentrated on new methods of teaching, teacher training and adaptation of the curriculum to the African context. Freire's work in Guinea-Bissau placed emphasis on the method of education, thus tackling the issue of discourse behind language (2.2.2.2). Reflecting on a particular

---

78 "aqueles que falavam minimamente o português ou pelo menos o crioulo, tinham adquirido hábitos urbanos e tinham o privilégio de um rudimento de escolarização"
79 "reafricanização das mentalidades"
80 "transformação radical do sistema educacional herdado do colonizador"

project in Guinea Bissau, Sedengal, where Portuguese and Crioulo where hardly spoken, Freire (1978) highlights the importance of the cultural action for freedom regardless of language. Freire (1978, p.72) points out that even if the interest for Portuguese vanishes (the language in which the literacy campaigns were conducted), "(t)he mastery of language, as "whole language", of expressiveness, will remain. Sedengal's experience will simply assert itself in another sense, as already evident today: in the "reading" and the "rewriting" of reality, without the learning of writing and of reading of linguistic signs"[81]. Freire's message regarding the hegemonic power of discourse behind language was highly important then as it is now. Unfortunately the lack of resources and qualified staff, and the option for Portuguese as language of instruction were problems that dictated the end of Freire's project in Guinea-Bissau (Costa L 2007). Thus since 1977, Portuguese language, has been spread, with traditional methods, through the national educational system, as I describe in section 4.2.2.1.

Unlike what had been anticipated by Cabral, the role of Crioulo in Guinea-Bissau became ambiguous. The graphic codification of Crioulo has remained an unsolved issue (awaiting governmental approval), while at the same time, mainly, civil society developments have equipped the language with adequate resources (dictionaries, grammars) that enable its use in teaching – which has happened experimentally as I will discuss in 4.2.2.2. These formal constraints have not affected the spread of Crioulo, which boosted by its symbolic role of unity in the 'liberation war' began to spread, reinforced, in particular, by the phenomenon of urbanization and maintained by the elites. Thus, after independence, the status of Crioulo developed, as the language was tentatively used in published literary works (books, short stories and poetry). Crioulo is also extensively used as an auxiliary language in the education system (unofficially), used orally in the radio and within the State apparel - areas where it competes with Portuguese. For instance, sources reported in 2002 that Parliament debated in Crioulo and only in official speeches Portuguese was used; the daily work in the ministries was also carried out orally in Crioulo. This situation has only marginally changed as I will describe later. There is thus a sharing of linguistic media between Portuguese and Crioulo - Portuguese for writing, Crioulo for speaking - within the official realm. Even literary production in Guinea-Bissau uses mostly Portuguese (Augel MP 2007). However, although the informal

---

81   "O domínio da linguagem, enquanto "linguagem total", da expressividade, permanecerá. A experiência de Sedengal simplesmente se afirmará noutro sentido, já evidente hoje: no da "leitura" e no da "re-escritura" da realidade, sem o aprendizado da escrita e da leitura dos signos linguísticos."

status of Crioulo and its corpus has developed, no official recognition has been granted.

Different explanations for this fact were found in my fieldwork. Semedo (researcher at INEP and former Minister of Education, 2002 interview) believed that the State was afraid to adopt Crioulo as a language of teaching, partially due to fear of losing international aid, namely from Portugal and also because most people in the urban areas perceived Crioulo as having a lesser status than Portuguese. She said those people would never put their children in a school that had Crioulo as a language of teaching. This attitude can be clearly linked to the colonial linguistic attitudes regarding Crioulo as 'broken' Portuguese. Thus Portuguese could be seen as having a utilitarian use, as a foreign language, for the state and for the individual people. Lemos (former Director of the Portuguese Cultural Centre in Bissau, 2002 interview) suggested that Guineans only want to learn Portuguese to migrate, since when actually in the country they do not need it - they will speak their own language, Crioulo or an African language. Portuguese, associated with the economic value of migration and development becomes a highly sought after commodity. In the same way as English or French as international languages connected to centres of power.

At the same time he also reported an ever present (probably subconscious) rejection of Portuguese language by the Guinean elite, given its association with the coloniser (Lemos 1999, p.,18): In 2002 sources indicated that Portuguese was still seen as the white man's language[82], therefore culturally it was viewed as negative to speak Portuguese (Gomes, LV, officer at the Fundo Bibliográfico para a Língua Portuguesa, Bissau, 2002 interview). This would explain the (unofficial) people's commitment to Crioulo.

Additionally there is the identification of Crioulo with a particular powerful group in Guinean society, as a social/cultural/economic label. Togolese political scientist Fafali Koudawo (2002 interview), a researcher at INEP in Guinea-Bissau, argued that the persistent doubts in Guinean society over the role of Crioulo language are connected with debates regarding Crioulo not being just an inter-ethnic language but being identified with an ethnic group, the *crioulos*, and their hegemonic relation over other groups. Koudawo finds a duality in Guinean elites: while the Guinean Crioulo elites originated from Portuguese-African intermarriage, had access to Portuguese; the non-Crioulo Guinean elites and the emerging elites connected with business (many rich traders who do not know how to read or write) have not had access to Portuguese, but wish to do so for the prestige it confers. In Guinea-Bissau, as elsewhere, access to the language

---

82   "Português é a língua do branco" / "Portuguese is the language of white people" (Gomes, LV 2002 interview).

that is considered to provide the most cultural capital is an important issue, thus the divide between those who speak and those who do not speak Portuguese appears to be a relevant fault line in society.

Unlike Mozambique, political instability has been the main characteristic of the Guinean political situation. The fight for power involves political, ethnic and economic interests, leaving the country in a state of extreme fragility. This has led some researchers to argue that

> In Guinea-Bissau, lacks the "project Guinea-Bissau". Mechanisms that foster and nurture that sense of belonging are missing. The precarious state of the schools network and the very low level of education are not adequate instruments for that task. What, above all, exists is the authoritarian, demagogic speech, guided by the national glory of the freedom fights.[83] (Augel MP 2007, p.27)

Portuguese language appears thus to be a no-choice, a legacy of colonialism for the instrumental construction of the state, while Crioulo remains in limbo regarding its role as language of national unity and the role of African languages remains undetermined. The lack of a communally imagined community, undermined by the chronic political instability, has not allowed clear linguistic choices, let alone a language policy, to mature and developed in the same way that has been happening in Mozambique. Nevertheless, the official commitment to Portuguese language has been maintained evidenced in the continuous efforts to spread and improve its acquisition through the educational system (section 4.2.2.1 and 4.2.3.1). Moreover the country has commitment to the Lusophone politico linguistic bloc, of which it is a founding member. These are reflected in the present linguistic debate that is reported to concern the authorities in Guinea-Bissau: the use of Portuguese language in the organizations of the sub-region, to ensure the full integration of the country, and associated with that the spread of Portuguese as the country's vehicular language (Gomes A, Ministry of Education, 2010 email).

Having highlighted the lack of an affirmative language policy in the construction of the Guinean state, I analyse in the following section how inadequately Portuguese has been spread in the Guinean education system.

---

83 "Na Guiné-Bissau, falta o "projecto Guiné-Bissau". Faltam mecanismos desencadeadores ou nutridores desses sentimento de pertença. O precário estado da rede escolar e o muito baixo nível de ensino não constituem instrumentos para tal. O que existe, sobretudo, é o discurso autoritário, demagógico, pautado na glória nacional das lutas libertárias."

4.2.2.1 Portuguese Language and Education in Guinea Bissau

Guinea Bissau's education system is placed in a context of rapid growth of the population (which is mostly young, rural and poor), leading the government to concentrate on the six years of basic education. Additionally the system comprises five more years of secondary education (non-obligatory). Limited vocational (teacher training, administrative, industrial and agricultural training) and higher education (university and colleges) is also available in the country. There are also informal schools that range from community schools to religious and private schools. Higher education is recent and limited. The first universities, one public and one private, started operating in 2004, supported by Portuguese universities. Other establishments include a law, medical and nursing school and institutions that prepare teachers for primary and secondary schools are also supported by foreign cooperation (Portuguese, Cuban, Brazilian). Thus it is not surprising that the intellectual elite of the country has normally studied abroad, in Portugal, as former colonial power, France, China, Cuba, Brazil, USA and in the countries of the former Soviet Union (depending on the scholarships available and denoting the socialist environment of the post-independence).

Education has always been an important issue for Guinea Bissau, as I demonstrated with Freire's involvement in the literacy campaigns. However the lack of resources and of political stability has forced the system into a situation of continual crisis. The insufficient number of teachers due to the poor employment conditions (meagre and late salaries and poor structures to support teaching), their lack of training and even grasp of the language being taught as well as the structural problems (lack of infrastructure and materials) all contribute to a poor level of education in Guinea-Bissau, and for the inadequate spread of any language. The school calendar is continuously compromised by teachers' strikes and a remark, attributed by Lemos (1999, p.58) to a Director-General in the Ministry of Education, summarises what still happens in the country: "in Guinea-Bissau, the teachers pretend they work and the State pretends it pays."[84]

In the midst of the chaos, the country has always committed to achieve the international targets set by the UN organizations regarding education. At present the country is aiming to achieve the MDGs, in particular, education for all in 2015. Reaching the international targets is a hard task for a country in the circumstances of Guinea-Bissau. The UNESCO-BREDA (2009) diagnosis of the country's education system has already concluded that 2015 is not considered a realistic deadline; instead, 2020 is adopted as mid range target to reach the 6 years of primary education for all.

---

84   "na Guiné-Bissau, os professors fingem que trabalham e o Estado finge que paga."

As in the case of Mozambique, international targets such as the MDGs are translated into internal political documents, some of which I examine in this section. It is important to note that although education is a major concern in Guinea-Bissau, language has not been an overt concern of policies.

Examples of the country's education policy in the 1990s are the National Education Plan for Human Development in Guinea-Bissau (1993-2000) and the National Medium Term Development Plan (1994-1997). Their focus was priority to basic education, emphasising quality and equity (gender balance), ensuring efficiency, improving the institutional context (timely payment of salaries) (Silva 1997). These are not dissimilar to what is described in the latest National Plan of Action *Plano Nacional de Acção: Educação para Todos* (2000-2015), aiming at reaching the goal of education for all, which sets a strategic vision to tackle the chronic problems of insufficient and inadequate supply of education services, poor outcomes (rates of repetition and drop-out) and large internal disparities (geographical and gender), uncertain financial sustainability and poor resource management and accountability.

The continuing crisis of the Guinean education system has been analysed by many international agencies throughout the years, and most times language in education is hardly mentioned, with perhaps the passing comment on the country's linguistic situation. It is therefore interesting to examine the series of constraints identified in the mid-1990s by the World Bank (World Bank 1994b) regarding the implementation of language policy in Guinea-Bissau that directly mention the issue of language. The constraints comprised the lack of:

- A nationally common mother tongue or second language;
- Well-prepared teachers;
- Appropriate and adequate textbooks and other learning and teaching materials;
- A national consensus on the best strategy;
- Objective and reliable data on the country's linguistic situation;
- And agreed criterion for the choice of the strategy.

Regarding the first constraint the Bank comments "Lack of a nationally common mother tongue in Guinea-Bissau makes it impossible to prepare teaching and learning materials that specifically address learning difficulties arising from the juxtaposition of the two languages: Portuguese as the foreign language, and the mother tongue that each student brings to school" (World Bank 1994b, p.2). The Bank advised the assignment of teachers geographically. As I indicate in the following section experiments in the use of mother tongue in education did take place. However, their emphasis was on using Crioulo as the language of

224

instruction, regardless on the mother tongue of the speakers, which, among other factors, contributed to the failure of the projects.

Thus in terms of language and quality of education, instead of addressing the issue by changing the language of instruction, the government has opted (with the help of the international donor community and particularly of Portugal - section 4.2.3.1) to improve the teaching of Portuguese, in a first stage, directly with the input of Portuguese teachers, and in a second stage, investing heavily on the training of the local teachers. This effort must be seen in the context of the lack of use of Portuguese in everyday life and with teachers, who often have a deficient mastery of the language, using (unofficially) Crioulo and local African languages as auxiliary languages in education. In 2000 the Declaration of Educational Policy (*Declaração de Política Educativa,* Ministério da Educação, Ciência e Tecnologia da Guiné-Bissau 2000, p.13) tentatively suggested a support role for national languages: "Basic Education will continue to be our main priority. Its main mission is to teach to read, write and count in Portuguese, from the mother tongues"[85]. Crioulo and the African languages have been officially used in literacy programs in non-formal education - when I visited the country in 2002 they were still being used - however in 2010 they were no longer used (Gomes A 2010 email).

The government has also shown concern over the lack of use of Portuguese language in its own institutions, where Crioulo is favoured. In July 2007, the Guinean National Assembly approved a law (*Lei 7/2007*) to enforce the use of Portuguese in the state institutions and in the media (local TV and radio stations to air at least 80% and 50% of its broadcast in Portuguese). Portuguese authorities have supported the measure by providing Portuguese language courses for the different professionals. However it is reported that the impact of the law and the language spread activities is still limited (Gomes A 2010 email). PAIGC deputy Lúcio Balencanti Rodrigues observed recently stated that "Some times when I speak in Portuguese to someone they automatically reply in Crioulo"[86] (Notícias Lusófonas 2010), an attitude which he explains by "the existence of a mental laziness and intellectual conformity not to speak Portuguese"[87]. Others might explain this by the fact that people feel more comfortable speaking their mother tongues and the languages with which they are more familiar or in which they are more fluent.

---

85   "O Ensino Básico continuará a ser a principal prioridade. A sua missão principalmente será a de ensinar a ler, escrever e contar em português, a partir das línguas maternas."

86   "Às vezes falo com alguém em português e responde automaticamente em crioulo"

87   "há uma preguiça mental e o conformismo intelectual para não falar o português"

The solution for the education (and overall) crisis in Guinea-Bissau has always been dependent on external support. Thus the relations with the international donor community have been essential to the country, although troubled at times, such as at the end of the 1990s, when most donor relations with the country broke down due to the 1998/9 conflict and following political instability, until 2003/4. The IMF, EU, the UN, many national development aid agencies directly or indirectly through the multilateral organisations, and NGOs finance and/or work with the Guinean government. For instance, in the area of education, and up to 2005, the World Bank continuously supported basic education development plans (Project *Firkidja*) in Guinea-Bissau and acted largely as a Ministry of Education. Currently, Portugal, Cuba and Japan are among the main donors supporting Guinea Bissau to achieve eliminating literacy by the year 2015, within the MDG. The coordination of this multitude of partners is still not very strong. Only this year, 2010, has the government set aside resources for the development of coordination between the international partners involved in the education process in Guinea-Bissau (Sambú 2009).

At present the UN system works with Guinea-Bissau to achieve the MDGs and other development objectives of the country. The latest strategic framework covering 2008 to 2012, based on the common assessment by the country (Documento de Estratégia Nacional de Redução da Pobreza DENARP) and the development agencies, following from previous similar program, focuses on three strategic cooperation axes: governance; growth and poverty reduction; and social protection and human development. Within this, support to the development of the education system is one of the continuous main aims of the program. Language of education is not mentioned at all in the document. The document also mentions the 'national appropriation' of the program, the involvement of the national actors in the definition and implementation of the program. Thus one can argue that international agencies work with the country to deliver what is commonly agreed to achieve the development goals. Since Portuguese language is the *de facto* official language of the country and the language of the education system, the issue of teaching language as one of the causes for the falling of the system becomes a non issue. The working of the international system although apparently working with a greater involvement of the developing countries, does not do more than perpetuate the establish *status quo*.

The language of teaching is an important factor in the failing of the education system of in Guinea-Bissau. Gomes A (2002 interview), then Director General of Secondary and Higher Education at the Ministry of Education, believed that was the biggest problem education faced in the country, since Portuguese was not mastered by students or teachers, being in practice a foreign language

226

for many of those starting education. Others, such as Bicari (1999), a teacher with 25 years of experience in Africa, believe the crisis of the educational system in Guinea-Bissau, and for that matter in the PALOP, is part of a wider crisis of the State. The European universal model was transplanted to Africa without having been adapted to African culture. The formal African education system is not an African system; it is a transplanted system that does not serve the purpose of development of African societies or the personal development of African youth. Still, others highlight the lack of resources and the lack of a national strategy. Padre Artur Neves (2002 interview), director of a Catholic school in Bissau, believed that, since independence, Guinean politicians did not know what they wanted regarding education. The different foreign cooperations – Portuguese, Brazilian, Swedish, French, and Cuban - all had a say, all had projects with the Ministry of Education, but a strategy was never achieved. Fafali Koudawo, researcher and now head of the private university Colinas de Boé, states the problems in the low levels of education in Guinea Bissau are caused not just by a lack resources of the State but because of a lack of an educational policy: "We just have some schools. Schools for what? The country needs to focus on a real discussion about National Education but since this reflection is not done yet, students are limited to low-level studies leaving school without any real education or training"[88] (Cardador 2009).

Authorities have always acknowledged the problems. The Education Minister, Artur Silva, has stated that a lot of work still needs to be done to make Portuguese language a reality in the country and defended further investment in the teaching of Portuguese (Notícias Lusófonas 2010). One of the measures he mentioned was the targeting of pre-school age children. He is reported to have said that it is necessary "to start from primary school, from a tender age to speak Portuguese, at home, in the families, in the streets and in the schools and in all the places"[89] (Notícias Lusófonas 2010). This declaration fits well with similar tenets exposed as fallacies by Phillipson (1992) regarding English, such as the early start and the maximum exposure.

The government thus seems to continue to be committed to Portuguese language. Nevertheless despite the successful enlargement of the teaching network and the improvement in literacy rates, quality and conditions of teaching are still an issue. Bernardo Ocáia, the president of the Associação Guineense de Profes-

---

88 "Nós limitamo-nos a ter algumas escolas. Escolas para quê? O País precisa de se concentrar numa verdadeira discussão sobre a Educação Nacional mas como essa reflexão ainda não está feita, os alunos limitam-se a fazer estudos de baixo nível saindo das escolas sem uma verdadeira instrução ou formação"

89 "começar desde o ensino básico, desde tenra idade a falar Português, em casa, nas famílias, nas ruas e nas escolas e em todos os lugares"

sores de Português (Portuguese Teachers Association of Guinea Bissau), is adamant that teaching conditions were better in the colonial times, and that since independence there has been a chronic lack of resources (Ferreira 2010). He is also very critical about the methodology for the teaching of Portuguese, which is reported to be the same as in the colonial era, thus not adapted to the plurilinguistic conditions of Guinea Bissau, where 90 to 95% of the population speak a local language, Crioulo and Portuguese. Moreover, Wilson Barbosa, Director of the Portuguese School of Guinea Bissau, observes that despite Portuguese being the official language of the country, there is a "lack of interest in the use of the [Portuguese] language"[90], stressing that "in the public bodies the language of communication is Crioulo"[91] and even in some state school Crioulo is used (Ferreira 2010). As Ocáia, above, he stresses that only a minority in Guinea Bissau speaks Portuguese, those living in the "praça" (that is the urban areas). It is evident that the language policy (or its absence) of the Guinean government does not reflect the linguistic reality of the country. The causes certainly go beyond the linguistic realm, as I have already pointed out in 4.2.2. Augel J (1997, p.253) hints at:

> Influences outside the pedagogical reflections that interfere in the decisions. Interests related to power and to the preservation of the extreme social stratification cause the country to practice since colonial times and also after independence (in 1973/74), a certain "educational Darwinism": the school is extremely selective and most are still denied access and formal education.[92]

Thus Portuguese, the language of a few, continues to be spread to the masses, however that is done in a limited (not reaching EFA) and deficient way (methodology and resources inadequate to reach adequate mastery of the language). The other languages, used daily, remain practically invisible in the governmental policy, as I demonstrate in the following section.

4.2.2.2 Crioulo and African Languages in Education

The use of Crioulo and African languages is increasing in Guinea Bissau due to demographic growth and, in the case of Crioulo also due to the urbanization

---

90   "desinteresse na utilização da língua"
91   "nas instituições do estado a língua de comunicação é o crioulo"
92   "influências fora das reflexões pedagógicas que interferem nas decisões. Interesses ligados ao poder e à conservaçao da extrema estratificação social fazem com que o país pratique, desde os tempos coloniais e também depois da independência (em 1973/74), um certo "darwinismo educacional": a escola é extremamente seletiva e a grande maioria continua excluída do acesso e educação formal."

process and increased job mobility (Benson 2010). I have alluded to the fact that the tension between the two, reflects some of the power struggles in society. Thus the expansion of Crioulo is criticized by some since "the Creole group is undoubtedly the most influential, the most "modern" and Westernized, the more assimilated to the habits introduced by the colonial power, and it is among them that we will find the meager percentage of Portuguese speakers"[93] - "(a)mong the least literate there is a fear that Crioulo, or the Guinean language, being a language spoken by those belonging to an urban culture identified with the hegemonic class of the country, may stifle the other ethnic languages"[94] (Augel MP 2007, p.81).

The fear is not unfounded as it is evident in research findings that, in Guinea-Bissau, discussions on language focus on the relation between Portuguese and Crioulo. African languages are hardly ever mentioned. Although the linguistic tension is between Portuguese and Crioulo, competing possibly for official language domains, the linguistic rights that seem to be more threatened in the long run are those of the speakers of African languages.

The discussions around language in Guinea Bissau are normally placed in the context of improving the quality of the education and finding a solution for the crisis of the education system. They focus on the difficulties that have arisen in the teaching/learning of Portuguese and this has led the Government to experiment with transitional programs. Several studies have been made to develop and use Crioulo and African languages in literacy programmes, and transitional literacy programmes to Portuguese have taken place in Crioulo and in the other ethnic languages (Mandinga, Fula, Manjaco e Balanta). The Ministry of Education of Guinea-Bissau assisted by SNV - Dutch Cooperation and by the Portuguese NGO CIDAC, conducted between 1987 and 1997 three experiments in three different regions of the country, occupied by speakers of Balanta, Manjaco and Bijagós, using crioulo as the language of instruction in the first two years of primary schooling. The project in the Bijagós Island, with a modified methodology, is the only one still active today (Gomes 2010 email), now developed by the FASPEBI (Fundação para o Apoio ao Desenvolvimento dos Povos do Arquipélago dos Bijagós / Foundation for the Support to the Development of the People of the Bijagós Archipelago) connected with the

---

93 "o grupo Crioulo é, sem dúvida, o mais influente, o mais "moderno" e ocidentalizado, o mais assimilado aos hábitos introduzidos pelo poder colonial, e é entre eles que se vai encontrar a magra percentagem dos falantes do português"

94 "entre os menos letrados existe um receio de o crioulo, ou língua guineense, sendo um idioma falando por pertencentes a uma cultura urbana, própria da camada hegemônica do país, poder abafar as demais línguas étnicas"

Catholic Church and also supported throughout the years by different donors such as the Portuguese government, Portuguese NGO CIDAC and the EU.

The mentioned transitional programs were instituted on the premise that Crioulo was understood and spoken by the great majority of the population (World Bank 1994a, p.46). However, the World Bank noted that "there is no consensus on how widely spread the use of Crioulo actually is, nor there is a consensus on how many in the teaching cadre can handle that language in ordinary communication, much less for using it to teach children" (World Bank 1994b, p.2). Therefore the transition system using Crioulo could not be fully justified. Benson (2010, p.329) who participated in the experimental projects acknowledged that the experiments with Crioulo was flawed in the sense that it ignored the African languages (L1): "In Guinea Bissau, the experiment that my colleagues and I evaluated in 1992/93 … was designated to use kiriol [crioulo], an L2 for most learners as well as for most Guineans, as a political compromise and practical solution to materials in diverse L1s and the lack of comprehensibility of Portuguese-medium education". However she states that "we were able to show that in the absence of L1 schooling, use of L2 kiriol supported learning and was preferable to all-L3 schooling [Portuguese], even in remote areas where children did not speak the L2 [Crioulo] when they began primary school" (Benson 2010, p.329). Additionally, set in a 'culture of pilot projects' (Benson 2005), the bilingual projects were characterised by lack of continuity, due to being financed by intermittent international aid and by lack of teachers (low and delayed salaries, refusal to go to the interior of the country) (Semedo 2002 interview). Thus it was difficult, having learnt from the experiment, to be able to use that for a following step in the process.

The use of Crioulo and of ethnic languages, as medium of instruction is still faced with the lack of political decision regarding the standardisation of their written forms. In 1998, the UN agencies sponsored the development of a proposal regarding the alphabet, orthography and word division of Crioulo, Mandinga and Fula. The project gathered a team of linguists from Guinea-Bissau, Mali and Senegal. With the 1998/9 conflict all came to a halt. The proposal in 2002, at the time of the study trip, awaited Ministerial approval (Semedo 2002 interview) and I have not identified further developments. Nevertheless, as I pointed out earlier, there is a defined educational policy that stipulates that the national languages are to be used in adult literacy - the 2000 Declaration of Educational Policy. However the policy is not in practice.

In February 2009 a UNICEF sponsored team returned to Guinea Bissau to investigate the potential for mother tongue-based schooling to be implemented to address access and quality issues to achieve Universal Primary Education by 2012 (Benson 2010, p.236). Benson (2010, p.236) reports that there was "evidence that the Portuguese-only policy has failed to promote either learning of curricular content or L3 proficiency. We also found that there is sufficient interest among educators, as well as human and linguistic resources, to begin strategic planning for multilingual education". Father Luigi Scantamburlo (2010), who runs the bilingual education project in the Bijagós, confirms a similar vision and believes Guinea-Bissau should rethink its educational strategy. He states:

> No one denies the value of Portuguese: My experience after nine years of implementation of bilingualism in some schools in the Bijagós Islands says bilingualism (learning to read and write in the mother tongue or in a language that the student knows), helps to better learn Portuguese, and especially gives students confidence, dignity and a tool to develop their own ability to communicate[95] (Scantamburlo 2010).

In light of the political and economic context of the country, the possibility of mother tongue schooling being further implemented in Guinea-Bissau is dependent on external support. In 2010, sources of the Ministry of Education indicate that nothing is being done regarding Crioulo or the African languages, and that the debate regarding, in particular, the use of Crioulo in the education system has died (Gomes A 2010 email).

Besides governmental action, other actors are very important in language spread in Guinea-Bissau. The work of the Catholic Church in Guinea Bissau is recognised as particularly important. Other religious denominations are also important in the country, such as the Madrassas (Koranic schools) and the protestant churches. Their missionary work involves language spread and research findings found evidence of both the reinforcement of Portuguese (FEC in section 4.2.3.1), and the development of resources in Crioulo and African languages. I mentioned the FASPEBI project, within which Father Scantamburlo has developed, building on previous work, educational resources for the teaching of Crioulo, such as a grammar and a dictionary - that incidentally have had the financial support of Portuguese cooperation. Research has also found indication of other missionaries developing work in Crioulo and African languages, namely SIL. American consultants David and Lynn Frank, of Wycliffe Bible Translators (USA), are working in translating the Bible in collaboration with other partners: "The translation work there [in Guinea Bissau] is happening sup-

---

95 "Ninguém nega a o valor do Português: a minha experiência depois de nove anos de implementação do bilinguismo nalgumas escolas das Ilhas Bijagós diz que o bilinguismo (aprender a ler e a escrever na língua materna ou numa língua que o aluno conhece), ajuda melhor para aprender também o Português, e sobretudo dá aos alunos confiança, dignidade e um utensílio para desenvolver a própria capacidade comunicativa"

231

ported by the local church, by a Brazilian organization called ALEM and by SIL, with one SIL member assigned there full-time as a language programs manager" (The Frank Family 2009). Despite the linguistic implications, the objectives of the Wycliffe Bible Translators are clearly religious, as is evident in their prayers: "That God will bless the translators and the plans in Guinea-Bissau, to communicate the Gospel clearly, accurately and naturally" (The Frank Family 2009). The linguistic work of these agents is extremely important and their achievements, resources and objectives must be taken into account when elaborating a national strategy. However their examination is outside the remit of this study.

4.2.2.3 French and English Languages

Apart from Portuguese, French and English are the other two European languages that have been given official attention due to their status of international languages. Despite the non-existence of recent statistical data regarding the use of foreign languages in Guinea Bissau, it is safe to assume as correct the perception that French is the most used foreign language in the country (Gomes A 2010 email) - which is not surprising as the country is set in a sub-region where French is predominant as official language.

In terms of language policy the 2000 Declaration of Educational Policy (*Declaração de Política Educativa*, Ministério da Educação, Ciência e Tecnologia da Guiné-Bissau 2000, p.14) mentions the functional role of foreign languages in its list of intentions: "Revise the education policy of foreign languages in Basic, Secondary and Vocational Education, having in mind the national languages, Portuguese as a second language, French and English as regional languages and of access to technology and science"[96]. The arguments are similar to the ones presented in Mozambique for the spread of the European international languages: regional and international links, modernity (language providing access to science and technology).

In terms of the languages taught in the education system, French was the first foreign language taught in the colonial education system. At present, the students take French or English optionally from the 7th grade (from the 10th /11th grade there is also German and Latin according to subgroups) (Gomes A 2002 interview and 2010 email). A project to introduce French in primary school, in the 5th grade, was started but the 1998 conflict put an end to it. Many of the

---

96 "Revisão da política do ensino das línguas estrangeiras no Ensino Básico, Ensino Secundário e Técnico-Profissional, tendo em conta as línguas nacionais, o português como língua segunda, o francês e o inglês como línguas regionais e de acesso à tecnologia e à ciência."

teachers trained for that project, given their good preparation, went on to work for international organisations or left the country and all the human resources investment was lost (Semedo 2002 interview). In 2002 English and French were courses available at the Escola Normal Superior Tchico Té (ENSTT) that trains teachers for secondary schools. I have not been able to establish if that is still the case, however my source at the Ministry of Education stated that the teachers of foreign languages had no special training to teach nor were they assisted by any external party (Gomes A 2010 email). It thus appears that the spread of English and French in the national education system is not being supported directly by foreign entities at the moment, although the teaching of French takes place at the French cultural center and the teaching of German language might also be receiving support from Germany.

A series of factors have been identified as contributing to the spread of French in Guinea-Bissau. According to Koudawo (2002 interview) these are:

- Geography. Guinea-Bissau has francophone neighbours;
- Ideology. The fight for independence in Guinea-Bissau is grounded in French writings: PAIGC fight against Portugal was orchestrated from Guinea-Conakry and all the top party responsibles spoke French and had absorbed ideology through French language;
- International aid. After independence many development workers came from Guinea-Conakry to help Guinea and they worked in key areas of the public administration and worked and taught French;
- Ethnic groups and migrations. There are very close connections between ethnic groups across borders. Given the porosity of the borders and the close connections, the migration of people, both ways, is very common. People come to Guinea-Bissau because the market is still developing and find more opportunity to exercise their skills, for instance, mechanics and masons. Many Guineans, especially from the Monaco and Manama ethnic groups, who live across the border of Senegal, maintain close contact and many send their children to study in the koranic schools there (UNICEF is seriously concerned with the implications of this practice and child trafficking in the sub-region) or go to France, via Senegal, and come back, through several generations;
- Regional economic integration. People and goods are free to travel across frontiers, open by the economic regional integration (ECOWAS and WAEMU).

At public administration level, French, more than English, is increasingly used due to the integration of Guinea-Bissau in regional organisations where French dominates. Also it is frequent that documents regarding Guinea-Bissau produced by international organisations, such as UNDP, UNESCO-BREDA, the World Bank (which often have their delegations in francophone countries of the sub-region) are written in French. France has persevered in its efforts to spread French in Guinea-Bissau as described in section 4.2.3.3.

However, in 2002 Gomes A. (2002 interview) reported that English was the clear preference at ENSTT. People enrolled more for the degree Portuguese/English than for the Portuguese/French - I was unable to confirm the trend in 2010. English and French continue to be taught in private schools in Guinea Bissau (Gomes 2010 email) and the website of the SOS schools (schools for orphans supported by the charity SOS Children's Villages UK) reports the teaching of both languages in their primary and secondary schools (www.sos-schools.org). The UK authorities have not developed official language spread activities in Guinea-Bissau. In practice, the honorary consul, owner of a company called Mavegro and of a radio with the same name, retransmits BBC World service programmes. In 2000 it featured an English language course ("Look Ahead") for Portuguese speakers. The British NGO VSO has operated in the country, supporting the teaching of English at ENSTT among other activities. The USA, until the 1998/9 conflict, spread English in Guinea-Bissau, mainly through the Peace Corps. In the country since the beginning of the 1990s, assisting economic liberalisation, the USA's main targets for LSP were entrepreneurs to whom they made available Commercial English courses and youth - reinforcing the teaching and training of teachers of English in secondary schools (Semedo and Koudawo 2002 interviews). These activities came to a halt when the USA embassy suspended operations, and the Peace Corps withdrew, from Bissau on June 14, 1998, and have not since come back. However, the seed was sown and with local efforts the spread of English continued at the time of my study trip in 2002, based on some of those trained by the Americans. Koudawo (2002 interview) mentioned a local ONG, National English Language Council (NELC), which provided English language courses. Some interviewees point out the availability of Internet cafes in Bissau and the growing interest of Guinean youth in Anglo-Saxon music and popular culture as causes for the increase in the demand for English. Reinforcing English in Guinea-Bissau was a migration wave of refugees from neighbouring Anglophone countries during the 1990s. Nigerian, Liberian and Sierra Leone political crises brought several waves of refugees to Guinea-Bissau which developed into an increasingly numerous Anglophone community that supports the spread of English (Koudawo 2002 interview).

4.2.3 External Language Spread Policies in Guinea-Bissau

Guinea-Bissau is a fragile state that has been struggling to find its own sense of direction in statehood and, in what concerns this study, language policy. Faced with a lack of a consistent and sustained political national project, in a context of extreme primary needs, the issue of language has never been given the attention it deserves. As in Mozambique, Portuguese, the language of the coloniser was adopted, here as a *de facto* official language, however its use and spread in the Guinean linguistic space has been hindered by a series of factors. These include the lack of consideration of the importance of other languages, in particular Crioulo but also of the other African languages; the methodologies employed in the teaching of Portuguese, since although being second or third language, Portuguese is normally taught as first language; the insufficient preparation of the teachers, and their meagre and uncertain salaries; the lack of infrastructures, with no or hardly no pedagogical resources or support; and overall the inability of Guinea Bissau to create and maintain a stable state to allow the policies to be discussed, decided, implemented and evaluated and provide the minimal conditions for teachers and children to interact.

It is not the objective of this study to discuss what national language policy should Guinea-Bissau follow. What I consider important to highlight in this section on external language spread policies in Guinea Bissau is that, given its circumstances, the country is in a fragile state. Not being a 'donor darling' as Mozambique and having less capacity for donor coordination, lacking a clear perspective on the national project, leaves Guinea Bissau more susceptible to external influences. The external donors' work reinforces the existing linguistic *status quo* in the country. That is, Portugal reinforces the position of Portuguese as official language, France that of French as first foreign language, the multilateral agencies validate the option for the European languages at the top of the linguistic hierarchies.

The external language spread policies identified in the case of Guinea Bissau were those of Portugal, Brazil and France, which I will analyse in the following sections. Additionally my research findings lead me to argue that, at present, Germany might be starting a process to reinforce German language spread in the country. I consider that the following information, mostly available from the German Federal Foreign Office website, substantiates my point:

1. German language is still taught in the 10th and 11th grade in Guinea Bissau (Gomes A 2010 email);
2. Since the Fall of 2007 the German - Guinea Bissau Friends Association, AGAA (Associação dos Guineenses Amigos da Alemanha) is providing

German language courses (Auswärtige Amt 2010) - considering the economic context of the country, examples of similar situations referred to in this study, and that this information was only available on the German Federal Foreign Office website (and only in the German version), I consider it safe to assume that the courses are not self financing and that the source of financing must be Germany;

3. German language is reported to be strongly represented in Guinea-Bissau due to formerly close relations with the former German Democratic Republic (Auswärtige Amt 2010). As in the case of Mozambique, Germany is able to harvest the long term effects of the language spread policies of the former GDR (scholarship program that trained many in the elite, which includes Malam Bacai Sanhá, a president of Guinea Bissau);

4. Germany between 2007 and 2008 donated 52 000 Euros for the renovation of INEP, the only research institution in the country (Auswärtige Amt 2010);

5. INEP is working with the University of Bayreuth and the Volkswagen Foundation in a social science project (Auswärtige Amt 2010);

6. In March 2007 a German portal for Lusophony, www.alemanja.org was inaugurated as an initiative of the German Embassy in Brazil.

German language spread is thus a case to follow in Guinea-Bissau. I now examine the established language spread policies, those of Portugal, Brazil and France.

4.2.3.1 The External Language Spread Policy of Portugal in Guinea-Bissau

Political relations between the two countries after independence were reported as good since they shared a similar left-wing ideological positioning. Koudawo (INEP researcher 2002 interview) mentioned a wave of Portuguese volunteer workers that came to Guinea-Bissau pushed by romanticism; he described it as an exciting and somewhat confused period, a very generous cooperation.

As explained in section 4.1.3.1, the external language spread of Portugal in the former colonies is more related to political reasons than to economic advantages. Education and culture have always been two of the most important areas for cooperation between the Portuguese government and Guinea-Bissau. The main projects relate to:

- Teaching of Portuguese language,
- Teacher training and scholarships,
- Cultural Centre.

236

The cooperation program 2008-2010, as in the cases of other foreign cooperations, sets the projects undertaken within the objectives of the Guinea Bissau government, described in DENARP. Thus Portugal supports the national objectives of expanding, improving access to and raising the efficiency and quality of education (Instituto da Cooperação Portuguesa 2008).

Both during the 1990s and most of the 2000s, Portuguese cooperation action has been dispersed in several institutions at source and target level. In Lisbon, the source of policies and financing has been the Ministry of Foreign Affairs with its related agencies, Instituto da Cooperação Portuguesa and Instituto Camões, and the Ministry of Education. Only in 2010, has the IC assumed the Ministry of Education's responsibilities for education abroad at primary and secondary levels. The activities developed in Guinea-Bissau also mirror those divides. Different Portuguese institutions concerned with language spread operate in Guinea-Bissau working alongside each other. However co-ordination among them is often weak. At the time of the study trip, 2002, conflicting lines of management were affecting the maximum use of the already limited resources available - reaching the point that the Portuguese language teachers were at times unable to use the transport vehicles to reach their schools because there was disagreement over who should pay the fuel since the vehicle was 'owned' by one institution and the teachers where under the tutelage of another – although both institutions belonged to the Portuguese government...

Portuguese language spread activities are centred around three main projects: Programa de Apoio ao Sistema Educativo da Guiné-Bissau / Support Program to the Educational System in Guinea Bissau (PASEG); Projecto de Apoio à Educação no Interior da Guiné-Bissau / Support Project to Education in the interior of Guinea Bissau (PAEIGB); support to higher education through cooperation between the Lisbon and Bissau's Law School and support to the Portuguese Department in Escola Normal Superior Tchico Té (ENSTT) by the Camões Institute.

Overall the support is provided by placing Portuguese teachers in the country to teach students and to support and train local teachers. Besides the government, Portuguese private foundations, such as the Fundação Calouste Gulbenkian and the Fundação Bissaya Barreto, also develop projects in the area of education on its own or in collaboration with the Portuguese government. Town twining projects also support this policy. Portuguese NGOs such as CIDAC and FEC operate in the area of education. Additionally most international organizations and NGOs operating in the country develop their activities in Portuguese reinforcing the spread of the language and its status as the official language of the country, in line with the government policy.

In terms of external LSP, educational cooperation at primary and seconday school level has been led by the Portuguese Ministry of Education (in 2010 the responsibility is in the process of being transferred to IC). PASEG, Support Program to the Education System in Guinea Bissau, links to an initial project, *Projecto África* or *Projecto de Ensino Aprendizagem da Língua Portuguesa para o Ensino Básico* (1987-1989; 1990-94), developed by a predecessor of IC, ICALP, to improve the quality of education through in-service teacher training in primary education. PASEG has been operating since 2000, and as clarified in official documents "was born in the context of bilateral cooperation relations, through a request formulated by the Guinean government" in 1999 (Instituto da Cooperação Portuguesa 2008). The stressing of the request by the target country is a recurrent and understandable act, but does not invalidate underlying factors such as the colonial legacy or the structural dependency. The Portuguese Ministry of Education and the Portuguese Cooperation Institute, place teachers mainly in Bissau to teach Portuguese and/or support other teachers at the secondary schools of Bissau. At the time of the study trip (2002) the Ministry of Education/ICP had 11 teachers in Bissau. Since, at the time, the new academic year had not started, the teachers were doing alternative work - Portuguese courses for workers of a communitarian radio, literacy classes for children, teacher training - in schools outside the formal educational system and other organisations such as local NGOs (AD), catholic schools (Liceu João XXIII), and the Portuguese School. Those teachers also teach the Portuguese language courses at IC's Centro Cultural Português, Portuguese Cultural Centre (CCP/IC) in Bissau.

Outside Bissau, the capital, support to education within the Support Project to Education in the Interior of Guinea-Bissau, PAEIGB, is developed by Fundação Evangelização e Culturas (FEC, Evangelisation and Cultures Foundation) a Portuguese Catholic NGO working with the Lusophone countries, financed by the Portuguese Cooperation Institute. FEC's work in Guinea Bissau also receives support from other partners such as the Catholic Church, the British NGO Plan and Action Aid, and from SNV – Dutch Cooperation and is increasingly in the last few years closer to the work of UNICEF developed in the country (FEC 2010). PAEIGB started in 2000 and aimed at improving (particularly primary) education in the interior of the country through capacity-building of teachers from all levels of education (except higher education), headmasters and librarians. Voluntary workers act as support teachers. In the morning they teach classes and in the afternoon they provide teacher training in terms of pedagogy and Portuguese language and they also have an important role in the development of socio-educational projects. The project revolves around the "promotion" of Portuguese language; training of teachers and supporting link projects between the school and the community in four regions of the interior of the country: Cacheu (Canchungo, Caió e Ingoré); Tombali (Catió e Cafal), Oio (Mansoa, Bissorã e Nhoma) and Bafatá (Bafatá, Geba e Bambadinca). In 2001, this involved 14 teachers/technicians who were able to reach 50 schools and 215 teachers. Additionally, FEC is involved with a Catholic local radio station, Rádio Sol Mansi, in Oio, supporting journalists in the areas of programme-making, production and Portuguese language. This particular project is aimed at the spread of Portuguese language through Catholic radio in Africa (FEC 2010). At the time of the study trip 2002, FEC's 12 volunteers, not necessarily teachers or even teachers of Portuguese, provided training and support to Catholic schools in the villages outside the capital. The volunteers had to have a strong spirit of mission given the harsh conditions they faced (e.g. riding a bicycle for 2 hours to reach a *tabanca* (village) and 2 hours back; using public transportation, that is irregular and insecure; not having running water or electricity; risking personal and health security (malaria, cholera, hepatitis are very common)). PASEG operated until 2007 and was then replaced in 2008/9 by Projecto + Escola with similar objectives. Currently the project is designated Djunta Mon, foreseen to operate until 2012 - although the name is now in Crioulo, the focus is still Portuguese language. The named objectives are: "to improve the quality of the elementary primary education in the target schools, focusing in the areas of Portuguese language, maths, integrated sciences, pedagogical competences, management and school administration"[97]; and "to increase the frequency of use of Portuguese language in everyday life in Guinea Bissau"[98] (Fundação Evangelização e Culturas 2010).

There is in many of these teachers, particularly in the ones working at primary and secondary school level, an individual commitment that brings to mind the romanticism Koudawo (2002 interview) described cooperation had in the first years of independence. However in most cases the well-meaning individual is spreading the mainstream discourse on language that incorporates Ansre's (1979) arguments in favour of European languages (section 2.2.2.1) and perpetuates (neo)colonial dependencies. One of the students I met informally during my study trip in 2002 said Guinea-Bissau was as "a house that belonged to Portugal"[99].

At higher education level the cooperation between Lisbon and Bissau's Law School has been in operation for 16 years. It is particularly important given that higher education in Guinea Bissau is extremely feeble. The other important pro-

---

97   "Melhorar a qualidade do ensino básico elementar nas escolas alvo, centrando-se nas áreas da língua portuguesa, da matemática, das ciências integradas, das competências pedagógicas e da gestão e administração escolar"

98   "Aumentar a frequência do uso da língua portuguesa no quotidiano guineense"

99   "uma casa que lhes pertence" (Roberto, student at the Liceu João XXIII, Bissau, 2002)

ject, that is particularly relevant for language spread is the support given by the Camões Institute to the Portuguese Language Department of the Escola Normal Superior Tchico Té (ENSTT), where it has established a Centro de Lingua Portuguesa (CLP/IC). In addition to the support to the Portuguese language degree (since 2002/3), CLP/IC and ENSTT have been developing, since 2006, the Projecto Unidades de Apoio Pedagógico/Pólos de Língua Portuguesa, a 3 year in-service training project, undertaken in 12 Pedagogic Units throughout Guinea-Bissau's regions to support Primary and Secondary School teachers (N'Tanhá 2010, Encarte JL 2010a). The project had the support of the World Bank which provided the infrastructures. The other costs are covered by the Camões Institute and Petromar, a Guinean company that is 85% owned by Portuguese Galp Energia. Interestingly and relevant to my earlier anecdotal reference to fuel costs, Petromar, which is the main fuel distributor in Guinea Bissau, provided part of its sponsorship in fuel and lubricants given the decentralised nature of the in-service training (Encarte Jornal de Letras 2010a). In a context of extreme need it is interesting to see how commercial, political and linguistic interests ally to consolidate influence by the sponsoring of projects. The first three-year project that ended in 2009 successfully trained 432 teachers. In 2010, 1,112 teachers are enrolled over three different levels reaching over 70,000 students.

Educational Portuguese cooperation also includes the provision of scholarships to Guineans to study in Portugal. In 2001 there were around 20, in 2002 they were reduced to 7. In 2002, the Portuguese government was unhappy with the level of return of the students to Guinea-Bissau – only 20%. Perdigão (2002 interview) commented that there were no mechanisms to ensure their return since there was no political will to put them in place. The solution found was the use of internal scholarships for students to attend the Portuguese School or any private school that has equivalence to the Portuguese educational system. The 2008-2010 cooperation agreement indicates that internal scholarships at secondary and higher education level are privileged, while external scholarships are given mainly for post graduate levels.

Another important element of Portuguese language and culture spread in Guinea Bissau is the Portuguese Cultural Centre, which opened in 1979 in Bissau, the capital, where a French cultural centre was already operating (Lemos 1999 and 2002 interview). The 1998/9 conflict would put a halt to the activities of the centre until 2002. The centre was later refurbished between 2005 and 2006, despite previous plans for a new one to be built. From the start the Portuguese centre had a library and Portuguese courses. In 1987 Portuguese for foreigners (non-Guineans) courses also started. The Portuguese language courses are still in operation today and reach between 200 to 300 students per year (Encarte Jornal de Letras 2008).

During the 1990s the activities of the Cultural Centre, mostly restricted to Bissau, due to transportation problems (lack of vehicles), targeted young people, especially at secondary school level, and the mass of civil servants that needed Portuguese to fulfil their roles. The activities were directed in three areas: growing provision of Portuguese language courses, development of the library and organisation of arts events promoting Portuguese and Guinean culture through the means of Portuguese language. This strategy developed by the then Director of the Cultural Centre, Mário Matos e Lemos (Lemos 1999, p.38-39) as he assumed his post in 1985 issued from a perceived antagonism against Portuguese language from Guinean and foreign intellectuals who pushed for the development of Crioulo. An antagonism that according to Lemos (1999, p.48) diminished during the 1990s: "the Guineans, once the years of rejection were past, really wanted to learn Portuguese"[100]. In my view the above perception of antagonism indicates a lack of understanding of the importance of mother tongue education, not uncommon then nor now, despite all the awareness work being developed internationally. By the time of my study trip in 2002 this strong attitude against Crioulo had toned down and IC was supporting publications in and about Crioulo. Moreover, the Portuguese teachers sent to the country un-officially used Crioulo to support the teaching of Portuguese in Bissau.

In 2007/8 the CCP/IC advertised itself as "Guinea Bissau's House of Culture"[101] to highlight the strong partnership it had developed with local cultural agents and the importance of the activities of the foreign cultural centres, given the absence in Bissau of a cinema, theatre or public library (Encarte JL 2008). CCP/IC was developing in parallel with a diverse and intensive arts programme, a series of training modules for cultural agents in the areas of theatre, cinema, puppetry, guitar, literature and creative writing, masks, photography and cultural promotion with trainers from the country, Portugal, Brazil, Cape Verde, Senegal and Germany. This particular activity is worth noting as it is an effort to strengthen the fabric of local cultural agents. Unfortunately the cultural attaché in 2010 was always unavailable to provide an updated of the present activities of the CCP/IC. However according to other local actors (Rocha, Cultural Affairs Co-ordinator of the Centro Cultural Brazil – Guiné-Bissau, 2010 interview and Le Beller, Director of the Centro Cultural Franco-Bissau-Guineense, 2010 email), they were going through a quiet phase emphasising more language than culture, which leads me to assume that in comparison with the immediate period, there was a significant drop in the number of cultural activities.

---

100 "os guineenses, passados os anos da rejeição, queriam mesmo aprender Português."
101 "A Casa da Cultura da Guiné-Bissau"

In order to reinforce Portuguese language spread, television in Guinea-Bissau was installed by Portugal in 1989. In addition to the national channel, in 1995 the country gained access to RTP International, replaced in 1998 by RTP África. Not just the Portuguese variety is spread, since as is the case in Mozambique, the cultural and linguistic influence of the Brazilian *novelas* is significant.

4.2.3.2 The External Language Spread Policy of Brazil in Guinea-Bissau

Brazil, Guinea-Bissau and Mozambique, as former colonies of Portugal, share a historical, cultural and linguistic bond that opens the possibility for increased relations on different levels. Although the focus of this study is on specific policies relating to language spread (which I associate with cultural ones), the importance of language in the broad area of cooperation must be highlighted. In the case of the relations between Brazil and Guinea-Bissau, language spread *per se* does not appear as a dominant concern, but it is an underlying and important factor. Brazil is an important partner (on its own and as a purveyor of trilateral cooperation, with countries such as Japan, USA and Norway) for Guinea-Bissau, developing important technical cooperation projects, particularly in the areas of health, agriculture and professional training. Recently Brazil has financed the Professional Training Centre in Guinea-Bissau - open in 2009 - a USD$ 1.4 million project which makes technical and professional training possible in areas such as civil construction, carpentry, welding and services. Brazil is also helping Guinea-Bissau tackle being the hub of a new cocaine trafficking route from South America via West Africa to supply growing demand for illegal drugs in Europe. Brazil is investing in the creation and capacity-building of a police academy in the country supporting the National Plan to Fight Drugs and Crime, supported by the UNODC Regional Office for West and Central Africa (Nansil 2009). In terms of health and agriculture, besides the importance of the common language in the delivery of the programs, the countries are also able to explore advantages in terms of similar problems that they face (malaria) and climate conditions (e.g. protection of mangrove areas). All these projects, although not specifically related to language, have linguistic consequences: they reinforce the position of Portuguese language in the country and expose the Guineans to another variant of Portuguese.

The mid 2000s saw a rapprochement of the countries. The Brazilian President visited the country in 2005 and the Guinean President visited Brazil in 2007. Brazil's relations with Guinea-Bissau are officially presented within a "need to strengthen South-South cooperation, by means of active solidarity, of further intensifying trade relations and investments, of exchanging scientific and

242

technological resources and of sharing knowledge" (Ministério das Relações Exteriores do Brasil 2007). In political terms, it is significant to note Brazil's commitment, since the end of 2007, to the restructuring and reconstruction of Guinea Bissau, by leading at the UN the Peacebuilding Guinea-Bissau's Configuration Commission (Nansil 2009).

As in Mozambique, the external cultural policy of Brazil – which includes language spread - is developed through the CEB (Centro de Estudos Brasileiros), renamed in 2008 Centro Cultural Brasileiro - Guiné-Bissau (CCBGB), which is its most dynamic and visible element. The Brazilian cultural centre is under the direction of the head of the diplomatic mission and has as main mission to execute the Brazilian external cultural policy (already discussed in 4.1.3.2). The present Coordinator for Cultural Affairs of the CCBGB described the mission of the centre as "the promotion of Lusophony and of Brazilian culture in interaction with the local culture, highlighting the similarities, the things that unite us, without loosing track that they are the cultural arm of the Brazilian Ministry of External Relations"[102] (Rocha interview 2010). The activities of the centre follow the general guidelines from Brasília, which include: the teaching of Portuguese language (the Brazilian variant), promotion of Brazilian literature (including publishing activities), music and cinema, distribution of information on Brazil, and the organisation of exhibitions, shows and talks to make Brazilian culture available to the local publics (Ministério das Relações Exteriores do Brasil 2010b). The other important program, also developed in Mozambique, but that is particularly important in Guinea Bissau, is the student program Programa de Estudantes-Convênio, which the Brazilian Ministry of Foreign Relations, Itamaray, justifies thus: "Brazil contributes to the training of qualified human resources; provides knowledge of Brazilian reality, cultural exchanges and the expansion and deepening of the vision of the Other"[103] (Ministério das Relações Exteriores do Brasil 2010b).

Culture and language, both in 2002 and at present, are important visible areas of cooperation between Brazil and Guinea-Bissau. The CEB, now Centro Cultural Brasil – Guiné-Bissau (CCBGB), opened in 1988 in Guinea-Bissau. In terms of infrastructure the center houses a multimedia library, multipurpose rooms and classrooms and an outdoor area. As recently as 2009 the centre was

---

102 "a promoção da lusofonia e da cultura brasileira de uma forma interactiva com a cultural local, destacando as semelhanças , as coisas que nos unem, sem perder de vista que são o braço do Departamento Cultural do Ministério de Relações Exteriores do Brasil"

103 "o Brasil contribui para a formação de recursos humanos qualificados; proporciona o conhecimento da realidade brasileira, o intercâmbio cultural e a ampliação e aprofundamento da visão do outro"

refurbished and a café area, additional classrooms and an open-air theatre (100 places) have been built. Only in 2010 has the center been able to be fully operational (Rocha 2010 interview).

Before I analyse the activities developed by the centre, it is important to note that the CEB was closed from 2005 to 2008. This was due to differences between the Director of the Centre, at the time, and the Ambassadors regarding his work contract and the mission of the CEB. At the time of my visit to Bissau in 2002, the director of the CEB, Arnaldo Lima said the center used to be an open space to everyone, but now its use as a cultural center was being limited and it had turned into a school, since the teaching of the language became a main point for the Ambassador (Lima 2002 interview). Lima acknowledged that there was a rivalry between the embassy and the CEB. At the time the center also struggled with the need for space and with the updating of the library. According to Lima, Guinea-Bissau was not a priority for Brazil. Working conditions had deteriorated. Since 2001, the CEB directors were hired locally and paid in the local currency - there were no guarantees, he said. It was a measure taken by the Brazilian government to reduce internal and external debt. The divergences led three years later to the resignation of the Director and to the closing of the center between 2005 and 2008 (Rocha 2010 interview). In 2008, the center reopened under a double co-ordination, one responsible for co-ordination of academic affairs and the other for cultural affairs. Unlike the previous Director, those presently responsible for cultural affairs, are part of staff of the Brazilian Ministry of Foreign Affairs. Human resources problems are not uncommon with personnel hired for external spread activities and the Portuguese IC has had many problems regarding the terms and conditions of the work contract of teachers and lecturers hired to work in its network.

On of the strongholds of the activities of the Center have been the Portuguese language courses. In 2002 they provided courses of introduction to literacy for children (pre-school level, since 1993), basic Portuguese and Brazilian literature. In 2001/2 they also had literacy courses for adults. In the past, CEB had also promoted courses of Portuguese for foreigners (1989/90) (Lima A 2002 interview). During the period of closure, the Portuguese classes were suspended. They reopened in 2008, with the placement of a Brazilian lecturer in the CCBGB that is in charge of the academic affairs and at present delivers "Brazilian culture and Portuguese language reinforcement classes"[104] (Rocha 2010 interview) to 800 students from the 9th grade onwards (secondary school students) – but there is a waiting list of 900! This clearly evidences the eagerness of students to improve their skills in Portuguese language, and makes

---

104 "aulas de reforço da língua portuguesa e cultural brasileira"

them a preferential target group for the activities of the center (It is also worth noting that all the activities of the center are free, which given the economic conditions of the population, is an extremely attractive offer). In these classes there is also a concern with the promotion of citizenship and the development of oral and communicational skills (Rocha, Cultural Affairs Co-ordinator at the CCBGB, 2010 interview). This provision intends to reinforce and support the Guinean education system, which as pointed out has extreme problems. The provision of the Portuguese language classes and Brazilian literature and culture classes was justified by the Coordinator of Cultural Affairs as being for the "promotion of Lusophony"[105] (Rocha 2010 interview). This mention of the concept of Lusophony regarding the teaching of Portuguese at CCBGB indicates that the concept is acceptable and useful in the Guinean context, unlike in Mozambique. The extreme weakness of the Guinea state and education system and its desperate need for external aid and support are not alien to this predisposition. I will return to this issue in Chapter 5.

Although at present the CCBGB clearly divides in terms of structure, language and culture, they work in synergy. From the issues debated in Portuguese class, the coordinators are able to single out subjects (e.g. delinquency) that concern youth and explore these in the cultural activities of the center. They will have talks, workshops or focus the work of one of their permanent groups on the particular issue to be discussed. This integration of the academic and cultural areas is visible, for instance, in the activity of the CCBGB theatre group *Lingua de Bode*. The youth theatre group works in the adaptation of classic Brazilian literary works to the Guinean reality; they work the language and the oral skills and present their work at the Center and in the community (e.g. schools). The poetry group *Vida Verso* develops a similar work. Although the work of these groups is mainly developed in Portuguese, Crioulo is also used in some occasions to present part of the work they develop to particular audiences. It was interesting to register the observation of the Coordinator for the Cultural Affairs of CCBGB that in Guinea Bissau "people think their things are of less worth"[106] and that the work that was being developed at the Center was also aimed at changing that attitude by showing respect for Crioulo, as a language, in the interactions that they developed in classes and talks (Rocha 2010 interview). This indicates that there is awareness of the underlying power issues of language relations, however this sort of attitude is still dependent on the individual managing the center/service and not issuing from a clear central political directive.

---

105 "perspectiva da promoção da lusofonia"
106 "As pessoas têm um sentido que as coisas deles são menores"

The CCBGB, like the CEB before, promotes the Brazilian culture by organizing cinema sessions (this was the only cultural activity of the Center that continued during the closure thanks to the good will of a local Embassy employee), exhibitions, musical shows, theatre plays and poetry readings. CEB also promoted a literary competition, the *Prémio Literário José Carlos Schwarz*, created in 1991 - of which the Portuguese Cultural attaché was normally part of the jury. The cultural activities although promoting Brazilian culture integrate elements of the local culture appealing both to the local and expatriate communities. For instance, one of their significant projects *Bissau canta Brasil* (Bissau sings Brazil) the local artists are encouraged to include Brazilian music in their repertoire.

The cultural activities at CCBGB, besides interacting with the academic part, are also connected to the technical cooperation projects developed by Brazil in Guinea-Bissau. At present one of the cooperation projects focuses on the promotion of the civil register of births and on the promotion of human rights in education (Incidentally, the programme developed to promote the fundamental rights of the children is not concerned with the use of African languages in education! – Rocha 2010 interview) and the CCGB is promoting debates, cinema sessions and the launch of a book around the same subjects. The book "Brasil-Guiné-Bissau Olhares Cruzados pela Identidade" is part of a series that gathers testimonies of children from Brazil and other countries regarding identity. Besides working with the other embassy services, and with a wide range of Brazilian partners (government bodies, foundations, NGOs), the CCBGB establishes partnerships locally with governmental structures (Instituto da Biodiversidade e das Áreas Protegidas / Institute of Biodiversity and Protected Areas), local NGOs (AD, Aifa-Palop) and occasionally with the other cultural centres – I return to this point in section 4.2.3.4. The centre also has a radio programme, *Movimento Brasileiro*, in the Catholic Church local radio station, *Sol Mansi*.

The development of the cultural programmes at the CCBGB is limited by the financial procedures dictated by the Brazilian Ministry of Foreign Affairs. The Coordinator proposes and discusses the activities with the local Ambassador and then these have to be authorized by the Ministry, only then will financial resources be available (Rocha 2010 interview). This does not leave much maneuvering space to the local structure – they can obviously make use of the infrastructure, but any decision that involved spending of monies need previous authorization, which takes some time. This constrains the flexibility of the structures to respond to any short notice local needs and projects. However it is not a problem specific to the Brazilian center in Bissau - in Mozambique the Director also noted similar problems, and the Portuguese structures are not alien to the same issues. Only the bi-national French centers, in both case studies, are autonomous financially, which allows them great flexibility.

In 2002 limited financial resources and internal divergences in strategy (between the Director of the centre and the Ambassador) hindered the already circumscribed impact of the centre. Even more in Guinea-Bissau, that in Mozambique, the foreign cultural centres concentrate their activities in the capital, due to the deterioration of the transport network and issues with security. At present the economic crisis, in addition to the mentioned constraints, hinders the development of activities by the CCBGB. The planning of activities is defined locally, as mentioned, and no main strategies are issued from central structures. Long term planning is made difficult by the short missions staff serve in the countries, normally two, or three, years (Rocha 2010 interview).

In terms of educational cooperation, Brazil made available to Guinean youths – as it did in the Mozambican case - the *Programa Estudante Convénio* (Student Covenant Program) that offers vacancies to students in bachelor and post-graduation courses in Brazil. In 2002, around 250 Guinean students were in Brazil, and 50 of them received scholarships. In 2004 it was estimated that the number of Guineans studying in Brazil under that programme would reach 400 (Embaixada do Brasil na Guiné-Bissau 2007). Although the cultural center was closed from 2005 to 2008, the Programa de Estudantes-Convênio was able to continue thanks to the efforts of local embassy workers. The countries have "agreed to seek to further strengthen cooperation in the training of Guinean students, which has already made it possible for around 900 Guinean citizens to carry out their education in Brazilian higher education and post-graduate institutions, between 2000 and 2007" (Ministério das Relações Exteriores do Brasil 2007). At present the CCBGB is developing activities to reinforce the preparation of the students of Guinea Bissau to attend the Brazilian establishments and support their integration. As the Coordinator of Cultural Affairs noted, since Portuguese is a foreign language in Guinea Bissau, the students struggle with the use of the Portuguese language (highly influenced by Crioulo). Their level of mastery of Portuguese has often been found not to be sufficient to secure positive outcomes of attending the courses in Brazil. The centre tests the students on their Portuguese linguistic competences and that becomes part of the selection process for the Programa de Estudantes-Convênio. The Programa de Estudantes-Convênio is particularly important for Guinea-Bissau given that the higher education structures in the country are extremely weak (unlike Mozambique).

Brazil's external LSP is concurrent with the country's national policies and with Portugal's external LSP in the spread of Portuguese language in Guinea-Bissau, although the two countries do not co-ordinate their actions or have significant collaboration. I return to this issue in section 4.2.3.4. No issues about varieties of Portuguese have been identified, either in 2002 or in 2010. This is explained first by the extreme need of Guinea-Bissau in receiving support to implement its national educational and developmental policies, and secondly, by the increased multilateral commitment of the Lusophone countries in the management of Portuguese language (orthographic agreement) and the development of an international strategy (section 4.1.4.3). Thus as the cultural co-ordinator of the Brazilian centre (Rocha 2010 interview) explained the matter of variety was not important, as long as it was a standardised variety, a *norma culta*, which only the European and the Brazilian varieties of Portuguese are - for the moment.

4.2.3.3 The External Language Spread Policy of France in Guinea-Bissau

Despite newly independent Guinea-Bissau's relationships with the international community being centred in the Soviet Union countries, French cooperation was, from the start, involved in the development of the country. The 1990s were characterised by a large wave of French language spread in Guinea-Bissau. Until the 1998/9 conflict French cooperation was very active and occupied key sectors. French external LSP included a very dynamic cultural centre that focused both on cultural exchange and language teaching, also providing support for the training of teachers with the objective to spread French through the national education system at secondary school level - a similar strategy to the one followed in Mozambique. Several interviewees stressed the great investment made by the French in the years prior to the conflict and saw the Franco-Guinean Cultural Centre, a sort of Georges Pompidou Centre, as the major symbol of this era. The 1998 conflict led to a breakdown in the relations of the two countries that were re-established in 2000. Progressively French external LSP projects have been reinstated and it is particularly relevant to note that the cultural centre was rebuilt and reopened in 2004. The economic relations between the countries are very modest (Ambassade de France à Bissao 2010). However the justifications for French language spread in Guinea-Bissau must be viewed in a context of the maintenance and reinforcement of Francophony in Africa, a policy objective still valid in French contemporary policy (Remiller 2008, Assemblée Nationale de France 2010).

With the outbreak of hostilities in Bissau in 1998/9, France had to evacuate its diplomatic personnel, as the buildings that housed the embassy and the Franco-Guinean Cultural Centre were destroyed. French interests were targeted because it was popular belief that France was backing the deposed government through Senegal. Verschave (1998 and 2000), as mentioned in section 2.1.3.4, wrote extensively exposing French policy in Africa as being aimed at exploiting the geopolitical and natural resources of the Francophone countries. In his book, *Noir Silence*, published in 2000, he denounced France's involvement supporting the Senegalese troops that came to Bissau in support of President Nino Vieira in the 1998/9 conflict, in the name of economic and military interests: corruption and arms, drugs and diamonds trafficking benefiting the elites of the countries involved. INEP researcher, Fafali Koudawo (2002 interview) that witnessed the 1998/9 conflict and the hostility against France believed that the wave of rage quickly faded and did not damage France's influence in the country:

> In reality, in my opinion, there was no break in France's influence capacity here. I would actually say the opposite, because the country now is more weakened, therefore needs more help. The country is in an area whose godmother or godfather is France. France has something to say about everything concerning the finance in the Franc zone. And Guinea-Bissau being the weakest country in the area is at the mercy of France. France has an immense direct influence.

> France also has influence through Senegal. But the relations between the two countries are now stable.[107]

The present partnership agreement between France and Guinea-Bissau (2008-2012) establishes the teaching of French, cultural cooperation and student mobility as transversal programmes supporting the country plans to reinforce human capital as describes in its DENARP. The document justifies the intervention: "To ensure its stability, boost economic development and strengthen its human capacity, Guinea-Bissau wishes to improve its regional integration and to have the means to make exchanges with Francophone Africa and to work with their corporations"[108] (Ministère des Affaires Etrangères 2008, p.9). As in the Mozambican case study, the 'request for language spread' is always attributed to the target country, and here, as the case of English in Mozambique, justified by the economical regional integration of the country, and also by the affiliation to specific politico linguistic blocs - Guinea Bissau has been a member of the OIF

---

107 "Na realidade, para mim, não houve uma quebra na capacidade de influência da França aqui. Diria até pelo contrário, porque o país agora está mais enfraquecido, pelo que precisa mais de ajuda. O país está numa zona cujo padrinho ou madrinha é a França. A França tem voz sobre tudo o que pode acontecer no domínio financeiro na zona do Franco. E a GB sendo o país mais fraco da zona, está à mercê da França. A França tem uma influência directa imensa."
"A França também tem influência interposta através do Senegal. Mas as relações estão estabilizadas entre os países."
108 "Para assegurar a sua estabilidade, dinamizar o seu desenvolvimento económico e reforçar as suas capacidades humanas, a Guiné-Bissau deseja aperfeiçoar a sua integração regional e dotar-se de meios para intercambiar com a África francofona e para trabalhar com as suas empresas."

249

since 1979. Thus the teaching of French is presented as "a priority of education programs and is object of a strong demand by a significant proportion of the population, which sees it as a vehicle for economic and social advancement and inclusion in the job market" (*ibid.*). Again, as in Mozambique, French (and the European languages) is presented as a tool for development. The functional arguments stress the usefulness of French to access modernity ("advancement") and jobs. The Service de Coopération et d'Action Culturelle (SCAC) of the French Embassy in Guinea-Bissau aims to promote French culture and language thought Francophony and cultural diversity (Ambassade de France en Guinée-Bissao 2007, Ambassade de France à Bissao 2010). The cultural diversity argument as a backdrop for the spread of French in Mozambique has already been discussed (section 4.1.3.4) and I will discuss it in Chapter 5.

The teaching of French in Guinea-Bissau targets specific publics: the initial and in-service training of teachers; young people that just finished their education; government administration; corporations (Ministère des Affaires Etrangères 2008, p.9).

Education and youth, administration and business were also addressed as priorities by the British Council Mozambique in the spread of English, particularly at the turn of the century. These areas are key in the sustained spread of foreign international language: through the education system there is a first contact with the language being spread– and for the ones that distinguish themselves, the potential elite, there is often the chance to develop their knowledge further through scholarships. Consolidating the linguistic skills of the administration allows people to be more at ease using that particular language and to use it more often in regional/international domains. Since Guinea-Bissau integrates economic regional blocs dominated by French as an international language, it is important for business to have the necessary linguistic skills to interact in the region.

The partner organizations in the diffusion of French are indicated in the 2008-2012 partnership agreement as being the national administrations of the countries, OIF, the Associação dos Professores de Francês da Guiné-Bissau and to have the support of the Centro Cultural Franco-Bissau-Guineense (CCFBG) (Ministère des Affaires Etrangères 2008, p.9). In the process of research I have found no references to the work of OIF in Guinea Bissau, apart from the International information Data Bank of Francophone States that operated between 1996/97 - 2001 having INEP as its partner institution. In 2002 the project was being re-evaluated but during its lifetime it was very active.

Since 1986 France supported the teaching of French in secondary schools (teacher training and materials), special courses for adults (mainly in the State administration) and the training of Guinean teachers at the French department of

250

Escola Normal Superior Tchico Té, by sending French teachers and by enabling training in France and in neighbouring Francophone countries (Senegal). When the conflict took place they were starting to spread French in the regions (Gomes, LV and Mancanha, 2002 interviews). The French department at Tchico Té was destroyed in the conflict and the French School in Bissau, also closed at the time of the 1999/8 conflict. The French Department was rebuilt but the school was not reopened. However in 2001 a group of parents created a local association to open a private international school, Ecole Internationale de Bissau, where they could educate their children according to the French educational programme. After the conflict, France diplomacy returned to Guinea Bissau in 2000. The responsible for the Cultural and Cooperation Services of the French Embassy, Christophe Laniese (2002 interview) said that after evaluating the situation of the country they decided to concentrate on three main areas: finance, health and media. Finance, because it was the basis of the recovery of the country; health, because of the need of the populations; and media, as a means to achieve democratisation in the country. Regarding the diffusion of French, they continued supporting the French department at Tchico Té. However, in 2002 there were only 4 teachers whilst before the conflict there were 7 (Mancanha 2002 interview). In 2002 French authorities were also subsidising the French association of teachers and providing around 20 new scholarships per year to study in the sub-region (most to Senegal). In 2008 France re-examined the scholarship program and decided to focus on particular areas of more demand of the job market and in line with the priorities of the bilateral cooperation program (finance, public administration, infrastructures, health) (Ministère des Affaires Etrangères 2008, p.9). The French local embassy information website indicates the scholarships available are for the duration of 2 years in a country of the sub-region - no other information was obtained. Unfortunately it was also not possible to obtain any update regarding the support to Tchico Té - however the absence of reference to this institution in the information received from the embassy could be seen to indicate that the support has been terminated. Regarding the teachers' association, the relations between partners might have been strained as I indicate further in the text.

The bulk of the language spread activities of French cultural diplomacy in Guinea-Bissau are concentrated on the Centre Culturel Franco-Bissao-Guinéen (CCFBG). In 2004 the refurbished CCFBG reopened in Che Guevara Square and is one of the few places for cultural events in Bissau (theatre, concerts and exhibitions). CCFBG is a bi-national cultural centre, as the one in Mozambique, a local law institution constituted by the Guinean Ministry of Foreign Affairs and the French Embassy. The facilities of the centre also include a multimedia library and among the activities developed are: French language courses, a wide range of arts events, technical courses, conferences. French courses are very popular. The courses are organized in 6 to 7 sessions of 4 weeks, each lasting 40h, and attended by over 350 students per session (Roussey and Le Beller 2010 emails). The arts events cover all different artistic areas and French, Francophone and Guinea-Bissau work. In their activity the CCFBG also uses commercial sponsors. These activities are similar to the activities previously developed by the fist incarnation of the centre, the Centro Cultural e Pedagógico Francês de Bissau, which started working in 1975. Regarding that first period of activity there was a focus on the promotion of French through language courses for the general public and the State, including the use of radio to transmit French courses in Portuguese and, interestingly, in Crioulo (Expresso 13.06.87, reference in Appendix 7).

The present aims of the CCFBG are described on its website (http://www.ccf-bissau.fr/, last accessed 4.07.2010) as: to "favour the teaching and the availability of French language in the Republic of Guinea-Bissau"[109]; "be a meeting place for all that share the wish of the language and of French thought as well as the cultures in French language"[110]; "favour the cultural interchange between the Republic of Guinea-Bissau and France"[111]; "be a space of study, debate and leisure"[112]. These aims place an important responsibility on the CCFBG in terms of language spread that seems to be growing. The partnership document, referred to earlier, mentioned as one of the partners in the spread of French, the Associação dos Professores de Francês da Guiné-Bissau (French Teachers Association of Guinea Bissau) (Ministère des Affaires Etrangères 2008, p.9). However, information provided by the responsible for French cooperation and culture (Roussey 2010 email) reports that the CCFBG, since 2007, gave leave to the teachers association that managed the French courses at the center (which I presume is the same as the one referred to in the other document, and this is why I mentioned earlier the possibility of a strain in the relationship between the partners). The CCFBG undertook the management of the courses, hired more staff and obtained contract work that was contributing to a financial balance in relation to the SCAC subvention - although the self-financing of the courses was not seen as possible given the economic situation of the country (Roussey 2010 email). Additional information points to further expansion of the courses, as the Center will recruit three more teachers from September 2010 (Le Beller 2010 email). These teachers will be 'native' speakers (two French and

---

109 "favorecer o ensino e a divulgação da língua francesa na República da Guiné-Bissau"
110 "servir de lugar de encontro para todos os que compartilham o desejo da língua e do pensamento francês bem como culturas da língua francesa"
111 "favorecer intercâmbios culturais entre a República da Guiné-Bissau e a França"
112 "propôr aos seus aderentes um espaço de estudo, de debate e de lazer"

another from Quebec). I attribute this choice to the fact that "The number of qualified teachers (that is to say, having both a satisfactory mastery of the language and teacher training) is limited in Bissau in relation to the needs"[113] (Roussey 2010 email). However I would like to argue that given the placing of Guinea-Bissau in a predominantly Francophone sub-region, it is surprising the teachers are coming from Western developed countries - a sort of first circle of Francophony to use Kachru's (1985) terminology of concentric circles of English. Could it be that no sufficiently qualified teachers were available in the sub-region or could this choice be underpinned by the native speaker fallacy (Phillipson 1992)?

4.2.4 Perceptions and Discourses about Languages and Policies in Guinea-Bissau

In this section I discuss perceptions and discourse about languages and policies in Guinea Bissau that are important for external language spread in the context of this study. These include: language relations and competition; external language spread policies and politico linguistic blocs; and the cultural center as an instrument of external cultural policy.

4.2.4.1 Language Relations and Competition

As in the case of Mozambique, the late 1980s and 1990s witnessed numerous articles (Appendix 7), mostly in the Portuguese press, alluding to threats to Portuguese language in Guinea-Bissau and identifying French language as a competitor for the status of official language. These perceptions omitted the internal debates regarding language relations and competition revolving mainly around Portuguese and Crioulo. The Director of the Portuguese Cultural Centre in Bissau during most of the 1990s, Mário Matos e Lemos (Lemos 1999, p.29-30) contextualizes the perception:

> The Portuguese press has often transmitted the idea that Portuguese was dangerously threatened by the unstoppable spread of French, an idea echoed by many Portuguese travelers, impressed to find people speaking French while shopping in Mercado do Bandim. They did not know, however, that the majority of the Bandim vendors were from Senegal, Mauritania or Mali. The few Guinean sellers that said «bonjour» or

---

113 "Le nombre d'enseignants compétents (c'est-à-dire possédant à la fois une maîtrise satisfaisante de la langue et une formation pédagogique) est limité à Bissau par rapport aux besoins"

«oui» did not know Portuguese, but regarding French did not speak more than that.[114]

However Lemos (1999, p.28) confirms that, from 1995, there was a growing interest in learning French which led to an increasing number of language courses being on offer at the then Instituto de Cooperação Franco-Guineense (Franco-Guinean Cooperation Institute, the official name of the French Cultural Centre at that time). He (1999, p.35) also believed French intellectuals and authorities, Swedish development aid and namely the Portuguese NGO, CIDAC, through their support given to literacy in Crioulo, were indirectly 'attacking' Portuguese language in Guinea-Bissau. In his opinion the French did not do it directly given their close relations with Portugal in the EU. This attitude indicates unawareness of the benefits of mother tongue education in multilingual contexts – an attitude than it is not uncommon, but is particularly serious when is displayed by those involved in cultural diplomacy.

Despite the indication by Lemos above of foreign aid support to Crioulo, overall, the international agencies, the NGOs and the different national aid agencies have been constant partners of the Guinean State in the development of the national education system and, therefore, in the spread of Portuguese language.

Unlike Mozambique, the discourses relating to threats to Portuguese as official language have not disappeared. As recently as February 2010, the state newspaper Nô Pintcha, published an article entitled "Portuguese doesn't want to lose space in Guinea Bissau"[115] (N'Tanhá 2010). The article reports declarations of Besna Na Fonta, Secretary of State for Teaching (Secretário de Estado do Ensino). The Secretary of State is reported to state that Portuguese, despite being the official language is not that used in Guinean society - which is a commonly acknowledged fact. He is also reported to have shown concern "over the space Portuguese language has been losing for French, due to Guinea-Bissau's integration in the sub-regional organisations" and to have stated that "Portuguese may disappear, if the CPLP countries, in particular Portugal, do not take the neces-

---

114   "a imprensa portuguesa tem transmitido frequentemente a ideia de que o Português se encontrava perigosamente ameaçado pelo avanço imparável do Francês, ideia de que muitos viajantes portugueses se faziam eco, impressionados por irem às compras ao Mercado do Bandim e encontrarem a falarem Francês. Não sabiam, porém, que na sua maioria os vendedores do Bandim eram senegaleses, mauritanos ou malianos. Os poucos negociantes guineenses que diziam «bonjour» e «oui» não falavam Português, mas em questão de Francês por ali se quedavam."

115   "Português não quer perder espaço na Guiné-Bissau"

sary preventive measures"[116] (N'Tanhá 2010). There is evidence that regional integration (where French dominates) - as in the case of Mozambique - is an important factor for the spread of regionally dominant international languages. Correspondence with the sources at the Guinean Ministry of Education (Gomes 2010 email) has also pointed out this situation. Additionally, looking at information sources on Guinea Bissau, such as international organisations reports, it is very common to find those exclusively in French - something the CPLP is now trying to target with the development of a multilateral strategy for the spread of Portuguese as an international language through the approval in July 2010 of the *Declaração de Brasília*. The second relevant point of that article is the attribution of responsibility to Portugal, and also to the CPLP, in the maintenance of Portuguese in Guinea-Bissau. During the 2002 study trip, I identified on the Guinean side that same view on the historical responsibility of Portugal to help the Guinean State to spread Portuguese. As pointed out earlier, the weak state of Guinea-Bissau, politically and economically, has made the country extremely reliant on external support.

Koudawo (2002 interview) foresaw in the long run (25/30 years) the possibility of Portuguese becoming a residual language. Koudawo claimed that the Creole elite that kept Portuguese influence alive rested on a dead economy, depending on the State; the emerging elite was non-Creole and financially grounded on trans-bordering commerce, with the Francophone countries. He saw the emergence of a new important piece of data: the overwhelming islamisation of the population and the importance of islamisised sub-regional immigration.

In addition to the perception of French language threat, the perception of a potential Arabic language threat to Portuguese was identified in the early stages of my research as issuing from demographic and social factors. Lemos (2002 interview) believed a Muslim elite would replace the present elite of Guinea-Bissau, the westernised Crioulo-speaking elite, in 20 years time. He said that while the Crioulo-speaking elite who studied in Portugal and in France are attracted to stay in Europe and do not wish to return to Guinea-Bissau; the Guinean Muslims that study in Saudi Arabia or similar countries do return to the country, prepared and with a sense of mission. He saw the overwhelming islamisation of the population and the importance of islamisised sub-regional immigration as an important new piece of data. Lemos (2002 interview) also suggested that Portuguese authorities had been ignoring the requests to support the teach-

---

116 The extract of the article reads "Besna Na Fonta mostrou-se preocupado com o espaço que a língua portuguesa tem vindo a perder em detrimento do Francês, devido a integração da Guiné-Bissau nas organizações da Sub-Região.
Perante esta situação, disse que o português pode vir a desaparecer, se os países da CPLP, em particular Portugal, não tomarem medidas de prevenção necessárias."

ing of Portuguese by Muslims communities in Guinea-Bissau – again in this case, Portugal is seen as "responsible" for the maintenance and spread of Portuguese. However this perception of threat is not shared locally by all. Former Guinean Minister of Education, writer and researcher, Odete Semedo (2002 interview) did not see the use of Arabic as being a threat, since it is a cultural characteristic of the Islamic ethnic groups in Guinea-Bissau. She also pointed out that Koranic schools have shown interest in integrating the national educational system, teaching along the Koran and of Arabic language, also scientific disciplines, such as maths and science, and Portuguese language.

In the efforts to update the information for this study I have not identified new references to Arabic language; however it might be that the importance of Islam for the Guinean elites is being reinforced. Former President Kumba Yalá (2000-2003) and candidate to the 2009 elections, converted to Islam in 2008; if this was a strategy to appeal to the Muslim vote or if it has other relevance has not been determined. Given the high percentages of Muslim religion in Guinea Bissau and the multilingual nature of the linguistic landscape, I would argue that Arabic spreads mainly as a religious language - in a similar but higher percentage than in Mozambique - and is not competing with other languages in other fields of communication. However the importance of Islam amongst the elites is an open question.

4.2.4.2 External Language Spread Policies and Politico Linguistic Blocs in Guinea-Bissau

The main external language spread policies identified in Guinea-Bissau were that of the Portuguese government assisting Guinea-Bissau to maintain Portuguese as its official language and spread it in the country, with the concurrence of Brazil, and that of France, spreading French as first foreign language. These policies intertwine and are reinforced by some foreign policy choices of the Guinean state. Ultimately they influence national language policy.

The country is a member of the Francophony (since 1979) and is also a founder member of CPLP (1996). The participation in CPLP is explained by the historical connection and the linguistic legacy of colonialism. The participation in Francophony can be explained by a mix of historical, political, economical and geographical reasons:

– Guinea-Bissau is geographically part of a 'Francophone' sub-region. Both border countries (Senegal and Guinea-Conakry) and most neighbouring countries are Francophone countries and members of the Francophonie.

- Guinea-Conakry was the headquarters of the PAIGC during the armed fight for independence.
- Along all the borders there is an intense migratory movement due to the separation of ethnic groups by the colonial borders.
- Guinea-Bissau participates, since 1997, with its neighbours in UEMOA, in an economic zone promoted by France.
- With the fall of the Berlin wall, Guinean foreign policy adopted a pragmatic approach and established new rapports with Europe. France became a strong partner (temporarily estranged by the 1998/9 conflict).

The perceptions of external LSP found during research revolved around three main issues. The first is that language spread was seen as a part of international cooperation, a much needed and welcomed help to the country. The second relates to Portugal having historical responsibility in the continuation of the spread of Portuguese in Guinea-Bissau and the insufficiency of its actions. For instance, several Guineans the researcher met at a Portuguese language course in a secondary school in Bissau questioned why Portugal didn't do more. The third issue relates to cooperation with France, perceived by most Guineans as not competing with the Portuguese in the areas of language spread, but as an important and wealthy international donor, and perceived as language competition by Portuguese based authors (and also used by some Guineans to 'prick' Portugal's pride).

These perceptions all point to the importance of the colonial legacy, linking Portugal and Portuguese to Guinea-Bissau, and to the dependency of the country in relation to the external donors. In that sense the belonging to politico linguistic blocs, in the case of Guinea-Bissau, Francophony and Lusophony, implies also a positioning of the country within, at times, potentially conflicting networks. As I mentioned earlier, research findings indicate at present that one of the relevant debates in the country regarding language is the use of Portuguese in the regional international organisations where French (and English) predominate. Thus at the same time that Guinea-Bissau is a member of the Francophony, it also defends Lusophony - which within an official perspective of Francophony as an organisation that defends cultural diversity is not problematic. Boutros-Ghali, the Secretary-General of Francophony, visiting Guinea-Bissau in January 1998 (before the conflict) said his visit was in the context of the enlargement of the Francophony to the political dimension[117]. He intended to demonstrate the importance of multiple partnerships, as was the case of Lusophony and Francophony, in the defence of cultural diversity and pluralism (Banobero, Intégra-

---

117 Previously just cultural and economic, the political dimension is a consequence of the Cotonou Summit and the decisions made in Hanoi.

tion, Le supplément en français de Banobero, Ano I, N.º 00, 10/02/98). However, French research Cahen (1998) believed there is an evident stance of France in defending and extending its area of influence. Portuguese authorities have always toned down this perception of competition, however the then President of the Instituto Camões, Jorge Couto, in an interview to the Portuguese daily newspaper Público (18.11.98), acknowledged French was a competitor in Guinea-Bissau.

In Guinea-Bissau, the concept of Lusophony is an instrumental concept. Lusophony is not seen as a cultural entity but as a financing entity (Djaló 2002 interview). Fafali Koudawo (2002 interview) observed that while Portuguese cooperation saw their influence as cultural in Guinea-Bissau, the elite of the country saw language from a utilitarian perspective: the more languages the better, the more people they can communicate with. So they saw language spread not as negative but value added. The problems Guinea-Bissau has in sponsoring their officials to participate in IILP/CPLP meetings and the lack of resources to pay its quotas are well known - they were even mentioned by Calane da Silva, Mozambican intellectual, researcher and Director of the Centro Cultural Brazil - Moçambique (2010 interview) in the Mozambique case study. Gomes A (2002 interview), in 2002 Director General of Secondary and Higher Education at the Ministry of Education and also the Guinean representative of the IILP/CPLP, said that if there was no solidarity between the CPLP members, the IILP would be an incomplete body, and the missing part would surely be Guinea-Bissau.

The thematic of Lusophony and Francophony seems to be enduring in Guinea Bissau, and is echoed periodically in the programmes of the CCFBG. The CCFBG celebrated last March 2007 the Francophony day by organizing, among other events, a conference entitled "Portuguese and French, Latin Languages, Sister Languages", which highlighted the importance of language diversity in Africa for Francophony and the complementarity of Portuguese and French in Guinea-Bissau (Ambassade de France en Guinée-Bissao 2007). This event echoes the words of Boutros Boutros-Ghali, secretary general of the Francophonie who in his 1998 visit to Guinea-Bissau stated that there was no contradiction between Lusophony and Francophony: "they are two cultural, political and economical groupings that cooperate having in mind the same objective, the defence of cultural diversity and plurilinguism"[118] (Banobero, Intégration, Le supplément en français de Banobero, Ano I, N.º 00, 10/02/98). In May 2009 there as

---

118 "ce sont deux groupements culturels, politiques et économiques qui vont coopérer, tout en ayant le même objectif, à savoir la défense de la diversité culturelle et du plurilinguisme" (Banobero, Intégration, Le supplément en français de Banobero, Ano I, N.º 00, 10/02/98)

a debate on "Guinea-Bissau at the Luso-Francophone Crossroads"[119] (Ministério das Relações Exteriores do Brasil 2009). In 2010, the celebration of the 40 years of Francophony, at the CCFBG, which included a speech by the Guinea Bissau Minister of Foreign Affairs, also presented a series of forums that explored different facets of Francophony (political actor, instrument of development, vector of education, space of freedom and for the imagination) and ended with a debate on the future of French language (Centre Cultural Franco-Bissau-Guineen website www.ccf-bissau.fr 2010). Unfortunately I was not able to access any content on the debates. However just the fact that these events are taking place, and their titles, signifies that the subject of the spread of French language in Guinea Bissau continues to be important and relevant to the country.

4.2.4.3 Cultural Centres as an Instrument of External Cultural Policy

The foreign cultural centres represent extremely important infrastructures in Bissau given the fragile political and economical situation of the country that leaves little room for investment in culture. As pointed out by the French officer responsible for cooperation and cultural action, Gilles Roussey (2010), "Cultural life in Guinea-Bissau is placed in a *sui generis* and economically difficult environment in which artists, if they have not emigrated, show a creativity that is expressed in manifold ways"[120].

The first foreign cultural centre to open in Guinea-Bissau was the French cultural centre, then Centro Cultural e Pedagógico Francês de Bissau, in 1975, becoming bi-national in a 1990 agreement. The centre was destroyed in June 1999 and reopened in 2004. The Portuguese centre opened in 1979 (closed for refurbishment in 2005/6 but continued to organised events with local partners). The Brazilian CEB, now CCBGB, opened in 1988, and was closed from 2005 to 2008. Even the life of these infrastructures denotes the fragile economic and political situation of the country, as evident in CEB's problems relating to work conditions and salaries and the CCFGB being destroyed in the 1998/9 conflict. The Centre Culturel Franco-Bissau-Guinéen (CCFBG) is in Bissau the most important cultural infrastructure: "because of its location, its premises, the nature and number of the activities that are undertaken"[121] (Roussey 2010). The only other infrastructures that are able to accommodate large audiences are hotels and

---

119 "Guiné-Bissau na encruzilhada Luso-Francófona"
120 "La vie culturelle en Guinée-Bissau s'inscrit dans un contexte sui generis et économiquement difficile dans lequel les artistes, lorsqu'ils n'ont pas émigré, manifestent pourtant une créativité qui s'exprime de façon multiforme."
121 "tant par sa situation, ses locaux, que la nature et le nombre des activités qui s'y déployent"

corporations. The Portuguese and the Brazilian centers' infrastructures have a smaller dimension.

Given the overall scarcity of infrastructures and resources, it would be expected that the centers, as in Mozambique, would maintain close relations, coordinating and pooling their resources. This is not the case. My research findings in Guinea Bissau suggest that there is at presented limited collaboration between the centres and no coordination of activities. In my 2002 visit, the French responsible for the cultural and cooperation services, Laniese (2002 interview) said the European countries met at least once a month and they exchanged information regarding their activities, the situation of the country and future perspectives. They did not, however, have common projects.

It could be argued that the present apparent lack of collaboration and coordination between the cultural centres is consequence of a series of factors: limited financial resources and autonomy of the local services (dependent on central budgets and inflexible procedures – particularly in the case of Portugal and Brazil) that complicate the establishment of partnerships; the lack of strong personal relationships (or even the will to foster them) and the lack of any established procedures for co-ordination (the personal relationships could encourage the informal coordination); absence of political will to cooperate or coordinate activities issuing from perceptions of cultural and linguistic competition.

At present, the cooperation between the Brazilian and the French centres although restricted exists and the relations are good. Given the financial difficulties, mentioned by the responsible of the cultural affairs of the Brazilian centre, it could be argued that that is the main obstacle to further collaborations. The Director of the CCFGB said of the relations with CCBGB: "Excellent relations, regular and sustained" [122] (Le Beller 2010 email). The CCBGB and the CCFGB had in 2009 a series of events celebrating the year of France in Brazil that included exhibitions, talks, dance and musical events taking place in both infrastructures.

During the 1990s the Portuguese cultural centre had some events in partnership with CEB but never with the French centre, although they had good relationships. At present, regarding the relations with the Portuguese centre, both the Brazilian and French counterparts indicated the near absence of relations apart from courtesy. The Director of the Cultural Affairs of CCBGB mentioned the relations between the centres not being very close. However the responsibles for the centres promoted and attended each other's events (Rocha 2010 interview). The Director of the CCFGB confirmed the promotion of each other's events, but noted the further absence of the relations with the Portuguese cultural centre:

---

122 "Excellentes relations, régulières et soutenues"

"Scarce relations, virtually nonexistent in terms of collaboration and exchanges"[123] (Le Beller 2010 email). He further commented that it was difficult for him to explain the situation and said:

> It seems that, after the reopening of the French Cultural Centre in 2004, following the 1998 conflict, the French-Portuguese relations in Bissau, in terms of cultural exchanges, remained at a level close to zero ... Question of conflict? Which? It is worth noting that the Portuguese focus on language, not so much on culture, which is not our case. In any event it is difficult to give you a clear and precise answer[124] (Le Beller 2010 email).

I interpret this comment as indicating a perception of competition between the two cultural diplomacies directly connected with the language spread of French and Portuguese in Mozambique.

The Brazilian responsible for the cultural affairs, Rocha (2010 interview) noted that the Portuguese cultural centre, during the time she had been in the post (since 2008) appeared to be in a quiet phase for reasons she was unaware of - she noted being told that the person in charge of the Portuguese centre before was very active. This could reinforce the argument that the level of cultural activities developed by the cultural diplomacy structures depends to a great extent on the individuals in charge locally. Unfortunately the person responsible in 2010 for the Portuguese Cultural Centre was always unavailable to supply any information for this study, which prevents me having access to 'the other side of the story'... The situation may in itself be significant and interpreted as lack of transparency in the development of cultural diplomacy.

4.2.5 Conclusion

As in Mozambique, language policy (or in real terms the lack of it) in Guinea-Bissau does not reflect the linguistic situation of the country. It reflects the lack of a clear national project that is caused mainly by the instability of political power and the need for national reconciliation. The elite inherited the colonial language and despite initial ideals to use Crioulo as a language of national unity that would also be used in education, bridging between Portuguese and African languages, was not able to translated that into reality. Although the elite has

---

123 "Relations rares pour ansi dire inexistantes en matière de collaboration et d'échanges"
124 "Il semblerait que, depuis a réouverture du CCF en 2004, suite au conflit de 1998, les relations franco-portugaises à Bissau, en matière d'échanes culturels, soient toujours restés à un niveau proche du zéro...Question de conflits ? Lesquels ? Il faut savaoir que les portugais mettent l'accent sur la langue, peu sur le culturel ce qui n'est pas notre cas. En tout état de cause difficile de vous donner une réponse claire et precise."

remained stable, with the adding of new elements with the opening up of the country to democracy and liberal economy in the 1980s and 1990s, its functioning as a steering group of the nation appears to be undermined by corruption and ethnic tensions, thus not allowing the rhetoric of the freedom fighters to be replaced by a clear sense of nationhood in the construction of a modern state.

The multicultural and multilingual reality of Guinea-Bissau, the linguistic rights of its people and the problems with the use of Portuguese in education have not been given enough consideration, despite the occasional encouragement provided by external partners. Given the overall context of the country, one might argue that other needs have priority. However, education has been considered a main priority in the development of the country, and language is a fundamental issue in education.

The construction of the Guinean state has linguistically rested on the legacies of colonialism: Portuguese as the official language and Crioulo and African languages remaining undefined under the occasional label of national languages. Portuguese continues to be spread in the education system and Crioulo and the African languages are thriving through demographic trends and are very much alive in everyday life. Although international missions have verified the existence of conditions for mother tongue education in Guinea-Bissau (Benson 2010), the political commitment to Portuguese as teaching language has not changed or shown any indication that it will.

As argued throughout this study, linguistic relations reflect power relations in society. The external language spread policies developed in Guinea Bissau reinforce the role of European international languages, Portuguese, as official language, and potentially of vehicular language, and French, English, German foreign languages used in regional/international communication. If no internal change takes places – namely a national consensus on the construction of nationhood that attributes clear roles to Crioulo and/or African languages - the structural power of international European languages, linguistic legacies of colonialism and the economic external dependency of the country will continue to be the main determinants of the langue policy of Guinea-Bissau.

If no changes occur, it is also worth reflecting on how, in the long run, the linguistic rights of the Guinean population can be accounted for. As Guinean society is more and more penetrated by the educational system, subject to processes of development according to Western patterns and included in the processes of globalisation, and the European languages continue to accumulate the most cultural capital and reward its speakers with the best jobs, how will the other languages be able to sustain the linguistic competition and survive? Will the roles of language of tradition and family be sufficient? Probably not.

262

Chapter 5   Discussion and Conclusions

In this final chapter I discuss and evaluate the findings of the study. In the discussion section I analyse the differences and similarities between the case studies and, in the light of the theories and findings, discuss the topic. In the second section I return to the research questions and present the final conclusions, explain how these contribute to the development of knowledge, reflect on the research process and suggest key issues for further research.

5.1 Discussion

In the following subsections I discuss the similarities and differences of the cases studies, examine the transferability of the findings across Lusophone Africa, and identify threads and themes of the findings relating them to the theoretical issues discussed in Chapter 2.

5.1.1 Similarities and Differences in the Case Studies

In Chapter 3 Methodology I presented the case studies' similarities, namely, being sub-Saharan African multilingual countries, former colonies of Portugal and occupying lower ranks in the Human Development Index. I have also identified a series of independent variables (section 3.4) for the case studies - language relations and policies, political stability, economical development, regional context, donor interest - that arguably explains different situations in the case studies regarding being the object of external LSPs (the dependent variable). I also noted that the former colonial countries also have differences (overall capability and economic development, foreign policy range and objectives, strategies that privilege or not language activities) among themselves that explain the different deployment of external LSPs.

I will now discuss these variables in relation to the findings of the research. Regarding the similarities of the case studies, three important points must be made. First, the multilingual reality of both countries has limited impact on the main language policies adopted by the countries. They also manage that situation differently, and I will come back to this point. Secondly, the colonial legacy has had the major impact in the language relations and policy of the independent African countries. As is the case with other ex-colonies, Mozambique and Guinea-Bissau adopted Portuguese, the ex-colonial language, as official language and language of the education system. The elite groups created during the period of colonialism played a significant role in this process. Portuguese, as European ex-colonial language, had the most valued cultural capital, which was further reinforced by becoming the common language in the building of nationhood in the new African states in the tradition of Western nation building (in the case of Guinea-Bissau, Crioulo was supposed to play that role, but remained undefined). The spread of Portuguese, as the official language, became a fundamental policy in both case studies. The extension of the education system and the improvement of its quality are continuous policy objectives in both countries. Thirdly, both countries occupy the lower ranks in the Human Development Index, indicating the fragile situation of their citizens and also of their states. The states are not able to provide the conditions for their citizens to achieve certain threshold levels to live a long and healthy life, access education and have a decent standard of living. Mozambique and Guinea-Bissau are designated 'developing' countries. I have used this terminology and would like to note that the use of 'developed' and 'developing' to classify countries in this study indicates different unequal positions in the international system. Development is a concept set in Western terms and thus the placing of the countries operates within those parameters; the adjectives thus reflect the contemporary discourse. Africa is still dependent on the 'developed' world through increasing economic globalisation, predominance of Western discourses of development and dominance of European languages; they are victims of colonialism and of the structures of the international system. It is thus important to note that Mozambique and Guinea-Bissau's state budgets are extremely dependent on the international donor community.

In terms of the independent variables of the case studies, Mozambique and Guinea Bissau show important differences. In terms of language relations and policies, although Portuguese is the official language and the language of the education system in both countries - and the one with most cultural capital - in Guinea-Bissau it has faced the informal competition of Crioulo. Crioulo is considered the language of national unity and identity by a large majority of the elite but it is not politically assumed as such. This lack of a clear language policy and a defined role for the different languages may be, besides a continuity of colonial language attitudes and a sign of dependency, a reflection of the chronic political instability of Guinea-Bissau. This political instability contrasts with the Mozambican situation which is dominated by a stable and continuous political elite. Mozambique, from the mid-1980s, economically linked to World Bank and the IMF policy influences, with the regional economic integration in the SADC, and with the signature of the Peace Accords that officially ended the civil war in 1992, had the necessary conditions to receive and apply international development funds. Guinea-Bissau's political instability (in particular the period of the 1998/9 conflict and its aftermath) on the other hand caused 'donors' fatigue' and damaged the attraction of foreign investment to the country. These facts have important implications for economic development. Guinea- Bissau has a GDP per capita of US$ 225 and Mozambique a GDP per capita of US$ 397 (2007 data in Pôle de Dakar 2010). Mozambique is considered a success case in international development and a 'donor darling'. Guinea-Bissau's state is struggling, and the country is mired in international drug trafficking. In terms of the regional context both states are deepening their economic integration.

One of the underlying concerns of this study is the defence of cultural and language diversity and linguistic human rights in the case study countries. In this regard it is important to report that although African languages are thriving in Lusophone Africa (the Ethnologue only reports one extinct language in Angola - and despite the fragility of the available statistical data, in particular for Guinea-Bissau), their place of majority languages in the linguistic spaces of these countries is not translated into language policy. As I mentioned, Portuguese, as ex-colonial European language retains the hegemonic position in the policies of these countries, reflecting the value languages are ascribed in society and the power relations in those societies. Clear fault lines are evident in both countries between those who speak Portuguese and those who do not. Portuguese, besides benefiting from the arguments that position European languages at the top of the linguistic hierarchies (Ansre's (1979) identified arguments mentioned in section 2.2.2.1 are still very much alive, despite research indicating otherwise), is continuously sustained and reinforced internally, as its cultural capital offers the best rewards (education, best paying jobs, access to a bigger market), and externally by the structures, policies and agencies in the international system. The external LSPs play here a very important role, which will be discussed next. However to conclude my brief discussion about the role of the African languages in the case studies, it is important to note that the work that is being done remains at political/linguistic level, not at an economic level. Thus is the case of Mozambique, where there is a fairly large project of bilingual education; African languages are recognised as national languages; and there are resources devoted to them. However, African languages need to be valued in the economic sense to be able to survive in the long run in face of the competition of European languages that dominate the realms of power and money.

Individual choice of languages is not in the remit of this study. However the national language policies of governments are extremely important in the choices made available to the citizens and thus the state is able to manipulate the linguistic and cultural capital available. The choice of national language policies does not take place within a political and ideological vacuum. I have mentioned the colonial legacy, which is the most important factor found to have determined national language policies in the case studies, and the spread of Portuguese as ex-colonial European language. The issue of language attitudes, the spread and promotion of European languages in Africa needs to be understood within a larger context of the structure of the international system (nation/states, blocs of states, international organisations), the dependency of the African countries on the exterior (international donor community and powerful bilateral donors), the objective of achieving goals and objectives (Education for All, Millennium Development Goals) externally imposed and measured, all of which are based on a predominantly Western conception and are mediated mainly by European international languages.

African languages are perceived as important in their representation of the cultural heritage of the countries. In Mozambique there is a development of the awareness of the importance of the multicultural and multilinguistic character of the country, and African languages are now also seen as an asset for national cohesion and conscience (Agenda 2025) - which, a national language policy, currently being prepared, may translate into practice. Nevertheless, in both case studies is visible the pervasiveness of international European languages that has been fostered by the history, structure and functioning of the international system. Portuguese as the legacy of colonialism, and the language of an important politico linguistic bloc, French and English as languages associated with access to development and modernity and languages used by international and regional organisations, and to a lesser degree, German as a European language also associated with development and modernity and connected, like the other European languages, to a center of economic power, are imbued with significant cultural and linguistic capital that places them at the top of the linguistic hierarchies in the case studies.

Associated with these languages are external language spread policies that support in different measures (and, in some cases, are at the origin of) the internal language spread policy of the African countries. In Mozambique, my research identified overt external language spread policies undertaken by the governments of Portugal, Brazil, France, UK and Germany. In Guinea-Bissau, research identified external language spread policies undertaken by the government of Portugal, Brazil, France and Germany. Germany's policy was not declared.

Among these external LSPs, Portuguese language spread has a special position, as it is the official language in the case study countries. Portuguese language and its worldwide presence is central to Portugal's concept as a nation and also part of the national project of the PALOP that are now co-partners in the spread and internationalisation of Portuguese language. Portugal willingly and to the maximum of its capacity cooperates with them, as Portuguese language is considered its compared advantage or valued added in relation to other countries offering aid (although that advantage is less visible in non-linguistic areas, as there is a general rise in multilingual teams amongst aid providers). Portuguese language spread brings multiple benefits to Portugal, of which the political seem to be the most prominent, although there are also economic/financial benefits. The push for the internationalisation of Portuguese aims particularly at trying to unlock the economic potential of the language. This internationalisation has as a crucial basis the fact that Portuguese is the official language in eight countries (nine since 20th July 2010, with the adoption by Equatorial Guinea of Portuguese as its third official language, after Spanish and French); this represents the main argument for the presence of the language as official or work language in international organisations. CPLP represents that bloc of countries in international relations (the full membership of Equatorial Guinea is being negotiated). Although known, an often forgotten fact in official discourse is that the number of the citizens of the countries does not add up to the number of 'advertised' Portuguese speakers – which is, in particular, the case of the Guinea-Bissau and Mozambique. Part of the undeclared objective of Portuguese external LSP, officially developed under development aid, educational cooperation, cultural diplomacy or external cultural policy, is to make the real situation (multilingual and where Portuguese is still a minority language) match the political image. Thus in both case studies, Portugal, in the measure of its financial capacity, cooperates with the Mozambican and Guinean governments to support their efforts to spread Portuguese and reinforce its status. In both countries, education has been and is a priority in the relations with Portugal. Language is at the core of Portuguese cooperation. In terms of the development of cultural diplomacy, although the existence of other cultures is widely stated, practice shows that Portuguese language is effectively the only accepted medium to develop cultural activities.

Given that Portuguese is the official language of the African countries studied, they also benefit from the strengthening of its international position - within the established Western framework of international relations. Significantly, at the CPLP 2010 summit in Luanda (23.07.2010), the Angolan President, José Eduardo dos Santos declared "Each of our countries are inserted in different regions of four continents, which gives us the privileged status of spokespersons of each other and encourages the expansion of our influence to areas far away from our respective geographic space"[125] (Dos Santos 2010, p.2). He added:

---

125 "Cada um dos nossos países está inserido em regiões diferentes de quatro continentes, o que nos confere o estatuto privilegiado de porta-vozes uns dos outros e potencia o alar-

"CPLP becomes an important tool to develop and strengthen the assertion of our countries in the regional and international levels, ensuring our fair and effective participation in the shaping of the global political and economic order"[126] (Dos Santos 2010, p.3). Both Mozambique and Guinea-Bissau are able, according to their capacities, to exercise Portuguese external language spread – namely within the regional organisations that they are part of - as mentioned in Chapter 4.

In both case studies, the external language spread policies of Portugal and Brazil spreading Portuguese language are concurrent (although not coordinated) and no issues regarding the difference in varieties were noted. Portugal has the advantage of being the former colonial power and the source of the dominant variety of Portuguese in both linguistic spaces. As demonstrated, external language spread does not appear to be a priority of the Brazilian government.

I would like to discuss now, based on the findings of the case studies, the justifications of the actors involved regarding external LSP. The source countries justify their external LSPs using the following reasons: request of the target countries / support the African countries in their educational choices (e.g. national choice of Portuguese as official language, with particular emphasis for its role as medium of teaching; support of English or French as foreign languages in the educational system) and in their development; European languages enable communication with the outside world (regional and international links); provide access to knowledge, training, science and technology and thus contribute to development, governance, capacity-building and poverty reduction; contribute to cultural and linguistic diversity (a favourite argument of French language spread); give access to the job market. The African target countries justify the acceptance of external LSPs by: affirming a neutral view of language, e.g. Portuguese is seen as ideologically liberated (which indicates a change in the perception of the ownership of the language); Portuguese as a common language that provides the basis for national identity and unity; global and regional status of languages connected with access and participation in the structures of the international system (interstate relations, regional blocs, international organisations); diversification of languages that enables access to development resources (scholarships, training, IT, research, tourism); participation in the global market; promotion and management of poverty reduction and economic growth; and helping the migration of individual citizens.

---

gamento da nossa influência para zonas muito distantes do nosso respectivo espaço geográfico."

126 "a CPLP converte-se num instrumento importante para desenvolver e fortalecer a afirmação dos nossos países nos domínios regional e internacional, garantindo a nossa participação justa e efectiva na configuração da ordem Política e Económica Mundial."

This long list of arguments/justifications for the promotion and acceptance of the spread of European ex-colonial languages can be explained by the following clusters of reasons:

1. Historical, connected with the colonial legacy: European languages were taught in the (foreign) education systems, Portuguese as medium of education, French as main foreign language (a position that issues from French language status as the previous international lingua franca and French political and intellectual influence in Portugal), and English as a second foreign language.

2. Political and economic: In connection with the previous reasons, the European languages serve as a basis for the construction of the nationhood models - in the case studies, Portuguese (in the tradition of Western European nationalism) - of the African countries by the elites created by the colonial system. European languages are structurally favoured by the international system - they dominate interstate relations, economic processes of globalisation, and the international organisations that appropriate thinking and resources for international development. They are also the basis of important international politico linguistic blocs that represent added opportunities to enhance the profile of the African countries, their economic chances and the access to development resources. At regional level, because of the colonial legacy and the lingering dependencies, European languages are important in the construction of regional blocs.

3. Cultural imperialism: European languages and the countries associated with them are perceived as models of modernity and development. Given their structural power, European languages – and English in particular – became gateways to science and technology. Relations between source countries and the elites of the target countries, can be viewed within the framework of 'soft power'.

It is interesting to note, regarding justifications for external language policies, that, while discourses of the local representatives of external language spread policies present their action as a reply to a request of the African country, at source, discourses tend to be more open regarding underlying motivations. For instance, the UK is clear in its intent to create a platform of influence to support its long-term interests (Davidson 2007). Portugal's government programmes continuously stress the maintenance and spread of Portuguese worldwide as a statement and reinforcement of national identity. In a similar way French is important for France, although justifications for French language spread have changed in the 1980s and 1990s from the greatness of French culture and the beauty of French language to stressing the defence of cultural diversity, and to helping development through supporting French in foreign educational systems. Multilateral support of Portuguese, through CPLP, uses similar justifications: at the Luanda Summit (23.07.2010), which had as theme Solidarity in Diversity, the importance of the cultural diversity and multilingualism of the different countries was formally stressed. Germany aims to contribute to modernisation and development through intercultural dialogue. Regardless of the justification used, external language spread policy is part of foreign policy, and thus "part of the business in the projection of power and influence, of gaining friends and deterring enemies" (Fox 1999, p.1). External language spread policy projects a national linguistic image that can harness power and influence. The benefits of these policies are achieved in the long term and it is not always easy to evaluate their outcome. To use the 'buzzword' of the times, external LSPs are a privileged instrument of 'soft power'; they influence behaviours and predispose attitudes (particularly through the elites) - and can be a good business too (at present, particularly, for English language agents).

In the case studies, given the situation of the countries, as 'developing', thus aiming to reach 'development', the existence of external language spread policies is justified and matched by the source countries of these policies to the internal documents of the target country that describe the steps to achieve established (in a framework appropriated by the international institutions) objectives of capacity-building, governance, poverty reduction, economic development, etc. Moreover, in the case studies, the cultural centers or akin structures, which are symbols of external language and cultural spread policy, often carry a denomination that includes the names of the two countries (source and target) - as I will describe later - denoting a concern in moulding a positive perception of their activities by using an inclusive title. This operational mode, although in line with the rules of engagement between independent countries, masks the inherent dependency of the African countries in relation to donors, the contemporary policy objectives of the European countries and the political and historical background that contextualises those relationships.

In terms of organisation, the European countries are converging to a model to develop their cultural diplomacy that focuses on trademark institutions that contribute to enhance their strategies of nation branding. The UK through the British Council (1934), Germany through the Goethe Institut (1951), Portugal through the Instituto Camões (1992), the short-lived Brazilian Instituto Machado de Assis (2006), and France planning to bring together its cultural network abroad under the Institut Français (2010). Given their character, the local institutions representing the different cultural diplomacies are also symbolic of their source countries. Thus in Mozambique there is a British Council - Mozambique, a Instituto Cultural Moçambique - Alemanha, a Instituto Camões - Centro Cultural Português de Maputo, a Centro Cultural Brasil - Moçambique and a Centro Cultural Franco-Moçambicano. These centers, as mentioned, have tended in their designation to include the country/town in which they are. This reveals a concern with the stress of a two-way relationship. In the case of the Brazilian centres the change of name took place in 2008. The French center in Mozambique, as well as in Guinea-Bissau, is a bi-national cultural centre, the target country is the owner of the premises and the source country pays for the running costs and activities - the decisions on the programmes have been increasingly shared. In Guinea-Bissau the structures are similar; there is a bi-national Centre Culturel Franco - Bissau Guinean, an Instituto Camões - Centro Cultural Português de Bissau, and a Centro Cultural Brasil - Guiné-Bissau. These centers develop both cultural activities and pure language spread activities such as language courses. These centers may or not be also involved in coordinating other external language spread activities that are deployed in support of educational system of the target countries. In the case of France, the Service de Coopération et d'Action Culturelle is normally in charge of that, freeing the cultural centers and their Directors to focus on cultural activities. In the case of Portugal, up to 2010, the different ministerial remits translated in having various responsibilities, accumulated or not in different people regarding, for instance, support to higher education, suport to secondary and primary education, and cultural activities. These revealed themselves on the ground, at times, difficult to concilliate and coordinate.

The European countries, source of external LSPs in the case studies, develop those activities in two main areas, cultural diplomacy - mainly identified with the cultural centres which I discuss further in section 5.1.3 - and development aid - in which I include the support to the educational systems. In some cases, as was the case of France, in 1998/9, organisational rearrangements at ministerial level, that joined those two areas into a single Ministry of Foreign Affairs, had some impact on the work developed on the ground bringing to Africa officers developing work without properly considering local realities (section 2.1.3.4). Also in the case of Portugal (section 4.1.3.1) there appears to exist a political tension between language as instrument of foreign policy and as instrument of development. Moreover in the British case there was a clear political indication by DFID that English Language Teaching *per se* was not suitable for developmental work - however that work continued through the British Council (section 4.1.3.3). This apparent duality is evidence of the complex context in which external language spread activities and the intentions/objectives of the actions are defined and deployed.

The strategies of the countries identified were similar in their support to the internal structures of the target countries (e.g. university departments, teachers' associations, native teacher placement, local teachers' training), and in their deployment of their own structures (e.g. cultural centre model) that developed cultural activities enhancing the profile and increasing the attraction of the source country and the language they represent, at the same time they directly develop language spread activities (courses, exams). Scholarships are an important means to create enduring links between the elites of the target country and the source country. Alumni networks and associations of formers students were also identified as an effective means of maintaining those links active.

It is particularly significant to note in Mozambique that English and French language spread have been fostered by the UK and France to become self-sufficient in terms of spread. In the case of English, although the language was already present in the educational system, its expansion could not sustain the teaching of English without external support. Research findings indicate that the Mozambican government made the request to the UK authorities and these, through British advisers, helped in the draft of the project, that they latter financed, for the training of teachers throughout the country. In this case, it appears that the structural power of the English language (international organisations, donor community) and its regional dominance (SADC) were major factors in the event. In the case of French, its teaching had stopped with independence, and it was the suggestion and financial support of France, that were decisive in its reintroduction. This case evidences the commitment and investment of France in relation to French language. In Guinea-Bissau, France had, before the 1998/9 conflict, proceeded with similar plans. The present apparent absence of this strategy of external LSP in Guinea-Bissau is arguably connected with the unstable situation of the country and the mentioned 'donor fatigue'. In the above context, I would like to highlight the important role foreign advisers and consultants have on the definition of policies in developing countries. This issue affects the whole spectrum of 'aid' - often the models of the 'developed' world are applied without proper consideration of the local conditions. This is part of Africa's dependency.

Overall the external language spread policies reveal the hegemony of the European languages. However, Germany, tentatively, by teaching Changana in Maputo, may be evidencing a potential shift in paradigm in the development of cultural diplomacy and external language spread policies; as is the attitude of concern over the self-deprecating language perceptions of Guineans identified of staff at the Centro Cultural Brasil - Guiné-Bissau. Portuguese as official language, besides the concurrence of Portugal and Brazil in its spread, also benefits from the overall support of the framework of the international system and the work of international organisations. For instance, in terms of reaching the objective of Education for All, Portuguese, despite being at the basis of the failing of

272

the system (being a foreign language for the majority of the learners), is the language considered to be the medium of development (given its formal status of official language) - and that has remained unchallenged. In terms of the domain of external communication, the international European languages compete for foreign language use - and have niche markets according to blocs of countries.

Before ending this general discussion of the case studies it is necessary to stress the duality of some of the arguments used for external language spread policy. I will focus on two. One used by Germany, "Language is the basis of dialogue" (German Information Centre Pretoria 2010), and the other, complementary, often used by France "a dialogue with other languages and cultures in the world in order to promote cultural diversity" (Ministère des Affaires Étrangères 2007c). Language is the basis of communication and dialogue, and promoting a language is *per se* a good thing. I find the secondary title of an overview of the German programme Aktion Afrika, to be self-explanatory: "The many faces of cultural cooperation" (German Information Centre Pretoria 2010). External language spread policies are both good and bad for African countries. After all languages are means of communicating and, as many of my interviewees suggested, the more the better! However, are external language spread policies deployed in the case studies, and overall, with altruistic purposes? At this point I would like to recall that cultural relations integrate an element of self-interest (any perceived positive outcome obtained from the engagement), only the awareness and willingness to respond/satisfy the needs/interests/objectives of the '*Other*', will dictate the outcome of the relationship for either engaging country. Cultural diplomacy can have positive aspects (presenting yourself and knowing the '*Other*') although it can also contribute to cultural imperialism, since it promotes the values and structures of a dominating center (Schiller 1976 in Phillipson 1992). External language spread policies can thus be viewed as part of linguistic imperialism, as they promote the language of a dominating ex-colonial center. Fundamentally, all external LSPs examined implied asymmetrical linguistic relations - predominance of European languages - which undermine the positive benign context in which cultural relations are officially portrayed as happening. And like a cuckoo (Phillipson 2006a) they create means for their self-perpetuation.

My critique of the spread of European languages must be seen in the context of my stand in defence of a balanced linguistic societal equilibrium, one that has cultural and linguistic diversity as an ideal and that defends linguistic human rights. I find that the external language spread polices of the European countries in Africa promote and reinforce the structural advantage of their international languages and contribute to the lack of use of the other languages. While, in the contemporary world, the need for international (European) languages is undeniable, governments actively seeking to spread them should also foster the use and valorisation of other languages - in the case of Africa, part of their cultural/language spread budgets and know-how should also be applied to the local languages.

5.1.2 Transferability of Findings to Lusophone Africa

In section 3.2.2, I mentioned I would attempt transferability of the findings of the study to Lusophone Africa. Lusophone Africa shares a common colonial history and legacy. Portuguese is the official language of all PALOP. In Angola, Portuguese shares the linguistic space with 39 African languages - 6 of these have had a significant corpus development and have been used in experimental bilingual educational projects, besides being used in ad hoc literacy projects. The other two PALOP, Cape Verde and São Tomé and Príncipe, face less linguistic diversity: Portuguese and Creoles of Portuguese base. In Cape Verde there are plans to make the local Creole also an official language. Nevertheless, despite the political signs that favour the status of the African languages, in practice the status of Portuguese language remains undisputed. The colonial legacy (and its implications in the lower status and lack of development of the African languages) appears as the main determinant of the internal language policies of the African Lusophone countries, regardless of their linguistic makeover (more or less diverse).

I would argue that the patterns regarding external LSPs occurring in the cases examined can be observed in the other Lusophone countries.

As previously mentioned, all countries of Lusophone Africa are founding members of CPLP and IILP, which, at multilateral level, evidences their commitment to Portuguese, their official language. With the exception of Angola, they are members of the OIF (although Mozambique only has observer status). As I mentioned in section 2.3.1.1, the importance of this belonging is relative. Angola, for instance, although not being a member of OIF is still the target of bilateral external language spread policy of France. I will now briefly explore the deployment of external LSP by France in the other Lusophone countries to support my argument of the transferability of the conclusions of this study to other Lusophone countries.

All African Lusophone countries are part of the French Zone de Solidarité Prioritaire, and France's external language spread policy has been active in all of Lusophone Africa, as shown in the following table:

Table 5.1 French Cultural Network in Lusophone Africa (2010)

	Embassy services (SCAC)	Centre Culturel	Alliance Française
Angola	✓		✓
Cape Verde	✓	✓	✓
Guinea Bissau	✓	✓	
Mozambique	✓	✓	
São Tomé and Príncipe	✓		✓

The official justifications for French external LSP in Lusophone Africa are connected with the use of French language as a language of communication with neighbouring countries and as a language of emigration. The Haut Conseil de la Francophonie (1997, p.506) reported: "In Cape Verde, Guinea-Bissau and São Tomé e Príncipe (Portuguese official language), French is firstly a language of communication with the francophone neighbouring countries and of migration: Senegal and France for Cape Verde, Gabon for São Tomé."[127] The vast number of refugees returning to Angola has also meant the increase in speakers of French and English, the official languages of the countries that received them during the conflicts. Moreover, a vast number of Francophones and Francophiles existed in the PALOP at independence, since, during colonial times, French was the first foreign language to be learnt in the educational system of the African Portuguese colonies (following the system of metropolitan Portugal). Present French external language spread fosters the local teaching of French language as a main instrument for the sustaining of Francophony in those countries.

The proactiveness of French external LSP in Lusophone Africa is self-evident. In 1997, Cape Verde undertook an education system reform that suppressed the teaching of French at primary school level and set up an optional system (English/French) for secondary level. In reaction to that decision, French Cooperation reinforced its services to the Ministry of Education and the Pedagogical Institute, in order to "aid reflection"[128] regarding the reinforcement of the teaching of French in the country (Haut Conseil de la Francophonie 1999, p.29). The French government has continuously sponsored projects to spread French in Cape Verde. For instance, from 1999 to 2003, a project of 380 000 Euros supported the Ministry of Education in the development of this language

---

127 "Au Cap-Vert, en Guinée-Bissau et à São Tomé e Príncipe (portugais officiel), le français est d'abord la langue de communication avec les pays francophones voisins et d'émigration: Sénégal et France pour le Cap-Vert, Gabon pour São Tomé."

128 The French original is quite enlightening: "La coopération française a renforcé son dispositif auprès du ministère de l'Éducation et de l'Institut pédagogique pour aider à la réflexion sur la réintroduction du français dans les deux dernières années du primaire et son obligation au niveau supérieure."

policy regarding French by availing technical staff; other projects focused on the training of teachers, and, from 2004, there is an ongoing project, budgeted at 700 000 Euros, that aims to reinforce the presence of French inside and outside the education system (Ambassade de France au Cap-Vert 2007b). In practice, since 2000, French language in Cape Verde has been taught at secondary level: children entering secondary school choose either French or English, but in the second cycle (last two years) the students must study both languages, for 3 hours per week (Ambassade de France au Cap-Vert 2007a). Overall, in Cape Verde the elites and the business circles use French as international language. However, a decline in Francophony has been noted among young people and those that leave the school system (Ambassade de France au Cap-Vert 2007a) - an observation that could be seen to question the effects of French investment in external LSP in Cape Verde.

The relationship of French external LSP and Angola is also relevant. The example that follows denotes how priorities change over time for the targeted country. Early in 1994, the then French Minister for Cooperation, M. Michel Roussin (1994, p.241) announced that the Angolan government had made available an infrastructure - Palácio de Ferro - to be refurbished and transformed into the Centre Culturel Franco-Angolais. However, the building was later renovated with money from Endiama, the Angolan national diamond society, with the support of Brazilian construction companies, and its use is still to be decided. No Franco-Angolan cultural centre exists to this day. It would be interesting to research the cause of this change. Despite any eventual troubles in the relationship, France's commitment to the spread of French in Angola did not wane, being developed through the work of its local SCAC service and the linguistic and cultural presence of three Alliance Française branches (Luanda, Cabinda e Lubango). At present, France in Angola is developing similar strategies to the one I have described for Mozambique. Alongside the offer of scholarships, in the Autumn of 2008, the implementation of a project budgeted at 840,000 Euros was initiated. The project includes: the setting up of language center and a masters degree on the teaching of French as a Foreign Language at University Agostinho Neto; support to distance learning for teachers and the use of IT for the teaching of French; along side overall support of existing structures (French teachers association, other government institutions that teach French) and the creation of a team of supervisors for the teaching of French (Ambassade de France à Luanda 2010).

Despite France's bilateral efforts accounting for most of French language related initiatives, multilateral efforts seem now to be arising in Lusophone Africa. For instance, an international conference has taken place in Praia (Cape Verde) in November 2007 regarding the teaching/learning of French and

276

Portuguese in the African multilingual context[129]. The conference was organised by the Latin Union (an organization to which all the PALOP are members) and the Cape Verdian Institut of Higher Education, in partnership with the Agence Universitaire de la Francophonie (connected with OIF), the Instituto Internacional da Língua Portuguesa (connected with CPLP) and the Université Cheikh Anta Diop (Senegal). This mix of multilateral Francophone and Lusophone institutions seems to indicate that the policy pioneered by France to promote dialogue between *Xphonies* (Calvet 2002a) at the turn of the century is bearing some fruit.

Although France is recognised by its political concern and financial investment in Francophony (and thus it is not surprising its scope of action to include Lusophone Africa), other countries also operate external language spread policies in the Lusophone countries.

Signs from American sources indicate that the USA might be reinvesting in external language spread policies to back up its public diplomacy. Kerry's (2009, p.2) *U.S. Public Diplomacy – Time to Get Back In the Game* report to Members of the Committee on Foreign Relations of the United States Senate recommends "The Department of State should engage in the teaching of English using American or American-trained teachers hired directly by the embassy ...This will ensure that the Department has full control over the content and quality of the education, and will go far to advancing our Public Diplomacy efforts". A John Brademas Center for the Study of Congress (2009, p.4) report on American cultural diplomacy prepared by academic and cultural actors after President Obama's 2008 election also points to the use of cultural activities with the same purpose: "this report recommends that international arts and cultural exchanges be integrated into the planning strategies of U.S. policymakers as a key element of public diplomacy". Research found evidence of strong external language spread investment by the USA in Angola. Donation of educational resources, teacher placement (in anticipation of the opening of the English Language Teaching Department) at the Instituto Superior de Ciências da Educação, part of the Universidade 11 de Novembro; offer of scholarships (both financed by the USA government through USAID and by private corporations such as Esso); and the agreement of a Peace Corps project to place American volunteers as English teachers in secondary schools throughout Angola, are part of the activities developed by American services in Angola (PANA 2010, Batista 2010, Angop 2010 and Televisão Pública de Angola 2009). American Ambassador Dan Mozena justifies: "To promote English language is an idea of the President

---

129 Brochure available at http://dpel.unilat.org/DPEL/Promotion/Manifestations /Praia/Documents/brochure.pdf

of the Republic and other leaders from Angola. Angola is the natural leader of southern Africa, but to lead is necessary to speak English. It is the language of the international market, so we have some programs to promote the teaching of English language"[130] (Batista 2010). The arguments are similar to the ones presented for British ELT in Mozambique.

The UK is not totally absent from ELT in Angola. The British Council made its reappearance in Angola in 2005 (since 1943-1946), with the Peacekeeping English Project (British Council 2007) that aims to improve the skills of military personnel participating in international missions. Discussions regarding the opening up of a permanent British Council presence there are recurrent; this needs to be viewed in relation to Angola's importance as producer/supplier of oil, gas and diamonds (Fotheringham 2002 interview, Vines 2009).

Germany has also demonstrated increasing attention to the Lusophone world, as I mentioned in the case studies. Germany through the programme 'Aktion Afrika', launched in February 2008, has intensified its cultural and linguistic spread in Africa. The Goethe Institut opened in Angola in June 2009.

Spain also has intensified cooperation with Africa. One of the main objectives of the Africa Plan 2006-2008, the Spanish action plan for sub-Saharan Africa, included "the strengthening of cultural co-operation and of mutual understanding an appreciation" and "the promotion of Spanish" (Ministerio de Asuntos exteriores y de Coopéracion, Gobierno de España 2006, p.1). The plan for 2009-2012 reinforces Africa as a strategic and political priority for Spanish foreign policy and also stresses the importance of language:

> Language is a key driver of rapprochement and mutual understanding of cultures, as well as a factor of cultural enrichment and identity. This Plan aims to promote and to adequately respond to interest in the study of Spanish in Africa, counting on the collaboration of Equatorial Guinea, the only Spanish-speaking country on the continent. At the same time, seeks to promote respect for and protection of African linguistic richness and variety, a cultural heritage of Humanity[131] (Ministerio de Asuntos exteriores y de Coopéracion, Gobierno de España 2009, p.18)

---

130 "Promover a língua inglesa é uma ideia do Presidente da República e de outros líderes angolanos. Angola é a líder natural da África Austral, mas para liderar é preciso falar inglês. É a língua do mercado internacional, por isso, temos alguns programas para promover o ensino da língua inglesa"

131 "La lengua es un vector clave de acercamiento y conocimiento mutuo de las culturas, así como un factor de riqueza cultural e identidad. El presente Plan deberá contribuir a fomentar y a dar respuesta adecuada al interés por el estudio de la lengua española en África, contando para ello con la colaboración de Guinea Ecuatorial, único país de habla española del continente. Al mismo tiempo, tratará de promover el respeto y protección de la riqueza y variedad lingüística africana, uno de los patrimonios culturales de la Humanidad"

According to information available on the Spanish Ministry of Foreign Affairs website (www.maec.es), Mozambique was, in 2009, the country of sub-Saharan Africa in which Spain invested more official development aid. Mozambique and Angola (where there is an 'Aula Cervantes') are in tier 2 of the top priority countries, while the other three PALOP are place in a second tier of importance called "countries of specific interest" (there is a third category called "Countries to be closely followed") (Ministerio de Asuntos exteriores y de Coopéracion, Gobierno de España 2006, p.1). The Plan Africa 2009-2012 announced that Spain and Mozambique would continue their cultural cooperation:

> Cultural cooperation will continue to intensify. A chapter on "culture" will be included in the VII Joint Commission and the learning of Spanish will be encouraged, in 2009 the first examinations will be held in Mozambique to obtain the diploma of Spanish as a Foreign Language (DELE).[132] (Ministerio de Asuntos exteriores y de Coopéracion, Gobierno de España 2009, p.124)

Different countries have similar strategies to spread ex-colonial European languages. It is urgent that African countries take in their own hands the decisions regarding their linguistic policies.

I find that the above facts confirm the transferability of the patterns regarding external LSPs in the case studies to Lusophone Africa. Moreover the above evidence also indicates a strong possibility of its transfer to Africa overall and even beyond (for instance in the case of the USA).

5.1.3 Threads and Themes

From the different threads of research that traverse this study I have selected four main themes to discuss further. These are:

1. Language and the construction of the national project
2. Language and Education
3. Elites, External LSP and Cultural/Linguistic Affinities
4. Portuguese language politico linguistic bloc

---

132 "Se continuará con una intensa actividad en el ámbito de cooperación cultural. Se incorporará un capítulo "cultural" en la celebración de la próxima VII Comisión Mixta y se fomentará el aprendizaje del español, siendo 2009 el primer año en que se celebrarán en Mozambique exámenes para la obtención del diploma de español como lengua extranjera (DELE)"

Language and the construction of the national project

Language represents an important means to create and maintain a sense of nationhood in the sovereign political association that is the state (section 2.1). Language policies are thus at the very heart of the state (Lewis 1980 cited in Rassool 2008). The African countries have adopted the ideology of linguistic nationalism in the construct of their national projects. Mozambique elected Portuguese language as official language and language of national unity and identity, *intra*nationally and *inter*nationally. In the case of Guinea-Bissau, the *de jure* official status of Portuguese language and its use in the official communication and as language of teaching in the education system, also indicates a similar situation. However, given the extensive use of Crioulo in official oral communication and as a vehicular language in the country, its corpus development and prestige within important groups of Guinean society, there is a potential for change in the language policy. The national identity as an ideological creation (Billig 1995) is a form of social life that cannot not be regarded as a homogenized entity. Moreover, as Anderson (1991) pointed out, common languages should not be treated as emblems of nationhood but as building particular solidarities. Thus there is ample scope for the integration of the African languages in the respective national projects. The multidimensionality of nationality and identity in a globalising world (Hobsbawn 1990) should be taken into account by the governments of the African countries (which are inherently multilingual and multicultural) in the definition of their national projects. The definition and construction of the national language policy is undertaken by the elites of a country. Trudell (2010) notes the ambivalence of the positioning of the elite as agents of the West and responsible for the development of local languages. For instance, literature in Mozambique and in Guinea-Bissau is mainly developed in Portuguese language. In my interviews with Mozambican writers, Mia Couto (2002 and also in Couto 2009) and Calane da Silva (2010) it was clear their condemnation of the African countries' attitude of victimisation and culpabilisation about the past – they believed the African countries should assume their own linguistic choices. At the same time, Mia Couto, who writes in 'his' Mozambican Portuguese, is a strong defender of African languages. In contrast, others in Guinea-Bissau maintain the attitude that Portugal should help – an attitude deriving from multiple economic and political factors, but also arguably from a lesser appropriation of Portuguese language, due to the Crioulo already making the bridge between Portuguese and African languages. The Portuguese language in Mozambique is an appropriated language, at linguistical level (e.g. Português Moçambicano variety in development), at political level (official language, common language of the nation), at social level (mother tongue of an

280

increasing urban population). The local variety of Portuguese at the same time that emerges from the everyday use of the language, is poltically fostered.

Languages are dynamic and the linguistic situation in Africa should not be read as a simple dichotomy of European versus African languages in a positive/negative balance. As it has been deployed, the process of spread of official languages in Africa leads to their *de facto* supremacy and can be read as a 'glottophagic'/language cannabalism process (Breton 1991, Calvet 2002b). It is thus imperative that a strong political will supports policies for African languages allowing the maximum participation of the people in the governing process and promoting socio-cultural independence from the outside world (Heine 1992). Given that national identity is an ongoing creation, Guinea-Bissau, in particular, is in a situation that potentially can lead to a redefinition with important reflections on language policy. However the dependency of the country on external donors, bilateral and multilateral, will make any redefinition difficult.

Language in Education

In the case studies, as in other African countries, education is one of the main governmental priorities. However, despite international (e.g. UNESCO and even the World Bank 2005) recognition that one of the main causes of the failing of the education systems in Africa is the language of education (European languages are not familiar to the pupils) - this is an issue that largely remains ignored.

The education systems in the case studies are mainly all Portuguese language assimilationist systems (with the mentioned exceptions of the bilingual projects and the fact that African languages are - mostly unofficially - used as auxiliary languages given the lack of mastery of the teaching language by teachers and pupils). Underlying the systems are most of the fallacies identified by Phillipson (1992) (section 2.2.3.1) regarding English language teaching. Thus the systems for the teaching of Portuguese in the case studies (where effectively it is mainly a foreign language) still rely on monolingualism (Portuguese the exclusive language of teaching). I have mentioned the bilingual projects that are transitional and short term; the ideal of the native speaker (although local varieties of Portuguese are developing and increasing their prestige, the ideal teacher/norm is still European Portuguese); early start (as noted the education system has Portuguese as teaching language and in the development of pre-education systems the issue of early exposure to Portuguese has been stressed, particularly in Guinea-Bissau); maximum exposure (predominant negative attitude to the use of African languages as auxiliary languages, although this is changing, especially in Mozambique); and, to a lesser degree, the subtractive fallacy that sustains that the use of other languages will drop the standards of the language being promoted. This links with the previous tenet and there are signs of change in the case studies, namely the development of the bilingual projects. Official and academic discourses indicate that the methods for the teaching of Portuguese in the PALOP have been adapting to methodologies of second/foreign language teaching, however evidence of the case studies (particularly Guinea Bissau) indicates that the transition is still circumscribed in practice.

Regarding teaching in African languages, Mozambique has in place a short-term transitional bilingual model that is applied to 16 languages and Guinea-Bissau has a transitional bilingual model Crioulo/Portuguese being implemented in the Bijagós Islands. These models are an improvement to a 'foreign' monolingual system, since, in most cases, Portuguese, the language of both educational systems, is not spoken by the children entering school for the first time. However, the bilingual project in Guinea-Bissau is quite limited geographically and linguistically (Crioulo/Portuguese) and even the one in Mozambique being a short-term model is considered, by the standard of contemporary education research (Heugh 2009), insufficient to build meaningful indigenous linguistic capital. As Benson (2010) notes, African language policy (bilingual models) has been influenced by the Northern models and its transposition needs to be given more thought in terms of local application. Moreover, the future of the bilingual project in Mozambique was not clear in the findings - doubts appeared to cloud its future expansion. In Guinea-Bissau, there was sensibility amongst some international partners (UNESCO as reported by Benson 2010) for the support of mother tongue education, but will that be enough to withstand pressures favouring monolingual Portuguese education? Time will tell, but the signs are not auspicious.

At present the countries are aiming to achieve Education for All by 2015. That target has already been deemed non-reachable in Guinea-Bissau at that date, and 2020 was advanced as mid-range target (UNESCO-BREDA 2009). Tackling quality of education is a major concern; however the issue of the use of mother tongue in education remains, mostly, absent from the political agenda and the governments remain firm in their investment in European languages. African countries have progressed in enlarging their education access but the system remains limited and transition rates are low. In Guinea Bissau, in 2000, 48% of children were out of school (UIS Statistics), in 2005/6 the percentage decreased to 34% (RESEN 2009) but there is still a quarter of the population that does not have access to school. Moreover school life expectancy is only 6.2 years (RESEN 2009), that is, roughly corresponding to the primary cycle. The percentage of those finishing secondary school is very low: 17% of those that

282

attend school (2005-2009 data, Pôle de Dakar 2010). In Mozambique, the situation is slightly better, only 20% of children are out of school (2008 data UIS statistics) and the school life expectancy is 8.2 years (2005 data UIS statistics). However the percentage of those finishing secondary school is 5% (2006-2007 data, Pôle de Dakar 2010).

Thus, despite improvements, the situation remains problematic, so why the continual insistence on European languages? External pressures (structural power of international European languages, international system working for maintenance of status quo, dependency at economic/financial level and of thinking about education models, bilateral and multilateral external LSPs, etc) and internalised ideologies (prevalence of common language ideal in the construction of nationality, language attitudes influenced by colonialism) play a fundamental role in the maintenance, reinforcement and spread of Portuguese. Linguistic imperialism remains a valid theory in the interpretation of the disadvantaged situation of these countries. Linguistic imperialism entails unequal exchange, communicative rights and benefits between people/groups defined in terms of their competence in specific languages in a system that legitimates such exploitation (Phillipson 1992, 1998).

Elites, External LSP and Cultural/Linguistic Affinities

External LSPs through their strategies of operation target mainly the elites. Even its apparent mass spread through the target countries educational systems will in practice reach limited sections of the student population. In the available statistics there is a low number of pupils reaching secondary school levels. In Mozambique the gross enrolment ratio at the cycle of secondary school is 27%, and in the second cycle is 7% (2006/7 data, Pôle de Dakar 2010), and in Guinea-Bissau is 37% for the first cycle and 20% for the second cycle (2005/6 data, Pôle de Dakar 2010) - the percentages refer to the pupils that are in the education system and do not include the ones the system does not reach. Thus, since foreign European languages tend to be placed at the end of the secondary school cycle, they reach a limited number of pupils. This reinforces their position as languages of a small elite group. Only those few that reached the end of the secondary school system are able to go to university and those will potentially be the elite of the country - besides the minority that is able to study abroad and/or go to private school. Nevertheless, research highlighted a tendency for the earlier introduction of these languages in the education system - namely French and English in Mozambique - which will increase the number of pupils reached.

The most successful students will receive scholarships from Western countries (and despite an increasing trend for provision of internal and regional scholarships, postgraduate development is still largely available). These periods of study and the links they create, in the case studies, tend to benefit the elites of those countries. The elites that in the colonial period had a strong identification with Portugal, began diversifying their influences, first, due to the Marxist-Leninist inclinations of the post-independence, to Soviet countries, and latter on, to the other European ex-colonial countries, that still played regional hegemons and were keen to established those links. That closeness between the elites and those other countries was mentioned by the interviewees (e.g. Matusse 2002 interview, regarding the UK); it was apparent in the way that former student associations acted as gateways for further language spread (e.g. Germany in Mozambique and Guinea-Bissau). The links are various, not always evident or able to be proven. I would like to reinforce this with the example of Mozambique's financial system, where those occupying the most powerful positions in the banks connected with Portuguese capitals - which, by the way, dominate the market - (such as Banco Internacional de Moçambique and Banco de Investimento) are Mozambicans who had studied in Portugal. Similarly, in those banks connected with South Africa (e.g. the First National Bank and the Standard Bank) and UK (Barclays Bank) capitals, the recruitment for top positions favours those educated in those countries. The reason advanced, by my (non-attributable) source, is that those people would understand better the business philosophy of those banks, given that they had studied in the country of origin of the capital banks. This example clearly connects financial/economic and cultural/linguistic factors that impact on the development of Africa.

Additionally, the cultural centers, located in the capital cities of the countries, are a flagships/symbol of the power of the source countries that, as instruments of cultural diplomacy, interact with the political, economic, intellectual/cultural elite of those countries. In the findings it was also noticeable, particularly, in the case of Mozambique, given its economic development and support of the international community (donors and NGOs) that reflected in a greater dynamic of civil society, that cultural relations were starting to be developed beyond the governmental scope and thus moving away form the national base to direct relations between arts organisations. In this case the previous existence of linguistic/cultural links (e.g. constructed and maintained through external LSPs) can represent a significant factor of influence.

The mentioned tripartition of Africa resulting from the linguistic areas formed by English, French and Portuguese in sub-Saharan Africa, as Breton (2003) observed, resulting, for example, in the constitution of politico linguistic blocs, is another example of the strength of cultural forces (Mazrui and Mazrui 1998c) which I highlighted several times in the findings.

Although 'cultural' and linguistic affinities are not mutually exclusive they represent an important pull factor for African governments and elites.

Portuguese Language Politico Linguistic Bloc

Since 1996, the Lusophone countries have joined forces in the construction of a Portuguese language politico linguistic bloc, through the setting up of two main organisations, CPLP and IILP. The lack of financial resources pooled for the development of these organisations - originating mainly from Portugal and Brazil, and to a lesser extent from Angola and Mozambique - have dictated that the organisations have remained political forums more than source of active policies.

Portugal, although reported as not being at the origin of the idea, has been one of its great promoters, and arguably one of the countries that can most benefit from it. In the case of Portugal, the international status of Portuguese is of paramount importance in its self-image as a nation and an important factor of prestige in the international system - this relies on the maintenance of Portuguese as official language in the other CPLP countries and its spread to its citizens. This is evidenced in the governmental programmes (available at http://www.portugal.gov.pt/) and in the official discourses (for example the President of the Republic speeches are a paramount example - available at http://www.presidencia.pt/). For instance, on the 5th May 2010 the "Day of Portuguese Language and Culture of the CPLP" was celebrated for the first time, at a ceremony in Lisbon. The President of the Portuguese Republic stressed among several 'facts' that Portuguese was spoken by 250 million citizens, and that in 20 years the forecast was of 350 million speakers (Presidência da República 2010b). This type of discourse describing the expansion of Portuguese language as an international language (fact, fable, or somewhere in between) is an expression of the banal nationalism that ideologically sustains Portugal as a nation. This ideology is translated in the dominance of Portuguese language in Portugal (where migration is turning language into an issue in need of governmental attention - for the moment in the sense of integration and assimilation of migrants into Portuguese culture and language) and the fostering of its spread internationally and within the CPLP. That is, politically there is an ongoing effort through external language spread activities (teacher training, teacher placement, scholarships, educational resources, etc) to transform the non-Portuguese speakers citizens of the CPLP grouping into Portuguese language speakers. It is no doubt a multilateral and bilateral political engenieering of a multinational linguistic situation.

Regarding the focus of Portugal on the omnipresence of Portuguese language within CPLP, it is interesting to note the words of the Portuguese President of the Republic on a visit to Cape Verde in July 2010 encouraging the valorisation and the spread of the common language and, in that, 'deproblematising' the existence of other languages:

> It is visible the importance assumed by Creole in the communication between Cape Verdians and I do not think this is a matter of concern. Portuguese is not defined, nor never shall, in opposition to any other language or dialect. Quite the contrary, the richness of *our language*, of Portuguese language, and his prodigious plasticity owe much to its *ability to integrate words and expressions* of the cultural mosaic of people who speak it.[133] (Presidência da República 2010a, my emphasis in italics)

Thus the political integrity of Portuguese language is affirmed, while linguistically is allowed to "integrate" words and expressions of other languages. I have mentioned the "Day of Portuguese Language and Culture of the CPLP" - celebrated for the first time on the 5th May 2010 - the title in itself is indicative of the continual dismissal (although rhetorically acknowledged) of the multilingual nature of namely the continental African countries, not to mention Timor-Leste and Brazil - a situation Do Rosário (2007) attributes to Portuguese authorities with the neutral complicity of the Brazilians (section 1.2). The economic lead of the organisation relying on Portugal and Brazil (Nery 2002 interview, Calane da Silva 2010 interview) allows these countries to set the political agenda.

Although cultural diversity seems to be acceptable in the Portuguese language politico linguistic bloc, linguistic diversity only recently began to be clearly mentioned. I would argue that this indicates a political inability to deal with the concept of linguistic diversity in the construction of political spaces - that still relies on the ideology of the common hegemonic language. There is a continual lack of consideration of the issue of mother tongues within CPLP, which is also connected with a lack of a defined language policy for the organisation. In the *Plano de Ação de Brasília* (2010) the issue of other national languages in each state is mentioned to note the need of adaptation in the learning/teching methodologies of Portuguese for multilingual contexts - within that concern, the study and teaching of those national languages is advised

---

133 "É patente a importância assumida pelo crioulo na comunicação entre os cabo-verdianos e não creio que tal mereça preocupação. O português não se define, nem nunca se definirá, em oposição a qualquer outra língua, idioma ou dialecto. Muito pelo contrário, a riqueza da nossa língua, da língua portuguesa, e a sua prodigiosa plasticidade muito devem à sua capacidade para integrar palavras e expressões próprias do mosaico cultural dos povos que a falam."

(Conselho de Ministros da CPLP 2010). The implementation of this policy and the extent to which the advice given is followed through would be an interesting issue for future research.

The promotion of Portuguese as global language is expected to bring political and economic benefits for all the participating countries in the bloc to operate in the international system. This strategy can be seen to partially involve hegemonic processes, as Portuguese was a legacy of colonialism. The Portuguese politico linguistic bloc represents for the participating countries part of their multiple collective entities; it represents, among others, a set of cultural, political and economic affiliations, of which the countries make different use depending on circumstances. Countries must be seen as multidimensional. Thus the positions of Portuguese, French, English languages in the case studies and the affiliations to different politico linguistic groups reveal at case study level the inter-linked hegemonies existing in the world system (Frank and Gills 1995/2001) (section 2.3.2.1).

5.2 Conclusions

This study explored the argument that Postcolonial Africa has been the setting for competing external language spread policies (LSPs) by ex-colonial European countries at the turn of the 21st Century. The main research question was: "Are there languages at war in Lusophone Africa?" To explore the topic I chose the case studies of Mozambique and Guinea-Bissau, to be analysed in the time frame of the 1990s to the present. The overarching questions guiding the research were:

1. How and why did Portuguese become and how and why has it been sustained as official language in Mozambique and Guinea-Bissau? Why is this important in the context of the case studies? Is the Portuguese language being threatened in Mozambique and Guinea-Bissau? If yes, by which languages, how and why? If no, why has that perception occurred?
2. Are competitive external LSPs being developed in Mozambique and Guinea-Bissau? If yes, by which countries, how and why? How are the policies perceived? What are the implications for the countries involved? If no, why has that perception occurred?
3. Is the language spread policy of ex-colonial countries a good or a bad thing for postcolonial societies?
4. What is the place of European languages in postcolonial African societies?

The following section presents a summary of the conclusions of this study by answering the main research questions. Additionally it is explained how this study contributes to the development of knowledge in the area of external language spread policies amongst ex-colonial European governments in postcolonial African countries and to the broader debate on Portuguese language spread.

5.2.1 Summary of Conclusions and Contribution to Knowledge

The study concludes that there are languages at war in Lusophone Africa. Research identified in Mozambique external language spread policies originating from Portugal, Brazil, France, the United Kingdom and Germany and in Guinea-Bissau from Portugal, Brazil and France, non-withstanding concurrent and competing policies from other actors, within the period from the 1990s to the present.

In the context of the case studies, English as international/regional language of inter-communication, French as second international/regional language of inter-communication, and Portuguese as the former colonial language and now official language, as language of national identity and unity and as language of a substantial international linguistic bloc, are seen as substantial contenders in the competition for linguistic space in sub-Saharan Africa, where African languages mostly remain circumscribed to non-official domains. This linguistic inequality reflects the power relations enacted in society and internationally. It further raises issues of linguistic/cultural human rights and the defence of language and cultural diversity that this study argues for.

Perceptions of Portuguese language being threatened in both case studies, particularly present in the 1980s and 1990s (but still identified at present in Guinea-Bissau), reveal a realist understanding of international relations issuing from a neo-colonial mindset akin to the spheres of influence resulting from the scramble for Africa in 1884-1885. Portuguese language, as a legacy of colonialism, was maintained by the independent countries of Lusophone Africa as official language and the language used in the construction of the state/nationhood of the independent African countries, through the inheritance of the colonial structures and the embryonic national elites constituted in the colonisation period. The maintenance of the status of Portuguese and its spread have been supported by external LSPs of Portugal and Brazil and reinforced by the structure of the international system, through linguistic nationalism, linguistic imperialism and dependency. Portuguese, language as official language in these countries, does not appear to be threatened, on the contrary Portuguese language is a threat to the African languages, as its dominance of the official domains (education, media, and official communication) and similarly a lack of concern for African languages limits the development of the corpus and status of the latter.

However Portuguese language has to compete with other European ex-colonial languages as language of international inter-communication. English and French are the objects of external language spread policies of ex-colonial European governments, namely the UK and France, with the concurrence of other actors, and/or are also reinforced by the structure of the international system, which confers and maintains the status of these languages, regionally and internationally, as the languages to be used in international inter-communication. External LSPs reinforce and extend the spread of the European ex-colonial languages in Africa - however their consequences reach far beyond the linguistic arena. External LSPs, as government policies aimed at spreading the language of a state abroad (Ammon 1992a), part of foreign policy, are instruments for the projection of the national image and a tool for pursing the national interest of the source countries. These policies operate through a variety of activities that include: supporting the inclusion of the language in the education system of the target country; making scholarships available for the best students; supporting and/or offering language courses directly to the local publics; developing cultural activities that have a foreign language component and/or promote the cultural image of the source country, thus making its language also attractive. The spread of the European languages favours the influence of the European countries through communicational advantages, which may be used in negotiations, business/investment and the attraction of elites. For African countries they represent an instrument of communication that allows them to participate (although still in a dependent position) and be heard in the international system - which in turn has been constructed by the West on its own (political, economic, ideological) terms.

In Lusophone Africa, as indicated by the case studies of Mozambique and Guinea-Bissau, ex-colonial countries compete to spread their languages, within the development of their foreign policies. The development of external LSPs has an impact on the internal language policies of the African countries. The internal language spread policies of the African countries are able to influence to a great degree the linguistic options of their citizens, in particular through their presence in the national education systems and their value (or not) for official communication. The choices of the speakers can, thus, be strongly influenced by governments. In that linguistic competition (even multilingualism has a limit), speakers will accord different values to each language and acquire languages accordingly (which may vary throughout life). In that sense, the development of external LSPs represents a factor in the choices of the speakers, as it makes languages available and promotes their attraction value (economic benefits, cultural symbols). The consequences of those policies are both positive and negative. They are positive in the sense that, undoubtedly, they represent opportunities for communication with others. They are negative if they perpetuate the ideology of linguistic imperialism and the stereotypical arguments against the use of African language - within a larger imperialist/neocolonialist framework that tends to stress that West is Best!

European languages do have their place in postcolonial African societies. With the increasing globalisation of the world, no country in the world can ignore them and the important role they play in international communication. Thus the African countries must include them in their educational system as foreign languages. Moreover, ex and postcolonial countries are set in a web of relationships at bilateral and multilateral level, in which language represents a particular powerful link. In that complex context, I examined the development of external LSPs - which are still mainly developed bilaterally - and observed the importance of the construction of politico linguistic blocs, accounting for the underlying legacies of colonial ties, the dependency towards Western frameworks and the increasing globalisation of the world. The language link, bilateral and multilateral, represents an important means for the attraction and deployment of development aid projects that given the dependent situation of the African countries within the international structure cannot be overlooked.

Moreover, the African countries examined, as is the case with many others, have used the European ex-coloniser language as official language and language used in the construction of their state/nationhood. Thus, internally, the European languages have a fundamental role; nevertheless one that can be performed by African languages if a political option so determines and the financial resources to back it are made available.

The unequal divide between mother tongues and official language in the educational system of most African countries must be bridged. The relevance of each language must be recognised in terms of the local context and national project. Africa's future relies on a new way of conceiving development and education and on a new role for African languages and cultures. Most authors now believe the best option for African states is a balanced policy of European and African languages (Bokamba 1995, p.23). The development of the corpus and the status of African languages are paramount to the participation of the citizens in their respective economies and polities. European languages are important to connect African countries to other countries and to enable them to operate in the global economic market. English plays, nowadays, an important role in international communication that no country in the world can ignore. As Rassool

(2007, p.149) argues "excolonial languages, and particularly Standard English, represent preferred linguistic capital within the global cultural economy".

The language-in-education debate is a very important issue, particularly in postcolonial societies (although with the present migration movements it is an increasing pressing issue worldwide), and normally is centred on access to language. The debate generally highlights the need of access to mother tongue education and the need to promote the status of those languages in relation to the use of dominant/official/international languages. Access to language is important but insufficient. As argued by Pennycook (1998b, p.84) the question of voice (relationship between language, discourse and subjectivity) is extremely important. The crucial issue for Pennycook (1998b, p.84) is "how languages intersect with, on the one hand, discursive frameworks of meaning, and on the other hand, the individual desire to make meanings. We need access to the domains in which languages and discourses combine to construct our lives."

My aim with this study was to contribute to the development of knowledge in the area of external language spread policies amongst ex-colonial governments in postcolonial countries and to the broader debate on Portuguese language spread. I chose to develop my study through the case studies of Mozambique and Guinea-Bissau, as I viewed the countries in the confluence of several external language policies. I have examined their national circumstances, in particular their language policies, and the external language policies foreign countries deploy in their territory. These policies, at the centre of my study, were examined with the intention to clarify their underlying motivations, at the same time as understanding how these policies operate, what are their consequences and how are these policies perceived by the actors involved (both in the source and the target countries). I have done so through transdisciplinary analysis using elements of sociology of language, sociolinguistics and international relations. I believe that I have demonstrated how external language policies are deployed in practice and how the example of Portuguese language spread is relevant to the understanding of other ex-colonial European languages.

Portuguese is placed among the European languages that compete in the domain of international communication. The monitoring of the activities developed and the analyses of its outcomes allows to understand how government policy is able to be implemented within a context of more resourceful actors and how the development or not of a multilateral action is able to support language spread and in what way. Portuguese external LSP is also important to be analysed in terms of linguistic imperialism, since its underlying ideology, Lusophony, rests on the central position of Portuguese language as mediator of the culture of eight countries. The official rhetoric of Portuguese language spoken by more than 200 million people around the world does not correspond to the reality of large numbers of the African countries' populations not being (fully) proficient in the Portuguese language.

5.2.2 Reflection on the Research Process and Key Issues for Further Research

The initial assumptions of this study (section 3.2) and the iterative grounded strategy (section 3.4) enabled an interesting research process, not without personal and academic challenges. Departing from a quite narrow theoretical background of international relations and cultural diplomacy, the emergence of crosscutting issues, as the research process developed, made it necessary to explore other academic fields, namely sociology of language and linguistics. Within a constructivist approach to the nature of social reality and the character of knowledge, maintaining validity for the work was extremely important, which was sought through triangulation. Given the predominantly political nature of the topic and its sensitivity, it was at times difficult to explore beyond the public statements and the political correct discourse. Moreover, the transdisciplinary and transnational context in which the external LSPs were being explored made it imperative for the researcher to constantly have to challenge her interpretation at linguistic, academic and discoursal level. It was no doubt a very rewarding experience - in particular the interaction with the interviewees and all those that directly and indirectly contributed to the research.

Of the numerous areas for further research, the obvious step is the monitoring of the situation in the case studies - for instance focusing on the situation of the African languages and observing the multilateralisation of language management and development of the membership and activity of CPLP/IILP. Another strand would be the expansion of the scope of research to include the other countries of Lusophone Africa and look into the situation in Timor-Leste, where at present the relationship between local languages, Portuguese and English is being discussed. In Africa, it would be interesting to examine the external LSPs being deployed in Rwanda and Madagascar and to analyse their impact. These countries, considered 'francophone', have recently added English as official language and language of teaching. Rwanda in 2009 became a member of the Commonwealth - the second country after Mozambique to be admitted to the organisation without having historical colonial ties with the UK. Could it be that the processes of external LSP are similar?

The collection of financial data available for the area of external LSPs and cultural diplomacy would be a key issue for future research. This is a challenging piece of research given the differences in national frameworks and the different calculations. However it would be of great value to be able to compare the investment of the different countries. Through the process of research for this study I noted an evolution in the availability and disclosure of budgets for cultural diplomacy in particular from Portugal. This was a strand of research that I had initially envisaged for this study, but was forced to drop, due to its complexity.

Another, fundamental, area for future research is the appropriation of language. How is this achieved? When does the mind become de-colonised? This also connects to analyses of the individual choices in terms of linguistic repertoire and their link with national and external language policies.

Additionally, comparisons between language spread undertaken in 'developed' and 'developing' countries would be able to contribute to a better understanding of dependency situations and eventual paradigm shifts from traditional cultural diplomacy to cultural co-operation (Fisher 2009). Maybe that only happens 'amongst equals'?

Research is an endless task - the disentanglement of discursive and parallel strands to form a seemingly logical and articulated body of work. I hope that I have achieved that in this study.

References

Aberbach, Joel D. and Rockman, Bert A. (2002). Conducting and Coding Elite Interviews. *PS: Political Science & Politics*, 35 (4), December, pp.673-676.

Achebe, Chinua (1975) *The African Writer and the English Language*, pp.428-434. Extract Available at http:www.fb10.uni-bremen.de/anglistik/kerkhoff/africanlit/Achebe/Achebe428.htm to 434.htm [05.06.2007].

Adegbija, Efurosibina (1994) *Language Attitudes in Sub-Saharan Africa: a Sociolinguistic Overview*. Clevedon: Multilingual Matters.

Agência Brasil (2010) Cultura brasileira influencia modo de vida em Moçambique. Quinta-feira, 12/05/2010 às 06h35. Available at http://www.nominuto.com/noticias/brasil/cultura-brasileira-influencia-modo-de-vida-em-mocambique/52659. [27.06.2010]

Alexander, Neville (2007) Linguistic diversity in Africa in a global perspective. In Alexander, Neville and Busch, Brigitta (2007) *Literacy and linguistic diversity in a global perspective: an intercultural exchange with African countries*, pp.13-22. Strasbourg: Council of Europe Publishing. Available at http://www.ecml.at/documents/A3_LDL_E_web.pdf [08.05.2010]

Alidou, Hassana (2004) Medium of Instruction in Post-Colonial Africa. In James W. Tollefson and Amy B. M. Tsui eds. *Medium of Instruction Policies: Which Agenda? Whose Agenda?* London: Lawrence Erlbaum Associate Publishers, p. 195-214.

Ambassade de France à Bissao (2010) Relations économiques. Available at http//www.ambafrance-gw.org/france_bissao/spip.php?article261 [07.06.2010]

Ambassade de France à Luanda (2010) La France en Angola: Service de Coopération et d'Action Culturelle. Available at http://www.ambafrance-ao.org/france_angola/spip.php?article20 [17.07.2010]

Ambassade de France au Cap-Vert (2007a) La langue française au Cap-Vert. Available at http://www.ambafrance-cv.org/article.php3?id_article=405 [13.11.2007].

Ambassade de France au Cap-Vert (2007b) Les projects de cooperation. Available at http://www.ambafrance-cv.org/article.php3?id_article=293 [13.11.2007].

Ambassade de France au Mozambique (2002) Appui à l'Enseignement du Français au Mozambique. Available at: www.ambafrance-mz.org/appuifle.html [06.09.2002].

Ambassade de France au Mozambique (2007) La France au Mozambique et au Swaziland. Available from: www.ambafrance-mz.org/ [10.03.2007].

Ambassade de France au Mozambique (2010a) La coopération régionale. Available at http://www.ambafrance-mz.org/spip.php?article134 [07.06.2010]

Ambassade de France au Mozambique (2010b) Le soutien à la diversité culturelle. Available at http://www.ambafrance-mz.org/spip.php?article1017 [24.06.2010].

Ambassade de France au Mozambique (2010c) Les projets du Fonds de Solidarié Prioritaire (FSP). Available at http://www.ambafrance-mz.org/spip.php?article123 [07.06.2010].

Ambassade de France en Guinée-Bissao (2007) Ambassade de France en Guinée-Bissao. Available at http://www.ambfrance-gw.org/ [13.08.2007]

Ammon, Ulrich (1992a) Editor's Preface. *International Journal of the Sociology of Language*, 95, pp.5-9.

Ammon, Ulrich (1992b) The Federal Republic of Germany's policy of spreading German. *International Journal of the Sociology of Language*, 95, pp.33-50.

Ammon, Ulrich (1994) Editor's Preface. *International Journal of the Sociology of Language*, 107, pp.5-6.

Ammon, Ulrich (1997) Language-Spread Policy. *Language Problems and Language Planning*, 21 (1), Spring, pp.51-57.

Anderson, Benedict (1991) Imagined Communities: Reflection on the Origins and Spread of Nationalism. Revised Edition. London: Verso.

Angop (2010) Formação: EUA e Esso oferecem bolsas a municipes do Cazenga. 20 May 2010. Available at http://www.portalangop.co.ao/motix/pt_pt/noticias/educacao/2010/4/20/EUA-ESSO-oferecem-bolsas-municipes-Cazenga,855495e4-42ba-4397-b3cd-822650a6d003.html [17.07.2010].

Anholt, Simon (2009) The importance of national identity. Available at http://www.fco.gov.uk/en/about-us/publications-and-documents/publications1/pd-publication/national-reputation [21.06.2010].

Ansre, Gilbert (1979) Four Rationalisations for the Maintaining of European Languages in Education in Africa. *African Languages: Languages and Education in Africa*, 5 (2), International African Institute, OAU, Inter-African Bureau of Languages, pp.10-17.

Appadurai, A. (1990). Disjuncture and difference in the global culture economy. *Theory, Culture, and Society*. 7: 295-310.

Appadurai, Arjun (1996) *Modernity at Large: Cultural Dimensions of Globalization*. Minneapolis: University of Minnesota Press.

Assemblée nationale de France (2010) La francophonie en Afrique: quel avenir? 24 Juin 2010. Available at http://www.assemblee-nationale.fr/13/evenements/images/programme_afrique_francophonie.pdf [08.07.2010].

Augel, Johannes (1997) O crioulo da Guine Bissau. In *Afro/Asia*, 19/20, pp.251-254.

Augel, Moema Parente (2006) O crioulo guineense e a oratura. In *SCRIPTA*, Belo Horizonte, v. 10, n. 19, p. 69-91, 2° sem. Pp. 69-91. Available at http://www2.pucminas.br/imagedb/documento/DOC_DSC_NOME_ARQ UI20070621145422.pdf [06.07.2010].

Augel, Moema Parente (2007) *O Desafio do Escombro: Nação, Identidades e Desafios no Pós-Colonialismo na Literatura da Guiné Bissau*. Rio de Janeiro: Editora Garamond.

Auswärtige Amt / German Federal Foreign Office (2010) Guinea Bissau: Kultur und Bildungspolitik. Mars 2010. Available at http://wwwauswaertiges-amt.de/diplo/de/Laenderinformationen/GuineaBissau/Kultur-UndBildungspolitik.html [08.06.2010].

BALL, Rodney (1997) *The French-Speaking World: A Practical Introduction to Sociolinguistic Issues*. London: Routledge.

Ball, Stephen (1994) *Education reform: a critical and post-structural approach*. Buckingham: Open University Press.

Banco de Portugal (2009) Evolução das Economias dos PALOP e de Timor-Leste 2008/2009. Lisboa: Departamento de Relações Internacionais. Available at http://www.bportugal.pt/pt-PT/PublicacoeseIntervencoes/Banco/Cooperacao/Publicacoes/00_EEPTL_2009.pdf

Bandeira, José Gomes (1998) Entrevista a José Soares Martins. *Jornal de Notícias*, 10 March. Lisbon.

Baptista, Charles (2005) Vamos aprender mandarim? *Correio da Manhã*, 16 December. Maputo.

Bartholomew, Ann, Takala, Tuomas and Ahmed, Zuber (2009) Avaliação a Meio Percurso da Iniciativa 'Fast Track' da EPT. Estudo Nacional: Moçambique, esboço. Available at http://www.camb-ed.com/fasttrackinitiative/download/FTI_Mozambique_CR-Portuguese.pdf

Batista, Ricardo (2010) Embaixador americano em Luanda defende que Angola tem grande potencial de investimento, mas a "corrupção é real". 16 June 2010. Available at http://www.construir.pt/2010/06/16/embaixador-americano-em-luanda-defende-que-angola-tem-grande-potencial-de-investimento-mas-a-corrupcao-e-real/ [17.07.2010].

BBC para Africa (2006) Moçambique adere à Francofonia como observador. Available at: http://www.bbc.co.uk/portugueseafrica/news/story/2006/09/printable/060928_francophone.moztl.shtml [11.11.2006].

297

Bennett, James C. (2002) An Anglosphere Primer. Available at: http://www.pattern.com/bennettj-anglosphereprimer.html [22.11.2006].
Bennett, James C. (2003) Networking Nation-States: The Incoming Info-National Order. *The National Interest*, 74, Winter 2003/2004, pp.17-30.
Bennett, James C. (2004) The Anglosphere Challenge: Synopsis. Available at: http://anglospherechallenge.com/book.html
Benson, Carol (2004) *The importance of mother tongue-based schooling for educational quality: Commissioned study for EFA Global Monitoring Report 2005*. Available at http://unesdoc.unesco.org/images/0014/001466/146632e.pdf
Benson, Carol (2005) Bilingual Schooling as Educational Development: From Experimentation to Implementation. *ISB4: Proceedings of the 4th International Symposium on Bilingualism*, ed. James Cohen, Kara T. McAlister, Kellie Rolstad, and Jeff MacSwan, 249-258. Somerville, MA: Cascadilla Press. Available at www.cascadilla.com/isb4.html
Benson, Carol (2009) Designing Effective Schooling in Multilingual Contexts: Going Beyond Bilingual Models. In Skutnabb-Kangas, Tove, Phillipson, Robert, Mohanty, Ajit K. and Panda, Minati ed. (2009) *Social Justice Through Multilingual Education. Bristol: Multilingual Matters*, pp. 63-81.
Benson, Carol (2010) How multilingual African contexts are pushing educational research and practice in new directions. In *Language and Education*. Vol. 24, Issue 4, 2010, pp.323-336.
Bicari, Lino (1999) Crise da Escola Pública em África, Demissão do Estado, Respostas da Sociedade. Unpublished article supplied by the author.
Bickley, Verner C. (1982) Language as the Bridge. In Stephen Bochner, ed. *Cultures in Contact: Studies in Cross-Cultural Interaction*. Oxford: Pergamon Press, Chapter 5, pp.99-125.
Bijeljac, Ranka and Breton, Roland (1997) *Du Langage aux Langues*. Paris: Gallimard.
Billig, Michael (1995) *Banal Nationalism*. London: Sage Publications.
Blamangin, Olivier (2000) Introduction à la cooperation multilatérale. In Observatoire Permanent de la Coopération Française, *La Coopération Educative de la France*. Paris: Karthala, pp.167-189.
Bokamba, Eyamba G. (1995) The Politics of Language Planning in Africa: Critical Choices for the 21st Century. In Martin PÜTZ ed. *Discrimination Through Language in Africa? Perspectives on the Namibian Experience*. Berlin: Mouton de Gruyter, pp. 11-27.
Bound, K., Briggs R., Holden, J. and Jones, S. (2007) Cultural Diplomacy. London: DEMOS. Available at http://www.demos.co.uk/files/Cultural%20diplomacy%20-%20web.pdf

Bourdieu, Pierre (1991) *Language and Symbolic Power*. Cambridge: Polity.

Braga, António (2010) Os Centros Culturais em Moçambique e especificidades da sua actuação. A version of this document was due to be published in Jornal de Letras, Portugal. This version was provided by the author to the researcher by email in June 2010.

Brann, Conrad B. (1985) *Official and National Languages in Africa: Complementary or Conflict?* Québec: Centre International de Recherce et Aménagement Linguistique.

BREDA-UNESCO (2009) RESEN Elèments de Diagnostic du Système Educatif Bissau-guinéen: Marges de manouevre pour le développement du système éducatif dans une perspective d'universalitation de l'enseignement de base et de reduction de la pauvreté. Document supplied by M. Guillaume Husson, educational systems analyst responsible for Guinea-Bissau's report at the Pôle de Dakar, 05.07.2010, email.

Breton, Roland (1991) The Handicaps of Language Planning in Africa. In David F. Marshall, ed. *Language Planning: Focusschrift in honor of Joshua A. Fishman*. Amsterdam: John Benjamins Publishing Company, pp.153-174.

Breton, Roland (2000) Can English Be Dethroned? *The UNESCO Courier* April, pp.23-24.

Breton, Roland (2003) Sub-Saharan Africa. In Jacques Maurais and Michael A. Morris, ed. *Languages in a Globalising World*. Cambridge: Cambridge University Press, pp.203-216.

British Council (1990) Annual report and accounts: 1989/90. London: The British Council.

British Council (1991) Annual report and accounts: 1990/91. London: The British Council.

British Council (1993) Annual report and accounts: 1992/93. London: The British Council.

British Council (1998) Annual report: 1997/98. London: The British Council.

British Council (2006) *Making a World of Difference: Cultural Relations in 2010*. London: The British Council.

British Council (2006a) Annual report: 2005/06. London: The British Council.

British Council (2007) Corporate plan 2008-11. Available at http://www.britishcouncil.org/home-aboutus-corporate-plan.pdf [20/06/2010].

British Council (2009) Annual report 2008-09. Available at http://www.britishcouncil.org/new/about-us/annual-report-2009-09/?startPagingAt=1&page=2 [20.06.2010].

British Council (2010) Mozambique English Language Courses. Available at http://www.britishcouncil.org/africa-mz-english-language-courses.htm [27.06.2010].

British Council Mozambique (2002) Country Brief: British Council, Mozambique. Maputo: British Council [Printed two page document supplied by Simon Ingram-Hill].

British Council Mozambique (2007) Young Learners. Available at: http://www.britishcouncil.org/mozambique.htm [12.04.2007].

Brocard, Hervé (2002) Appui à l'Enseignement du Français: Synthèse du Project. Maputo [Printed four pages document supplied by the author].

Brookes, Emily (2009) Globo's colonial connections. 22 April 2009. C21 Media 2010. Available at http://www.c21media.net/common/print_detail.asp?article=49147 [27.06.2010].

Bryman, Alan (2004) Social Research Methods. 2nd ed. Oxford: Oxford University Press.

Buchmann, Claudia (1999) Poverty and Education Equality in sub-Saharan Africa. In Prospects, vol. 29, no.4, December 1999, pp.503-515.

Burnham, Peter et al. (2004) Research Methods in Politics. Basingstoke: Palgrave.

Cahen, Michel (1998) A França só vê um rival em África: os EUA. Entrevista com Michel Cahen. Público, 09 July, p.46. Lisbon.

Calvet, Louis-Jean (1974) Linguistique et colonialism: Petit traité de glottophagie. Paris: Payot

Calvet, Louis-Jean (1994) Les Politiques de Diffusion des Langues en Afrique Francophone. International Journal of the Sociology of Language, 107, pp.7-24.

Calvet, Louis-Jean (1996) Les Politiques Linguistiques. Paris: PUF.

Calvet, Louis-Jean (1998) Language Wars and Linguistic Politics. English translation of the 1987 French original. Oxford: Oxford University Press.

Calvet, Louis-Jean (2000) Users are choosers. The UNESCO Courier, April, pp.35-36.

Calvet, Louis-Jean (2002a) Le Marché aux Langues: Les Effets Linguistiques de la Mondialisation. Paris: Plon.

Calvet, Louis-Jean (2002b) Linguistique et Colonialisme. Pocket edition of the 1974 book. Paris: Éditions Payot & Rivages.

Canagarajah, A. Suresh (1998) Book Review: Linguistic Imperialism, Robert Phillipson. Multilingual Matters, 17 (5), pp.404-408.

Canagarajah, A. Suresh (1999) Resisting Linguistic Imperialism in English Teaching. Oxford: Oxford University Press.

Cardador, Luís (2009) Educação guineense à procura de uma 'visão'. 16 July 2009. Available at http://www.bbc.co.uk/portugueseafrica/news/story/2009/07/090716_gbeducationmt.shtml [03.07.2010]

Cavacas, Fernanda (1994) *O Texto Literário e o Ensino da Língua em Moçambique*. Lisboa: CIDAC, Colecção Sete.

Chaudenson, Robert (2000) *Mondialisation: La langue Française a-t-elle encore un avenir?* Institut de la Francophone, Diffusion Didier Erudition.

Christie, Iain (1996) *Mozambique: land of peace and promise*. Maputo: Bureau de Informação Pública.

Coelho, Eduardo Prado (1986) A língua dos «infantes» in *Revista ICALP*, no.5, July 1986, p.60-64.

Commonwealth Secretariat (2003) News: Commonwealth and La Francophonie to collaborate on trade 7 November 2003. Available at: http://www.thecommonwealth.org/press/31555/34582/35106/commonwealth_and_la_francophonie_to_collaborate_on.htm

Commonwealth Secretariat (1995) *Report of the Commonwealth Secretary-General 1995*. London: Commonwealth Secretariat.

Commonwealth Secretariat (2008) The Commonwealth. Available at: http://thecommonwealth.org/subhomepage/151236 [08.01.2008]

Conselho de Ministros da CPLP (2010) Plano de Ação de Brasília para a Promoção, a Difusão e a Projeção da Língua Portuguesa. Available at http://www.fao.org/fileadmin/templates/cplpunccd/Biblioteca/General/PA_Brasilia_PromoDivul_LP.doc [06.06.2010].

Costa, Larissa (2007) Educação como prática da liberdade? Alfabetização freireana em Guiné-Bissau. *Tempo Presente*, Year 2, n. 25. Available at http://www.tempopresente.org/index.php?option=com_content&task=vie w&id=2932&Itemid=147 [08.07.2010].

Coulmas, Flourian (1998) Language Rights – Interests of State, Language Groups and the Individual. In *Language Sciences*, vol. 20, Number 1, January 1998, Special Issue 'Language Rights'. Pergamon, pp. 63-72.

Couto, Mia (1981) Ainda o Problema da Língua: Submissão Cultural? *Tempo*, 536, 18 January, Maputo.

Couto, Mia (1995) Uma Luso-Afonia? *Público* 28 March, p.46. Lisbon.

Couto, Mia (2009) *E se o Obama fosse africano? E outras interinvenções*. Editorial Caminho.

Cox, Robert W. (1981) Social Forces, States and World Orders: Beyond International Politics Theory. In John A. Vasquez, ed. (1996) *Classics of International Relations*. 3rd ed. London: Prentice Hall, pp.126-134.

CPLP Comunidade dos Países de Língua Portuguesa (2007) Comunidade dos Países de Língua Portuguesa. Available at: http://www.cplp.org [27.03.2007].

Cristovão, Fernando (2008) *Da Lusitanidade à Lusofonia*. Coimbra: Almedina

Crystal, David (1997) *English as a Global Language*. Cambridge: Cambridge University Press.

Culturando (2010) Comunicado de Imprensa – Feira do Livro de Maputo – 1ª Edição. Available at http://kutsemba.com/Documents/Feira%20do%20 Livro%20de%20Maputo.pdf [11.06.2010].

Cunguara, Benedito and Hanlon, Joseph (2010) Poverty is not being reduced in Mozambique. Working Paper no.74, Development as State-making. *Crisis States Working Papers* Series No.2. London: London School of Economics. Available at http://macua.blogs.com/files/poverty-is-not-being-reduced-in-mozambique.pdf [24.06.2010].

Da Silva, Jaime F. and Gunnewiek, Lisanne Klein (1992) Portuguese and Brazilian Efforts to Spread Portuguese. *International Journal of the Sociology of Language*, 95, pp.71-92.

Dalsgaadr, Peter (2009) Language and Language Policy in Mozambique. Available at http://www.eb-moz.dk/ and http://www.tindzimi.dk/

Davidson, Martin (2007) A UK perspective on public diplomacy and cultural relations in a time of conflict. Iowa 6 December 2007. Available at http://uscpublicdiplomacy.org/pdfs/Martin_Davidson_Speech.pdf [20.06.2010]

Davies, Alan (1996) Review Article: Ironising the Myth of Linguiscism. *Journal of Multilingual and Multicultural Development*, 17 (6), pp.485-496.

De Almeida, Miguel Vale (2004) *An Earth-Colored Sea: 'Race', Culture and the Politics of Identity in the Post-Colonial Portuguese Speaking World*. English translation of the 2000 Portuguese original. Oxford: Berghahn Books.

De Almeida, Miguel Vale (2008) Portugal's Colonial Complex: From Colonial Lusotropicalism to Postcolonial Lusophony. Available at http://site. miguelvaledealmeida.net/wp-content/uploads/portugals-colonial-complex.pdf [14.09.09].

De Magalhães, José Calvet (1990) *Breve História Diplomática de Portugal*. Mem-Martins: Publicações Europa-América.

De Swaan, Abram (1998) A political sociology of the world language system (1): The dynamics of language spread. *Language Problems and Language Planning*, 22(1), Spring, pp.63-75.

De Varennes, Fernand (1997) To speak or not to speak: The rights of persons belonging to linguistic minorities. Available from: http://www.unesco. org/most/1n2pol3.htm [12.02.2002].

Denzin, Norman K. and Lincoln, Yvonna S. eds. (1998) *Collecting and Interpreting Qualitative Materials.* London: Sage.

Denzin, Norman K. and Lincoln, Yvonna S. eds. (2003) *Strategies of Qualitative Inquiry.* 2nd ed. London: Sage.

Do Couto, Hildo Honório (2007) *Ecolinguística: estudo das relações entre língua e meio ambiente.* Brasília: Thesaurus Editora.

Do Rosário, Lourenço (2007) Lusofonia: Cultura ou Ideologia. *IV Simpósio Internacional de Língua Portuguesa.* Maputo, Maio de 2007. Available at http://www.saber.ac.mz/handle/123456789/1684

Do Rosário, Lourenço (2010) A Língua Portuguesa: encontros e desencontros. Communication presented at the celebrations fo the Day of Portuguese Language and Culture of the CPLP, on the 5th May 2010, at the Camões Institute in Maputo. Availble at http://macua.blogs.com/ moambique_para_todos_/2010/06/a-1%C3%Adngua-portuguesa-encontros-e-desencontros.html#more [10.06.2010].

Dos Santos, José Eduardo (2010) Discurso do Presidente da República de Angola na Sessão de Abertura da VIII Conferência de Chefes de Estado e de Governo da CPLP, 23 July 2010, Luanda, Angola. Available at http://www.cplp.org/Files/Filer/cplp/CCEG/VIII_CCEG/Discursos%20C CEG/scan0017.jpg [24.07.2010].

Dovring, Karin (1997) *English as Lingua Franca: Double Talk in Global Persuassion.* Westport, Connecticut, USA: Praeger Publishers.

Duer, Kreszentia (1999) *Culture and sustainable development : a framework for action.* Washington DC: World Bank. Available at http://www-wds.worldbank.org/external/default/WDSContentServer/WDSP/IB/2005/ 12/16/000011823_20051216164530/Rendered/PDF/34671.pdf [2010].

Dunn, Kevin C. (2001) Introduction: Africa and International Relations Theory. In Kevin C. Dunn, and Timothy M.Shaw, eds. *Africa's Challenge to International Relations Theory.* London: Palgrave, pp.1-8.

Duvernois, Louis (2004) *Pour une nouvelle stratégie de l'action culturelle extérieure de la France: de l'exception à l'influence.* Available at: http://www.senat.fr/rap/r04-091/r04-0911.pdf [13.11.2007].

Eduardo, Tomé and Uprichard, Eddie (1995) *The Proceeding of the First National Conference on English Language Teaching in Mozambique.* Research Report No.7. Maputo: INDE.

Embaixada da Alemanha Maputo (2010) Relações culturais bilaterais. Available at: http://www.maputo.diplo.de/Vertretung/maputo/pt/06/Bilaterale__ Kulturbeziehungen/Bilaterale__Kulturbeziehungen.html [24.06.2010].

Embaixada do Brasil na Guiné-Bissau (2007) Cooperação. Available at: wwww.guine.org/cultural.html [13.08.2007].

Encarte Jornal de Letras (2008) Centro Cultural Português: «A Casa da Cultural da Guiné-Bissau». *Encarte Jornal de Letras*, No.126, 4 June 2008, Suplemento do Jornal de Letras no. 983, ano XXVIII. Available at http://www.instituto-camoes.pt/encarte-jl/centro-cultural-portugues-a-casa-da-cultura-da-guine-bissau.html [08.05.2010].

Encarte Jornal de Letras (2010a) Guiné Bissau: Professores de Português concluem formação. No. 149, 10 March 2010, Suplement *Jornal de Letras*, No.1029, Year XXIX. Available at http://www.instituto-camoes.pt/encarte-jl/guine-bissau-professores-de-portugues-concluem-formacao.html [04.07.2010].

Encarte Jornal de Letras (2010b) O Instituto Camões e o ensino do português nos PALOP. 5 May 2010. Supplement to *Jornal de Letras* (JL) no.1033, year XXX. Available at http://www.instituto-camoes.pt/encarte-jl/o-instituto-camoes-e-o-ensino-do-portugues-nos-palop.html [30.06.2010].

Errante, A. (1998). Education and national personae in colonial and post-colonial Portugal. *Comparative Education Review*, 42 (3), 267-308.

Esperança, José Paulo (2008) Uma Abordagem Ecléctica do Valor da Língua: O Uso Global do Português/An Eclectic Approach to Language Valuation: The Global Influence of the Portuguese Language. Available at http://www.instituto-camoes.pt/noticias-ic-portugal/lingua-representa-17-do-pib-em-portugal.html [2010].

Evans, Graham and Newnham, Jeffrey (1998) *Dictionary of International Relations*. London: Penguin Books.

Fairclough, Norman (2001) *Language and Power*. Longman. Pearson Education. Harlow: England. Second edition.

Fairclough, Norman (2006) *Language and Globalization*. Routledge, Oxon.

Faraco, Carlos Alberto (forthcoming) A lusofonia: impasses e perspectivas. In *Sociolinguistics Studies*. Vigo.

Featherstone, Mike ed. (1990) *Global Culture: Nationalism, Globalization and Modernity: A Theory, Culture & Society Special Issue*. London: Sage Publications.

Ferreira, André (2010) Professores de português na Guiné-Bissau reunem-se para analisar métodos de ensino. Entrevista com Bernardo Ocáia, presidente da Associação Guineense de Professores de Português, e Wilson Barbosa, diretor da Escola Portuguesa da Guiné-Bissau [10.05.2010].

Available at http://www.portugues.rfi.fr/africa/20100510-professores-de-portugues-na-guine-bissau-reunem-se-para-analisar-metodos-de-ensino [03.07.2010].

FIPF, Fédération Internationale des Professeurs de Françis (2008) Le français au Mozambique. Interview with Josefina Comé-Menete, 30th Septembre 2008. Available at http://www.fipf.info/index.php?post/2008/09/30/Le-francais-au-Mozambique

Fisher, Rod (2009) From Cultural Diplomacy to Cultural Co-operation? Briefing session, 18th November 2009, Brussels: Summary Report. Document supplied by the author.

Fishman, Joshua A. (1977) English in the Context of International Societal Bilingualism. In Joshua A. Fishman, Robert L. Cooper, and Andrew W. Conrad ed. *The Spread Of English: The Sociology of English as an additional language*. Rowley: Newbury House Publishers, pp.329-336.

Fishman, Joshua A. (1996a) Introduction: Some empirical and theoretical issues. In Joshua A. Fishman, Andrew W. Conrad, and Alma Rubal-Lopez, ed. *Post-Imperial English: Status Change in Former British and American Colonies*, 1940-1990. Berlin: Mouton de Gruyter, pp.3-12.

Fishman, Joshua A. (2006) Language Policy and Language Shift. In Ricento, Thomas (ed.) *An Introduction to Language Policy: Theory and Method*. Blackwell Publishing, pp.311-328

Fishman, Joshua A., Conrad, Andrew W. and Rubal-Lopez, Alma eds. (1996) *Post-Imperial English: Status Change in Former British and American Colonies*, 1940-1990. Berlin: Mouton de Gruyter.

Flavell, Roger H. (1993) *Report on a Visit to Mozambique: Secondary English Project*. London: University of London, Institute of Education.

Flick, Uwe (2005a) Design and Process in Qualitative Research. In Uwe Flick, Ernest Von Kardorff and Ines Steinke, eds. *A Companion to Qualitative Research*. Reprint of 1st English ed. London: Sage, 2005a, pp.146-152.

Flick, Uwe (2005b) Triangulation in Qualitative Research. In Uwe Flick, Ernest Von Kardorff and Ines Steinke, eds. *A Companion to Qualitative Research*. Reprint of 1st English ed. London: Sage, 2005a, pp.178-183.

Flick, Uwe (2009) *An introduction to qualitative research*. London: Sage.

Flick, Uwe, Von Kardorff, Ernest and Steinke, Ines (2005a) What is Qualitative Research? An Introduction to the field. In Uwe Flick, Ernest Von Kardorff and Ines Steinke, eds. *A Companion to Qualitative Research*. Reprint of 1st English ed. London: Sage, 2005a, pp.3-11.

Foreign and Commonwealth Office (2006a) Public Diplomacy Board: Terms of Reference. In Foreign and Commonwealth Office *Promoting the UK, Pu-*

blic Diplomacy Board. Available at http://www.fco.gov.uk/Files/ kfile/TORs,O.pdf [24.11.2006].

Foreign and Commonwealth Office (2006b) *White Paper: Active Diplomacy for a Changing World. The UK's International Priorities*. Available at http://www.fco.gov.uk/resources/en/pdf/active-diplomacy [21.06.2010].

Fox, Robert (1999) *Cultural Diplomacy at the Crossroads: Cultural Relations in Europe and the Wider World*, a Report on a Conference Organised Jointly by the British Council and Wilton Park. London: Networking Europe.

Frank, Andre Gunter and Gills, Barry K. (1995/2001) The Five Thousand Year World System in Theory and Praxis. Available at http://www.rrojasdatabank.info/agfrank/theory_praxis.html [25.05.2010].

Freire, Paulo (1970) *Pedagogy of the Oppressed*. London: Penguin.

Freire, Paulo (1978) *Cartas à Guiné-Bissau: Registo de uma Experiência em Progresso*. Rio de Janeiro: Paz e Terra. Available at http://www. didinho.org/Cartas%20a%20Guine%20Bissau.pdf [07.07.2010].

Fundação Evangelização e Culturas (2008) Relatório de Avaliação Intercalar Projecto + Escola, Setembro 2007 – Agosto 2008. Available at http://www.fecongd.org/fec/pdf/FEC_GB_Escola_Relatorio2008.pdf [05.06.2010].

Fundação Evangelização e Culturas (2010) Fundação Evangelização e Culturas website. Available at http://www.fecongd.org/ [05.07.2010].

Gadelli, Karl Erland (1999) *Language planning: Theory and practice. Evaluation of language planning cases worldwide*. UNESCO.

Galito, Maria Sousa (2006) *Impacto Económico da Língua Portuguesa Enquanto Língua de Trabalho*. Available at http://www.ciari.org/investigacao/ impacto_econ_lingua_portuguesa.pdf [12.09.2007].

Gellner, Ernest (1983, 2006) *Nations and Nationalism*. Oxford: Basil Blackwell. 2nd edition.

German Information Centre Pretoria (2010) "Aktion Afrika": The many faces of cultural cooperation. Available at http://www.germanyandafrica.diplo.de/ Vertretung/pretoria__dz/en/08__AA/Aktion__Afrika__Intro.html [08.07.2010].

Giroux, Henry A. (1987) Introduction: Literacy and Pedagogy of Political Empowerment in Freire, Paulo and Macedo, Donaldo (1987) *Literacy: Reading the Word and the World*. Routledge and Kegan Paul, pp.1-27.

Glaser, Barney G. and Strauss, Anselm L. (1967) *The discovery of grounded theory : strategies for qualitative research*. New York: Aldine.

Goethe Institut (2008) Foco regional: África subsaariana. Available at http://www.goethe.de/prs/pro/afrika-initiative/imprensa.pdf [11.06.2010].

Goethe Institut / ICMA (2010) Quem somos. Available at http://www.goethe.de/ ins/mz/mao/uun/ptindex.htm [11.06.2010].

Gonçalves, Perpétua (2000) (Dados para a) História da Língua Portuguesa em Moçambique. Available at http://cvc.instituto-camoes.pt/hlp/geografia/ portuguesmocambique.pdf.

Gouteyron, Adrien (2008) Rapport d'Information fait au nom de la Commission des Finances, du Contrôle Budgétaire et des Comptes Economiques de la Nation sur l'Action Culturelle de la France à l'Étranger. France, Sénat 2007-2008, No.428. Available at http://www.senat.fr/noticerap/2007/r07-428-notice.html

Graça, Pedro João Borges (1992) A Informação Cultural de Portugal: Introdução ao seu Estudo no Contexto Lusófono e Internacional. *Estratégia*, 4, pp.189-297.

Graddol, David (1997) *The Future of English?* London: British Council.

Graddol, David (2006) *English Next*. London: British Council.

Gramsci, Antonio (1971) *Selections from the prison notebooks of Antonio Gramsci*. Lawrence & Wishart.

Grando, Cristiane (2009) O Centro Cultural Brasil-República Dominicana e os Centros de Estudoes Brasileiros (CEBs) in Revista de Cultura, 67, January/February 2009. Brasul: Fortaleza, São Paulo. Available at http://www.revista.agulha.nom.br/ag67bienalgrando.htm [07.06.2010].

Guba, E. G., & Lincoln, Y. S. (1994). Competing paradigms in qualitative research. In N. K. Denzin & Y. S. Lincoln (Eds.), *Handbook of qualitative research* (pp. 105-117). London: Sage.

Guba, E.G. (1978) *Toward a methodology of naturalistic inquiry in educational evaluation*. Los Angeles: UCLA, Center for the Study of Evaluation.

Guirrugo, Osvaldo (2009) O Ensino Bilingue em Moçambique: Um Desafio Político Estratégico. *Folha de Linguística e Literatura* 11, UEM Abril/Outubro 2008, pp.19-25. Available at: http://www.flcs.uem.mz/ images/pdf_files/folha_14.pdf

Hamel, Rainer Enrique (2005) Language Empires, Linguistic Imperialism and the Future of Global Languages. Available at http://www.hamel.com.mx/ Archivos-PDF/Work%20in%20Progress/ 2005%20Language%20Empires.pdf [10.02.2010].

Hamilton, Russel (2001) Vernacular, Literary, Vehicular, and Official: The Portuguese Language in Africa. In Asela Rodríguez de Laguna, ed. *Global Impact of the Portuguese Language*. London: Transaction Publishers, 2001, pp.181-188.

Hantrais, Linda and Mangen, Steen eds. (1996) *Cross-National Research Methods in the Social Sciences*. London: Pinter.

307

Harrison, Graham (1998) Political identities and social struggle in Africa. In Anne J. Kershen, ed. *A Question of Identity*. Aldershot: Ashgate, pp.248-270.

Haut Conseil de la Francophonie (1997) État de la Francophonie dans de le Monde: Données 1995-1996 et 5 études inédites. Paris: La Documentation Française.

Haut Conseil de la Francophonie (1999) État de la Francophonie dans de le Monde: Données 1997-1998 et 6 études inédites. Paris: La Documentation Française.

Heine, Bernd (1992) Language Policies in Africa. In Robert K. Herbert, ed. *Language and Society in Africa: The Theory and Practice of Sociolinguistics*. Cape Town: Witwatersrand University Press, pp.23-35.

Heine, Bernd and Nurse, Derek, ed. (2000) African Languages: An Introduction. Cambridge: Cambridge University Press.

Heugh, Kathleen (2007) Language and Literacy Issues in South Africa. In Rassool, Naz (2007) *Global Issues in Language, Education, and Development: Perspectives from Postcolonial Countries*. Clevedon: Multilingual Matters, pp.187-217.

Heugh, Kathleen (2009) Literacy and Bi/multilingual Education in Africa: Recovering Collective Memory and Expertise. In Skutnabb-Kangas, Tove, Phillipson, Robert, Mohanty, Ajit K. and Panda, Minati ed. (2009) *Social Justice Through Multilingual Education*. Bristol: Multilingual Matters, pp. 103-124.

Hobsbawm, E. J. (1990) *Nations and Nationalism since 1780. Programme, Myth, Reality*. Second edition. Cambridge University Press.

Hornberger, Nancy (ed.) (2008) *Encyclopedia of Language and Education*. New York: Springer.

Huntington, Samuel P. (1993) The Clash of Civilizations? Foreign Affairs 72 (3), Summer, pp.22-49.

Huntington, Samuel P. (1996) *The Clash of Civilizations and the Remaking of World Order*. London: Touchstone Books.

Instituto Camões (1992) Criação do Instituto Camões: Discursos e documentos. Lisboa: Instituto Camões.

Instituto Camões (2005a) Cooperação Portugal-Brasil e Instituto Machado de Assis in IC Notícias, 28 November 2005. Available at http://www.instituto-camoes.pt/noticias/noticia144.htm [14.09.2007].

Instituto Camões (2005b) Novo Ano Académico in Jornal de Letras (JL) supplement, 914, XXV, IC encarte 91, 12 October. Available at http://www.instituto-camoes.pt/encarte/encarte91a.htm [14.09.2007].

Instituto Camões (2010) Dia da Língua Portuguesa e da Cultura da CPLP, Moçambique, Terça, 04/5 Maio 2010. Available at http://instituto-camoes.pt/mocambique/dia-da-lingua-portuguesa-e-da-cultura-da-cplp.html

Instituto da Cooperacão Portuguesa (1999a) Integrated Portuguese Cooperation Programme 1999. Lisboa: Ministério dos Negócios Estrangeiros.

Instituto da Cooperação Portuguesa (2002f) Programme for Development Cooperation. Lisboa: Ministério dos Negócios Estrangeiros.

Instituto da Cooperação Portuguesa (2008) Programa Indicativo de Cooperação 2008-2010 Portugal: Guiné-Bissau. Available at http://www.ipad.mne.gov.pt/images/stories/Publicacoes/picguine0810.pdf [08.05.2010]

Instituto Nacional de Estatística (1999) II Recenseamento Geral da População e Habitação 1997: Resultados Definitivos. Moçambique. Maputo: Instituto Nacional de Estatística.

Instituto Português de Apoio ao Desenvolvimento (2007) Indicative Cooperation Programme: Portugal – Mozambique: 2007-2009. Available at http://www.ipad.mne.gov.pt/images/stories/Publicacoes/IPAD_Mozambique_net.pdf [17.03.2010].

Instituto Português de Apoio ao Desenvolvimento (2008) APD Moçambique 2008. Available at http://www.ipad.mne.gov.pt/index.php?option=com_content&task=view&id=67&Itemid=98 [27.07.2010]

Jackson, Robert and Sørensen, Georg (2007) *Introduction to International Relations: Theories and Approaches.* Third edition. Oxford University Press

Jacomb, Martin (1995) Projecting British Values, Education and Culture. *Britain in the World: A one day Conference* organised by the Royal Institute of International Affairs in association with Her Majesty's Government. Wednesday 29 March 1995. London, pp.136-138.

Janson, Tore (2002) *Speak: A Short History of Languages.* Oxford: Oxford University Press.

John Brademas Center for the Study of Congress, Robert F. Wagner Graduate School of Public Service, New York University (2009) *Moving Forward: A Renewed Role for American Arts and Artists in the Global Age: A Report to the President and the Congress of the United States of America.* December 2009. Available at: http://www.nyu.edu/brademas/pdf/Brademas%20Arts%20Report%2012.09.pdf [13.04.2010]

Jona, Sara (2008) Reflexões sobre Educação Intercultural em Moçambique: da (in)tolerância linguística à coabitação com a diferença - um sonho adiado ou uma realidade possível? Paper presented at the V Simposium Internacional De Língua Portuguesa – Escola Portuguesa de Moçambique and in the Conference Colóquio Mestiçagens Sócio-culturais e Procura de Iden-

309

tidade na África Contemporânea, CODESRIA and UNICV, Cape Verde/Praia). 2008. Published in *Proler*, October 2009. Available at http://www.saber.ac.mz/handle/123456789/1665

Juppé, Alain and Schweitzer, Louis (2008) Livre blanc sur la politique étrangère et européenne de la France: La France et l'Europe dans le Monde 2008-2020. Available at http://www.diplomatie.gouv.fr/fr/IMG/pdf/2LIVREBLANC_DEF.pdf

Juvane, Virgilio and Buendia, Miguel (2000) National Languages, Education and Citizenship. *Mozambique National Human Development Report 2000*. Maputo: United Nations Development Programme, pp.52-53.

Kaplan, Robert B. and Baldauf Jr., Richard B. (1997) *Language Planning: from Practice to Theory*. Clevedon: Multilingual Matters.

Kaplan, Robert B. et al. (2000) Editorial: Current Issues in Language Planning. *Current Issues in Language Planning*, 1 (1), pp.1-10.

Katupha, J.M.M. (1991) Language situation and language use in Mozambique in (1991) *Conference on African Languages, Development and the State*. Centre of African Studies, University of London and EIDOS, p.2-14.

Kergueris, Joseph (2010) Rapport sur le projet de loi relatif à l'action extérieure de l'État. Sénat français, rapport N° 262, 3 February 2010. Available at http://www.senat.fr/rap/l09-262/l09-262.html

Kerry, John F. (2009) U.S. Public Diplomacy – Time to Get Back In the Game. A Report to Members of the Committee on Foreign Relations, United States Senate. U.S. Government Printing Office: Washington. Available at: http://www.fas.org/irp/congress/2009_rpt/pubdip.pdf [13.04.2010]

Koening, Matthias (1998) *Democratic Governance in Multicultural Societies*. UNESCO.

Laitin, David D. (1992) *Language Repertoires and State Construction in Africa*. Cambridge: Cambridge University Press.

Laranjeira, Pires (1995) *Literaturas Africanas de Expressão Portuguesa*. Lisboa: Universidade Aberta.

Leech, Beth L. (2002b) Interview Methods in Political Science. PS: *Political Science & Politics*, 35 (4), December, pp.663-664.

Lemos, Mário Matos (1999) *Política Cultural Portuguesa em África: O Caso da Guiné Bissau*. Lisboa: Publicações Europa-América.

Leonard, Mark, Stead, Catherine and Smewing, Conrad (2002) *Public Diplomacy*. London: Foreign Policy Centre

Lewis, M. Paul (ed.), 2009. Ethnologue: Languages of the World, Sixteenth edition. Dallas, Tex.: SIL International. Online version: http://www.ethnologue.com/

Lijphart, Arend (1971) Comparative Politics and the Comparative Method. *The American Political Science Review*, 65 (3), September, pp.682-693.

Liphola, Marcelino M. (2009) Desafios na Gestão da Diversidade do Património Linguístico em Moçambique. *Folha de Linguística e Literatura* 11, UEM Abril/Outubro 2008, pp. 9-19. Available at http://www.flcs.uem.mz/images/pdf_files/folha_14.pdf

Liphola, Marcelino Marta (1988) As Línguas Banto de Moçambique: Uma Pequena Abordagem do Ponto de Vista Sócio-Linguístico. *Revista AEMO*, 1, Maputo.

Lopes, Armando Jorge (1998) English in Mozambique: Jogging the Collective Memory. *Revista da Associação Portuguesa de Estudos Anglo-Americanos* 1 , pp. 39-45.

Lopes, Armando Jorge (2001) Language Revitalisation and Reversal in Mozambique: The Case of Xironga in Maputo. *Current Issues in Language Planning* 2 (2&3), pp. 259-267.

Lourenço, Eduardo (1998) Intervenção em Mesa Redonda. *Discursos*, 15, April, pp.64-68.

Lourenço, Eduardo (1999) *A Nau de Ícaro e Imagem e Miragem da Lusofonia*. Lisboa: Gradiva.

Lüdi, Georges (2006) Migration, Language, Linguistic Impotence. Available at http://www.goethe.de/dll/prj/mac/ver/en1275558.htm [17.05.2006].

Macaringue, Júlio (1990) Moçambique: Vamos aprender inglês? "Yes, it's very important?!" *Tempo*, 02 December. Maputo, pp. 17-27.

Malone, Gifford D. (1988) *Political Advocacy and Cultural Communication: Organizing the Nation's Public Diplomacy*. University Press of America.

Margarido, Alfredo (2000) *A Lusofonia e os Lusófonos: Novos Mitos Portugueses*. Lisboa: Edições Universitárias Lusófonas.

Mar-Molinero, Claire (1997) *The Spanish-Speaking World: a practical introduction to sociolinguistic issues*. London: Routledge.

Mar-Molinero, Claire (2000) *The Politics of Language in the Spanish-Speaking World: From Colonisation to Globalisation*. London: Routledge.

Massingue, V. (1995) *The process of education policy formation in Africa: the case of Mozambique*. Paris: Association for the Development of Education in Africa.

Mata, Inocência (2002) A língua portuguesa e a diversidade dos falantes nas literaturas dos países da CPLP. Comunidade dos Países de Língua Portuguesa (2002b) Instituto Internacional de Língua Portuguesa. *Cadernos CPLP*. Lisbon: CPLP, pp.60-64.

Matsinhe, Sozinho Francisco (2005) The Language Situation in Mozambique: Current Developments and Prospects. In Brock-Utne Birgit and Hopson,

311

Rodney Kofi (ed.) *Languages of Instruction for African Emancipation: Focus on Postcolonial Contexts and Considerations*. Dar es Salaam: Mkuki N Nyota Publishers. Cape Town: Centre for Advanced Studies of African Society (CASAS), pp.119-146.

Matusse, Renato (1991) Porquê Promover as Línguas Moçambicanas? (1) *Domingo*, 01 December, Maputo.

Matusse, Renato (1997) The future of Portuguese in Mozambique in Herbert, R. K., ed. (1997) *African linguistics at the crossroads: papers from Kwaluseni*. Köln: Rüdiger Köpe, p.541-554.

Matusse, Renato (1998) Moçambique ou Mozambique? Um Olhar sobre Falsas Prescrições Oftálmicas. Paper presented at the V Congresso Luso-Afro-Brasileiro de Ciências Sociais. Maputo. [Copy supplied by the author.]

Matusse, Renato (2002) Com a Independência, também libertámos a língua portuguesa. Maputo. [Copy supplied by the author.]

Maurais, Jacques (2003) Towards a New Global Linguistic Order? In Jacques Maurais and Michael A. Morris, ed. *Languages in a Globalising World*. Cambridge: Cambridge University Press, pp.13-36.

Mazrui, Alamin M. (2004) *English in Africa After the Cold War*. Clevedon: Multilingual Matters.

Mazrui, Ali A. (1998) Language and Race in the Black Experience: An African Perspective. In Ali A. Mazrui and Alamin M. Mazrui ed. *The Power of Babel: Language & Governance in the African Experience*. London: Villiers Publications, pp.13-29.

Mazrui, Ali A. and Mazrui, Alamin M. (1998a) Conclusion: The Linguistic Balance Sheet: Post-Cold War, Post-Apartheid and Beyond Structural Adjustment. In Ali A. Mazrui and Alamin M. Mazrui ed. *The Power of Babel: Language & Governance in the African Experience*. London: Villiers Publications, pp.192-211.

Mazrui, Ali A. and Mazrui, Alamin M. (1998b) Introduction: Africa's Linguistic Legacy: Between Expansionism and Nationalism. In Ali A. Mazrui and Alamin M. Mazrui ed. *The Power of Babel: Language & Governance in the African Experience*. London: Villiers Publications, pp.1-10.

Mazrui, Ali A. and Mazrui, Alamin M. (1998c) Language in a Multicultural Context: The African Experience. In Ali A. Mazrui and Alamin M. Mazrui ed. *The Power of Babel: Language & Governance in the African Experience*. London: Villiers Publications, pp.69-84.

Mazrui, Ali A. and Mazrui, Alamin M. ed. (1998d) *The Power of Babel: Language & Governance in the African Experience*. London: Villiers Publications.

Mazula, Brazão (1995) Educação, Cultura e Ideologia em Moçambique: 1975-1985. Available at http://www.macua.org/livros/mazula.html

McCraken, Grant (1988) *The Long Interview*. London: Sage.

McKinnon, Don (2007) The Modern Commonwealth – challenges in the 21st Century. London School of Economics, 12th November 2007. Available at http://www.thecommonwealth.org/shared_asp_files/gfsr.asp?NodeID=17 2338&attributename=file

McManus, Lisa (2010) British Council Mozambique. [Four page document about the context and activities of the BC Mozambique sent by email by the Director, Ms Lisa MacManus, on 26.06.2010]

Medeiros, Paula Cristina Pacheco (2005) Lusofonia: discursos e representações In *Cabo dos Trabalhos*, 1, Centro de Estudos Sociais, Faculdade de Economia. Coimbra: Universidade de Coimbra. Available at http://cabodostrabalhos.ces.uc.pt/n1/documentos/200611_lusofonia_discu rsos_representacoes.pdf

Melissen, Jan (ed.) (2007) *The New Public Diplomacy: Soft Power in International Relations*. Basingstoke: Palgrave Macmillan.

Meneses, Maria Paula (2007) Pluralism, Law and Citizenship in Mozambique: Mapping the Complexity. *Oficina* n. 291. Centro de Estudos Sociais, Universidade de Coimbra. Available at http://www.ces.uc.pt/publicacoes/ oficina/291/291.pdf

Meneses, Maria Paula and Santos, Boaventura Sousa (2008) Mozambique: the Rise of a Micro Dual State. Paper presented at the CODESRIA 12th General Assembly Governing the African Public Sphere, 07-11/12/2008, Yaoundé, Cameroun.

Merken, Hans (2005) Selection Procedures, Sampling, Case Construction. In Uwe Flick, Ernest Von Kardorff and Ines Steinke, eds. *A Companion to Qualitative Research*. Reprint of 1st English ed. London: Sage, 2005a, pp.165-171.

Miguel, Victor (1994) *Língua Portuguesa: Língua Ameaçada em Moçambique?* Tese de Licenciatura, BA Thesis, Unpublished. Faculdade de Letras, Departamento de Letras Modernas. Maputo: Universidade Eduardo Mondlane.

Ministère des Affaires Étrangères (2000) *A Cooperação Franco-Moçambicana em 1999: Um Olhar sobre 10 anos de Cooperação*. Maputo: Ministère des Affaires Étrangères – Coopération et Francophonie.

Ministère des Affaires Étrangères (2006) Document Cadre de Partenariat France – Mozambique – DCP – (2006-2010). Available at http://www.diplomatie.gouv.fr/fr/actions-france_830/aide-au-developpement_1060/politique-francaise_3024/instruments-aide_2639/documents-cadres-partenariat-dcp_5219/document-cadre-partenariat-france-mozambique-dcp-2006-2010_44312.html [10.03.2007].

Ministère des Affaires Étrangères (2006) Document Cadre de Partenariat France – Mozambique – DCP – (2006-2010). Available at http://www.diplomatie.gouv.fr/fr/actions-france_830/aide-au-developpement_1060/politique-francaise_3024/instruments-aide_2639/documents-cadres-partenariat-dcp_5219/document-cadre-partenariat-france-mozambique-dcp-2006-2010_44312.html [10.03.2007].

Ministère des Affaires Etrangères (2008) Documento de Parceria França – Guiné Bissau 2008-2012 . Available at http://www.diplomatie.gouv.fr/fr/IMG/pdf/DCP_Guinee_Bissao_PT.pdf [06.06.2010].

Ministère des Affaires Étrangères et Europèennes (2007c) Promoting French. Available at http:/www.diplomatie.gouv.fr/en/france-priorities_1/francophony-french-language_1113/French-language1934/promoting-french_4450/index.html [18.11.2007].

Ministère des Affaires étrangères et européennes (2009) Promoting French Around the World. Document of the Direction générale de la mondialisation, du développement et des partenariats. Available at http://www.diplomatie.gouv.fr/en/IMG/pdf/promouvoir_GB_p-p-2.pdf [25.04. 2010].

Ministério da Educação do Brasil (2004) Ata da primeira reunião plenária da Comissão para definição da política de ensino, aprendizagem e pesquisa da Língua Portuguesa no Brasil e de sua internacionalização. Available at http://portal.mec.gov.br/sesu/arquivos/pdf/MachadodeAssis/atadereuniao.pdf [14.09.2007].

Ministério da Educação do Brasil (2006c) Instituto Machado de Assis – Apresentação. Available at http://portal.mec.gov.br/sesu/index.php?option=content&task=view&id=690&Itemid=303 [14.09.2007].

Ministério da Educação, Ciência e Tecnologia da Guiné-Bissau (2000) Declaração de Política Educativa. Bissau.

Ministério das Relações Exteriores – Brasil (2010) Difusão Cultural. Available at http://www.itamaraty.gov.br/temas/difusao-cultural [07.06.2010].

Ministério das Relações Exteriores do Brasil (2007) Nota a Imprensa nº 549: State visit of the President of the Republic of Guinea-Bissau, Mr. João Bernardo Vieira, to Brazil - Brasilia, November 12 to 14, 2007 - Joint Communiqué. 14/11/2007. Available at http://www.itamaraty.gov.br/sala-de-imprensa/notas-a-imprensa/2007/11/14/state-visit-of-the-president-of-the-republic-of [02.07.2010].

Ministério das Relações Exteriores do Brasil (2009) Centro Cultural Brasil – Guiné-Bissau. Available at http://www.dc.mre.gov.br/lingua-e-literatura/centro-cultural-brasil-guine-bissau [28.07.2010].

Ministério das Relações Exteriores do Brasil (2010b) Educação. Available at http://www.itamaraty.gov.br/temas/difusao-cultural/educacao [2.06.2010].

Ministerio de Asuntos Exteriores y de Coopéracion, Gobierno de España (2006) Africa Plan 2006-2008, Executive Summary. Available at http://www.maec.es/es/Home/Paginas/20060605_planafricaingles.aspx [11.06.2010].

Ministerio de Asuntos Exteriores y de Coopéracion, Gobierno de España (2009) Plan África 2009-2012. Available at http://www.casafrica.es/casafrica/Inicio/PlanAfrica2009-2012.pdf [25.06.2010].

Mitchell, John M. (1986) *International Cultural Relations*. London: Allen & Unwin Ltd.

Mondlane, Eduardo (1995) *Lutar por Moçambique*, 1st.ed. 1969. Maputo: Centro de Estudos Africanos.

Monteiro, José Oscar (2006) O Estado Moçambicano entre o modelo e a realidade social. Palestra. Maputo. Available at http://www.sislog.com/ta/IMG/doc/palestra.doc [2010].

Mufwene, Salikoko (2005) Globalization, and the Myth of Killer Languages. In Graham Huggan and Stephan Klasen, ed. *Perspectives on Endangerment*. In press, pp.19-48. Available from: http//humanities.uchicago.edu/faculty/mufwene/publications/globalization-killerLanguages.pdf [18.05.2006].

Mühlhäusler, Peter (1996) *Language Change and Linguistic Imperialism in the Pacific Region*. London: Routledge.

Murray, Neil (2001) VSO's Support to Secondary and Technical Education Project (STEP) in *Mozambique: A View from the Trenches*. Maputo: VSO.

Myers-Scotton, Carol (1982) Learning lingua francas and socio-economic integration: evidence from Africa. In Robert L. Cooper (ed.) *Language Spread*, pp.63-94. Bloomington, Indiana: Indiana University Press.

N'Tanhá, Nelinho (2010) Português não quer perder espaço na Guiné-Bissau. 11 February 2010. Jornal Nô Pintcha. Available at http://www.jornalnopintcha.com/nacional/431-portugues-nao-quer-perder-espaco-na-guine-bissau.html [03.07.2010].

Nansil, Sumba (2009) Guiné-Bissau: Ministro das Relações Exteriores do Brasil visita o país. In Bissau Digital, 2009-10-22 Available at http://www.bissaudigital.com/noticias.php?idnoticia=4972 [02.07.2010].

Newitt, Malyn (1995) *A History of Mozambique*. Bloomington and Indianapolis: Indiana University Press.

Ngunga, Armindo S. (2001) Language policy for education and the media in Mozambique: An alternative perspective in Trewby, Richard and Fitchat,

Sandra, ed. (2001) *Conference Proceedings: National Institute for Educational Development*, 11 – 13 April 2000. Gamberg Macmillan, p.94-108.

Notícias Lusófonas (2007) Guiné Equatorial admite adoptar língua portuguesa [Online] Available at: http://macua.blogs.com/moambique_para_todos/ 2007/07/guin-equatorial.html [07.01.2008].

Notícias Lusófonas (2010) Guiné-Bissau quer apostar forte no ensino do Português. 8 May 2010. Available at http://timorlorosaenacao. blogspot.com/2010/05/guine-bissau-quer-apostar-forte-no.html [06.07.2010].

Nsiku, Edouard Kitoko (2008) Dogs' Languages or Peoples Languages? The Returning of Bantu Languages to Primary Schools in Mozambique. *Folha de Linguística e Literatura* 11, UEM Abril/Outubro 2008, pp. 7-17.

Nye, Joseph (2010) Soft Power and Public Diplomacy in the 21st Century. Inaugural British Council Parliamentary Lecture 20 January 2010. Available at http://www.britishcouncil.org/new/PageFiles/11706/2010%2001%2022% 20Joe%20Nye%20Soft%20Power.pdf [20.06.2010].

Nye, Joseph S. (2002) *The Paradox of American Power: Why the World's Only Superpower Can't Go It Alone*. Oxford: Oxford University Press.

Nye, Joseph S. (2004) *Soft Power: The Means to Success in World Politics*. New York: Public Affairs.

Obeng, Samuel Gyasi and Adegbija, Efurosibina (1999) Sub-Saharan Africa, In Joshua A. Fishman, ed. *Handbook of Language & Ethnic Identity*. Oxford: Oxford University Press. CH.23, pp.353-368.

Obondo, Margaret Akinyi (2008) Bilingual Education in Africa: An Overview. In Hornberger, Nancy (ed.) *Encyclopedia of Language and Education*. Volume 5: Bilingual Education, Springer Science,pp.151-164.

OECD/DAC (1997) 1997 Development Co-operation Review of Portugal: Summary and Conclusions. Available at http://www.oecd.org/document/ 58/0,2340,en_2649_33721_2087354_1_1_1_1,00.html [17.03.2007].

OECD/DAC (2004) 2004 France DAC Peer Review: Main Findings and Recommendations. Available at http://www.oecd.org/dataoecd/31/40/ 32556778.pdf [03.10.2007].

OIF (2008) Abdou Diouf mandate des envoyés spéciaux sur la langue française, 12 juin 2008. Available at http://www.francophonie.org/Abdou-Diouf-mandate-des-envoyes.html?var_recherche=mozambique

OIF (2008) Missions. Available at http://www.francophonie.org/oif/ missions.cfm [08.01.2008].

Olson, David (2007) *Jerome Bruner: The Cognitive Revolution in Educational Theory*. London: Continuum.

Palmeira, José (2006) Xeoestratexia Lusófona na Era Global. Tempo Exterior, 12, January-June. Available at http://www.igadi.org/te/pdf/te_se12/ te24_12_011jose_palmeira.pdf [17.07.2006].

PANA (2010) Diplomata americano encoraja Angola a apostar no ensino do inglês. 8 April 2010. Available at http://www.panapress.com/ freenewspor.asp?code=por010543&dte=08/04/2010 [17.07.2010]

Panguane, Sílvia (2010) Dia da Língua e Cultura da CPLP comemorada no Camões. 06 de Maio de 2010, 15:12. Available at http://noticias.sapo.mz/ info/artigo/1063111.html

Pattanayak, D. P. (1991) *Language, Education and Culture.* Manasagangotri, Mysore: Central Institute of Indian Languages.

Peace Corps (2010) Mozambique. Available at http://www.peacecorps.gov/ index.cfm?shell=learn.wherepc.africa.Mozambique [16.06.2010]

Pennycook, Alaistair (2006) Postmodernism in Language Policy. In Ricento, Thomas (ed.) *An Introduction to Language Policy: Theory and Method.* Blackwell Publishing, pp.60-76.

Pennycook, Alastair (1994) *The Cultural Politics of English as an International Language.* New York: Longman Publishing.

Pennycook, Alastair (1998) The Right to Language: Towards a Situated Ethics of Language Possibilities. In *Language Sciences,* vol. 20, Number 1, January 1998, Special Issue 'Language Rights'. Pergamon, pp. 73-87.

Pennycook, Alastair (1998a) *English and the Discourses of Colonialism.* London: Routledge

Pennycook, Alastair (1998b) The Right to Language: Towards a Situated Ethics of Language Possibilities. In *Language Sciences,* vol. 20, Number 1, January 1998, Special Issue 'Language Rights'. Pergamon, pp. 73-87.

Pennycook, Alastair (1999) Development, Culture and Language: Ethical Concerns in a Postcolonial World. The Fourth International Conference on Language and Development, October 13-15, 1999. Available at http://www.languages.ait.ac.th/hanoi_preceedings/pennycook.htm [01.12.2009].

Pennycook, Alastair (2000) English, Politics, Ideology: From Colonial Celebration to Postcolonial Performativity. In Thomas Ricento, ed. (2000c) *Ideology, Politics and Language Policies: Focus on English.* Amsterdam: John Benjamins Pub, pp.107-119.

Phillipson, Robert (1992) *Linguistic Imperialism.* Oxford: Oxford University Press.

Phillipson, Robert (1998) Globalizing English: are linguistic human rights an alternative to linguistic imperialism? In Benson, Phil, Grundy, Peter &

Skutnabb-Kangas, Tove (eds). Language rights. Special volume. *Language Sciences* 20:1, 101-112.

Phillipson, Robert (2000) English in the New World Order: Variation on a Theme of Linguistic Imperialism and "World" English. In Thomas Ricento, ed. (2000c) *Ideology, Politics and Language Policies: Focus on English*. Amsterdam: John Benjamins Pub, pp.87-106.

Phillipson, Robert (2006) English, a cuckoo in the European higher education nest of languages? *European Journal of English Studies*, 10/1, 13-32.

Phillipson, Robert (2007) Linguistic imperialism: a conspiracy, or a conspiracy of silence? In *Language Policy*, 6/3-4, pp.377-383.

Phillipson, Robert (2008) The linguistic imperialism of neoliberal empire. In *Critical Inquiry in Language Studies*, 5/1, pp.1-43.

Phillipson, Robert (2009a) *Linguistic Imperialism Continued*. London: Routledge / Orient Black Swan.

Phillipson, Robert (2009b) Some partner languages are more equal than others. Presented at the *Bamako International Forum on Multilingualism*, organised by the African Academy of Languages, Bamako, Mali, 19-21 January 2009. Available at http://uk.cbs.dk/forskning/institutter_centre/institutter/isv/menu/medarbejdere/menu/videnskabelige/videnskabelige/professor_emeritus/phillipson [29.07.2010].

Phillipson, Robert and Skutnabb-Kangas, Tove (1995) Language Rights in Postcolonial Africa. In Tove Skutnabb-Kangas and Robert Phillipson, eds. *Linguistic Human Rights*. Berlin: Mouton de Gruyter, 1995, pp.335-345.

Pieterse, Jan Nederveen and Parekh, Bhikhu (1995) Shifting Imaginaries: Decolonization, Internal Decolonization, Postcoloniality. In Jan Nederveen Pieterse and Bhikhu Parekh, ed. *The Decolonization of Imagination: Culture, Knowledge and Power*. London: Zed Books, pp.1-19.

Pinto-Bull, Benjamin (1989) *O Crioulo da Guiné-Bissau: Filosofia e Sabedoria*. Lisboa: ICALP – ME.

PNUD (2006) Rapport National 2006 sur le Développement Humain en Guinée-Bissau: Réformer les Politiques pour Atteindre les Objectifs du Millénaire pour le Développement en Guinée-Bissau. Available at http://www.gw.undp.org/rndhgw.pdf [30.04.2010].

Pôle de Dakar (2010) Analyse Sectorielle en Education: Entrée pays. Available at http://www.poledakar.org/ [08.07.2010].

Presidência da República (2010a) Discurso do Presidente da República na Sessão de Encerramento do Colóquio Internacional sobre Língua Portuguesa e Diálogo Cultural, Universidade de Cabo Verde, Cidade da Praia, 6 de Julho de 2010. Available at http://www.presidencia.pt/?idc=22&idi=44083 [18.07.2010].

Presidência da República (2010b) Intervenção do Presidente da República no Dia da Língua Portuguesa e da Cultura da CPLP, Escola Secundária Eça de Queirós. Available at www.presidencia.pt/?idc=10&idi=40183 [08.07.2010].

Radio Moçambique (2010) Escritor Mia Couto defende equiparação entre línguas moçambicanas e o português. Available at http://www.mozclick. com/rm/noticias/anmviewer.asp?a=3241&print=yes

Rassool (2004) Sustaining linguistic diversity within the global cultural economy: issues of language rights and linguistic possibilities. *Comparative Education*, vol. 40, number 2, May 2004, pp.199-214.

Rassool (2008) Language policy and education in Britain. In Hornberger, Nancy (ed.) *Encyclopedia of Language and Education*. Volume 1: Language Policy and Political Issues in Education, Springer Science,pp.267-284.

Rassool, Naz (1995) Theorizing Literacy, Politics and Social Process: Revisiting Maktab Literacy in Iran in Search of a Critical Paradigm. In *International Journal of Educational Development*, Vol.15, No.4, Pergamon, pp.423-436.

Rassool, Naz (1998) Postmodernity, Cultural Puralism and the Nation-State: Problems of Language Rights, Human Rights, Identity and Power. In *Language Sciences*, vol. 20, Number 1, January 1998, Special Issue 'Language Rights'. Pergamon, pp. 89-99.

Rassool, Naz (2007) *Global Issues in Language, Education, and Development: Perspectives from Postcolonial Countries*. Clevedon: Multilingual Matters.

Rassool, Naz (forthcoming) Language and Development: examining the concept of 'indigenous' language capital amongst refugee groups in Sub-Saharan Africa. In *International Journal of the Sociology of Language*. Special Issue on Language and Development in Sub-Saharan Africa.

Redacção Sapo (2010) "As línguas não divergem, complementam-se". Quinta 06 Maio 2010, 08:36. Available at http://opais.sapo.mz/index.php? option=com_content&view=article&id=5912:as-linguas-nao-divergem-complementam-se&catid=82:cultura&Itemid=278

Remiller, Jacques (2008) La Politique de la France en Afrique. Rapport d'information pour l'Assemblée Nationale de France. Available at http://www.assemblee-nationale.fr/13/rap-info/i1332.asp

República de Moçambique (1995) Política Nacional de Educação. Available at http://www.portaldogoverno.gov.mz/docs_gov/fold_politicas/eduCult/poli tica_educacao.pdf [28.07.2007]

República de Moçambique, Ministério da Educação (1998) Plano Estratégico de Educação 1999-2003: Combater a Exclusão, Renovar a Escola. Maputo.

República de Moçambique, Ministério da Educação e Cultura (2006) Plano Estratégico de Educação e Cultura 2006-2010/11: Fazer da escola um polo de desenvolvimento consolidando a Moçambicanidade. Available at http://planipolis.iiep.unesco.org/upload/Mozambique/Mozambique_PEEC .pdf

República de Moçambique, Ministério da Educação e Cultura (2009) II Conferência Nacional Sobre Cultura: Termos de Referência. Maputo, 14-16 May 2009. Available at http://www.mec.gov.mz/img/documentos/ 20090506100535.pdf

República de Moçambique/Comité de Conselheiros (2003) Agenda 2025: Visão e Estratégias da Nação. Maputo. Available at http://www.dnpo.gov.mz/ documents/p_governo/agenda_2025.pdf

Ribeiro, Fátima (1993) Preservar e Divulgar o Português, Uma das Línguas "Nacionais" de Moçambique. In *AMOLP*, Especial, December 1993-February 1994, pp.2-6.

Ribeiro, Fátima (2007) Ensino Bilingue em Moçambique: Preocupações que deviam ser de todos. Available from: http://oficinadesociologia. blogspot.com/ [06.08.2007].

Ricento, Thomas (2000) Historical and Theoretical Perspectives in Language Policy and Planning. In Thomas Ricento, ed. (2000c) *Ideology, Politics and Language Policies: Focus on English*. Amsterdam: John Benjamins Pub, pp.9-24.

Ricento, Thomas (ed.) (2006) *An Introduction to Language Policy: Theory and Method*. Blackwell Publishing.

Robinson, Clinton D. W. (1996) *Language Use in Rural Development: An African Perspective*. Berlin: Mouton de Gruyter.

Robson, Colin (2002) *Real world research: a resource for social scientists and practitioner-researchers*. Blackwell.

Rothkopf, David (1997) In Praise of Cultural Imperialism? *Foreign Policy* 107 Summer, pp.38-53.

Roussin, Michel (1994) Allocution du ministre de la Coopération, M. Michel Roussin à l'occasion du diner offert en l'honneur du Président de la République d'Angola, M. José Eduardo dos Santos. Politique Étrangère de la France – Textes et Documents – Février 1994. Paris: La Documentation Française, pp.240-241.

Routh, H.V. 1941. *The diffusion of English culture outside England*. Cambridge: Cambridge University Press.

Rubin, Herbert J. and Rubin, Irene S. (2005) *Qualitative Interviewing: The Art of Hearing*. 2nd ed. London: Sage.

Safran, William (1999) Nationalism. In Joshua A. Fishman, ed. *Handbook of Language & Ethnic Identity*. Oxford: Oxford University Press. Ch.6, pp.77-93.

Saiete, Jorge (2008) Não falem a língua do cão! 16th May 2008. Available at http://debateereflexao.blogspot.com/2008/05/no-fale-lngua-do-co.html

Sambo, Emildo (2007) Ensino bilingue pouco se faz sentir. Canal de Moçambique – 07.02.2007 Available at http://macua.blogs.com/moambique_para_todos/files/ensino_bilingue_pouco_se_faz_sentir.doc

Sambú, Homba Sana (2009) Combate ao Analfabetismo nas Regiões Leste do País. Available at http://www.gaznot.com/imprimer_article.php?id=203 [16.06.2010].

Saunders, Frances Stonor (1999) *Who Paid the Piper? The CIA and the Cultural Cold War*. London: Granta.

Saute, Nelson (1990) O Escritor Moçambicano e a Língua Portuguesa. *Tempo*, 11 February. Maputo, pp.42-46.

Scantamburlo, Luigi (2010) Comentário a Notícia sobre "Guiné Bissau quer alfabetizar população até 2015". 17 June 2010. Available at http://www.jornaldigital.com/noticias.php?noticia=22422 [03.07.2010]

Schraeder, Peter J. (2004) *African Politics and Society: A Mosaic in Transformation*. Second Edition. London: Thomson/Wadsworth.

Semedo, Maria Odete da Costa (2005) Educação como direito. Available at http://www.dhnet.org.br/redes/guinebissau/semedo_educacao_como_direito.pdf [15.06.2010]

Sen, Amartya (2006) *Identity and Violence: The Illusion of Destiny*. London: Allen Lane, Penguin Books.

Sendela, Rafael (2007) Ensino bilingue conta com 15 mil alunos. *Jornal de Notícias* (Maputo), 01.08.2007, p.1.

Silva, Paulo (1997) Letter of the Minister of National Education of Guinea-Bissau to the President of the World Bank. World Bank: Project Appraisal Document for a Basic Education Support Project – Annex 1B. Available at http://go.worldbank.org/0FWE787641 [12.08.2007].

Silverman, David (2003) *Interpreting Qualitative Data: Methods for Analysing Talk, Text and Interaction*. 2nd ed. London: Sage.

Skutnabb-Kangas, Tove & Phillipson, Robert (eds.) (1995), *Linguistic Human Rights. Overcoming Linguistic Discrimination*. Berlin: Mouton de Gruyter

Skutnabb-Kangas, Tove (1988) 'Multilingualism and the education of minority children' in Skutnabb-Kangas, T and Cummins, J (eds.) 1988 *Minority Education: From Shame to Struggle*, Clevedon: Multilingual Matters, pp.9-44.

Skutnabb-Kangas, Tove (1998) Human Rights and Language Wrongs in *Language Sciences*, vol. 20, Number 1, January 1998, Special Issue 'Language Rights'. Pergamon, pp. 5-27.

Skutnabb-Kangas, Tove (2000) *Linguistic Genocide in Education - or Worldwide Diversity and Human Rights?* London: Lawrence Erlbaum Associates.

Skutnabb-Kangas, Tove and Robert Phillipson (2008) A human rights perspective on language ecology. In Angela Creese, Peter Martin and Nancy H. Hornberger eds. *Ecology of Language*, volume 9 of Encyclopedia of Language and Education, 2nd edition,. New York: Springer, 3-14.

Smith, Anthony D. (1983) *State and Nation in the Third World. The Western State and African Nationalism*. Brighton: Wheatsheaf Books.

Smith, Anthony D. (1991) *National Identity*. Reno: University of Nevada Press.

Spencer, John (1985) Language and Development in Africa: The Unequal Equation. In Nessa Wolfson and Joan Manes, ed. *Language of Inequality*. Berlin: Mouton Publishers, pp.387-397.

Spolsky, Bernard (2004) *Language Policy*. Cambridge: Cambridge University Press.

Stevenson, Patrick (1997) *The German-Speaking World: a practical introduction to sociolinguistic issues*. London: Routledge.

Stiglitz, Joseph (2001) *Joseph Stiglitz and the World Bank: the rebel within*. London: Anthem Press

Stiglitz, Joseph (2002) *Globalization and its discontents*. London: Penguin

Stiglitz, Joseph (2006) *Making globalization work*. London: Allen Lane.

Sumich, Jason and Honwana, João (2007) Strong Party, Weak State? Frelimo and State Survival Through the Mozambican Civil War: An analytical narrative on state-making. *Crisis States Research Centre*, Working Paper No. 23. London: London School of Economics. Available at http://www.crisisstates.com/download/wp/wpSeries2/wp23.2.pdf

Taboroff, June (ed.) (2001) The Kimberley Consultative Workshop on Culture in Africa: synthesis report. Pretoria: World Bank Group. Available at http://www-wds.worldbank.org/external/default/WDSContentServer/WDSP/IB/2006/09/14/000090341_20060914095508/Rendered/PDF/37253.pdf

Tardif, Jean (2004a) From "Cultural Exceptionalism" to Cultural Pluralism. Translated from the French version by Paule Herodote. Available from: http://www.planetagora.org/english/theme1_suj2_note.html [02.11.2006].

Tardif, Jean (2004b) Globalization and Culture. Translated from the French version by Paule Herodote. Available from: http://www.planetagora.org/english/theme1_note.html [15.06.2006].

Tardif, Jean (2004c) Identidades Culturales y Desafíos Geoculturales. In *Pensar Iberoamerica, Revista de Cultura*, 6, May-August. Available from: http://www.campus-oei.org/pensariberoamerica/ric06a03.htm [16.06.2006].

Tardif, Jean (2004d) The Hidden Dimension of Globalization: What is at Stake Geoculturally. Available at http://www.planetagora.org/english/theme1_suj1_note.html [02.11.2006].

Taylor, Philip M. (1997) *Global Communications, International Affairs and the Media since 1945*. London: Routledge.

Teles, Ana Filipa (2009) *Dimensão Cultural da Política Externa Portuguesa: Da Década de 90 à Actualidade.* Dissertation presented for Master Degree in the Teaching of Portuguese as a Second Language/Foreign Language. Universidade Nova de Lisboa - FCSH - Departamento de Estudos Portugueses Lisboa. Available at http://cvc.instituto-camoes.pt/component/docman/doc_details.html?aut=2111

Televisão Pública de Angola (2009) Embaixador americano promete apoiar ensino da Língua Inglesa. 9 February 2009. Available at http://www.tpa.ao/artigo.aspx?sid=2ae44602-f73b-4162-92ca-dc32d216aefa&cntx=2TWvsJImYdxsV%2Bv21HJ0cDEDDHfWSTZg0c qbejLEh2LT%2FcF%2B8Xi3F6ciC9fnsXWA [17.07.2010]

Tengan, Alexis B. (1994) European Languages in African Society and Culture: A View on Cultural Authenticity. In Martin PÜTZ ed. *Language Contact, Language Conflict*. Amsterdam: John Benjamins Publishing Company, pp.125-137.

The Frank Family (2009) The Frank Family 2008-2009 Annual Report. Available at http://www.thefrankfamily.org/2008-2009annualreport.pdf [08.06.2010]

Thiong'O, Ngũgĩ Wa (1986) *Decolonising the Mind: The Politics of Language in African Literature*. First edited in 1981. London: James Currey.

Thurston, Alex (2008) China in Africa. Available from http://www.theseminal.com/2008/01/03/china-in-africa/ [24.05.2008].

Tomalin, Barry (2004) Cultural Branding – An Instrument of Cultural Diplomacy. In *Standing Group on International Relations Fifth Pan-European Conference*, September 9-11. The Hague. Available from: http://www. sgir.org/conference2004/papers/Tomalin%20%20Cultural%20dimensions %20of%20International%20Relations.pdf [07.11.2006].

Totaro-Genevois, Mariella (2005) *Culture and Linguistic Policy Abroad: The Italian Experience.* Clevedon: Multilingual Matters.

Trudell, Barbara (2010) When 'Prof' speaks, who listens? The African elite and the use of African languages for education and development in African communities. In *Language and Education*. Vol. 24, Issue 4, 2010, pp.337-352.

UNDP (2006) Mozambique National Human Development Report 2005: Human Development to 2015: Reaching for the Millennium Development Goals. Maputo: United Nations Development Programme. Available at http://hdr.undp.org/en/reports/nationalreports/africa/mozambique/MOZA MBIQUE_2005_en.pdf [30.04.2010]

UNDP (2009) Human Development Report 2009 – Guinea Bissau. Available at http://hdrstats.undp.org/en/countries/country_fact_sheets/cty_fs_GNB.ht ml

UNDP (2009) Human Development Report 2009 – Mozambique. Available http://hdrstats.undp.org/en/countries/country_fact_sheets/cty_fs_MOZ.ht ml

UNESCO (2004) World Data on Education: Mozambique. Available at http://nt5.scbbs.com/cgi-bin/om_isapi.dll?clientID=273550458&depth =3&infobase=iwde.nfo&record={7D9584B0}&softpage=PL_frame [01.05.2007].

UNESCO (2006) UNESCO/ACALAN meeting "Joining forces for preserving Africa's linguistic diversity": Preliminary Notes, 23 -25 March 2006 in Bamako (Mali). Available at http://www.unesco.org/culture/ ich/doc/src/00212-EN.pdf

Vaux, Tom, Mavela, Amandio, Pereira, Joao and Stuttle, Jennifer (2006) *Strategic Conflict Assessment: Mozambique*. DFID. Available at http://www.dfid.gov.uk/pubs/files/strategic-conflict-assessment.pdf [10.11.2007].

Verschave, François-Xavier (1998) *La Françafrique: Le plus long scandale de la République.* Paris: Stock.

Verschave, François-Xavier (2000) *Noir silence: Qui arrêtera la Françafrique?* Paris: Les Arènes.

Vilela, Mário (2002) Reflections on Language Policy in African Countries with Portuguese as an Official Language. *Current Affairs in Language Planning*, 3 (3), pp.306-316.

Vines, Alex (2006) UK Policy toward Angola and Mozambique. Available at http://ieei.pt/files/Paper_AlexVinesfinal.pdf [26.05.2008].

Vines, Alex (2009) Angola Fact Sheet. Programme Paper AFP 2009/02. Chatham House. 5 June 2009. Available at http://www.chathamhouse. org.uk/files/14163_angola_fact_sheet.pdf [20/06/2010]

Walt, Stephen A. (1998) International Relations: One World, Many Theories. In *Foreign Policy*, 110, Spring, pp.29-46.

Wardhaugh, Ronald (1987) *Languages in Competition: Dominance, Diversity and Decline*. Oxford: Basil Blackwell.

Weiβ, Johannes and Schwietring, Thomas (2006) The Power of Language: A Philosophical-Sociological Reflection. Available at http://www.goethe.de/dll/prj/mac/prj/bez/enindex.htm [17.05.2006].

Wendt, Alexander (1992) Anarchy is what states make of it: the social construction of power politics. *International Organization*, 46 (2), Spring, pp.391-425.

Williams, Raymond (1988). *Keywords*. First published in 1976, revised and expanded edition published in 1983. London: Fontana Press.

Wolff, H. Ekkehard (2000) Language and Society. In Bernd Heine, and Derek Nurse, ed. (2000) *African Languages: An Introduction*. Cambridge: Cambridge University Press, pp.298-347.

Woliver, Laura R. (2002) Ethical Dilemmas in Personal Interviewing. PS: *Political Science & Politics*, 35 (4), December, pp.677-678.

Woods, Paul (2001) Mozambique Country Plan 2001-02. Maputo: British Council Mozambique [Five page document emailed by Louise Waddingham at the headquarters of the British Council, 23.05.2002].

World Bank (1994a) Republic of Guinea-Bissau: Poverty Assessment and Social Sectors: Strategy Review. Vol I. Report No. 13155-GUB. Available at http://go.worldbank.org/8611WYTSK0 [12.08.2007].

World Bank (1994b) Republic of Guinea-Bissau: Poverty Assessment and Social Sectors: Strategy Review: Guinea-Bissau: Language of Instruction. Vol III: Annexes: Annex II-1. Report No. 13155-GUB. Available at http://go.worldbank.org/SFGBG1TFM0 [12.08.2007].

World Bank (2005) Education Notes: In their Own Language…Education for All. Available at http://siteresources.worldbank.org/EDUCATION/Resources/Education-Notes/EdNotes_Lang_of_Instruct.pdf

World Bank (2006) Guinea-Bissau Integrated Poverty and Social Assessment (IPSA): Transition from Post Conflict to Long-Term Development: Policy Considerations for Reducing Poverty. Vol. I: Main Report. Report No. 34553-GW. Available at http://go.worldbank.org/Z8SJ7PPDC0 [12.08.2007].

World Bank (2007) Promoting Shared Growth through Empowerment of Citizens and Institutions. Mozambique: Country Partnership Strategy 2008-2011. Available at http://siteresources.worldbank.org/MOZAMBIQUEEXTN/Resources/Mozambique_CPS_2008_2011.pdf

Wyszomirski, Margaret J. (2003) Overview. In Margaret J. Wyszomirski, Christopher Burgess and Catherine Peila ed. *International Cultural Relations: A Multi-Country Comparison*. Columbus: The Ohio State University.

Available at http://www.culturalpolicy.org/pdf/MJWpaper.pdf [18.01.2007].

Wyszomirski, Margaret J., Burgess, Christopher and Peila, Catherine ed. (2003) *International Cultural Relations: A Multi-Country Comparison.* Columbus: The Ohio State University, pp.1-26. Available at http://www.culturalpolicy.org/pdf/MJWpaper.pdf [18.01.2007].

Yin, Robert K. (2003) *Case Study Research: Design and Methods.* 3rd ed. London: Sage.

Zúquete, José Pedro (2008) Beyond Reform: The Orthographic Accord and the Future of the Portuguese Language. In *South European Society and Politics,* 13: 4, 495 - 506. Available at http://dx.doi.org/10.1080/13608740902738418

Appendices

Appendix 1

List of interviewees by alphabetical order of surname

Includes reference to position, organisation and place of interview

A

Amaro - Portuguese teacher. Maputo, Mozambique.

Amur, Sheikh Abdul Ramarrene - Muslim local leader. Ilha de Moçambique, Mozambique.

Angius, Matteo - Librarian, Instituto Camões - Portuguese Cultural Centre. Maputo, Mozambique.

B

Baldé, Djibrilo - Director of Teaching and Literacy, Ministry of Education. Bissau, Guinea-Bissau.

Barbosa, Fátima - National Institute for Development and Education (INDE). Bissau, Guinea-Bissau.

Beaumont, Sue - Planning Officer, British Council. London, United Kingdom.

Belorgey, François - Director, Franco-Mozambican Cultural Centre. Maputo, Mozambique.

Bicari, Lino - Former Portuguese teacher in Guinea-Bissau. Lisboa, Portugal.

Braga, António - Portugal's Cultural Attaché and Director of the Instituto Camões - Portuguese Cultural Centre. Maputo, Mozambique.

Brocard, Hervé - French Department, Pedagogical University. Maputo, Mozambique.

C

Castro, Helena - Responsible for Guinea-Bissau, GAERI, Ministry of Education. Lisboa, Portugal.

Chambel, Alexandra - Officer from the Department of Studies, Projects and Evaluation, Portuguese Cooperation Institute. Lisboa, Portugal.

Comté, Josefina - Government Officer, French Department, Ministry of Education (MINED). Maputo, Mozambique.

Correia, Ana Carla - Responsible for Mozambique, Portuguese Cooperation institute. Lisboa, Portugal.

Costa, Fernando - Responsible for Cooperation, Portuguese Embassy. Maputo, Mozambique.

Couto, Mia - Writer. Maputo, Mozambique.

D

Da Fonseca, Luís Adão - Former President of the Camões Institute (1992-1995). Porto, Portugal.

Dâmaso, Fernanda - Technical assistant, SNV, Bissau, Guinea-Bissau.

De Carvalho, António Jorge Jacob - Portuguese Ambassator. Bissau, Guinea-Bissau.

De Souza e Silva, Manoel - Director, Centro de Estudos Brasileiros (Brazilian Cultural Centre). Maputo, Mozambique.

Dinis, José - Director, Instituto de Línguas (Languages Institute). Maputo, Mozambique.

Djaló, Iaguba - Library Director, Instituto Nacional de Estudos e Pesquisa (INEP). Bissau, Guinea-Bissau.

Do Rosário, Lourenço - President, Bibliographic Fund for the Portuguese Language. Maputo, Mozambique.

E

Eduardo, Tomé - Director, Voluntary Service Overseas (VSO). Maputo, Mozambique.

Encarnação, Jorge - Responsible for Guinea-Bissau, Portuguese Cooperation Institute. Lisboa, Portugal.

Esslemont, Vivien - English Language Teaching co-ordinator, British Council. Maputo, Mozambique.

F

Fernandes, Jorge - Responsible for the Portuguese Language Center, Instituto Camões / Escola Superior Tchico Té. Bissau, Guinea-Bissau.

Fotheringham, Andrew - Director of Planning, British Council. London, United Kingdom.

G

Gomes, Alfredo - General Director of the Secondary and Higher Education, Ministry of Education. Bissau, Guinea-Bissau.

Gomes, Liberata Viegas - Bibliographic Fund for the Portuguese Language, Autonomous Sector of Bissau. Guinea-Bissau.

I

Ingram-Hill, Simon - Director, British Council Mozambique. Maputo, Mozambique.

J
Jamú, Sheikh Hafiz Abdu Razak - Muslim local leader. Ilha de Moçambique, Mozambique.
Jao, Mamadú - Director, INEP. Bissau, Guinea-Bissau.
Juma, Imtiaz - Executive Director, Fundação Aga Khan, Centro Ismaili. Lisboa, Portugal.

K
Koudawo, Fafali - Research Director, INEP. Bissau, Guinea-Bissau.

L
Lage, Margarida - Former responsible for the cultural centers at the Camões Institute (1995-1997). Presently officer at the Portuguese Institute of the Book and Libraries. Lisboa, Portugal.
Laniese, Christophe - Cultural and Cooperation Services, French Embassy. Bissau, Guinea-Bissau.
Lemos, Mário Matos e - Former Director of the Portuguese Cultural Center in Bissau (1985 to 1998). Lisboa, Portugal.
Lemos, Sandra - Fundação Evangelização e Culturas. Lisboa, Portugal.
Lima, Arnaldo - Director, Centro de Estudos Brasileiros (Brazilian Cultural Centre). Bissau, Guinea-Bissau.
Lopes, António Soares - Alias 'Tcheca, Toni' , Journalist from Guinea-Bissau. Lisboa, Portugal.
Lopes, Armando Jorge - Professor and specialist in language policy, Linguistics Department, Eduardo Mondlane University. Maputo, Mozambique.
Lopes, Catarina - Coordinator, Fundação Evangelização e Culturas (FEC). Bissau, Guinea-Bissau.
Lopes, António Maria - Catholic priest. Ilha de Moçambique, Mozambique.

M
Mancanha, Henrique - French Teachers Association. Bissau, Guinea-Bissau.
Marquer, Alain - Director of International Relations, Alliance Française de Paris. Paris, France.
Martins, Ângela - Government Officer, English Department, Ministry of Education (MINED). Maputo, Mozambique.
Martins, Sara - Responsible for educational projects, Portuguese Embassy. Maputo, Mozambique.
Matusse, Renato - Secretary General and Co-ordinator for Culture, Information and Sport, Southern Africa Development Community (SADC). Maputo, Mozambique.

Melo, Manuela - Responsible for Mozambique, GAERI, Ministery of Education. Lisboa, Portugal.

Merali, Karim - Chief Executive Officer, Aga Khan Foundation. Maputo, Mozambique.

Meyer, Arthur V. Correa - Brazilian Ambassador. Bissau, Guinea-Bissau.

Micallef, Ronnie - Director of the British Council in Malta, formerly stationed in Mozambique. London, United Kingdom.

Miguel, Victor - co-founder of the Associação Moçambicana da Língua Portuguesa, AMOLP (Mozambican Association of Portuguese Language). Maputo, Mozambique.

Montenegro, Teresa - Editor. Bissau, Guinea-Bissau.

Moreira, Sandra Luísa - Portuguese teacher, Nampula's Catholic University, Camões Institute's Language Centre. Nampula, Mozambique.

N

Nahara, Trindade - English Language Department, National Institute for Educational Development (INDE). Maputo, Mozambique.

Navarro, Júlio - Responsible for the editoral services and co-founder of the Associação de Escritores Moçambicanos, AEMO (Mozambican Writers Association), also senior officer at the Instituto Nacional do Livro e do Disco (Book and Record National Institute). Maputo, Mozambique.

Nery, Afonso Celso - Deputy for Education, Sports and Culture, Comunidade dos Países de Língua Portuguesa (CPLP). Lisboa, Portugal.

Neves, Artur - Catholic priest, Director of the Escola António José de Sousa. Bissau, Guinea-Bissau.

Neves, João Laurentino - Responsible for the Language Centers, Instituto Camões. Lisboa, Portugal.

Ngunga, Armindo - Dean, Faculty of Arts, Eduardo Mondlane University. Maputo, Mozambique.

P

Palha, Isabel - Responsible for the Portuguese Network of Lusophony, Portuguese Institute of the Book and Libraries. Lisboa, Portugal.

Patel, Samima - Specialist in language policy, Mozambican languages, Linguistics Department, Eduardo Mondlane University. Maputo, Mozambique.

Perdigão, Daniel - Portugal's Cultural Attaché and Director of the Instituto Camões – Portuguese Cultural Centre. Bissau, Guinea-Bissau.

Pereira, Ciro - Responsible for the arts and cultural animation, Instituto Camões - Portuguese Cultural Centre. Maputo, Mozambique.

Pereira, José Silva - Portuguese Cooperation Attaché. Bissau, Guinea-Bissau

Pereira, Luís Filipe - Director, Oikos (Portuguese NGO). Maputo, Mozambique.

Pinheiro, Osíris - Librarian, Centro de Estudos Brasileiros, Bissau, Guinea-B.

R

Ramos, Francisco Nuno - Director of the Language Centers, Instituto Camões. Lisboa, Portugal.

S

Sanca, Armando - Firkidja Project, Ministry of National Education. Bissau, Guinea-Bissau.

Santos, Paulo - Director of Primary Schooling, Ministry of National Education, Bissau, Guinea-Bissau.

Scantamburlo, Luigi - Catholic priest responsible for managing a series of schools in the Bijagós Archipelago. Bissau, Guinea-Bissau.

Semedo, Odete Costa - INEP Researcher, former Minister of Education. Bissau, Guinea-Bissau.

Sendela, Rafael Mozambican Languages Department, National Institute for Educational Development (INDE). Maputo, Mozambique.

Sequeira, Elisabete - Senior member of Progresso (NGO). Maputo, Mozambique.

Simbine, Gabriel - Intelectual. Maputo, Mozambique.

Simões, Jorge - Director, Fundo de Bolsas de Estudo para Nampula (Nampula's Scholarships Fund). Maputo, Mozambique.

Siopa, Conceição - Portuguese teacher, Eduardo Mondlane University – Instituto Camões Readership. Maputo, Mozambique.

Szalay, Jacques - Cultural and Cooperation Services, French Embassy. Maputo, Mozambique.

T

Tchibutane, Feliciano - Co-founder of AMOLP. Maputo, Mozambique.

U

Ussene, Assane - English Teacher, Nampula's Secondary School. Nampula, Mozambique.

W

Waddingham, Louisa - Responsible for operations in Southern Africa, Geographical Directorate, British Council. London, United Kingdom.

Appendix 2

Information Update - Interviewees, type and date of contact by institution

Mozambique

Ministry of Education and Culture	
Moisés Mabunda, officer at the French Department	Telephone and Emails, 4/8.06.2010
Auzinda Domingos, officer at the English Department	Telephone June 2010, Email 13.07.2010

Instituto Nacional de Desenvolvimento Educacional	
Rafael Sendela, Bilingual Education Co-ordinator	Telephone and Emails, June/July 2010

Portuguese Embassy in Maputo	
António Braga, Cultural Attaché and Director of the Centro Cultural Português de Maputo	Telephone and Emails, June 2010
Mónica Tavares, Responsible for Education	Email and telephone contact June 2010, but no information was received.

French Embassy in Maputo	
Richard Mouthy, Cultural and Cooperation Services	Email and telephone contact June 2010, but no information was received.
Patrick Schmitt, Director, Centro Cultural Franco-Moçambicano	Telephone interview, 22.06.2010

British Council Mozambique	
Lisa McManus, Director	Email 26.06.2010

Centro Cultural Brasil – Moçambique	
Raúl Calane da Silva, Director, Mozambican writer and journalist	Telephone interview, 11.06.2010

Guinea-Bissau

Ministry of Education	
Alfredo Gomes, Senior officer, former Ministry of Education	Email 09.06.2010.

SNV-Dutch Cooperation	
Fátima Barbosa, former officer at the Instituto Nacional de Desenvolvimento e Educação	Several email contacts, June/July 2010.

Portuguese Embassy in Bissau	
Maria Ermelinda Árede, Director of the Centro Cultural Português	Several telephone and email contacts, June 2010, no information received.
French Embassy in Bissau	
Gilles Roussey, Cooperation and Cultural Action Officer	Email
Bruno Le Beller, Director of the Centre Culture Franco-Bissao Guinéen	Several telephone and email contacts, June 2010
Centro Cultural Brasil – Guiné-Bissau	
Sónia Rocha, Responsible for Cultural Affairs	Telephone and email contacts June/July 2010. Telephone interview 02.07.2010
FASPEBI – Bilingual Project in the Bijagós Islands	
Father Luigi Scantamburlo, President	Emails 27/28.07.2010

United Kingdom

Commonwealth Secretariat	
Virgílio Juvane, Education adviser, former Director of Planning at the Ministry of Education in Mozambique (1980-2004)	Face-to-face interview, London, 16.07.2010

Brasil

Carlos A. Faraco, retired Professor at Universidade Federal do Paraná	Emails, December 2009

Appendix 3

Schedule of research trip to Mozambique

4th to the 19th of October 2002

Maputo
Nampula
Ilha de Moçambique

04/10/02, Friday
21.00 Check-in at Lisbon's International Airport

05/10/02, Saturday
10.30 Arrival at Maputo's International Airport
14.00 Exploring Maputo's sights
17.00 Attended the II Annual Popular Dance Festival at the Franco-Mozambican Cultural Centre, with the presence of the Mozambican President Joaquim Chissano

06/10/02, Sunday
Around Maputo: Namaacha and Pequenos Libombos Dam

07/10/02, Monday
11.00 *José Dinis*, Director, Instituto de Línguas (Languages Institute)
14.30 *Karim Merali*, Chief Executive Officer, Aga Khan Foundation
16.00 *Elisabete Sequeira*, senior member of Progresso (NGO)
16.30 *Júlio Navarro*, Responsible for the editoral services and co-founder of the Associação de Escritores Moçambicanos, AEMO (Mozambican Writers Association), also senior officer at the Instituto Nacional do Livro e do Disco (Book and Record National Institute)

08/10/02, Tuesday
10.00 *Fernando Costa*, Responsible for cooperation, Portuguese Embassy in Maputo
15.00 *Victor Miguel*, co-founder of the Associação dos Amigos da Língua Portuguesa, AMOLP (Mozambican Association of Portuguese Language)
16.30 *Ciro Pereira*, Responsible for the arts and cultural animation, Instituto Camões - Centro Cultural Português / Maputo (Camões Institute - Portuguese Cultural Centre)

09/10/02, Wednesday

09.30 *Lourenço do Rosário*, President, Fundo Bibliográfico para a Língua Portuguesa (Bibliographic Fund for the Portuguese Language)

16.00 *Renato Matusse*, Secretary General and Co-ordinator for Culture, Information and Sport, Southern Africa Development Community, SADC

17.00 *Matteo Angius*, Librarian, Instituto Camões - Centro Cultural Português / Maputo (Camões Institute – Portuguese Cultural Centre)

10/10/02, Thursday

08.30 *Simon Ingram-Hill*, Director, British Council Mozambique

11.00 *Luís Filipe Pereira*, Director, Oikos (Portuguese NGO) and Amaro, Portuguese teacher

12.00 *Conceição Siopa*, Portuguese teacher, Eduardo Mondlane University – Instituto Camões Readership

15.00 *Manoel de Souza e Silva*, Director, Centro de Estudos Brasileiros (Brazilian Studies Centre / Brazilian Cultural Centre)

16.30 *François Belorgey*, Director, Centro Cultural Franco-Moçambicano (Franco-Mozambican Cultural Centre)

11/10/02, Friday

08.00 Census research at the Bureau de Informação Pública, BIP (Public Information Bureau)

11.00 *Mia Couto*, writer

14.00 *Feliciano Tchibutane*, co-founder of AMOLP

16.00 Revolution Museum

17.00 Art Museum

22.00 Drinks at the Polana Hotel with *José António Teles Gomes*, a former Co-operation university teacher, now consultant, based in Lisbon

12/10/02, Saturday

08.10 Flight to Nampula (North of Mozambique)

10.30 Transfer to Ilha de Moçambique (Mozambique Island, Colonial Mozambique's first capital)

14.00 Arrival at Ilha de Moçambique

15.00 Sightseeing of the Stone Town

17.00 *António Maria Lopes*, Catholic priest

13/10/02, Sunday

07.30 Attended Catholic Mass celebrated in Portuguese and Makua (the local language)

10.00 Visit to the mainland off Mozambique Island: Chocas beach

15.00 Tour of Ilha de Moçambique: Stone Town and Makuti Town

14/10/02, Monday
10.00 *Hafiz Abdu Razak Jamú*, Muslim local leader
11.00 *Abdul Ramarrene Amur*, Muslim local leader
15.00 *Jorge Simões*, Director, Fundo de Bolsas de Estudo para Nampula (Nampula's Scholarships Fund)

15/10/02, Tuesday
06.00 Transfer to Nampula
10.00 *Sandra Luísa Moreira*, Portuguese teacher, Nampula's Catholic University, Camões Institute Language Centre
12.00 *Assane Ussene*, English Teacher, Nampula's Secondary School
17.40 Flight to Maputo

16/10/02, Wednesday
08.30 *Armindo Ngunga*, Dean, Faculty of Arts, Eduardo Mondlane University
10.00 *Josefina Comté*, Government Officer, French Department, Ministry of Education, MINED
14.00 *Vivien Esslemont*, English Language Teaching co-ordinator, British Council Mozambique
15.00 *António Braga*, Portugal's Cultural Attaché and Director of the Instituto Camões - Centro Cultural Português / Maputo

17/10/02, Thursday
10.00 *Jacques Szalay*, Cultural and Cooperation Services, French Embassy
10.15 *Hervé Brocard*, French Department, Pedagogical University
11.30 *Gabriel Simbine*, Intellectual
15.00 *Tomé Eduardo*, Director, Voluntary Service Overseas (VSO) Mozambique
Photocopying at the British Council: documents provided by Vivien Esslemont
19.00 Dinner at the Polana Hotel with *Simon Ingram-Hill* and his wife, *Ann*, who worked for AusAid (Australian Government Overseas Aid Program)

18/10/02, Friday
08.30 *Ângela Martins*, Government Officer, English Department, Ministry of Education, MINED
10.00 *Armando Jorge Lopes*, Professor and specialist in language policy, Linguistics Department, Eduardo Mondlane University
11.30 *Samima Patel*, specialist in language policy – Mozambican languages, Linguistics Department, Eduardo Mondlane University

14.00 *Rafael Sendela*, Mozambican Languages Department, Instituto Nacional de Desenvolvimento Educacional, INDE (Educational Development National Institute)

14.30 *Trindade Nahara*, English Language Department, Instituto Nacional de Desenvolvimento Educacional, INDE

15.30 *Sara Martins*, Responsible for educational projects, Portuguese Embassy in Maputo

19/10/02, Saturday
Personal visits
18.00 Check-in at Maputo's International Airport

Appendix 4

Schedule of research trip to Guinea-Bissau

23rd of November to the 7th of December 2002

Bissau
Bijagós: Bubaque

23/11/02, Saturday
08.00 Check-in at Lisbon's International Airport
10.25 Flight to Bissau
14.35 Arrival at Bissau. Meet by the Portuguese Cultural Attaché, *Daniel Perdigão*
15.30 Getting settled at Bairro da Cooperação (private condominium on the outskirts of Bissau where most Portuguese cooperants reside)
17.00 Exploring some of Bissau (including the use of a communitary taxi[134]!)

24/11/02, Sunday
Personal visits: Quinhamel. Mangrove area 40 minutes by car away from Bissau.

25/11/02, Monday
10.00 *Iaguba Djaló*, Library Director, Instituto Nacional de Estudos e Pesquisa, INEP (Studies and Research National Institute)
12.00 *Odete Costa Semedo*, INEP Researcher, former Education Minister
16.00 *José Silva Pereira*, Portuguese Cooperation attaché
16.45 *Daniel Perdigão*, Portuguese Cultural attaché

26/11/02, Tuesday
09.00 Research at INEP's Public Library
10.30 *Liberata Viegas Gomes*, Fundo Bibliográfico para a Língua Portuguesa (Bibliographic Fund for the Portuguese Language), Sector Autónomo de Bissau (Autonomous Sector of Bissau)
17.00 *António Jorge Jacob de Carvalho*, Portuguese Ambassator in Guinea-Bissau
18.30 *Teresa Montenegro*, Editor

---

134 A communitary taxi takes, at various times during its route, as many passengers as can be fitted in the vehicle and drops them off in their destinations in order of their successive geographical proximity. Price is individually negotiated according to the number of passengers already in the taxi, their destination and your destination.

27/11/02, Wednesday

09.00 *Catarina Lopes*, Coordinator, Fundação Evangelização e Culturas, FEC

10.00 *Osíris Pinheiro*, Librarian, Centro de Estudos Brasileiros (Brazilian Studies Centre)

11.00 *Arthur V. Correa Meyer*, Brazilian Ambassador in Guinea-Bissau

12.00 *Mamadú Jao*, Director, INEP

12.30 *Fafali Koudawo*, Research Director, INEP

16.00 *Fernanda Dâmaso*, Technical assistant, SNV, Dutch based development organisation

28/11/02, Thursday

08.00 *Artur Neves*, Catholic priest, Director, Escola António José de Sousa (Catholic Church Primary School)

10.00 *Christophe Laniese*, Cultural and Cooperation Services, French Embassy

14.00 AD (Guinean NGO), Bairro do Quelélé: visit to educational projects with children and radio broadcasters. Observation of the class and informal conversation with the participants.

17.00 Liceu João XXIII: visit to Portuguese class for teachers of Portuguese. Observation of the class and informal conversation with the participants.

29/11/02, Friday

09.00 Research at INEP's Public Library

15.00 Departure to the island of Bubaque, in the Bijagós Archipelago, Biosphere Reserve

20.00 Arrival at Bubaque

30/11/02, Saturday

07.30 Attended Catholic Mass celebrated in Portuguese

08.30 Informal conversation with the local catholic priests (two Italians and one Filipino)

10.00 Visit to Bubaque's Market

Personal visits: Bruce beach

01/12/02, Sunday

07.30 Attended Catholic Mass celebrated in Portuguese and Creole (the Guinean vehicular language)

10.00 Visit to Bubaque's Market

11.00 Personal visits: local beach

14.00 Return to Bissau

18.00 Arrival in Bissau

342

02/12/02, Monday
09.30 *Alfredo Gomes*, General Director of the Secondary and Higher Education, Ministry of Education
16.00 *Luigi Scantamburlo*, Italian priest running a series of schools in the Bijagós Archipelago using Creole as a teaching language

03/12/02, Tuesday
09.30 *Henrique Mancanha*, French Teachers Association
10.30 *Jorge Fernandes*, responsible for the Portuguese Language Center, Instituto Camões / Escola Superior Tchico Té

04/12/02, Wednesday
09.15 *Djibrilo Baldé*, Director of Teaching and Literacy, Ministry of Education
12.30 *Fátima Barbosa*, Instituto Nacional de Desenvolvimento e Educação / National Institute for Development and Education (INDE)
16.10 *Arnaldo Lima*, Director, Centro de Estudos Brasileiros

05/12/02, Thursday
09.00 Literature research at INEP's Public Library
11.00 *Paulo Santos*, Director of Primary Schooling, Ministry of Education
12.00 *Daniel Perdigão*, Portugal's Cultural Attaché and Director of the Instituto Camões - Centro Cultural Português / Bissau
16.00 *Armando Sanca*, Firkidja Project, Ministério da Educação Nacional, Ministry of National Education

06/12/02, Friday Holiday: End of the Ramadan
The holiday was decreted Thursday afternoon.
This was quite an unexpected set back in my schedule.

07/10/02, Saturday
Personal visits.
16.00 Check-in at Bissau's International Airport

343

Appendix 5

UK's rationale for English in Mozambique

Transcript of document authored by Simon Ingram-Hill, Director of the British Council Mozambique, to demonstrate to DFID the importance of English. Supplied by the author, 17 October 2002, Maputo, Mozambique.

The Case for English as a language for development and poverty elimination (with particular reference to African countries where English has not got official status

- *Language of immediate access to (global) information* about international standards, ideas, fashions, interests, science, technology, arts and commerce through the internet, English medium written an audio-visual, satellite TV, CD rom materials. (in contrast, in Mozambique, Portuguese requires translation and filtering, and is far more limited in range)
- *Language of development:* provides access to largest pool of capacity building providers, enables formation of transnational partnerships, provides access to the globalised non-formal private sector (itself an increasingly important instrument for development).
- *Access language for training opportunities* (and therefore international expertise) in English-speaking countries, or from English-speaking countries e.g. in Mozambique to visiting consultants, on-the-ground firms or via www. First world, Anglo-Saxon education is still regarded as marker for quality standards.
- *Language for choice:* offers greater choice of what one wants to learn, where and from whom.
- *Language of inclusion:* and away from isolation. e.g. SADC and Commonwealth: membership of the club, awareness and potential appreciation of its valued. In-country English can be the language crossing ethnic boundaries, where mother tongues are restrictive.
- *Language of governance:* it provides a window on democratic values through the media, internet, exchange of personnel, international initiatives and pressure groups.
- *Language of key groups in development*
  - the authority generation: (e.g. in Mozambique – internationally-trained Frelimo hierarchy speak good English)
  - the successor generation: young professionals want English for advancement and Youth want it for inclusion, identity and fashion
- *A Language of gaining power:* with developed negotiation, presentation and management skills
- *A Language for formal learning:* Medium of instruction at secondary or tertiary level schooling in countries without an internationally accepted alternative e.g. many African countries – Ethiopia, Kenya, Sudan
- *A force for poverty elimination:* language of donor coordination, and, through capacity building, of means to meet target poverty reduction indicators

Appendix 6

France's Rationale for French in Mozambique

Transcript of document supplied by Comté (2002 interview): printed four-page document containing no direct indication of source, but clearly attributable, by its content, to the participants in the French Mission to Mozambique in preparation for the project of the reintroduction of French language in secondary education, 14 to 21 October 1990.

Transcript of four typed pages (numbered page 2 to page 5):

- 2 -

Notre mission en République populaire du Mozambique, qui s'est déroulée du 14 au 21 octobre 1990, avait pour objet d' établir le bilan et les perspectives de l'opération que nos appellerons "réintroduction du français dans l'enseignement secondaire" ainsi que ses conséquences sur le plan de la formation, effectuée tant au Mozambique qu'en France, et d'identifier d'autre part les besoins exprimés en matière de conseil et d'assistance, essentiellement dans le domaine des enseignements supérieurs.

Elle était conduite dans la suite logique de la mission de suivi et d'orientation qui s'était déroulée du 9 au 14 juillet, et dans la perspective de l'établissement de l'aide mémoire préalable à la tenue en décembre prochain de la commission mixte.

Nous l'avons effectuée conjointement avec le Professeur Pierre DUMONT de Université Paul Valéry de Montpellier, dont l'Institut forme déjà des professeurs de français mozambicains, et plus généralement lusophones.

Nous ne pouvons manquer de remercier M. Denis BOSSARD, Conseiller à la mission de Coopération et d'action culturelle qui a organise avec efficacité l'emploi du temps de notre mission.

I – LE CONTEXTE DE L'ENSEIGNEMENT AU MOZAMBIQUE

Dans ce pays en proie à la guerre civile, on observe une baisse de la scolarisation: de 1 377 000 en 1981, le nombre des scolarisés est passé à 1 200 000 en 1988; la guerre continue d'entraîner la destruction des écoles (plus de 50% des locaux détruits entre 1981 et 1988). En outre l'entretien des locaux, ce fut confirmé par quelques visites, est inexistant.

La part de l'Education Nationale, dans des dépenses de l'Etat est passée de 17,9% en 1980 à 8,7% en 1987, alors que le budget militaire doublait.

L'enseignement secondaire général (classes de 8ème et 9ème, la 9ème équivalant à la 3ème en France) accueille 26 000 élèves, l'enseignement pré-universitaire (9ème et 10ème), 2 500 (1 000 en 1980), reportés dans seulement 5 lycées. Le diplôme de fin d'études n'est pas un examen et permet d'entrée à la Université. Une onzième année va être crées.

Le corps professoral est mal payé et la fonction enseignante ne présente pas d'attrait particulier. On peut penser que certains diplômés de français, à leur retour de France, se dirigeront vers d'autres fonctions !

- 3 -

Le Ministre de l'Education Nationale, qui est assisté d'un Vice-Ministre et d'un Secrétaire d'Etat à l'enseignement professionnel, n'exerce pas une autorité directe sur l'Université, dont le Recteur prend parfois part aux réunions di Conseil de Ministres.

Dans cette situation de crise où toute aide est accueillie avec gratitude, les autorités ne peuvent qu'être satisfaites de tous les appuis apportés à l'équipement de classes ou à leur réhabilitation, opérations mineures mais jugées complémentaires des actions pédagogiques comme celle de l'introduction du français.

II - LA REINTRODUCTION DE L'ENSEIGNEMENT DU FRANÇAIS DANS L'ENSEIGNEMENT SECONDAIRE ET LA FORMATION DES PROFESSEURS

Nous renvoyons pour le détail de l'opération et de la stratégie de formation au rapport de M. le Professeur Pierre DUMONT, que nous joignons en annexe, nous bornant ici aux grades lignes du projet.

Le français n'est plus enseigné depuis l'indépendance, mais il y a une réelle volonté de le réintroduire dans l'enseignement. Les raisons en sont une volonté d'ouverture vers le monde francophone, un souhait de faciliter l'accès aux formations supérieurs et technologiques en français et aussi un souci de ne pas accorder un monopole, puissant attrait du monde anglophone omniprésent aux frontières.

Les autorités ont doc décidé l'introduction du français en février 1991 dans un lycée de Maputo, sur un nombre limité de classes ; l'extension progressive de cet enseignement devrait conduire à son insertion dans les programmes comme seconde langue étrangère.

Pour ce faire l'enseignement dans sa première phase, ne pourrait, selon le Ministre, être confié qu'à des Français, de même que – nous le citons – 'on ne confiait pas celui du portugais à des Brésiliens'.

Il convient donc de mener de front cinq actions majeures, auxquelles s'ajouteront d'autres interventions dans ce même domaine.

1) **Introduire le français dans le secondaire proprement dit**

L'établissement choisi est l'Ecole secondaire Francisco Manyanga, le plus grand lycée de Maputo qui atteint le chiffre de 6 000 élevés (au cours diurnes et nocturnes), adolescents et adultes.

Le français sera introduit en février 1991, à la raison de 4 heures par semaine en 10éme puis en 11éme. 40 heures de cours seront ainsi assurées par deux coopérants, et ce volume porté à 80 heures en février 1992 avec l'ouverture de deux nouveaux postes.

Un local a été réservé à cet effet, qui sera réhabilité par la Mission et équipé en matériel pédagogique audiovisuel, en excluant, là comme ailleurs, le laboratoire de langues, instrument inadapté à ce genre d'opérations.

L'opération, considérée les deux premières années comme expérimentale, serait élargie aux autres établissements avec l'arrivée en 1992 des professeurs formés en France. Les quatre postes de coopérants seraient alors redéployés sur des fonctions de conseillers pédagogiques assurant le suivi des nouveaux professeurs mozambicains.

2) **Assurer la pré-formation à l'Institut des Langues** des futurs boursiers qui se rendront à l'Université de Montpellier. L'opération est en cours depuis 1986 et connaît un réel succès, le Professeur DUMONT se félicitant du niveau général des boursiers arrivant de Maputo. Cet Institut mène une action pédagogique intelligente, produisant ses propres instruments méthodologiques; toutefois un complément d'équipements, de matériel audiovisuel et de documentation apparaît indispensable.

Un poste de VSN est à ouvrir en octobre 1991 pour assurer la pré-formation de la nouvelle promotion de 20 candidats à la formation dispensée à Montpellier. La Mission précisait par ailleurs que ce VSN serait chargé en outre du sous-titrage des émissions de Canal France et que le poste serait redéployé en 1993 sur le Centre Culturel français, alors achevé.

3) **Former à l'Université Paul Valéry de Montpellier** les futurs professeurs du secondaire (une trentaine à ce jour, auxquels viendra s'ajouter un groupe supplémentaire de 20 candidats, annonce fait à l'occasion de notre mission).

En 1994 ou 1995, quelques formations en D.E.A. pourraient être assurées afin de pouvoir d'un encadrement de Département de Français de l'I.S.P.

4) Mettre en place à l'Institut Supérieur Pédagogique (I.S.P.) un Département de Français, qui assurera le relais de la formation dispensée à Montpellier, avec le soutien d'un accord interuniversitaire liant cette Université à l'I.S.P. d'une part et à l'Université Eduardo Mondlane (U.E.M.) d'autre part.

Cet accord permettrait de garantir un niveau de qualité et d'assurer la continuité de formation de formateurs de l'I.S.P.

Un assistant technique est arrivé en fin octobre pour mettre sur pies ce Département aux côtés de sa responsable.

L'I.S.P. fondé en 1976 et restructuré en 1986, est le seul établissement de formation de professeurs depuis la fermeture en décembre 1989 de la Faculté d'Education de l'U.E.M. Il dispose d'un annexe à Beira et compte en ouvrir une à M[N]ampula en 1991, pour atteindre en 1992 le total de 1 500 étudiants.

Si la coopération française peut apporter un appui documentaire dans les diverses disciplines, il est évident que l'essentiel de notre action portera sur le Département de Français, qui ouvre avec l'arrivée d'une coopérante. Un cours livre y sera dispensé dans un premier temps ; en coordination avec Montpellier y sera préparé le futur cours de formation des professeurs, ainsi que le programme de français du secondaire. Un responsable de l'I.S.P. se rendra à Montpellier dans le cadre de l'accord.

5) Dispenser des cours de français au corps professoral et aux étudiants de l'Université

(cf. les demandes exprimées par la Faculté des Lettres)

Enfin, nos professeurs à l'Institut des Langues doivent, outre la pré-formation des futurs boursiers destinés à étudier en France, assurer des cours pour des cadres supérieurs du Ministère des Finances, dont une partie suivra par la suite des stages spécialisées en France.

A partir de février 1991, s'ajouteront des cours pour le Secrétariat d'Etat au Tourisme, la Société des Pétroles, et des responsables de service, professeurs et étudiants, de l'Université en attendant l'arrivée d'enseignants particuliers pour cette dernière en octobre 1991.

Nous citerons, à la marge, quelques autres indicateurs du renouveau de l'intérêt pour le français ; les demandes émanant des Séminaires des religieuses françaises et des Peres Salésiens qui reprennent dès lors que le pouvoir politique a autorisé l'ouverture des 'écoles communautaires', d'est-à-dire confessionnelles.

Appendix 7

Press articles on Portuguese language being under threat in Africa

Portugal

Source	Date	Headline / quote
Grande Reportagem	25.01.1985	Agonia do Português em África Fernando Gaspar "Portugal, ou cuida de encontrar um novo Português para África ou, melhor das hipóteses, como quem encomenda a alma ao criador, entrega o futuro nas mãos de missionários ainda por nascer. E pode bem ser, então, que os portugueses venham a descobrir, já tarde provavelmente uma língua agonizante promete ser o prato forte. E não se pense que o repasto ainda vem longe: estudos oficiais apontam para um prazo de cinco a dez anos. Se até lá não se fizer alguma coisa, não há bíblia que salve o português em África." (p.57) "Como responde Portugal Às suas responsabilidades? Ameaçado [na Guiné-Bissau] pela França, o país do Mundo que mais gasta com a divulgação dos seus valores culturais" (p.63)
O Dia	06.09.1987	Ministro garante Guiné vai permanecer lusófona "O secretário de Estados dos Negócios Estrangeiros da Guiné, Marcelino Lima, afirmou que a participação do seu país na cimeira francófona não significa de modo algum uma pretensão de abandonar o português." "Aquele membro do governo de Bissau salientou ainda que, quando o seu país assumiu a presidência do sub-comité da Formação de Quadros, Acção Cultural e Investigação Científica dos «Cinco», muito contribuiu para a introdução do português como língua de trabalho na Organização de Unidade Africana (OUA)."
Diário de Notícias	06.09.1987	Guiné-Bissau não pretende abandonar idioma português
Expresso	13.06.1987	Guiné-Bissau: a ofensiva francesa "O Francês já se impõe ao Português como língua de comunicação, através de uma política persistente e agressiva." "Um alto responsável guineense disse ... «Portugal está a empurrar a Guiné-Bissau com as duas mãos para a França». Não surpreende, por isso, o facto de já circularem ofícios e ordens de serviço em Francês por

		alguns Ministérios. «Eles terão de contar com a nossa resistência cultural», comentava um professor guineense, a propósito da ofensiva linguística da França. Só que a resistência tem limites – e sobretudo se lhe faltar o apoio da retaguarda."
Revista Elo	November 1990	O português repartido pelo mundo: Dupla tarefa na África lusófona A concorrência do francês "Situada num espaço francófono, a República da Guiné-Bissau ressente-se da hegemonia do francês." (p.18)
Diário de Notícias	11.09.1992	África: «Guerra» linguística apontada ao Português Assunção Almeida "As forças conjugadas sa Comunidade Britânica, dos Estados Unidos e da África do Sul irão desencadear uma incidência de três poderosos blocos, com recursos materiais potentes, tecnologia avançada e humanamente preparados para uma batalha de longo prazo, mas dispostos a ganhar a guerra «por capitulação dos portugueses», é o cenário lógico do conflito linguístico-cultural que já se está a esboçar no cone Sul de África."
Revista Elo	October 1993	França: o amigo irrecusável "Tudo aquilo que Portugal não é capaz, a França faz. Este podia ser o lema da Cooperação Francesa nos países africanos de língua portuguesa." (p.12)
Público	19.07.1993	Um Adeus Português: Língua Portuguesa perde força em Moçambique e há já quem pense no Inglês para "língua oficial" José Pinto de Sá quotes a document issued on the last day of the Conferência Nacional de Cultura: " "A língua portuguesa é a língua oficial", precisa um documento divulgado no último dia da Conferência Nacional sobre Cultural (CNC), "(mas não) se deve criticar a ideia de que o Estado moçambicano, soberanamente não possa vir a rever esta situação". A formulação é tímida, mas deixou de imediato todas as orelhas no ar, nos corredores da Conferência." "A lusofonia já perdeu Goa e Timor, na confusão entre política e cultura. Agora a Guiné-Bissau parece irresistivelmente atraída para a esfera da francofonia. Será que os Cinco viram Quatro? Ou viram Três)…" p.79
Público	10.09.1993	Moçambique: Cuba vai, França vem
Jornal de Notícias	29.05.1994	Moçambique nas Malhas da "Commonwealth"
Público	26.07.1995	Moçambique: "Quem tem medo da Commonwealth?" José Pinto de Sá

		"No seu editiorial se segunda-feira, o diário "Media-Fax" escrevia: "Nós imaginamos uma comunidade assente numa certa maneira de viver a vida, uma partilha dos encantos subversivos do piripiri, e Lisboa sempre a reduzir a comunidade a um exército defensor de uma língua. Para quê este tribalismo linguístico? Que é feito, afinal de contas, do pendor português para a mestiçagem?""
Público	28.08.1995	Debate na TV moçambicana: Portugal "versus" Commonwealth
Jornal de Notícias	19.11.1995	Moçambique "é uma dor de alma ver aquela ex-colónia afastar-se cada vez mais de Portugal, com o risco da perda do Português como língua oficial. Recorde-se que, já nos tempos coloniais, Moçambique, com a cumplicidade do Estado português, tinha adoptado hábitos e costumes ingleses, desde a condução pela esquerda à aculturação do Inglês e do Africander com o Português e línguas indígenas."
O Diabo	28.11.1995	Portugal enxovalhado "A Inglaterra, nossa aliada, vai conseguir agora com a Commonwealth o que não foi alcançado pela rainha Vitória"
O Diabo	28.11.1995	Na Commonwealth por excepção... "A pouco e pouco Moçambique vai cortando todos os laços de afinidade que o prendiam a Portugal."
Jornal de Notícias	08.12.1995	Portugal reagiu emocionalmente à adesão de Moçambique à Commonwealth – criticou o embaixador Brito e Cunha em Maputo
Público	27.07.1996	José Pinto de Sá Língua portuguesa perde terreno em Moçambique: A anglofonia não dorme "enquanto em português se discursa, na difusão do inglês investe-se a sério", p.4
Diário de Notícias	26.01.1998	Contra o Monopólio Português: Cooperação espanhola em Moçambique põe em causa a legitimidade da língua oficial do país e reabilita sistema de ensino

Mozambique

Source	Date	Headline or quote
Tempo	05.12.1993	Moçambique entre Fogo Cruzado Jorge de Oliveira, p.91 "Os moçambicanos, ou pelo menos alguns deles, começam a ter que se dividir em partes para poderem acompanhar o francês, inglês e português."
Tempo	02.01.1994	Salomão Manhiça, Secretário-Geral do Ministério da Cultura e Juventude "houve uma pessoa [José Pinto de Sá], desgraçadamente até moçambicana que escreveu um artigo e publicou-o num jornal português chamado «O Público», e depois disso a mentira pegou. É uma mentira que se vende bem em Portugal. O título era mais ou menos assim: Moçambique ou Mozambique». ...dizia que a Conferência Nacional sobre Cultural debateu muito e propôs que a língua portuguesa seja substituída pela língua inglesa. ...isto é uma pura mentira." P.30 "Infelizmente há muita gente, não só em Moçambique como em Portugal, que ainda quer tratar Moçambique e os moçambicanos como se fossem uma colónia de Portugal." P.31
Tempo	01.05.1994	O Neocolonialismo e as Insuficiências Africanas Ruy Duarte de Carvalho, referência literárias angolana, "Portugal tem mostrado desvantagem relativamente à acção de outros europeus. Talvez por incapacidade para competir com esses países, talvez, mais simplesmente, por falta de estratégia". (p.29) Jorge de Oliveira: "Portugal pode fazer bastante para ajudar a «sua» língua nos vários cantos do globo, mas uma certeza existe, a língua de Camões, o português, deixou de lhe pertencer, faz tempo."

354

Guinea-Bissau

Source	Date	Headline or quote
Nô Pintcha	23.08.1996	A CPLP é uma solução Alhadji Bubacar Djaló da Liga Guineense de Protecçaõ ecológica LIPE (p.8) "Portugal que pagou muito caro o bilhete de sua ingressão na União europeia, não tem meios financeiros consequentes para enfrentar as suas ambições extracontinentais. Além demais, o povo português, que tem mais sangue africano que europeu continua a buscar-se entre as razões económicas que o empurram para a Europa e o coração que não pode abandonar a África" "Fortunas inestimáveis dormem nas galerias subterrâneas de Angola, da Guiné-Bissau e de Moçambique que não esperam outra coisa senão serem valorizados par o bem das suas populações. O Brasil e Portugal poderiam ajudar a materializar este sonho."
Nô Pintcha	26.09.1997	Portugal tem responsabilidade histórica sobre o estado do ensino da língua portuguesa no país João Bernardo Vieira

DUISBURGER ARBEITEN ZUR SPRACH- UND KULTURWISSENSCHAFT
DUISBURG PAPERS ON RESEARCH IN LANGUAGE AND CULTURE

Herausgegeben von
Ulrich Ammon, René Dirven und Martin Pütz

Band   1   René Dirven / Yvan Putseys (Eds.): A User's Grammar of English: Word, Sentence, Text, Interaction - Part A. The Structure of Words and Phrases. 1989.

Band   2   René Dirven / Richard A. Geiger (Eds.): A User's Grammar of English: Word, Sentence, Text, Interaction - Part B. The Structure of Sentences. 1989.

Band   3   René Dirven / Wolfgang Zydatiß / Willis J. Edmondson (Eds.): A User's Grammar of English: Word, Sentence, Text, Interaction - Parts C & D. The Structure of Texts / The Structure of Interaction. 1989.

Band   4   René Dirven: (Ed.): A User's Grammar of English: Word, Sentence, Text, Interaction - Compact Edition. 1989.

Band   5   Martin Pütz / René Dirven (Eds.): Wheels within Wheels. Papers of the Duisburg Symposium on Pidgin and Creole Languages. 1989.

Band   6   Ulrich Schmitz / Rüdiger Schütz / Andreas Kunz (Eds.): Linguistic Approaches to Artificial Intelligence. 1990.

Band   7   Friedrich Lenz: Organisationsprinzipien in mündlicher Fachkommunikation. 1989.

Band   8   Luc Van Doorslaer (Hrsg.): Niederländische Literatur im Spiegel niederländischer Kultur. Aufsätze zur Gastprofessur von Prof. Dr. Marcel Janssens (Universität Löwen) in Duisburg, Sommersemester 1988. 1990.

Band   9   Frank Lüschow / Marita Pabst-Weinschenk (Hrsg.): Mündliche Kommunikation als kooperativer Prozeß. Sprechwissenschaftliche Arbeitsfelder. Festschrift für Elmar Bartsch. 1991.

Band 10   Susanne Niemeier: Ein Fall im Medienvergleich: Film- und Fernsehversion von "A Streetcar Named Desire". Beitrag zur Annäherung an eine Mediensemiotik. 1990.

Band 11   Paul Kent Andersen: A new look at the passive. 1991.

Band 12   Richard Kremer: The efficiency of English language teaching in smaller countries: Denmark. Basic English language teaching in Denmark and its wider context. 1991.

Band 13   Frank Lüschow: Sprache und Kommunikation in der technischen Arbeit. 1992.

Band 14   Gunter Kellermann / Michael D. Morrissey (Eds.): Diachrony within Synchrony. Language History and Cognition. Papers from the International Symposium at the University of Duisburg 26-28 March 1990. 1992.

Band 15   Wim Waumans (Hrsg.): Mit fremden Augen. Niederländisch: eine Sprache, verschiedene Kulturgemeinschaften. 1993.

Band 16   Eberhard Klein: Konditionalität in didaktischen und pädagogischen Grammatiken des Englischen. Prinzipien zur Erstellung von Lehr- und Lerngrammatiken. 1993.

Band 17   Xiaoan Zhu: "Wenn sich das Gras bewegt, dann muß auch der Wind blasen!" Studien zur Metapher in der deutschen politischen Pressesprache – unter besonderer Berücksichtigung der China-Berichterstattung. 1993.

Band 18   Fritz Ponelis: The Development of Afrikaans. 1993.

Band 19   Martin Pütz: Sprachökologie und Sprachwechsel. Die deutsch-australische Sprechgemeinschaft in Canberra. 1994.

Band 20 Heiner Pürschel (Ed.); Co-Editors: Elmar Bartsch, Peter Franklin, Ulrich Schmitz, Sonja Vandermeeren: : Intercultural Communication. Proceedings of the 17th Inter- national L.A.U.D. Symposium. Duisburg, 23-27 March 1992. 1994.

Band 21 Dominiek Sandra: Morphology in the reader's mental lexicon. 1994.

Band 22 René Dirven: Metaphor and Nation. Metaphors Afrikaners live by. 1994.

Band 23 Ralph Bisschops: Die Metapher als Wertsetzung. Novalis, Ezechiel, Beckett. 1994.

Band 24 René Dirven / Johan Vanparys (Eds.): Current Approaches to the Lexicon. A Selection of Papers Presented at the 18th LAUD Symposium, Duisburg, March 1993. 1995.

Band 25 Michael Schloßmacher: Die Amtssprachen in den Organen der Europäischen Gemein- schaft. Status und Funktion. 1996. 2., durchges. Aufl. 1997.

Band 26 Johan Vanparys: Categories and Complements of Illocutionary Verbs in a Cognitive Perspective. 1996.

Band 27 Hideaki Takahashi: Die richtige Aussprache des Deutschen in Deutschland, Österreich und der Schweiz nach Maßgabe der kodifizierten Normen. 1996.

Band 28 Angela Heidemann: The visualization of foreign language vocabulary in CALL. 1996.

Band 29 Kazuma Matoba: Referenzperspektive in Sprechakten. Ihre Funktion und Entwicklung in der deutschen und japanischen Sprache. 1997.

Band 30 Olaf Jäkel: Metaphern in abstrakten Diskurs-Domänen. Eine kognitiv-linguistische Unter- suchung anhand der Bereiche Geistestätigkeit, Wirtschaft und Wissenschaft. 1997.

Band 31 Birgit Smieja / Meike Tasch (Eds.): Human Contact through Language and Linguistics. 1997.

Band 32 Martin Pütz (Ed.): The Cultural Context in Foreign Language Teaching. 1997.

Band 33 Andrea Gerbig: Lexical and Grammatical Variation in a Corpus. A Computer-Assisted Study of Discourse on the Environment. 1997.

Band 34 Helga Bister-Broosen: Sprachkontakte und Sprachattitüden Jugendlicher im Elsaß und in Baden. Vergleichende soziolinguistische Untersuchungen in Colmar (Frankreich) und in Freiburg und Müllheim (Deutschland). 1998.

Band 35 Helga Bister-Broosen (Hrsg.): Niederländisch am Niederrhein. 1998.

Band 36 Alicja Sakaguchi: Interlinguistik. Gegenstand, Ziele, Aufgaben, Methoden. 1998.

Band 37 Benjamin Biebuyck / René Dirven / John Ries (Eds.): Faith and Fiction. Interdisciplinary Studies on the Interplay between Metaphor and Religion. A Selection of Papers from the 25th LAUD-Symposium of the Gerhard Mercator University of Duisburg on 'Metaphor and Religion'. 1998.

Band 38 Ulrich Ammon (Hrsg.): Sprachförderung. Schlüssel auswärtiger Kulturpolitik. 2000.

Band 39 El Hadj Ibrahima Diop: Das Selbstverständnis von Germanistikstudium und Deutschunter- richt im frankophonen Afrika. Vom kolonialen Unterrichtsfach zu eigenständigen Deutsch- landstudien und zum praxisbezogenen Lernen. 2000.

Band 40 Herman M. Batibo / Birgit Smieja (Eds.): Botswana: The Future of the Minority Languages. 2000.

Band 41 Harald Haarmann: Die Kleinsprachen der Welt – Existenzbedrohung und Überlebens- chancen. Eine umfassende Dokumentation. 2001.

Band 42 Dirk Scholten: Sprachverbreitungspolitik des nationalsozialistischen Deutschlands. 2000.

Band 43 Riana Roos Paola: Pro-active Language Teacher Education in a Multicultural Society. 2001.

Band 90 Maria-Antonia Kontostathi: Die Arbeit mit dem Europäischen Sprachenportfolio als Möglichkeit zum selbständigen Erarbeiten fremdsprachlicher Kompetenzen. 2012.

Band 91 Yu Chen: Verbessern chinesische Studierende ihre Sprechfertigkeit im Deutschen während des Fachstudiums in Deutschland? Eine empirische Untersuchung unter Berücksichtigung sozialer Aspekte. 2012.

Band 92 Jakob Haselhuber: Mehrsprachigkeit in der Europäischen Union. Eine Analyse der EU-Sprachenpolitik, mit besonderem Fokus auf Deutschland. Vollständige Dokumentation und Perspektiven für die Zukunft. 2012.

Band 93 Hans Wagener: Untergräbt Deutschland selbst die internationale Stellung der deutschen Sprache? Eine Folge der Förderung von Englisch im Bildungsbereich. 2012.

Band 94 G. Stickel / M. Carrier (eds.) · Language Education in Creating a Multilingual Europe. Contributions to the Annual Conference 2011 of EFNIL in London. 2012.

Band 95 Jun He: Die Auswirkungen der englischsprachigen Hochschullehre in Deutschland auf das Deutschlernen in China. 2013.

Band 96 Monika Reif / Justyna A. Robinson / Martin Pütz (eds.): Variation in Language and Language Use. Linguistic, Socio-Cultural and Cognitive Perspectives. 2013.

Band 97 Carla Figueira: Languages at War. External Language Spread Policies in Lusophone Africa. Mozambique and Guinea-Bissau at the Turn of the 21st Century. 2013.

www.peterlang.de